THE ENCYCLOPAEDIA OF THE PARANORMAL

THE ENCYCLOPAEDIA OF THE PARANORMAL

A Complete Guide to the Unexplained

Lynn Picknett

MACMILLAN
LONDON

First published 1990 by
MACMILLAN LONDON LIMITED
4 Little Essex Street, London WC2R 3LF
and Basingstoke

Associated companies in Auckland, Delhi, Dublin, Gaborone,
Hamburg, Harare, Hong Kong, Johannesburg, Kuala Lumpur,
Lagos, Manzini, Melbourne, Mexico City, Nairobi, New York,
Singapore and Tokyo

ISBN 0–333–49100–9

A CIP catalogue record for this book is available
from the British Library

Typeset by BP Integraphics, Bath, Avon, England

Printed in Great Britain by
Richard Clay Ltd, Bungay, Suffolk

To

LdV

and all Arcadians,
past, present and future

with love and honour

et in arcadia ego . . .

Contents

Acknowledgements

Of all the distinguished contributors to this book I should like to express enormous gratitude to Guy Lyon Playfair and Hilary Evans for their generous help above and beyond the call of duty; for unstinting professional help, advice and comfort, Esther Jagger and Rosemary Anderson, and at Macmillan, Katrina Whone and Beverley Cousins; to Dr Brian Roet and Professor Leo Vincent for providing the inspiration on all levels; to Sarah Litvinoff without whom this book and much else would never have been accomplished; and to Terry for help with these and many other words, and for all that words can never describe.

Contributors:

Vida Adamoli; David Alderton; Dr Dan Ben Or; Manfred Cassirer; David Christie-Murray; Joe Cooper; James Cunningham; Hilary Evans; Brian Inglis; Rachel Leedham; Jane Lyle; Guy Lyon Playfair; Lynn Picknett; Dr Brian Roet; Professor Archie Roy; Terence Sharkey; Dr Rupert Sheldrake; Val Stephenson; Larissa Vilenskaya

Introduction

It is worth stating at the beginning that, for the purposes of this book, the paranormal is considered to be very different from the 'occult'. The first may be defined as phenomena that orthodox science cannot or will not investigate or explain, while the second is much more a matter of choice – concerning societies we might join or pacts we might make with otherworldly entities, real or imagined. The paranormal arguably happens anyway, much as radio waves circulate the globe, with or without our permission, but the occult we may choose to 'dabble' in. Only where aspects of the paranormal have been manipulated by adepts of magical systems is the occult mentioned in this book.

It was, nevertheless, a daunting task to fit such an unruly subject into one volume and call it an encyclopaedia. What is one man's reason is another man's magic, but this book should at least cover aspects of the paranormal from UFOs to werewolves to thoughtography to poltergeists; from great controversies to sceptics; from iconoclasts to grey-beard eminents; from the dead to the living and all between . . . A strict editorial code was developed to justify the inclusions (and, to some extent, what was excluded). If an entry led naturally to be cross-referenced with others, then it was considered for inclusion. If it stood by itself then it was merely on call. The 'see also' paragraphs at the end of each entry are an essential part of the book's plan, and are sometimes deliberately provocative. The reader might like to use them for an overview of the subject. Accept them or reject them, the connections are there.

A distinguished list of contributors has produced a variety of authoritative entries, particularly in the field of science, psi research (especially that of the Eastern bloc), and ufology. Authoritative they may be, but even so they are boldly cross-referenced with other sections, which may not please purists, but seems to follow the way of the world of the paranormal. Unlike many parapsychologists, we have not pinned a label on each phenomenon and made it do for an explanation. These phenomena have been divided into sections only for convenience not because they accord with some Divine plan.

As the research for this book progressed clear themes emerged – although, like much of the paranormal, they tended to become elusive if sought too keenly. But even so, some themes positively shouted. Such subjects as thoughtography (the intriguing business of photographing one's thoughts), suspended animation, visions of the Virgin Mary, psychokinesis, thoughtforms, and the classic Philip Experiment all clearly attest to the power, in its literal sense, of the human mind. Even 'miracles' that have usually been thought to originate from someone or something 'out there' now suggest a complex interaction of external forces with the mind and brain in ways we are only beginning to guess at.

One major implication of some psi research is its practical use. Too often one bends a spoon paranormally and wonders at the futility of such an action. Surely this awe-inspiring subject is worth more than a party trick (and a growing collection of unusable cutlery)? Yet despite its apparent unpredictability, psi-functioning can be coaxed into repeating itself, and into performing a crucial function, as in the 'Eleventh-hour syndrome', and in Psi-Mediated Instrumental Response, both of which are jargon for what most people consider simply to be the answer to a prayer.

Theories and expositions are the backbone of an encyclopaedia, but people are its flesh and blood.

In this book we include some of the most remarkable people ever to have lived, from Jesus and the Apostles to mediums who materialise the dead; from stigmatics to UFO abductees; from those who merely levitate to those who heal the sick. The cast list includes names to conjure with (literally, in some cases) such as Dr John Dee, Helen Duncan, Jose Arigo, Aleister Crowley, Matthew Manning, Sai Baba – and Leonardo da Vinci, no stranger to encyclopaedias, but his first entry in one on this subject . . .

This book is not aimed at sceptics, for they tend to dismiss any unusual phenomenon – and the witness with it – before so much as listening to the facts. This is not very gentlemanly. Indeed, there are few other areas where witnesses to events are so maligned before their case is heard. Scepticism actively destroys – phenomena, careers, people – as one international committee of rationalists well knows. Our aim is not, like them, to condemn without mercy, but to coax and encourage those shy yet powerful aspects of life known as the paranormal. Research has shown that psi phenomena, including those that might be described as 'miracles', can flourish in an atmosphere of welcome, in a world where disbelief is suspended, if only for a short while.

Encyclopaedias are rarely modest, but few seek to be inspirational, cheering, and a good read – we can hope that nothing is impossible, and that this one is the exception to the rule.

Lynn Picknett
Editor
London, 1990

I The Power of Belief

Fairies ● Angels ● The Devil ● Witchcraft ● Spiritism ● Seance-room phenomena ● Levitation ● Apports ● Psychic music, art and literature ● Miracles of St Médard ● Psychic surgery ● Healing ● Holism ● End times cults ● Toad magic ● Ritual magic ● Great Beast 666 ● Old Testament Miracles ● New Testament Miracles ● Speaking in tongues ● The Resurrection ● Turin Shroud ● Haemography ● Paranormal portraits ● Images that bleed and weep ● Moving statues ● Stigmatics ● Visions of the Virgin Mary ● Incorruptibility ● Church of Jesus Christ of Latter Day Saints (Mormons) ● Buddhism

Mankind has proved that it can believe anything or nothing with equal facility and fanaticism. Faith and the desire to believe often obscure the facts, as in the vexed case of the Turin Shroud, where there may be evidence for belief having – literally – created the miracle through psychokinetic imprinting of the cloth. Where belief is strong and has been reinforced by the tradition of centuries, it assumes a life of its own, a kind of ideoplastic reality that challenges the so-called 'laws of nature'.

To believers in miracles, context is all. When Catholic saints defy the process of decomposition long after their death this is taken as a sure sign of their holiness, yet ordinary people who die outside the Church have also been found to be incorruptible – and this is seen as nothing more than proof that the anomaly happens. Stigmatics bleed and suffer the agonies of Christ, but the miracle was confined to the ranks of the faithful – until a ten-year-old black girl was also stigmatised for a few days. She was not a Catholic, nor was she particularly known for her saintliness, yet the phenomenon was real, attested by doctors and psychiatrists. Was this American girl's miracle a physical anomaly, a phenomenological freak? Did it indicate that more than mere belief is involved in stigmata? Or was it a mistake on the part of God (or the gods), or even a Cosmic Joke?

Similarly, when religious images are witnessed to bleed and weep it is taken as a sign of the divine

presence, and pilgrims flock to pray before the miracle. Yet research has shown that the images in ordinary family snapshots have also cried.

Miracles appear to be no respecters of persons or creeds, but may occur within any religion or cult – although, depending on the context, they may be attributed to a different source. When seagulls came in answer to Brigham Young's prayers and ate the marauding locusts this was seen as a sign of the favour with which God viewed the fledgling Mormon Church. Yet if the crops that were saved had belonged to an enemy this might have been seen as the malevolent workings of witchcraft.

The history of the paranormal is enlivened by the regular appearance of supernatural beings, such as fairies, angels, demons and a young girl frequently understood to be the Virgin Mary. Apologists for various religions and cults may insist that these creatures from elsewhere in the multiverse are essentially different in character and purpose, but nevertheless such encounters reveal remarkable similarities – and it may be that they tell us more about the visionaries than the visions.

Many phenomena appear to have complex sources; automatic writing, which is almost always a product of the writer's unconscious mind, may occasionally reveal genuinely paranormal knowledge, or seem to come from a discarnate spirit. When Mrs Curran tried her hand at automatic writing she was apparently taken over by 'Patience

Worth', whose literary ambitions, frustrated in her lifetime, were finally realised. Deceased composers and artists find expression for new works through living hands, as if creativity knows no bounds, not even those of bodily death.

The power to create by belief reaches its apotheosis in the rituals of the magical adept, whose meticulous self-discipline and lengthy preparations serve to focus his imagination and will, to bring about a change in reality. This may consist of summoning up his Guardian Angel, or an elemental spirit, with instruction and information to impart – for knowledge, to the adept, is power. The magical process is essentially about transformation; in its most popular form it is the basis for many fairy stories and in Britain it is celebrated every Christmas pantomime season in the 'transformation scene', in which Cinderella's pumpkin becomes a coach, and mice become its horses. On another level a profound form of magic is seen in the transubstantiation of the Catholic Church, where, at the climax of the Mass, the wine is believed to become Christ's blood and the wafer his flesh. The old pagan idea of killing the god and eating him to ensure fertility has become the heart and centre of Christianity.

Pagan sites, gods, spirits and beliefs were partially absorbed and subtly changed by the proselytising Church. For a few centuries this arrangement seemed to work, but the harsh tenets of the Middle Ages, with their emphasis on hellfire and damnation, led to an equally uncompromising rebellion. Where once there was Lucifer, Son of the Morning, the beautiful subversive, there was now the Devil with his terrifying goat's head and cloven hoofs, carrying with him the stench of brimstone. Where once there were wise women of the villages who were natural healers and seers, there were now witches, in league with the Devil, dedicated to evil and destruction. The wise women continued to exist, but many were swept away with the hundreds of thousands of innocent people who perished horribly in the great European witch-hunts.

Undoubtedly Devil worship existed, as it still does, but the vast majority of the accused had no knowledge of the evil practices for which they were condemned. Belief that can create anything – for good or evil – created the witchcraft heresy and provided it with its martyrs. The witch-hunt hysteria inevitably said much more about the accusers than the accused; when men come to power whose terror and bigotry is stronger than their humanity, the witch must always burn.

FAIRIES

Folklorists use the word 'fairy' in two broad senses. The first covers the whole range of supernatural creatures other than angels, devils and ghosts, and includes goblins and hobgoblins, merpeople, fairy animals and a huge variety of solitary, and often strictly localised hags, bogies and monsters. The second definition applies to one particular species, varying in size but more or less human in appearance. This type of fairy is known under a variety of names: elves in the Scottish Lowlands; the Daoine Sidhe in Ireland, and the Seelie Court, again in Scotland. Equally often they are referred to euphemistically as 'The Good Neighbours', 'The Strangers', or quite simply, 'Them'.

Fairies in this more specific sense have been the subject of much fanciful story-telling, but there are also innumerable accounts in traditional folklore that bear a curious ring of authenticity, if only because of the matter-of-factness – the lack of astonishment – with which encounters with fairies are described. One of the best authorities is the Scottish scholar and clergyman Robert Kirk (1644–92), minister of Aberfoyle; his manuscript book *The Secret Commonwealth of Elves, Fauns and Fairies*, the result of years of study of Highland fairy beliefs, ends with apparent conviction that such creatures exist. (After his death, Kirk himself was thought to have been abducted into captivity under a fairy hill.) Kirk believed that fairies were 'of a middle nature betwixt man and angel', and his account describes characteristics found in folklore tradition throughout Europe.

Fairies in the narrower sense defined above are not evil, although they may be mischievous or

Fairies and gnomes by artist Arthur Rackham. The tendency today is to dismiss the many tales of man's interaction with such creatures as unsophisticated imaginings – literally 'fairy tales'. Yet folklore cannot be so easily dismissed; over the centuries some perception of the fairy realm does seem to have occurred repeatedly, and, as Dr Jacques Vallée has shown, stories of abduction by the Little People are reflected in today's alleged epidemic of abduction by aliens. It may be that encountering beings from other dimensions is a physical reality, or a case of psychic interaction – or, in some way not entirely clear at the moment, both.

capricious. They have a code of honour which might be described as aristocratic, respecting generosity and hating meanness; they like cleanliness and neatness; they may wreak terrible vengeance if a bargain with them is broken, or if they are too closely spied upon, or if their own taboos are infringed. Their amusements are also aristocratic: they love music and dancing, hunting and riding in procession.

They exhibit a curious dependence upon mankind, suggesting that their stock is weak. From time to time fairies will abduct a human child, leaving one of their own – a changeling – in its place. Sometimes they will kidnap a human midwife to attend a fairy mother in childbirth, possibly because she is in labour with a human–fairy hybrid. Sometimes they will steal human food, extracting its nutrition and leaving a worthless husk behind.

Human encounters with them occur at specific times of the day, at particular seasons and in particular places; fairies were often believed to live underground or inside hills or mounds. When human beings, willingly or unwillingly, found themselves within the fairy realm, their experience of time would frequently be distorted in a mysterious way. After several days of feasting and dancing, for example, they would return to humankind to discover that only a few moments had passed. Or, more often, they would return from elfdom after what had seemed a short visit to find that human time had moved on by several years.

Fairies also had the power to control human perception – a power originally known as 'glamour'. They could, for instance, turn a damp cave into a magnificent palace or a wizened crone into a beautiful young woman.

Features like these are found in many hundreds of independent accounts, shared and believed in by hundreds of traditional communities, albeit with many variations. What do these tales mean, and what do fairies as a phenomenon represent? Folklorists in the nineteenth and early twentieth centuries offered three main theories:

1. Fairies were spirits of the dead, merged perhaps with residual pagan beliefs about local spirits. They were creatures of the collective mind of pre-Christian country folk living outside the sophisticated world of what the historian Edward Gibbon called 'the elegant mythology of the Greeks and Romans'.

2. They were a dwindled form of the gods and heroes of the old Celtic world, driven out by Christianity. The aristocratic lifestyle of the Irish, Scottish and Welsh trooping fairies, with their fondness for hunting and riding in procession, lends credence to this theory.

3. They represent a folk memory of an ancient European people, possible of Mediterranean stock, driven underground by the Celtic invaders of the Iron Age and both despised and feared by their conquerors. Again, the fairies' traditional fear of iron gives some support to this version of their origins, as does the implication that they used magical powers to compensate for their lack of physical strength.

The modern reader, however, may well note some striking parallels between the characteristics of fairies recorded in folklore and modern reports of encounters with extraterrestrial aliens. In his important book, *Dimensions: a Casebook of Alien Contact* (1988), the distinguished ufologist Jacques Vallée draws attention to the similarities in descriptions of physical appearance, the apparent distortion in the behaviour of time, the habit of abducting human subjects, and several other features. (He might also have pointed to the similarity between the dome shape of many reported UFOs and the mounds in which fairies were often said to live.)

Vallée, however, does not argue that fairies are an earlier form of extraterrestrial visitor; indeed, he has come to reject the extraterrestrial hypothesis (ETH) altogether. Instead he offers the view that UFOs and their occupants, along with fairies, angels, demons and a wide range of other supernatural creatures, may represent a universal phenomenon that is both physical and psychic in nature; that this phenomenon is perceived and explained differently according to the cultural framework in which it appears and that it may emanate from a multiverse beyond the familiar dimensions of space-time. Whatever this phenomenon may be, he argues, it may well be altering human unconsciousness by methods and for purposes that we cannot begin to understand.

SEE ALSO *Angels*; *Cosmic Joker*; *Cottingley fairies*; *The Devil*; *Entity enigma*; *Men in Black*; *Other dimensions*; *Ritual magic*; *Time*; *UFO Paradox*; *UFOs*; *Crop field circles*.

ANGELS

The word 'angel' is derived from the Greek word *angelos*, meaning 'messenger'. The idea of spiritual beings who mediate between God and the celestial realm on the one hand, and the terrestrial realm on the other, is common to Zoroastrianism, Judaism, Christianity and Islam. It is likely that the more developed notion of an angelic hierarchy was absorbed by the Jews from their contacts with the other religions of the Near East, where such beliefs were closely associated with astrology.

In the Old Testament only two angels (or archangels) are named: Michael, the warrior angel who is the guardian of Israel; and Gabriel, the heavenly messenger who is also the ruler of Paradise. The Old Testament Apocrypha mentions two others: Raphael, the healer and helper, and guardian of human spirits; and Uriel, who watches over the world and rules the underworld. *The First Book of Enoch* adds three more, Raguel, Sariel and Remiel, and develops the idea that the higher orders of angels, the cherubim and seraphim, guard and worship at the throne of God, while the lower orders concern themselves with the affairs of men.

A stone angel, with symbols of life and rebirth guards a doorway at Winchelsea Church. Angels, much beloved of the more saccharine Victorian sentimentalists, were merely the messengers of God in the Old Testament, and were often described as ordinary men. Winged beings, however, were described by visionaries such as Swedenborg and Blake, although the latter believed angels capable of human frailty, including deception and fornication.

Christianity took over this angelic hierarchy from Judaism and, following St Paul, added the further orders of virtues, powers, principalities, dominions and thrones. Into this belief-system was incorporated the idea of a War in Heaven, in the course of which Lucifer, the proud angel, was cast out and became the fallen angel, the messenger who deceives men, giving them a false notion of their place in the order of things and tempting them to challenge God. This idea, when merged with the Judaic concept of Satan, the prosecuting angel who urges God to punish men mercilessly for their sins, produced the medieval Christian Devil, who is both tempter and ruler of Hell (and, as universally acknowledged Trickster, he can also be seen in the Fortean idea of the Cosmic Joker).

Islam absorbed the angelic hierarchy from Judaeo-Christianity – it was the angel Gabriel who revealed the Koran and the true nature of Allah to Mohammed – and elevated to some importance the idea that man has two guardian angels, one of whom records his good and the other his evil actions.

The medieval idea of angels (and demons) was linked to a tripartite conception of the world of being Heaven, Earth and the Underworld, this was itself linked to the medieval cosmology in which Earth, at the centre of the universe, was surrounded by the celestial spheres. When this system collapsed at the end of the Middle Ages belief in the hierarchy of angels also lost much of its force. In recent times, however, some Christian theologians, following Freud, have linked the idea of Heaven, Earth and Hell with the three levels of man's spiritual nature: the *superego*, the *ego* and the *id*.

While, in popular belief, angels were portrayed in human form, though sometimes with wings and nearly always with an aura of supernatural beauty, medieval theologians insisted that their true nature was purely spiritual, and that they took on human form only so as to appear visible to mankind. It may be significant, however, that all the biblical accounts of angels coincide with popular belief: the angels have human bodies and human attributes. This fact gives some support to the contention of a leading contemporary ufologist, Jacques Vallée, that angels, demons, fairies and other supernatural beings are culturally determined manifestations of a single phenomenon, of which UFO-occupants are only the most recent version.

SEE ALSO *Astrology; Church of Jesus Christ of Latter Day Saints (Mormons); Aleister Crowley; John Dee; The Devil; Entity enigma; Fairies; Life after death; Men in Black; Near death experience; New Testament miracles; Old Testament miracles; Ritual magic; Speaking in tongues; UFOs; Visions of the Virgin Mary.*

THE DEVIL

In Christian belief the Devil is the prince of evil spirits, the tempter of mankind, the ruler of Hell and the embodiment of absolute evil. He is known by a variety of names, of which, Satan, Lucifer,

The most common image of the Devil: winged like a bat, hooved and horned. Yet he was believed to have been Lucifer, 'Son of the Morning', beloved of God.

Witches and the Devil ride on broomsticks to an unholy Sabbat – an enduring image of proponents of the 'Old Religion'.

Belial, Beelzebul (Lord of Flies), and Beelzebub (Lord of Dung) are the commonest. (Mephisto or Mephistopheles, the tempter of Faust, is essentially a literary name.)

At least two major strands are woven into Western beliefs about the Devil, his role and his powers. The monotheisic religions (Zoroastrianism, Judaism, Christianity and Islam) have the tradition of a proud angel, Lucifer, who challenges the supreme power of God and is cast out of Heaven and into Hell. At the end of time he will be condemned to the fires of Hell for all eternity, but for the moment he has considerable earthly powers and freedom of action. In this tradition he strives constantly to tempt man away from the path of redemption and eternal life and into the ways of sin, death and destruction. He may appear as a serpent, or as a woman, or (in the case of *Faust* and elsewhere) as an elegant and worldly gentleman. Milton, in *Paradise Lost*, portrays him as a figure who retains an angelic beauty and nobility of countenance.

In the Old Testament, Satan is not the adversary of God, but the merciless prosecutor of the heavenly court, urging God to punish sinful mankind without pity. It is in post-biblical Judaism and in Christianity that Satan becomes the prince of evil, but his older role may explain why it is he, the

The only known specimen of the Devil's handwriting. As his worshippers are known to follow the 'left-hand path' perhaps one may wonder if their master is actually left-handed?

embodiment of all sin, who presides in Hell over the punishment of sinners. The notion of the Devil as effectively a God of Evil probably emerged in the period between the sixth and fourth centuries BC, when the Jews came under the influence of Zoroastrianism. As the idea of a single deity – all-powerful and absolutely good – began to establish itself, it may be that, in order to explain the existence of evil, the need was felt to believe in an entity representing absolute evil. This archetype is seen as being tolerated for the moment by God in his inscrutable wisdom, but doomed to ultimate defeat and destruction.

In medieval art and literature (for example in Dante's *Inferno*) the Devil and his attendant demons are described or depicted as figures of horrifying ugliness, only partially human in appearance. These lurid images were meant to convey the ugliness of sin and to terrorise men and women away from any inclination to sinfulness (although they may also be the result of a certain perverse enjoyment on the part of the painters and writers). Where the Devil is depicted, as he often is, in semi-human form, with horns and the legs of a goat,

that image may represent yet another strand in his creation – the survival in folk memory of a prehistoric pagan deity. Some of the names of the Devil and his demons (Beelzebul, Asmodeus, Astaroth and Beherit, for example) are certainly the names of heathen deities whom the Jews encountered and rejected as their own monotheism developed.

Modern Christian belief tends to reject the lurid imagery of the Middle Ages, along with the material nature of the punishments of Hell. But the idea of a living principle of evil persists, by whatever name it is called, and orthodox Christian priests still practise exorcism for the casting out of demons.

Devil worship, or Satanism, takes several forms, which are not always distinguished. On the one hand there is an old theosophical tradition that the Devil so-called is the One True God whose rightful place has been usurped by the God worshipped by Jews and Christians. Then there is the Devil worship of the witches, which may well have stemmed from the belief of the poor that the Devil offered them power and pleasure that were denied to them in this life, and therefore denied to them by the God of Christianity. Finally there is Satanism proper, a perverse intellectual cult that – consciously and deliberately – rejects the Christian God and the Christian virtues, and cultivates evil in rituals which reverse or desecrate those of Christianity (as, for example, when Aleister Crowley baptised a toad as Jesus Christ and then crucified it).

SEE ALSO *Angels*; *Aleister Crowley*; *John Dee*; *Entity enigma*; *Life after death*; *Men in Black*; *Near death experience*; *Possession*; *The Resurrection*; *Toad magic*; *Witchcraft*.

Witches being burnt alive for their alleged pacts with the Devil. Most of these poor wretches were merely unpopular members of a hysterical society.

WITCHCRAFT

'To understand witchcraft,' wrote Jeffrey Burton Russell in his *Witchcraft in the Middle Ages*, 'we must descend into the deepest oceans of the mind.' To most modern researchers this advice refers more to those who persecuted, tortured and killed over two hundred thousand alleged witches in the European witch-hunts of the fifteenth, sixteenth and seventeenth centuries, than to the 'witches' themselves.

Psychologists and sociologists have noted that almost all the accused were women, and almost all the persecutors were men – many of them celibates, being priests or monks, as in the Spanish Inquisition. Any serious threat to sexual stereotyping was put down with such hysteria that it rings through the centuries. When Joan of Arc's voices told her to wear men's clothing, ride a horse and lead men into battle the threat to a male-dominated society was clear; she must be burnt as a witch. Sexual overtones were present in the questioning of the accused, and blatant sexual sadism rife in the tortures inflicted upon them. All of this is horrific, but none of it involves the paranormal.

Yet the witches were accused of paranormal deeds, of having been seduced by the Devil and of having made a pact with him that gave them the power to change shape; to destroy cattle, crops and people with a look; and to fly to unholy Sabbats

Modern Cornish witches dance 'skyclad' – naked – during an invocation in 1980. Adherents of 'wicca' today believe that there is a new wave of persecution about to be unleashed on them from the Christian fundamentalists.

where they ate meals of excrement and newborn babies' flesh, and kissed the Devil on the anus. In fact, for centuries men have believed certain women to be sorceresses, to come in the spirit to sleeping men and suck their vitality away. In more enlightened times although we can make the intellectual connection between the erotic dreams that lead to nocturnal emissions and fantasies about visiting witches, belief in vampires remains strong even today.

Most of the alleged witches were totally innocent of the charges brought against them. The mentally sick, the deformed, the loners and the feared were the first to find themselves in the hands of the torturers; confession to outrageous and disgusting deeds in the company of the Devil meant a merciful strangling before the flames reached them, whereas last-minute retraction, or an outright and bold statement of innocence, meant a lingering death at the stake. This was appalling enough, but it is easy for the twentieth-century commentator to overlook the fact that, to the average churchgoer of the Middle Ages, Hell was a reality, and a confession of consorting with the Devil was a sure passport to the infernal regions. To die unshriven, accused of such terrible sin, was the ultimate torture.

With the publication of the *Malleus Maleficarum* (*Hammer of the Witches*) in 1486 – less than fifty years

after the invention of printing – the craze took on a new formality. Rules for the interrogation and execution of witches were set out with such fanatical thoroughness that George Lincoln Burr, the American historian, described it as 'the terrible book which has . . . caused more suffering than any other work written by human pen'.

Different countries reacted in different ways to the threat of witchcraft. In England witches often got off with a ducking in the village pond and a hefty fine, although the coming to power of Matthew Hopkins, the Witchfinder General, in the 1640s meant the financial ruin, torture and hanging of hundreds. In France the inquisitors specialised in torturing suspects into confessing to the wildest occult crimes. In Spain the Inquisition became a byword for state-sanctioned sadism. In Germany the hysteria ran at the highest temperatures and special jails were built to house the witches passed through to the stake at a rate of a thousand a year in just one small area.

A kind of glee ran through the communities involved – old scores were being settled in the name of God – and members of the same family felt free to name each other as witches, just as the Nazis were to encourage the party faithful to spy on their relatives. Although various attempts were made by rational men to disabuse the public of its prejudices, the mass hysteria eventually seemed to run out of steam by itself. The last European witch was executed in Poland in 1793.

Belief in the power of the 'hex' – the witches' curse – remains, especially in rural areas with strong pagan roots. Since time immemorial, most small communities have had in their midst a natural psychic, usually a woman, whose powers may be used for good or evil, but who generally functioned as a natural healer. Ironically, today the potential power of the traditional village 'wise woman' is being appreciated. As more people become dissatisfied with orthodox medicine, her spells and herbal potions are coming into their own. Such people also frequently have the gift of prediction or prophecy – without having made a pact with the Devil.

Undoubtedly a small percentage of those executed as witches had taken the 'left-hand path' and sided with an evil sect, throwing themselves into sexual perversions, satanism and murder for 'kicks'. It happens today, as it always has. Some may have indulged in the orgies they described, or may have truly believed they had sex with a cold, dark stranger who gave them occult powers. There are several possible explanations for the experiences reported by self-confessed witches of old; they may have 'flown' to Sabbats during out-of-the-body experiences; alternatively they may have induced the sensation of flight by rubbing themselves with a powerful drug, or by sitting astride a broomstick smeared with ointment containing that drug, or by taking the drug orally.

A tiny proportion of those accused of witchcraft may indeed have become the playthings of objective, evil entities, who – true to form – deserted them as soon as they were arrested. There are many accounts, from all centuries and cultures, of such magical, and ultimately destructive, partnerships. Some are to be found in the annals of witchcraft, many in those of ritual magic, and others – described perhaps as the relationship of medium and spirit guide – in the records of seance-room phenomena.

The last person to be prosecuted under the British Witchcraft Act of 1735 was materialisation medium Helen Duncan, who was jailed for nine months in 1944. The charge against her and her three assistants was that they had 'conspired together to pretend to exercise conjuration that spirits of deceased persons should appear and communicate with living persons present...'. The Witchcraft Act was repealed in 1951 and replaced by the Fraudulent Mediums Act.

The 1960s on both sides of the Atlantic saw an 'occult explosion' in which thousands of people became involved with variations of modern witchcraft, ritual magic ('magick', if Crowleyan) and satanism. Much of the witchcraft allegedly drawn from 'wicca' or the 'Old Religion' is, in fact, less than a century old, being the disseminations of such as British occultist Gerald Gardner, who died in 1964. Gardnerian witchcraft, with its emphasis on sexual exhibitionism and nudity, had a large cult following during the years of Flower Power. Today greater stress is laid on achieving altered states of consciousness in order to contact the archetypal gods.

Prejudice against occultists and persecution appears to be increasing once again; witches are particular targets for fundamentalist Christians, who, it is claimed, have launched a concerted attack against groups and individuals to the extent that some witches have lost their jobs and have had to move house. The human rights group Amnesty International repeatedly failed to respond to serious pleas for help from one group of persecuted witches in 1988.

SEE ALSO *Angels; Case of Ruth; Church of Jesus Christ of Latter Day Saints (Mormons); Cosmic Joker; Cottingley fairies; Creative visualisation; Aleister Crowley; John Dee; The Devil; Helen Duncan; Entity enigma; Fairies; Fantasy-prone personalities; Hallucinations; Healing; Katie King; Levitation; Mass hysteria; Men in Black; Out-of-the-body experiences; Ritual magic; Seance-room phenomena; Tulpas; UFO classification; UFO paradox; UFOs; Vampires; Werewolves.*

SPIRITISM

This movement originated in France with the publication in 1857 of a book entitled *Le Livre des esprits* (*The Spirits' Book*). Somewhat confusingly, it featured the words 'Spiritualist Philosophy' on its title page. The author explained that 'everyone is a spiritualist who believes that there is in him something more than matter, but it does not follow that he believes in the existence of spirits'. For such a belief, he coined the words Spiritism and Spiritist.

The author, a former schoolteacher named Hippolyte Rivail, had already written twenty-two textbooks on educational reform, mathematics and French grammar. This book was quite different – it appeared under the pseudonym Allan Kardec, who insisted that this and four subsequent books were not written by him, merely 'compiled and set in order'. The true authors were the spirits.

At first, Rivail had taken little interest in the table-turning craze that swept Paris in the 1850s. 'If you study the sciences you will laugh at the superstitious credulity of the ignorant, and you will no longer believe in ghosts', he wrote in one of his early works. Told by a friend in 1854 that tables were not only leaving the floor but tapping out messages from the beyond, he replied, 'I will believe that only when I see it'.

Encouraged by his friend, the playwright Victorien Sardou, he eventually did see it, and detected 'something serious behind all this apparent triviality'. It seemed to be 'the revelation of a new law, which I decided to investigate thoroughly'. He concentrated on the work of automatic-writing mediums, especially a certain Mademoiselle Japhet. In an early example of what became known as 'experimenter effect' he noticed that, while messages could be frivolous, they could also be serious when addressed to him personally. He was particularly struck by 'the knowledge and charity that shine out from the serious communications', and he duly embarked on a long series of sittings in which he asked questions and the spirits, through the writing hand of the medium, provided the answers.

The result was *The Spirits' Book*. It was followed by *The Mediums' Book* (1861), *The Gospel According to Spiritism* (1864), *Heaven and Hell* (1865) and *Genesis* (1867). Kardec also founded and edited the *Spirit Review* in which he included his own original research into mediums, healers and some interesting poltergeist cases.

Kardec, who died in 1869 at the age of sixty-five, never intended to found a new religion. For him, Spiritism was a restatement of basic Christian principles that had become neglected by most churches, and a rational philosophy based on demonstrable fact. Unlike Swedenborg or Andrew Jackson Davis, who covered some of the same ground, he was neither mystic nor medium. According to himself, he was merely a collector of, and commentator on, the writings of other hands. If these were inspired wholly or in part by his own subconscious mind, they are no less clear and readable for that. His stated mission was 'to make a coherent whole of what has hitherto been scattered, to explain in clear and precise terms what has hitherto been wrapped up in the language of allegory; to eliminate the products of superstition and ignorance from human belief leaving only what is real and actual'.

Spiritism, he said, had dealt materialism a death blow and 'shown the inevitable results of evil and consequently the necessity of goodness', while the future life was no longer 'a vague imagining, a mere hope, but a fact'. Reincarnation, not accepted by all Spiritualists of the age, became a central tenet of Spiritism, according to which human evolution is a path towards perfection through successive incarnations, each the result of what we were, did or thought in the previous ones.

Spiritism enjoyed a vogue in France that proved short-lived. It still flourishes, however, in the Philippines and Latin America, especially in Brazil where it was introduced by the statesman Adolfo Bezerra de Meneses. Brazilian Spiritists, now in their millions, concentrate on welfare projects for the poor and handicapped, and on spiritual healing centres where the public receive free treatment.

SEE ALSO *Enfield poltergeist*; *Experimenter effect*; *Fox sisters*; *Eileen Garrett*; *Ghosts*; *Healing*; *Karma*; *Life after death*; *Matthew Manning*; *Ouija board and planchette*; *Psychic music, art and literature*; *Reincarnation*; *Chico Xavier*.

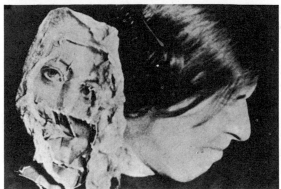

SEANCE-ROOM PHENOMENA

Seance-room phenomena seem to be based on the production by the medium of ectoplasm – a viscous, greyish-white substance that may take the form of the materialised dead. The American medium Margery Crandon is seen with an ectoplasmic hand emerging from under her skirts, while 'Eva C' partly materialises a ragged face that looks suspiciously like a cardboard cut-out.

Traditional seance-room phenomena are something of a rarity today, but they do take place. With some variations, the format for a 'materialisation' seance is almost universal. It takes place in conditions of semi-darkness or in a dim red light, which is supposed to be conducive to paranormal phenomena. The medium, more often a woman than a man, goes into a trance and her 'spirit' guide speaks through her, giving the sitters an uplifting lecture. The sitters are then encouraged to hold

hands and to sing. Believers claim this is to 'develop power', but sceptics point out that the noise provides potential diversion from the entry of accomplices, or the rigging of apparatus to produce fraudulent phenomena.

If the sitters are fortunate, the phenomena then begin. The first sign of paranormal activity (as in poltergeist attacks and spontaneous psi) usually takes the form of loud raps apparently emanating from the walls or furniture. Tiny dots of light, like electrical sparks, might be seen. Objects that were not previously in the room (which has usually been locked since the beginning of the seance) may fall from the air. These are known as 'apports' and are also familiar in the context of such experiments as those of the SORRAT group, and in poltergeist cases. Apports in seance rooms tend to be flowers, but in rare cases may be revealed to be familiar personal possessions of the sitters, such as an initialled handkerchief or a ring.

Undoubtedly the focus of all such seances is the 'spirit materialisation'. Figures purporting to be spirits of the dead take shape, becoming visible by 'clothing' themselves in the greyish-white substance which is apparently secreted through the orifices of the medium's body. This is 'ectoplasm', the very existence of which has been challenged by some psychical researchers, but which others have claimed to photograph with infra-red camera techniques. With a formidable psychic such as Eusapia Palladino as medium, ectoplasm has been witnessed to form 'pseudopods' – temporary levers and rods – with which to levitate tables or cause other physical phenomena to occur.

The ectoplasmic resurrected dead may walk and talk with the sitters, sometimes illuminating their faces by holding luminous cards up to them. Often, however, the materialisations are content to stand silently in the semi-darkness. Some rare seances have produced materialisations of animals or even monsters – the Polish medium Franek Kluski was photographed with a bird of prey across the back of his neck, and on another occasion with a ghoul-like creature by his side. At D. D. Home's seances, generally held in good light, disembodied hands and arms appeared and patted the sitters gently – whereas at those of Brazilian medium Carmine Mirabelli the dead materialised in full form, often reeking of the grave.

It is not unusual for a host of complementary phenomena to occur. They include sudden cold breezes, disembodied whispering, the levitation of the table around which the group are sitting; musical instruments may levitate and apparently be played by invisible hands. Many, if not all, of these effects are easily faked – the ectoplasmic rods and spirit materialisations are harder to produce fraudulently, and in some cases seem genuinely paranormal. The real problem that confronts the researcher is whether or not the phenomena constitute proof of survival, as the Spiritualists claim.

SEE ALSO *Angels; Apports; Kenneth Batcheldor; Black Monk of Pontefract; Boggle threshold; Case of Ruth; Consensus reality; Cosmic Joker; Aleister Crowley; The Devil; Helen Duncan; Ectoplasm; Entity enigma; Fairies; Fantasy-prone personalities; Gustave Geley; Ghosts; D. D. Home; Incorruptibility; Katie King; Levitation; Life after death; Carmine Mirabelli; Mysterious appearances; Eusapia Palladino; Parapsychology; Philip experiment; Coral Polge; Propensity for psi; The Resurrection; Ritual magic; Sex and psi; Society for Psychical Research; SORRAT; Doris Stokes; Thoughtography; Tulpas; Visions of the Virgin Mary; Witchcraft.*

LEVITATION

The ability to levitate, to defy the law of gravity and rise unaided into the air, is a rare, but well-documented paranormal ability that is usually (but not universally) attributed to the saints. St Francis of Assisi was often discovered to have risen in his religious ecstasy to the height of a beech tree. On at least one occasion a visiting monk 'beheld him lifted up in the air so high, and surrounded with such splendour, that he scarce could see him'.

That most practical medieval saint, Teresa of Avila, frequently fell into raptures and found herself levitated into the air. She was worried that her experiences might be delusions, and she vigorously denied her saintliness. Yet time and again she was lifted into the air in full view of the nuns, and several times in sight of the Bishop of Avila. Teresa found the experience embarrassing and occasionally tried to resist it, but afterwards found herself worn out 'like a person who had been contending with a strong giant'. Unresisted, the experience of the levitation was one of 'great sweetness'. Once Teresa was receiving Communion from the Bishop through the customary iron grille when she felt herself begin to rise. She grasped the grille in an effort to stop levitating, saying, 'Do not permit a creature as vile as I am to be taken for a holy woman.' The saint's inner conflicts and experiences are lucidly expressed in her *Life*, completed in 1565.

It was St Joseph of Cupertino (1603–63) who

*Victorian medium D. D. Home floats to the ceiling –
a feat that was often witnessed. Apart from levitation,
he was known for his apparent incombustibility.*

*Home floats out of a third-storey window at Ashley
House, London, in 1868 – and in through the next in
front of three reputable witnesses.*

showed the greatest, and most public, talent for
spontaneous levitation. As a child he had been
nicknamed 'open mouth' and was considered to
be simple, although his piety and the rigour of his
self-mortification were astonishing in one so
young. He was dismissed from the Capuchin order
because he lacked concentration to fulfil even the
most menial of tasks. A slip by the local bishop,
however, ensured him a place in a Franciscan monastery, where his austerities became even more
fanatical. His ecstasies also drew attention to him,
most of it unwelcome, and he was even questioned
by the Inquisition. Finding no fault with him, they
allowed him to worship in their own chapel, where
he experienced his first ecstatic levitation – sailing
through the air on to the high altar, while the nuns
screamed, 'He will catch fire!' Joseph remained
unburnt. On a visit to Rome he had an audience
with Pope Urban VIII – an experience that moved

him to such rapture that he flew into the air
instantly. On another occasion, walking in a garden with a fellow monk, he suddenly flew to the
top of a tree, but could not get down again and
a ladder had to be fetched.

Miracles and rumours of miracles had been
associated with him since his boyhood; one of the
best attested was his healing of a raging madman.
Commanding the sick man to commend himself
to God, Joseph grabbed him by the hair and they
both rose into the air, where they remained for
nearly an hour. This is the only known case of a
saint causing another to rise with him.

Not all those who levitate do so as a result of
their religious discipline. In 1657 the teenage Henry
(some reports call him Richard) Jones of Shepton
Mallet, Somerset, suddenly rose into the air until
his head touched the ceiling. He found himself constantly being uplifted and hurled by an invisible,

but apparently gentle, force; although he was once thrown nearly thirty metres over a wall, he was never hurt – merely astonished. After a year the abrupt levitations left him, never to return.

Two of the greatest Spiritualist mediums – D. D. Home and Carmine Mirabelli – were famed for their ability to rise into the air. Home's levitations were accompanied by sensations akin to those of a religious ecstasy, which he explained as the blessings of the spirits of the dead. On one occasion in 1868 he rose into the air and floated out through a third-storey window, then in through another window, before three witnesses of good repute. Mirabelli, who also favoured the Spiritualist explanation for his gifts, was photographed hovering near a ceiling.

Levitation of human beings is rare. However, objects frequently rise into the air during poltergeist attacks or during psi-induction experiments such as those of the SORRAT group.

SEE ALSO *Apports; Kenneth Batcheldor; Consensus reality; D. D. Home; Images that bleed and weep; Incorruptibility; Limits of science; Carmine Mirabelli; Moving statues; Mysterious appearances; Out-of-the-body experiences; Seance-room phenomena; SORRAT; Stigmatics; Witchcraft.*

Carmine Mirabelli, the great Brazilian medium, hovers at ceiling height. Extraordinary phenomena were frequently experienced in his presence. There seems no question that he was genuinely gifted as a psychic.

APPORTS

Objects that manifest paranormally are known as 'apports'. The term is generally associated with the seance room, where common apports are flowers, regarded as gifts from the dead to the living, but it can also describe mysteriously appearing objects in the context of poltergeists, religious miracles and spontaneous phenomena.

Presumably apports are also teleportations – they frequently show evidence of having travelled through solid matter, such as a door or wall. Stones flung by invisible attackers, as in poltergeist cases, are often warm to the touch, which may be linked to the suddenness with which their component atoms had been broken down and reassembled (on one side of a wall, for example, then on the other).

Very often the first sign of a poltergeist attack is the inexplicable movement of objects, a phenomenon which may be much commoner than might be supposed – it is often dismissed as 'absentmindedness' or 'just one of those things' (the JOTT syndrome). In parapsychological experiments the sudden appearance of objects is taken as a sign of success (or fraud); a huge stone was filmed – between frames – falling from thin air on to a table during one of Kenneth Batcheldor's psychokinesis experiments. Rubber rings were filmed linking inside SORRAT's 'minilab', then emerging through its glass wall, between frames of the film.

Hilda Lewis, the 'flower medium', caught in the act of cheating.

In the mid-1970s Uri Geller was staying with Professor John Hasted of London University when Mrs Hasted discovered the giblets from a frozen turkey lying beside the solid bird. On another occasion Spanish coins appeared in mid-air while Geller waited to speak to writer-researcher Colin Wilson – they were to work together in Barcelona.

It seems likely that some kind of psychokinetic force is involved, especially when deliberately invoked, as in the experiments of SORRAT. But it may be that Charles Fort's idea that the Earth is a refuse dump for an alien civilisation is an alternative hypothesis.

SEE ALSO *Kenneth Batcheldor; Black Monk of Pontefract; Boggle threshold; Church of Jesus Christ of Latter Day Saints (Mormons); Enfield poltergeist; Entity enigma; Fishfalls; Charles Fort; Uri Geller; Mysterious appearances; Other dimensions; Parapsychology; Psychokinesis; Seance-room phenomena; SORRAT; Thoughtography; Tulpas; UFO paradox.*

PSYCHIC MUSIC, ART AND LITERATURE

Rosemary Brown was first contacted by a discarnate musician when she was a young girl; her ghostly visitor turned out to be Franz Liszt, who promised that others would follow and write music through her mediumship. Since 1964 Mrs Brown, who has only a rudimentary knowledge of music, has acted as amanuensis for Beethoven, Chopin, Brahms and Stravinsky among others. She has often had to take instructions down phonetically, since some of the foreign composers relapse into their native languages when excited.

Although the music is considerably less than the best written by the composers in life, that is not the point of the communications. The late musicologist Sir Donald Tovey said, through Mrs Brown's mediumship:

In communicating through music and conversation, an organised group of musicians, who have departed from your world, are attempting to establish a precept for humanity, i.e. that physical death is a transition from one state of consciousness to another wherein one retains one's individuality ... We are not transmitting music to Rosemary Brown simply for ... pleasure ... it is the implications relevant to this phenomena [sic] which we hope will stimulate ... interest and stir many who are intelligent and impartial to consider and explore the unknown of Man's mind and psyche.

Not all musicians, however, have been critical of the posthumous works; Leonard Bernstein and Hephzibah Menuhin have met Mrs Brown and listened to the music – both were impressed. Richard Rodney Bennett had to admit: 'A lot of people can improvise, but you couldn't fake music like this without years of training. I couldn't have faked some of the Beethoven myself.'

Another psychic musician is concert pianist John Lill. He believes he is in touch with Beethoven, who has helped him further his musical career. As a nice gesture, the great composer dedicated one of his posthumous works to Lill, through Mrs Brown's mediumship. Recalling founder of the Society for Psychical Research Frederic Myers's 'frosted glass' analogy about the difficulties involved in discarnate communication with the living, Lill says: 'It's all to do with cleaning a window, and some windows are cleaner than others'.

The late Rosalind Heywood, an astute psychical researcher, believed that Mrs Brown (and those like her) is 'the type of sensitive whom frustration, often artistic, drives to the automatic production of material beyond their conscious capacity'. So is musical, artistic or literary genius latent within us all? Do we have to 'dress up' our genius in the guise of the famous dead in order to be able to accept it?

When Matthew Manning began to work in psychic art in the early 1970s he sought to contact certain artists, notably Pablo Picasso, who had only been dead three months when he first worked through Matthew. Works in the style of a huge variety of artists, from Elizabethan miniaturist Isaac Oliver to Aubrey Beardsley and Beatrix Potter, were to make up an impressive collection of psychic art, especially as many were apparently signed by the artists.

In 1978 the Brazilian psychic Luiz Gasparetto astounded viewers of BBC Television's *Nationwide* by going into a trance and producing 'new' Picassos, Cézannes and Renoirs so fast that many people thought the film had been shown too fast. (In fact the programme was live.) That evening he produced twenty-one works of art, sometimes working from the wrong side of the paper, often with

South London medium Rosemary Brown claims that dead composers, such as Liszt and Beethoven, use her as a channel through which they continue to compose music.

both hands simultaneously painting different pictures, and despite being upset by the studio lights – normally he works in the near dark. Both Matthew and Luiz regard the discarnate Picasso with caution – he broke several nibs of the British psychic's pens and, if anyone so much as whispers in front of the Brazilian when 'overshadowed' by Picasso, he throws the paper around.

In a monastery near Hong Kong several Buddhist monks of the order of the Red Swastika regularly become entranced and produce a wide variety of paranormally acquired knowledge and skill. One diagnoses and prescribes for illnesses, sometimes needing only a letter from the patient as a basis for his pronouncements. Another produces beautiful line drawings, in several separate pieces, often without looking at the paper as he does so. When put together, the pieces match exactly to make one perfect picture.

More difficult for discarnates is the practice of automatic writing, for words are products of the left brain, the hemisphere that actually retards intuition and mediumistic abilities. Inevitably, written communications are contaminated by the habitual thoughts and word associations of the medium, yet there are striking examples of this art. The Cross-correspondences comprise the most veridical and impressive of all automatic writing, for this project was planned with just such difficulties in mind. More overtly artistic, was the huge output of 'Patience Worth'.

In 1913 Mrs Pearl Curran, a housewife of St Louis, began to experiment with the ouija board. Very soon she had abandoned it as too clumsy for the work she was producing – poems and novels by the dead Quaker girl Patience Worth – and began to employ direct automatic writing. Patience was quaintly rustic, writing in the dialect of seventeenth-century Dorset (which she had left for America), and incredibly prolific. In one evening she wrote, through Mrs Curran's pen, twenty-two poems; over a five-year period her prose added up to nearly two million words. Several novels were published in the discarnate's name; *Hope Trueblood* was widely acclaimed and the talent of its mysterious author compared to that of the

Brontë sisters. Another full-length work, *The Sorry Tale*, concerned a contemporary of Christ and exhibited a profound scholarship that was certainly not that of Mrs Curran's conscious mind. (She honestly believed that the title of Tennyson's poem *The Lady of Shallott* was *The Lady of Charlotte*.)

Exhaustively investigated by Dr Walter Franklin, Prince of the Boston Society for Psychical Research, the work of Patience Worth remains impressive evidence for survival of the personality, and for the survival of burning literary ambition frustrated during life. Despite this, both prose and poetry are not to everyone's taste: one reviewer commented that her writing was 'feverish, high-flown and terribly prolix'. Patience, however, seemed to believe that there was a higher purpose than mere literary fulfilment at stake. She wrote: 'I weave not, nay but neath these hands shall such a word set up, that Earth shall burn with wonder.'

Mrs Curran died in 1938. Today there are many mediums who practise automatic writing – with greater or lesser skill and self-deception – but none so persuasive as Chico Xavier, whose 310 books produced by a wide variety of dead poets and novelists crash the boggle barrier.

Parapsychologists, many of whom entertain grave doubts about even such impressive scripts as the Cross-correspondences, are fond of labelling anomalous writing as 'telepathic psychokinesis' or ascribe it to the ubiquitous 'super-ESP'. Or it may be that dead musicians, artists and writers use mediums to carry on their earthly work. So far, however, no medium has reported a discarnate parapsychologist transmitting his quaint jargon through the process of automatic *explanation*.

SEE ALSO *American Society for Psychical Research*; *Boggle threshold*; *Case of Ruth*; *Cosmic Joker*; *Creative visualisation*; *Cross-correspondences*; *ESP*; *Explanations*; *Formative causation*; *Healing*; *Inspiration in dreams*; *Left and right brain*; *Life after death*; *Matthew Manning*; *Multiple personality*; *Ouija board and planchette*; *Palm Sunday case*; *Paranormal portraits*; *Parapsychology*; *Philip experiment*; *Coral Polge*; *Possession*; *Prodigies*; *Psychokinesis*; *Shamanism*; *Society for Psychical Research*; *SORRAT*; *Speaking in tongues*; *Spiritism*; *Telepathy*; *Thoughtography*; *Tulpas*; *Chico Xavier*.

Visitors to the Parisian churchyard of St Médard in the eighteenth century fall into convulsions, during which they exhibit astonishing immunity to pain – and are cured of their illnesses, no matter how grave.

MIRACLES OF ST MÉDARD

When François de Paris, the Deacon of Paris, died in 1727 the poor lamented, for he had a reputation as a healer among the underprivileged and sick. But it was at his funeral, in the churchyard of St Médard in Paris, that the most dramatic cures began, when a boy with a withered leg began to run and dance.

The news spread rapidly, provoking the wrath and condemnation of the Jesuits, who believed the cures to be either hoaxes or the work of the Devil. But most people who went to the churchyard went away shaken by what they had seen.

Those who had been healed – mostly women – were afflicted with extraordinary convulsions:

their bodies contorted into perfect hoop-shapes. They willingly underwent hideous tortures. Women invited onlookers to stab, bludgeon or burn them – yet no marks or blood appeared, and they came smiling through the ordeal. More remarkable still was the fact that the convulsionaries had the power to heal, sometimes sucking the septic matter from open sores. Others begged to be beaten or have their nipples twisted in wrenches – yet somehow in the process they were cured of lifelong deformities and tumours.

The outrageousness of these miracles became something of a scandal; many of the convulsionaries and their followers were thrown into the Bastille, and the churchyard was closed. Yet the faithful discovered that they could perform their miracles anywhere; there were sporadic outbreaks for several years after the clampdown. In 1759 a zealot called Sister Françoise regularly volunteered to be crucified for up to three hours at a time; although she showed pain, and blood flowed, she survived an ordeal designed to kill stronger people than herself.

The history of miracles is replete with stories of religious fanatics who seemed to transcend physical pain or to take extraordinary pain upon themselves, such as that associated with the stigmata. The convulsionaries seemed to exhibit an extreme form of mind over matter, often described as 'mass hysteria'. However, this is a label, not an explanation.

There are also similarities between the traumas experienced by the adherents of St Médard and the crises that frequently precede the onset of psychic abilities, poltergeist outbreaks or the phenomenon of images that bleed or weep. Mesmer had shown that inducing convulsions can bring about cures and temporary telepathic abilities; epileptics, such as Adrian Boshier, developed shamanistic talents; and electric shocks or blows to the head can make an ordinary person psychic. Clearly certain shocks to the system can induce such dramatic psi-functioning that it seems literally incredible – the crucifixion of Sister Françoise is just one of hundreds of such cases on record. The appearance of stigmata on the corpses of saints, or their bodily incorruptibility, may be the apotheosis of this phenomenon.

The strange story of the convulsionaries of St Médard reinforces the idea that the so-called 'laws of nature' may be mocked, given a certain – but so far mysterious – set of circumstances.

SEE ALSO *Boggle threshold; Consensus reality; Cosmic Joker; The Devil; Electric people; Explanations; Fireproof people; Healing; D. D. Home; Hypnosis; Hysteria; Images that bleed and weep; Incorruptibility; Limits of science; Mass hysteria; Mesmer; Possession; Psychic surgery; Psychokinesis; Rosenheim poltergeist; Sai Baba; Sex and psi; Shamanism; Stigmatics; Telepathy; Traumas and psi; Visions of the Virgin Mary; Witchcraft.*

PSYCHIC SURGERY

Thousands of sick people, desperate for the miracle cure that medical science cannot offer, annually arrive in the Philippines. They have come to visit the so-called 'psychic surgeons' who flourish there.

Time and time again investigators – and film crews – have exposed them as sleight-of-hand tricksters; on one occasion when the 'surgeon' appeared to have thrust his hand into a patient's stomach he simply buried his knuckles into the flesh, and the 'tumour' drawn out was discovered to be a chicken liver. Even the most famous of all the Filipino psychic surgeons, Tony Agpaoa, was exposed by an Italian film crew in 1973 when the so-called renal stones he produced from a patient's body were found to be pieces of pumice.

Although the motive for such trickery is hardly altruistic (Agpaoa has become very wealthy), these 'operations' do work. The power of suggestion, and the reinforcement of the sight of the blood, removed 'tumours' and so on, seem to have a remarkably powerful effect on even the most deadly and acute diseases. To some people the term 'operating theatre' may be taken in both senses, and the drama involved in such cures makes sick people well again.

The USA boasts a psychic dentist, Willard Fuller, who has been seen to provide instant fillings for bad teeth and even to cause new teeth to grow in the mouths of the aged. Although confirmation of his feats is hard to come by, the annals of healing contain reports of far weirder miracles.

SEE ALSO *José Arigo; Autosuggestion; Eleventh-hour syndrome; Valentine Greatrakes; Healing; Hysteria; Matthew Manning; Miracles of St Médard; Psi-mediated instrumental response; Psychokinesis; Sai Baba.*

HEALING

From the dawn of history healing through the laying on of hands, and through prayer, has been reported. In every known society there have been, and are now, healers claiming abilities to palliate and cure every possible symptom and illness. People receiving healing have felt heat, cold, tingling and other sensations during treatments. They often report marked reduction in all types of pain, with accelerated recuperation from their illnesses. In rare cases there are instantaneous cures, even of serious diseases such as cancer. Modern science has tended to doubt the efficacy of healing, assuming it to be no more than a ritual or magical belief, and asserts that the cures are spontaneous regressions of disease (for which modern science has no explanation, or even theory).

Recently, a few open-minded scientists have begun to listen to healers and to examine their reports more closely. Though the underlying mechanisms of healing are as yet a mystery, clues are emerging. Two broad yet distinct categories are apparent, present and distant (sometimes called 'absent') healing.

In his book on healing, *The Psi of Relief* (1989), Dr Daniel J Benor, an American psychiatrist, has reviewed the literature on healing research. He has found more than a hundred carefully performed experiments exploring the effects of the healing force on enzymes, yeasts, bacteria, protozoa, plants, animals and man. More than three-quarters of these show significantly positive effects, a few of which are summarised here.

In an examination of present healing, Dr Bernard Grad tested Oscar Estebany, an experienced healer, in his laboratory at McGill University in Montreal. Dr Grad anaesthetised a large group of mice and then made a small skin wound on the back of each of them. Estebany held the cages of some of the mice several times daily, giving them healing. Other mice were allowed to heal on their own. The wounds of the mice whose cages had been held by Estebany healed significantly faster than those of the others. Dr Grad repeated his experiment with more rigorous criteria, and again

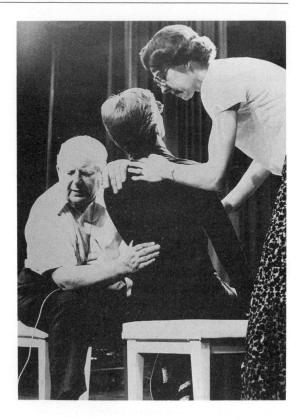

The late British healer Harry Edwards demonstrating his remarkable gift.

obtained significantly positive results.

A group of scientists at the Institute for Parapsychology in North Carolina performed more than a dozen experiments into distant healing using pairs of anaesthetised mice. They challenged various healers to waken one of each pair sooner than the other, and found that they were able to do so to a highly significant degree, even from behind a one-way mirror, with healers several metres away from the mice. The healers objected to having to switch the focus of their healing from one side of the table to the other, as the rules of the experiment initially dictated. When the researchers studied this, they found that the healing effect from one trial tended to linger and to influence mice placed subsequently on the same side of the table to waken earlier. Marilyn Schlitz, of the Mind Science Foundation in San Antonio, Texas, replicated these studies with automated timing for the waking of mice, and also found significant positive results.

Healers claim that most people have some healing ability. At St Joseph's University in Philadelphia, Dr Carroll Nash tested students' abilities to enhance and retard the growth of bacteria in laboratory cultures. The students who claimed no healing abilities, were successful at both tasks – using distant healing.

For her doctoral thesis, Joyce Goodrich, a New York psychologist, investigated whether distant healing could be detected through the sensations experienced by the human patients. She told them to expect healing at a certain time of day. Without their knowledge, distant healing was projected on some days but not on others. From the reports of the patients independent judges were able to differentiate when healing had and had not been sent.

Another of Dr Grad's experiments with present healing ended up as a test of healing through intermediary substances. He asked Oscar Estebany to treat mice to prevent the development of goitres that had been induced by a diet low in iodine. Estebany was reluctant to spend so much time on mice when he could be treating people, and suggested giving Dr Grad cotton wool that he had treated with healing. This, he said, would prevent the goitres if it was placed in the cages. Although sceptical, Dr Grad carefully considered Estebany's reports that he had healed people by having them hold various materials he had treated in this way, and decided to proceed with the modified experiment. He placed treated cotton wool in the cages of some iodine-deficient mice, and untreated cotton wool in the cages of others. The first group were significantly slower to develop goitres.

It is unclear what might be occurring with this type of healing. The suggestion is either that a healing energy is stored in the intermediary object, or that the object serves as a psychometric link between healer and patient to facilitate healing. Although many other studies have been done, it is too early to conclude precisely what healing is. It appears to be a most complex mechanism, acting on physical, mental, emotional and spiritual levels simultaneously.

Healing can, to a certain extent, be taught. At New York University Dr Dolores Krieger and Dora Kunz, a gifted clairvoyant and healer, developed the method of Therapeutic Touch healing. They have taught thousands of nurses and lay people in the United States and many other countries to develop their healing abilities. Dr Krieger and some of her students have performed experiments which demonstrated that Therapeutic Touch can elevate people's haemoglobin levels, reduce anxiety and relieve headaches.

In Therapeutic Touch, healers first 'centre' themselves by quieting and focusing their minds. Next, they pass their hands around the patient's body without touching it, scanning for sensations – such as heat, cold and tingling – which inform them of areas of health and disease. They then treat those areas that they feel have too much or too little energy by placing their hands on or near the body and visualising an energy transfer between themselves and the patients.

Dr Lawrence LeShan, a New York psychologist, has treated many cancer patients. He originally studied healing because he wanted to expose it as a dangerous sham that offered false hope, and, he then believed, led his patients to waste valuable time during which they might have had the benefit of conventional treatment. After sitting with a number of gifted healers, however, he came away impressed that healing works. He identified three steps to healing: concentration; caring for the patient; focusing on one's connection with the patient and with the All. Starting with meditation, he found he could reproduce these steps. He became a healer himself, and subsequently taught others these methods.

Many other methods and variants of healing have been described and are taught. British healer Matthew Manning runs highly successful healing workshops, designed primarily to awaken the healer's latent intuition.

Healers suggest that beneficial effects may occur on mental, emotional and spiritual levels, and are not put off when no physical results are noted. Faith is not necessary – the patient need not believe in the healer or in his methods in order for cures to occur, but he or she must believe in his or her own ability to change.

In the United Kingdom, most people learn to develop their healing abilities through one of the healing organisations, such as the National Federation for Spiritual Healing. The majority of these have united under the Confederation of Healing Organisations (CHO), which provides a code of conduct, conducts clinical trials to demonstrate the efficacy of healing, and works towards establishing a greater collaboration between doctors, the National Health Service and healers. Through the efforts of the CHO a third of the country's regional medical authorities have agreed to distribute to doctors lists of registered healers to whom patients can be referred.

In the United States, however, healing is a very individual matter. Although people may study particular techniques, there is no organisational framework within which to continue their practices.

Healing has no clear framework within conventional science around which to build a theory of how it works. But, modern physics contains hypotheses – of particle and wave, of action at a distance, and of interactions of the observer with matter – which suggest the beginnings of bridges between what has until now been folklore, but promises soon to become science.

SEE ALSO *José Arigo; Autosuggestion; Case for God; Church of Jesus Christ of Latter Day Saints (Mormons); Consensus reality; Creative visualisation; Eastern bloc psi; Explanations; Fireproof people; Valentine Greatrakes; Holism; Hysteria; Left and right brain; Limits of science; Matthew Manning; Mesmer; Miracles of St Médard; New Testament miracles; Old Testament miracles; Parapsychology; Psychic surgery; Quantum mechanics and the paranormal; Remote viewing; Ritual magic; Sai Baba; Shamanism; Soviet psi today; Spiritism; Stigmatics; Telepathy; Visions of the Virgin Mary; Witchcraft.*

tic therapy, the existence of the physical, mental, social and spiritual components of an individual's life is acknowledged, and he is encouraged to regain the balance that is essential if 'dis-ease' is not to be the result.

Practitioners of holistic therapy regard theirs as a gentle approach, one that seeks to mobilise the immune system – the opposite of conventional medicine, which tends to overpower the patient with drugs or surgery. Even the way in which hospitals are organised makes no sense to an advocate of holism: a patient under investigation must move from department to department, having various parts of his body tested – and treated – separately.

Holism is a challenge to the entire social structure, calling into question the way children are educated, for example. Many proponents of holism believe that it is counterproductive to teach arts and sciences separately. The pupil sees only a series of dislocated jigsaw pieces, some of which may be missing in the jumble.

Professor James Lovelock goes much further; he believes that the Earth and all that lives on it is part of one vast living organism that is capable of becoming diseased – and of being healed. This, the 'Gaia' principle, is widely accepted by adherents of New Age thinking as the ultimate form of holism.

SEE ALSO *Buddhism; Case for God; Formative causation; Valentine Greatrakes; Healing; Jung and the paranormal; Left and right brain; Limits of science; Matthew Manning; New Testament miracles; Sai Baba.*

HOLISM

The age of rationalism has seen the rise of specialisation in every area of life. The 'New Age' belief of holism is the direct counterpoint to this. Holism is seen at work most clearly in alternative or complementary medicine, where the whole patient – and not merely his symptoms – is treated. In holis-

END TIMES CULTS

A considerable number of people – some of them individuals who have been granted personal revelations, others members of organisations who are trustees of arcane wisdom handed down through the ages – believe they know the immediate future of mankind. Derived from a wide range of esoteric sources, the scenario almost always involves the arrival of an Antichrist. He will seize and rule our world for a while until Jesus Christ himself returns and defeats him in a successful battle – which, however, will involve Earth in considerable catastrophe. After this, Time, as we know it, will end, and some sort of timeless Golden Age will commence.

There are as many variations of this story as it has narrators. In its Christian form it is told only by those who regard Jesus as deity. For anthroposophists the role of villain is played by Ahriman. Believers in other divine powers offer alternative futures, similarly derived from ancient writings of uncertain authenticity. Of the many variations, the question on which opinions diverge most widely is how many of us will enjoy the eventual benefits. Many versions include a 'rapture' in which True Believers will be rescued in a flash of a second, just in time to escape the horrors of the final conflict.

It is an indication of the strength of man's sense that 'this life cannot be all' that there should exist a field of study so speculative as eschatology. It comprises the various anthropomorphic teachings concerning the 'last things' – the concept of a Day of Judgement, on which our earthly conduct will be assessed and retribution demanded for our failures to measure up to some undisclosed standard; millennial ideas involving some kind of compensation paid to those who drew the short straws in life's lottery; the catastrophic end of the world and its renewal; the resurrection (in some cases selective) of those already dead and buried; and the fate (also selective) of those still around to witness our planet's grand finale.

Virtually every religion, from the most primitive to the most sophisticated, embodies such teachings. Each version tends to reflect the cultural context in which it was formulated. Thus the Old Testament prophets foresaw, first, a period of 'Messianic woes', preceding a new order which would be inaugurated by God himself – characterised by the consumption of much food and drink and the begetting of numerous offspring.

The New Testament 'revelation' of St John of Patmos is considerably more refined. It introduces the idea of a final confrontation between good and evil, which has been taken literally by fundamentalist commentators ever since – despite the implausibility that a Power of Evil, possessed of a cosmic IQ presumably surpassing terrestrial measurements, would participate in a sequence of events that is preordained to culminate in his inevitable defeat on the battlefield of Armageddon.

At the time of Jesus's ministry, it was widely supposed among the Jews that these events were imminent. When the 'new order' failed to occur during Jesus's lifetime, theologians reread John and concluded that the year 1000 would probably see the awaited event. Prophecies accumulated around the millennium – all to be proved vain, but not without extraordinary displays of public alarm and subsequent relief.

Since then, established religion has gradually abandoned the notion that the destiny of Earth's inhabitants is somehow bound up with catastrophic events on the physical plane; but there has been no lack of others to carry such ideas to even greater extremes. In many cases, notably the popular millenarian movements in western Europe in the fourteenth to sixteenth centuries, beliefs reflected the social situation; they did so again in nineteenth-century Russia and in the twentieth-century movements among Melanesian cultures in the South Seas.

Today, the approach of the year 2000 has given a new impetus to literal interpretations of the kind that circulated a thousand years ago, although on an even flimsier basis of belief. Many UFO commentators have seen them as the vessels of Antichrist, and believe that Armageddon will literally be fought in the heavens between God's UFOs and those of Antichrist.

Typical are the speculations of Stuart Campbell, who in 1961 warned that 'the appearance of UFOs in our skies means the Devil is intensifying his campaign, because he knows his time is short. That means that something will happen soon.' Like other doomcasters, he found links between current trends and biblical prophecies; thus the boom in tourism is matched to Daniel's forecast that in the end time 'many shall run to and fro' – although this could apply equally well to the current craze for marathon races.

Campbell prudently refrains from naming the day, but others have been more explicit. The seventeenth-century prophet Brother Johannes was alleged by the French occultist Péladan to have predicted that 'somewhere about the year 2000 Antichrist will stand revealed', but there is always some doubt as to the authenticity of Péladan's sources. Ulrich von Mainz has interpreted them as signifying 1982, but an alternative reading points to 1992, so he could – as of the time of writing – still be proved right. Some of Nostradamus's commentators claim that he specified 1999 as the year of ultimate catastrophe, but his prophecies are notoriously malleable.

Many individuals have met beings who appear to be messengers announcing the end of time. In an interesting variant on the phantom hitch-hiker myth, the Reverend Swart, driving near Johannesburg in 1961, stopped to give a man a lift. His passenger warned him to prepare for the end of all things and the return of Christ – then vanished abruptly, as if the rapture had swept him up. Precisely the same thing happened to a couple near Buenos Aires in 1965; when they told their adventure at the next filling station, the attendant said they were the ninth customers that day who had told him that story. As a result of their experience the couple gave up their normal job and devoted themselves to a 'high Christian task'; their faith may have waned somewhat during the twenty-four years during which their hitch-hiker's prophecy has failed to materialise.

The best reference a prophet could offer would be a succession of fulfilled predictions; unfortunately there is not one whose track record encourages trust. Edgar Cayce, who seems to have displayed a remarkable ability to diagnose ailments while in an alternate state of consciousness, fared less well with his geophysical predictions. In 1958 he predicted for the near future cataclysmic changes in the western hemisphere, including 'new lands seen off the Caribbean Sea ... the greater portion of Japan must go into the sea. The upper portion of Europe will be changed as in the twinkle of an eye. . . .'

Another much-praised prophet is Jeanne Dixon, who is credited (erroneously) with predicting the Kennedy assassination. She foresees a world holocaust in 1999; however, she is also on record as saying (in 1969): 'I have seen a comet strike our earth around the middle of the 1980s ... our first

[US] woman president will surely be in the 1980s'. She says that the Antichrist was born around 1962 and is preparing his Satanic mission, which she sees as beginning to make real world impact in 1991–2. He will lead many souls astray, but eventually the grand deception of the 'Child in the East' will yield to Christ.

Self-deluded or self-seeking, many 'psychics' are making similar prophecies, creating a snowball effect – but with as little substance. All overlook the fact that 'the year 2000' is a man-made label devoid of significance – even for Christians, now that scholars agree that, even if Jesus existed, the birth date attributed to him is likely to be wrong.

The apparent convergence of predictions towards a *fin-de-siècle* cataclysm is as much a social artefact as the first millennial year, 1000. Writing in the journal *Meeting the Third Millennium*, editor Dan Lloyd commented: 'With the approach of the end of the century, apocalyptic fears have been aroused by the spectre of a yawning abyss into which a frenzied humanity seems bent on hurling itself.' It is to those who are so determined to torment themselves with such spectres that they will abandon all logic, all critical reasoning, that end-time prophecies make their appeal.

SEE ALSO *Angels; Astrology; Church of Jesus Christ of Latter Day Saints (Mormons); Cosmic Joker; The Devil; Divination; Entity enigma; Fate; Foaflore; Life after death; Mass hysteria; New Testament miracles; Old Testament miracles; Phantom hitch-hiker; Prophecy and prediction; The Resurrection; Time; UFO paradox; UFOs.*

TOAD MAGIC

In 1945 the body of old Charlie Walton was found near his home in the Warwickshire village of Lower Quinton; a cross-shape had been carved in the flesh of his chest with a bill-hook, and his head had been savagely pinned to the ground by a pitch-fork. There appeared to be no obvious murderer and no motive. When Detective Superintendent Robert

Fabian of Scotland Yard was called in, he suspected ritual murder, and lost no time in consulting Dr Margaret Murray, an anthropologist with expert knowledge of witchcraft. Although the case was never solved the locals believed Walton had been involved in the black arts, for he kept natterjack toads as pets.

The toad has been almost universally loathed and feared throughout history. Its hominid shape no doubt provided the psychological association with devils in medieval minds, and it was widely believed to be poisonous. In fact, the common European toads do produce a formidable arsenal of bactericides and fungicides and the hallucinogen bufotenin – which, if eaten or rubbed on the skin, produces the hallucination of flight. In recent years the introduction of the cane toad into Australia gave rise to the unpleasant practice of boiling the amphibians down and ingesting the results in a variety of ways to induce floating or flying sensations. Many recipes for witches' ointment made use of this basic substance; once the mess was rubbed all over their naked bodies they could attend their unholy Sabbats without leaving home.

Certainly some self-confessed witches did keep toads as familiars, and some even 'milked' them. In the fourteenth century a member of the heretical Waldensians of Turin confessed that the group worshipped a toad that represented the Great Dragon of Revelation, and that they drank a magical brew made with its faeces. (It should be noted, however, that the man told this interesting tale under torture. All 'heretics' were readily believed by the established Church to indulge in blasphemous practices. In most cases nothing could be further from the truth.)

Some occult groups kissed a toad, representing the Devil, on the anus (the *occulum infame*) in order to prove their allegiance and to gain esoteric knowledge. This ritual may have become the basis for the highly romanticised tale of the prince who was bewitched and turned into a frog, and who would only return to his human state when kissed by a princess. Master magician Aleister Crowley once ritually crucified a toad, and as late as 1939 witches (of the 'left-hand path') in rural France used tortured and crucified toads in their killing spells.

Throughout the centuries people have believed

Quarrymen find a toad inside a stone. Toads have often been discovered inside millenia-old stones, some of which have survived sudden exposure to the air.

the toad to be an enchanted creature that bears in its head a magical 'toadstone', a precious gem. Many have been killed in fruitless treasure-seeking.

Toads were at the centre of a huge controversy that spanned almost half the nineteenth century. In 1835 workers clearing away red sandstone to make way for the London–Birmingham railway track cracked open a piece of stone and discovered a toad inside. When exposed to the air it seemed 'oppressed' and gasped feebly; within ten minutes its colour changed from brown to black. It had been hurt when the rock was split and died four days later. But how could it have lived without food or air, inside stone, for geological ages?

Toads have often been discovered in cavities apparently formed around them, provoking out-

and-out sceptics such as the Victorian Captain Buckman to call the whole phenomenon 'a gross imposition', meaning that it was always a trick played upon the gullible by those who claimed to find the creatures. Others approached the problem more rationally, suggesting that the toad's rocky tomb was actually surrounded by microscopic fissures that let in air and insects – but this does not explain how the rock of two hundred million years came to lie over and around the living toad.

Tibetan Buddhists believe that such creatures are the reincarnated souls of evil men imprisoned in 'occasional Hells' outside the central Hell and found on the Earth. Using appropriate rituals, holy men can release the toad from its tomb – and the soul from its torment.

SEE ALSO *Buddhism; Cosmic Joker; Aleister Crowley; Curses; The Devil; Explanations; Charles Fort; Karma; Reincarnation; Ritual magic; Tulpas; Werewolves; Witchcraft.*

RITUAL MAGIC

Whereas religion is an appeal to the gods, it has been said, magic is an attempt to compel them. At the higher levels of European magic – which are derived from ancient Egyptian and oriental magic – the adept attempts to compel the Higher Powers to give him control over spirits so he can increase his personal power or add to his store of transcendental wisdom. Central to such attempts is the power of the word in the form of an incantation, and the recitation of the secret names of the spirits concerned. To the adept, the Bible's first statement, 'In the beginning was the word', is to be taken literally, and to know the name of a person or spirit is to begin to have power over him. The culminating incantation is always prefaced and accompanied by an elaborate ritual.

There are many types of ritual magic, each with its own techniques. The 'beginners' ritual is candle-magic, in which coloured candles are anointed and lit, with accompanying incantation, at the appro-

priate phase of the moon. Such simple ritual is scorned by the serious adept, however, whose preparation for each 'working' must be meticulous.

In the preceding ceremonial, the adept will spend several days – typically nine – preparing himself in body and spirit. This will involve fasting, sexual abstinence, ritual ablutions, prayer and meditation on the object of the 'working' he is about to undertake.

The date and time of the ceremonial will be chosen in accordance with the traditional laws of astrology and the phase of the moon. Workings for the purpose of increase of any sort (such as the gaining of knowledge or power) take place during the phase when the moon is waxing; workings concerned with decrease (such as in healing, which will come about when the sick cells diminish in number) take place during the waning of the moon. Highly charged rituals traditionally take place at the moment of the new and full moons.

The adept must assemble and consecrate the instruments of the ritual – all, if possible, made by himself from materials never before used. (Even in simple candlemagic the magician is urged to make his own candles, or at least to pay precisely the right amount of money for them.) These instruments will almost invariably include, for the serious working adept: the altar, the chalice, the tripod, the censer, the lamp and the rod. (Rituals devoted to the 'left-hand path' – black magic – also use the sword and the fork or trident.) The rod, probably the most precious of all these instruments, must be made from a wand of almond or hazel cut with a golden sickle in the early dawn and bound with rings of copper and zinc. It should also be blessed by another magician who possesses a consecrated rod himself.

As the ritual hour approaches, the adept will anoint himself with sacred oil (composed perhaps of myrrh, cinnamon, galingale and olive) and put on vestments appropriate to the time and purpose of the invocation (such as purple and gold on a Sunday, white and silver for Monday, or green if transcendental wisdom is the purpose). Again, the magician is urged to make the garments himself. He will also prepare the incense, using, for example, a blend of cedar, rose, citron, aloes, sandalwood and cinnamon.

Two forms of High Magic: the Catholic Mass (celebrated here by the stigmatic Padre Pio), where the wine and wafer are believed to be miraculously transmuted into the actual blood and flesh of Christ; and the climax of a ritual magic 'working', celebrated here by Aleister Crowley. But where religion attempts to placate the gods, magic attempts to control them.

The ritual itself begins with the drawing of appropriate diagrams, almost certainly a circle and one of the sacred triangles such as the Pentagram, each marked with appropriate magical symbols, and the adept will then proceed with a series of strictly ordained actions. These involve the traditional placing of the instruments, the lighting of the lamp, the burning of the incense, and, above all, the recitation of the invocation and the incantation.

At no point during the ceremonial must the adept move from inside the 'magic circle', which may be drawn or painted on the floor of the temple, or may be inscribed in the air with his hand before the ceremony begins. To step over the circle is asking for trouble, for if the invocation is successful then spirits are compelled to attend or even to appear, and submit to the adept's will. Many will be powerful and belligerent, waiting to pounce on the adept who crosses the line. A final, 'banishing'

ritual must conclude the ceremonial to compel the spirit to return harmlessly whence it came.

Rituals of this kind were conducted throughout the Middle Ages and the Renaissance by such adepts as John Dee and Nostradamus. Profound and ancient occult ceremonies have found eager adherents over the centuries through various 'heretical' groups such as the Templars, Rosicrucians and Masons, all of which flourish today. In their *The Holy Blood, the Holy Grail* (1982) authors Michael Baigent, Richard Leigh and Henry Lincoln provide persuasive evidence that all these hermetic societies are overshadowed by the mysterious Priory of Sion, still a force to be reckoned with in the late twentieth century. Despite the continued smear campaign of the established Church these societies neither worshipped the Devil nor appealed to the gullible and stupid. For example, one Rosicrucian adept – and a Grand Master of the all-powerful Priory of Sion – was Leonardo da Vinci (who is emerging as a strong contender as faker of the Turin Shroud, allegedly for purposes of deliberate anti-Christian propaganda).

Magical rituals culled from many of these sources were revived in the nineteenth century by societies such as the Hermetic Order of the Golden Dawn, and are – no doubt – still conducted in secret today by those who believe, with Eliphas Levi, that magic is the great science that 'reconciles faith with reason'. The testimony of reliable witnesses suggests that the results of properly conducted rituals – the uttering of 'the right words' – performed by experienced adepts can be sometimes remarkable, and often frightening.

The Church utterly condemns the occult and warns against 'dabbling' in it, yet its own rituals – for instance the transubstantiation of the wine and bread into the blood and body of Christ during the Mass – are extraordinarily similar to those of High Magic. And while it is undoubtedly true that practising magic lays the magician open to potential madness or even death, most ritual magicians are, as Dion Fortune said, protected by their own ineptitude.

The various elements that make up the rituals create the perfect psychological conditions for shifting from one state of consciousness to another – arguably from one plane of being to another. Everything about the ritual, such as cutting the ash for the wand and inscribing the magic circle, are devices for focusing the adept's will and sharpening his purpose. But behind it all lies one force the potency of which can only be guessed at – the harnessing of the imagination.

All occultists, psychics, artists and healers share the same capacity for creative visualisation, an ability latent in everyone. Once the imagination is fully engaged – by this one could mean the subconscious or the intuitive, right hemisphere of the brain – anything is possible. Hypnosis relies upon imagination, as does healing and any project that requires the use of intuition or creativity.

As for the spirits that may or may not be summoned by the ritual, the British magician J. W. Brodie-Innes once remarked that whether they 'really exist is comparatively unimportant; the point is that the universe behaves as though they do'.

SEE ALSO *Angels; Autosuggestion; Case of Ruth; Church of Jesus Christ of Latter Day Saints (Mormons); Consensus reality; Creative visualisation; Aleister Crowley; John Dee; The Devil; Entity enigma; Fairies; Fantasy-prone personalities; Formative causation; Great Beast 666; Healing; Hypnosis; Left and right brain; Men in Black; Philip experiment; Possession; Psychokinesis; Seance-room phenomena; Shamanism; Stigmatics; Thoughtography; Toad magic; Tulpas; Turin Shroud; Werewolves; Witchcraft.*

GREAT BEAST 666

The New Testament Book of the Revelation of St John the Divine describes the most evil man the world will ever know thus: 'Let him that hath understanding count the number of the beast: for it is the number of a man; and his number is Six hundred threescore and six.' The identity of the Beast has been the source of much speculation down the centuries. Using the ancient system of numerology, each generation has tried to find the number 666 in the names or lives of great dictators. The Emperor Nero was a strong contender for the role, despite the fact that his name only added up to 666 if an extra 'n' was added to it. Napoleon, Hitler and Stalin have also failed the test, to the great regret of their enemies.

The occultist Aleister Crowley, who died in 1947, believed that he was the Beast, and commonly signed himself either 'The Great Beast 666' or '*To mega therion*' – 'the Beast' in Greek, the letters of which add up to 666, using the Hebrew system of numerology. His conviction about his true identity came through a combination of pointed insults from fanatically religious members of his family and his eager reading of the New Testament in his formative years. Although he lived to see himself dubbed 'The Wickedest Man in the World' by the more sensational British newspapers, his notoriety was overshadowed by that of others in the mid-twentieth century.

Occultists and adherents of the New Age movement are reluctant to give up their search for the Beast. A whole new 'foaflore' (friend-of-a-friend-based folklore) has built up around the discovery of the number 666 on identity cards and the like. It was noticed that the British Post Office number for the Falkland Islands in 1982 was 666, but the wriest – or most sagacious – comment on the possible British connection with the number was made by the statesman Thomas Macaulay. He suggested that the Beast was a well-known British institution with 666 members (if one included servants, librarians and so on): the House of Commons.

SEE ALSO *Cosmic Joker*; *Aleister Crowley*; *The Devil*; *Divination*; *End times cults*; *Foaflore*; *Prophecy and prediction*; *Ritual magic*.

OLD TESTAMENT MIRACLES

The Old Testament records the evolution of the idea of deity in the history of a single Judaean culture from the primitive animism – the belief that all manifestations of nature have a soul – to the highly ethical, monotheistic worship of Yahweh (Jehovah). Its miraculous elements include veridical dreams (dreams that are confirmable by fact), mystical experiences, angelic appearances, healing, raising from the dead, divination, clairvoyance and clairaudience, precognition and paranormal fire. Psychical activities were regarded as legitimate, especially in later Judaism, only if practised under the auspices of Yahweh.

Many Old Testament legends appear unlikely enough though they cannot be disproved; but critics must be wary, for research shows that some incidents that would have been dismissed as myths a century ago could indeed have happened. Research, like that of the American Maimonides Dream Laboratory, supports the revelatory nature of dreams. So Jacob's ladder vision could have foreseen his return to the land of his youth, promised by God to his descendants; and Joseph knowing the reasons for the imprisonment of Pharaoh's

Exodus, Chap. 3.ᵈ Ver. 2ᵈ.

THE BURNING BUSH

Moses cowers before the mysteriously burning bush – one of the many biblical examples of spontaneous combustion.

butler and baker could have interpreted correctly the symbolism of their hope and fear. Moses, using his rod to find water in the desert, possibly used dowsing techniques. Miriam, punished with leprosy for opposing Moses, was restored to health by his prayer; and Naaman, a Syrian general, was cured of leprosy when Elisha told him to bathe in the river Jordan seven times. Since there are well-attested cases of chronic skin diseases being cured by hypnosis or distant healing, it would be unwise to reject such stories dogmatically.

The Old Testament also records various mystical experiences. Jacob wrestled with a mysterious but beneficent, supernatural being, and had encounters with other unworldly beings. An angel told Samson's parents of their hero-son's birth, then ascended in an altar-flame. Samuel, the seer (a possessor of 'second sight'), first learned of his gift when he heard clairaudiently the voice of God calling him as a child in the Tabernacle. Isaiah saw God attended by seraphim in the Temple. On the bank of the Euphrates Ezekiel saw four great wheels that appeared to be full of eyes – recalling to modern ufologists descriptions of alien craft.

Paranormal fire occurs frequently in the Old Testament; some of the instances are paralleled today by incidents of spontaneous combustion, including that of human beings. Such could have been the poetic justice visited on Nadab and Abihu, devoured by flames for offering 'strange fire' to Yahweh in rivalry to the high priest Aaron. And this is not the only story of the kind. On many occasions God 'answers by fire' igniting altars for Moses, Aaron, Gideon, David, Solomon and Elijah.

Sceptics and rationalists have found or invented natural factors that could explain some of the alleged miracles. The 'burning bush' from which God's voice called Moses to lead Israel from Egypt might have been a flickering wisp of gas from the oil-rich desert, ignited by the sun's rays and concentrated by the burning-glass of a crystalline stone. The plagues of Egypt could have occurred because excessive deposits of red clay turned the Nile to stagnant 'blood' that bred an excess of frogs; their piled, decaying bodies then bred lice, the larvae of swarms of flies that caused disease ('murrain') in cattle, and abscesses and death in humans.

It has been suggested that an earth tremor so weakened the jerry-built walls of Jericho that the rhythmic tramping of the invading army and the resonance of blasts from rams' horns were enough to bring them down (or had Joshua discovered the devastating potential of the sonic boom?). Elijah was fed twice daily by ravens which brought him food – but the Hebrew word for 'ravens' can also be translated as 'merchants' or 'Arabs'. The manna from Heaven that fed the Israelites crossing the desert may have been the exudation of tamarisk shrubs, which still feeds the modern Bedouin. Yet even today Fortean archives attest to anomalous falls of various substances, some of which are edible, besides instances of astonishing synchronicity that equal that of manna actually falling when it is needed. Indeed, the many instances of psi-mediated instrumental response (PMIR) – or answers to a prayer – on record would indicate that such events are not 'mere' coincidences.

SEE ALSO *Angels; Autosuggestion; Charles Fort; Curses; Eleventh-hour syndrome; Entity enigma; Explanations; Fate; Fireproof people; Fishfalls; Healing; Hypnosis; Inspiration in dreams; New Testament miracles; Precognition in dreams; Prophecy and prediction; Psi-mediated instrumental response; The Resurrection; Sai Baba; Shamanism; Spontaneous human combustion; UFOs.*

NEW TESTAMENT MIRACLES

The root meaning of miracle is 'something that causes wonder'; and since the authors of the New Testament regarded the events they recorded as a unique revelation of 'God with us', a breakthrough of eternal values into human existence, it is not surprising that their work is permeated with a sense of the wonderful. While it may be a profound error of judgement to ignore the so-called Gnostic Gospels – those rejected by the Church Fathers as too disruptive and controversial – even the four Gospels and Acts contain many accounts of miracles, some confirmed by references in the Epistles. Many of these – for example the Annunciation, the Virgin Birth, events surrounding the birth of John the Baptist, the Resurrection, and the Ascension – remain unique, even within the framework of psychical research.

The New Testament is dominated by the personality of Jesus Christ, who is still regarded as everything from God Himself in human form to a mythical character who never existed. His recorded personality is that of a supremely charismatic thaumaturge – a worker of miracles – who 'spoke with authority' and expressed his compassion for humanity by many miracles of healing. A growing number of commentators ascribe Jesus's miraculous abilities to his familiarity with the occult skills of the Essenes, a mystical Jewish sect whose teachings bypassed the established Church to surface in the 'heretical' groups such as the Cathars.

Twenty-six individual healing miracles are

Jesus walks on water. Was this an actual event, to be taken literally, or some form of deliberately induced mass hallucination?

recorded in the accepted New Testament, although some of these may be different versions of the same occasions. They embrace leprosy, palsy, fever, blindness, deafness, dumbness, lunacy, paralysis, curvature of the spine, dropsy and gynaecological problems, but he must have healed many more on the numerous recorded occasions when multitudes brought their sick to him. Two cures were effected at a distance, and several were of afflictions suffered from birth, or for many years. With the cures of Jesus may be considered those by Peter, Paul and other disciples, for the gift of healing was regarded as part of the ministry of the early Church.

It is known today that many illnesses are psychosomatic and can be cured by authoritative treatment from charismatic healers. There are also examples in the literature of orthodox, psychical and spiritual healing or inexplicable 'instantaneous regressions' of even fatal illnesses. Few pilgrims to Lourdes and similar shrines are cured, but there have been instances, attested by examining committees of doctors – some of them required by the Church to be non-believers – of cures as miraculous as any recorded in the New Testament. Examples of influence at a distance are to be found in hypnotic experiments, some of which have included healing. Jesus seems to have been universally successful except in places where 'he could do no mighty work because of their unbelief' – he suffered, like many psychics or sensitives, from the inhibiting influence of sceptical attitudes (today's 'experimenter effect').

Three raisings from the dead are attributed to

Jesus – Jairus's daughter; the widow of Nain's son on his way to burial; and Lazarus, summoned from his tomb on the fourth day after interment – and one to Peter, that of Dorcas at Joppa. Of Jairus's daughter Jesus said, 'She is not dead but sleepeth', which some have taken to imply coma. Modern evidence of dramatic resuscitation, even clinical death, make the others possible, even to sceptics. The only exception is the raising of Lazarus, which is inexplicable in any but supernatural terms and is rejected as fact by many biblical scholars. The authors of *The Messianic Legacy* (1968) suggest that this 'raising' was actually the symbolic death and rebirth of an initiation ceremony, possibly connected with the sect of the Essenes.

Jesus is also recorded as showing power over nature in the calming of a storm on a lake, the supply of a miraculous draught of fishes, walking on water, changing water into wine, and supernatural multiplication of provisions in the feeding of the five thousand and four thousand. He was also responsible for three signs which have troubled many believers; the sending of evil spirits from a healed demoniac into a herd of swine that then drowned themselves; the withering of a barren fig tree; and the payment of tax with a coin taken from a fish's mouth.

Some of these can be explained naturally, though fundamentalists prefer the supernatural implication. Large inland lakes among mountains are subject to very sudden storms which die away quickly. There is nothing exceptional about an observer on land, possibly on higher ground, seeing the sudden arrival at sea of a shoal of fish. In the story of the loaves and fishes, those who had the foresight to bring food with them were shamed by the example of Jesus's disciples into sharing their meagre supplies with strangers; so they divided their own provisions with their hungry neighbours, and as a result there was enough and to spare. The swine were panicked by the shrieks of the demoniac in the throes of being healed, and rushed down a steep slope into the sea; the disciples rationalised their action by attributing to Jesus words that he never spoke.

The fig tree episode has been explained either as coincidence or as a parable of Jewry's showy but fruitless religion reported as an actual incident.

Walking on the sea can be believed by all who accept the possibility of levitation, for which there is considerable evidence; and since quantum physics has shown all matter to consist of the same basic particles, the changing of one substance, such as water, into another such as wine, is no longer inconceivable. The coin story, the only miracle Jesus is reported to have done for his own benefit, is so uncharacteristic that many Christians believe it to be untrue, yet it is consistent with many of the tougher characteristics shown by Jesus in the Gnostic Gospels. Besides the healings already mentioned, *Acts* contains stories of the miraculous discomfiture of rival sorcerers and exorcists, three supernatural deliverances from prison, fulfilled prophecies and other wonders. There are examples of fulfilled precognitions in psychical research literature; and the deliveries from prison can be paralleled by the experience of the twentieth-century Christian Sadhu Sundar Singh, who claimed supernatural deliverance after three days from a dry well in which he had been left by Buddhists to die. The jealous sorcerers who tried to buy the Holy Spirit find modern counterparts among the conjurers who, as members of CSICOP, apparently seek to discredit all psychics and all miracles.

'Speaking in tongues', first heard at the Pentecost after Jesus's crucifixion, and a regular feature of some early Christian worship, can be heard in Pentecostalist churches today. At that first Pentecost the disciples, transported by the ecstasy of being filled with the Holy Spirit, may have repeated parts of the Temple liturgy – which were chanted in many vernaculars – without understanding what they were saying. In Christian congregations the tongues were probably *glossolalia* – inspired sounds that are not languages and have more of the nature of music than of speech. Such tongues, together with spiritual healing, are New Testament 'miracles' that have survived into the modern world.

SEE ALSO *José Arigo; CSICOP; The Devil; Experimenter effect; Explanations; Fate; Valentine Greatrakes; Healing; Levitation; Limits of science; Matthew Manning; Near death experience; Old Testament miracles; Possession; Prediction and prophecy; Quantum mechanics and the paranormal; The Resurrection; Sai Baba; Speaking in tongues.*

SPEAKING IN TONGUES

Seven weeks after Christ's crucifixion, the disciples were worshipping at the Temple in Jerusalem, surrounded by Jews from all over the East who had gone there to celebrate the Feast of Pentecost. Suddenly the disciples were seized with a divinely inspired ecstasy and began to preach 'in tongues' – in languages they had never learnt, yet were perfectly understood by the polyglot throng. This is *xenolalia*, or speaking in real languages through paranormal means. Unfortunately, since the advent of the tape recorder, only cases of *glossolalia* – speaking in unidentified tongues, or pseudo-language – have been recorded.

Today many charismatic and fundamentalist Christian sects encourage, or tolerate, speaking in tongues at the climax of their worship. The phenomenon is often heard at adult baptisms, when the joy of the 'born-again' Christian finds tongue. It is regarded as a gift from the Holy Ghost, or a sign that Christ is present except for the Roman Catholic Church, which banned speaking in tongues from the end of the first century. Even some born-again Christians warn against excessive indulgence in *glossolalia* regarding it as addictive and divisive, much as a working occultist might warn against too much time spent playing with the ouija board.

On tape, *glossolalia* typically sounds like 'refined gibberish'; the tongues have no syntax and very little vocabulary. Many Christians believe that these utterings, unintelligible to humans, may well be the language of angels. St Paul, however, counselled that only love really mattered, 'Though I speak with the tongues of men and of angels.'

On occasion, however, *glossolalia* sounds convincing. There are stories that are part of religious 'foaflore' about foreign visitors hearing their own language being spoken. The Church of Jesus Christ of Latter Day Saints (Mormons), for example, states in its articles of faith: 'We believe in the gifts of tongues ... and the interpretation of tongues.' Although increasingly discouraged, there was a strong grass-roots belief in the phenomenon that persisted into the 1960s. Mormon missionaries – commonly eighteen-year-old boys and slightly older girls – were sent, with the minimum of warning and training, to foreign countries to preach the word. In this sink-or-swim situation they tended either to panic or to pick up the language as fast as possible. Nevertheless it was believed that some would be granted the gift of tongues, and stories were told that this had happened. There were some absurdities: an Icelandic missionary who knew no English talked at her uncomprehending Yorkshire audience in her mother tongue for forty-five minutes, hoping for a linguistic miracle. It did not come; she never learnt the language and returned home within weeks.

Often, strange tongues are part of the nightmare of being possessed, which is why the Catholic Church banned the practice. The Ursuline nuns involved in the unpleasant and tragic events known as 'The Devils of Loudun' began to babble in languages allegedly recognised as Latin, Greek, Turkish, Italian, Spanish and, curiously, an American Indian dialect.

Historically a feature of heretical practice, speaking in tongues remains largely a fringe activity, although it may come upon anyone at any time. Even the Catholic stigmatic Teresa Neumann is believed to have cried out during her agonies in Aramaic, the dialect spoken by Christ and the disciples. This was taken, by the faithful, as a sign of her saintliness.

The English medium 'Rosemary', who recalled memories of former lives, also spoke in languages which she had known then, but by the 1930s were long since dead. Egyptologist Howard Hulme was sufficiently interested in her claims to talk to her in ancient Egyptian and record her answers on a gramophone record. She talked for over two hours in one session, maintaining the same guttural sounds and drawing on a consistent vocabulary and syntax throughout. Unfortunately no one knows how the ancient Egyptians spoke, so the tests were inconclusive.

Catherine Elise Muller, known as 'Hélène Smith', claimed to visit the planet Mars; its inhabitants taught her their language, which she spoke and wrote fluently. Investigated in the early twentieth century by Professor Theodore Flournoy of Geneva University, she obliged by also speaking

Hindustani, a language unknown to her conscious mind. The 'Martian' proved to fit a syntax remarkably similar to her native French, and many years after her death it has been proved that there are no Martians on Mars.

Writer-researcher Hilary Evans has coined the term 'producer' for the almost perversely creative part of our subconscious minds, which creates, for example, a fictitious Cambridge, in our dreams, even though there is no need, for we may be very familiar with the real university city. This over-enthusiastic producer may well be the origin of Hélène Smith's Martian – or the verbal outpourings of those believed to be possessed, besides those believed to be overtaken by the Holy Spirit. The real phenomenon may lie not in spiritual worlds, but in the 'Superself' – the world of raw creativity within the human mind.

SEE ALSO *Case of Ruth*; *Church of Jesus Christ of Latter Day Saints (Mormons)*; *Creative visualisation*; *Fantasy-prone personalities*; *Hypnosis*; *Left and right brain*; *Mysterious appearances*; *New Testament miracles*; *Other dimensions*; *Possession*; *Prodigies*; *Psychic music, art and literature*; *The Resurrection*; *Stigmatics*; *Visions of the Virgin Mary*; *Chico Xavier*.

THE RESURRECTION

Judged by the impact that Christianity has made upon the world, the Resurrection of Jesus Christ is arguably the most important paranormal event in history. Whether it actually happened or not, there can be no doubt that a number of Jesus's immediate circle were convinced that they had seen their risen Lord, and that the experience changed them in a matter of weeks from dispirited, terrified men into courageous evangelists, willing to undergo martyrdom for the truth they preached.

The principal records of what was believed about the Resurrection in the first century AD are contained in 1 Corinthians 15, Mark 16, Matthew 28, Luke 24, John 20 and 21, Acts and two incomplete apocryphal Gospels, Peter and Hebrews. All these have been studied exhaustively by scholars of every outlook from fundamentalist Christianity to convinced atheism.

The essence of the story is as follows. Jesus was arrested late on Thursday evening, condemned by the Sanhedrin, the supreme Jewish Council, for blasphemy and handed over to the occupying Roman authorities on an accusation of sedition. He was subjected to brutal treatment by Roman soldiers, flogged and crucified at about 9 a.m. on Friday. His death, at about 3 p.m., was confirmed by the centurion in charge after a spear had been thrust into Jesus's left side (although several modern commentators suggest that he was not, in fact, dead. Death by crucifixion commonly took much longer, even lasting for days). Taken from the cross, he was buried by Joseph of Arimathea before the Sabbath began – as required by Jewish law – at 6.p.m. in Joseph's own rock tomb near the crucifixion site. A great stone was rolled across the entrance to the tomb. A guard was mounted by the disciples (a detail rejected by many Christian and sceptical authorities alike).

On Sunday morning the grave was visited by a group of his women followers, who found it empty and the stone rolled away. A young man told them that Jesus had risen and they were to tell his disciples to return to Galilee, where he would meet them. Jesus then appeared separately to Mary Magdalene (who was repeatedly referred to in the Gnostic Gospels as 'the first disciple', and some researchers believe she was actually Jesus's wife); Peter; two disciples walking to a place near Jerusalem called Emmeus; James, his (half?) brother; twice to the eleven remaining apostles; to St Paul (though this seems a vision different from the others); and possibly on other occasions. The appearances ended with the Ascension, which convinced his followers that Jesus had returned to God his Father, whence he would shortly come back in glory to the Earth.

Both Christian and hostile critics have questioned every detail in the story. There was no guard, they have suggested. Jesus's tomb was not empty – the women visited the wrong grave. If it was empty, Jesus was merely unconscious when buried; he then recovered, appeared to his disciples and died later – some say much later, such as at the Siege of Massada in AD 66. Alternatively his body was

The Resurrection *by Sir Stanley Spencer, depicting the fundamentalist Christian belief that the dead will rise from the grave on Judgement Day.*

removed by a gardener, by Joseph of Arimathea (who had lent his own tomb only temporarily), by the Roman or Jewish authorities, by thieves, or by the disciples perpetrating a pious fraud.

The inconsistences in the accounts are emphasised; one tradition places the appearances in Galilee, happening probably some days after the Resurrection, while another ascribes them to Jerusalem on the Sunday of Christ's rising. Peter places the Ascension immediately after the Resurrection, Luke apparently on the Sunday evening (though he contradicts himself in Acts with the phrase 'being seen of them forty days', an idiom meaning 'for a moderately long time'). Several of the accounts state that Jesus was not immediately recognised and that some 'doubted' – the acknowledgement at least suggests their author's honesty.

The quasi-physical nature of Christ's risen body, which could eat and be touched, yet at the same time move through locked doors and dematerialise at will, has also inspired hostile criticism to ascribe the appearances to veridical hallucinations or other psychological quirks. If the grave was empty and Christ's body was truly a glorified development of the physical organism that had occupied it, problems arise for philosophy and theology. The body was certainly different from seance materialis-

ations, which are allegedly formed from ectoplasm drawn from the medium and do not leave graves even temporarily unoccupied. It was also different from tulpas, quasi-physical thoughtforms allegedly created by magical adepts, sometimes so expertly that they can be seen by others. Some believe that the process of resurrection caused, or released, a huge burst of light (or even radiation) that magically imprinted Jesus's image on his winding-cloth, the controversial Turin Shroud.

Many of the critical theories cancel each other out, and it is possible for ingenious conservative scholars to iron out most of the inconsistencies and create a concordant account of what could have happened. What any scholar accepts is, however, a matter of his personal faith, or his scepticism. The only certainty is that Jesus's followers, convinced beyond regard for their own safety, preached Christ resurrected some six weeks after the crucifixion – and changed the history of the world.

SEE ALSO *Case of Ruth; Consensus reality, Helen Duncan; Ectoplasm; Explanations; Fantasy-prone personalities; Hallucinations; Incorruptibility; Katie King; Life after death; New Testament miracles; Paranormal portraits; Quantum mechanics and the paranormal; Thoughtography; Tulpas; Turin Shroud; Visions of the Virgin Mary.*

TURIN SHROUD

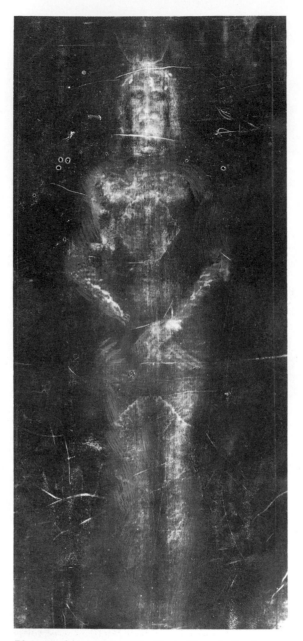

Photographic negative of the Turin Shroud, clearly showing the image of a crucified man. Long believed by the Church faithful to be the shroud in which Jesus was wrapped, and which was mysteriously imprinted with his image, the cloth remains an intriguing mystery. Several attempts to subject the cloth to radio-carbon dating have resulted in ambiguous, or even contradictory, datings. Meanwhile, believers continue to revere it as the true image of Jesus.

The Turin Shroud is a 4.3-metre length of linen cloth that bears the faint images of the front and back of a male body, slender and muscular and just over 1.8 metres in height. The head and body are marked with many wounds consistent with New Testament descriptions of the scourging and crucifixion of Jesus Christ. Many Christians have believed for centuries that it is the shroud provided by Joseph of Arimathea and wrapped around the body of Christ before he was laid in the tomb, and that the image it bears is, therefore, an authentic portrait of the crucified Son of God.

The Shroud first appeared in Europe in the mid-fourteenth century, when it was exhibited in a small French country church by the impoverished widow of a minor nobleman, Geoffrey de Charny. No record survives of how the relic may have come into his possession, but some modern scholars believe that the Shroud might be identical with the Mandylion, another mysterious image of Christ which was known to the Byzantine Empire, but which disappeared during the sacking of Constantinople by Crusaders in 1204. The Mandylion may have been brought to France by the Knights Templar, who, it was widely believed, preserved it in secret for use in their ceremonies. In 1453 de Charny's daughter presented the precious relic to the House of Savoy, which has owned it ever since, although the Archbishop of Turin is its custodian.

The authenticity of the Shroud has been an article of faith for many Catholics since the fourteenth century, but many bishops have condemned it as a forgery and the Church has never officially vouched for its genuineness. Until the end of the nineteenth century, scientists and secularists on the whole dismissed it as a superstitious absurdity. In 1898, however, it was photographed for the first time by an Italian photographer called Secondo Pia. On Pia's negative the image on the cloth sprang to life, showing the anatomical features and the details of the wounds with astonishing clarity. The question immediately sprang to mind: why would a fourteenth-century forger create an image that could only be clearly seen as a photographic negative, a concept unknown before the nineteenth century?

The Shroud quickly became the subject of intense scientific interest, and of increasingly sophisticated testing. Paradoxically, every scientific test until the late 1980s tended to strengthen, rather than weaken, the case for the Shroud's authenticity. Some of the more remarkable features which emerged in the 1970s were these:

1. Microscopic traces of cotton fibres among the linen weave, and of pollen dust, suggested that the cloth originated in the Middle East.

2. No trace could be detected of any kind of pigment. The image appeared to result from superficial discoloration of the linen fibres, darker and lighter shades being produced by closer and looser groupings of the discoloured fibres.

3. The bloodstains were certainly human in origin.

4. The hair was worn in an unbound pigtail, a fashion common among young Jewish males in the first century AD.

5. The wounds were consistent to a remarkable degree with those to be expected from a scourging by a Roman flail and with crucifixion, and reveal a knowledge of morbid anatomy that is unlikely to have been available to most fourteenth-century forgers. In particular:

(a) The blood flow is consistent with a crucified man's agonised raising and lowering of his body in order to breathe.

(b) The nail wounds in the hands are in the bones of the wrist and not in the palms, which could not have withstood the weight of the body.

(c) The thumbs are not visible – a particularly telling point, since a nail driven into the wrist at the point indicated on the Shroud would have severed the median nerve, causing the thumbs to curl tightly into the hand.

The image clearly shows a swollen abdomen, the result of asphyxiation, which was the normal cause of death after crucifixion. Space-age techniques have revealed that the image is directionless – showing no signs of brush-strokes – which suggest that it was produced in some way by the body lying underneath the cloth. NASA's image enhancements have shown that the image is three-dimen-sional, its density varying precisely according to the distance between the cloth and the parts of the body that would have been lying beneath it. This characteristic, seemingly impossible to fake, enabled scientists to produce a detailed model of the body that might have lain in the Shroud; arguably a scale model of the actual body of Christ.

In the light of results like these, some at least of the scientist members of the 1978 Shroud of Turin Project concluded that the image had been formed in some unexplained way by a real corpse. The most likely explanation seemed to be that the image had resulted from scorching of the linen fibres, as if the body had emitted a burst of heat and/or light. Several holy people – such as Padre Pio, the stigmatic who died in 1968 – are recorded as having given off extraordinary heat or light in the form of a halo, and lightning and radiation have been known to project lasting images of objects or people on to their surroundings. At Hiroshima there is a clear image of a fallen man on a doorstep, caused by the intense radiation from the atom bomb. (Perhaps significantly in this context, the child hero of the film *Empire of the Sun* (1988) is given the lines: 'I learnt a new word today – "atom bomb". Like God taking a photograph.')

On the Shroud, the details of the wounds included signs of severe beating; head wounds that might have been caused by a crown of thorns; a likely spear wound in the side; and the fact that the legs had not been broken, as was commonly done to speed the death of the victim. All these suggested that the body that had produced the image was that of Jesus Christ, and not of any ordinary crucified man.

For some time it had been suggested that part of the Shroud might be submitted to radio-carbon dating, the technique that dates very old organic artefacts by measuring the amount of residual carbon-14 in them. The suggestion was for a long time resisted by the Turin authorities on the grounds that the tests would involve the destruction of a significant amount of the Shroud's material. Eventually, when the technique had been developed so that only a minute amount of material was required, consent was given, and samples were sent to laboratories at Zurich, Oxford and Tucson, Arizona for independent testing. In 1988 all three laboratories reported that the cloth dated from some time after 1000 AD – probably the fourteenth century.

Radio-carbon dating, then, has apparently declared the Shroud a forgery, although the technique is by no means infallible. If the relic is a forgery, then given its extraordinary details and properties (which radio-carbon dating in no way explains) it is one of the most remarkable forgeries of all time. The hypothetical medieval forger emerges as a prescient genius whose work surely ranks with that of the greatest artists, sculptors, photographers and holographers. However, the truth may be that the forger was indeed one of these greatest of men, for evidence is emerging (although unconfirmed as yet) that the Turin Shroud is the handiwork of no less than Leonardo da Vinci. Dovetailing research and inspirations of a network of Europeans, involving documents' scholars, secret societies and even psychics have uncovered not only evidence for Leonardo's personal involvement, but also a little of his method and even his motive.

The story goes that there was indeed a Shroud imprinted with a mysterious image of a crucified man and that, in 1492, Leonardo was asked by the de'Medicis to sharpen it by painting over it. Exceeding his brief for various reasons of perfectionism and personal belief, the master painter secured a dead (or dying?) body from a charnel house where he regularly carried out his anatomical research, and scourged and crucified it. Dressed with pungent unguents – every detail authenticated by research – the body was laid under a winding-sheet and subjected to a carefully controlled (al)chemical treatment, followed by a blinding flash of light (some say lightning). The body was left wrapped in the cloth for two days and when unwound a faint image was discernible on the cloth.

The motives for this trickery were not merely those of financial gain or the professional challenge involved. Leonardo, a Rosicrucian adept and Grand Master of the Priory of Sion, had always been careful to hide his heretical activities behind a smokescreen of scepticism and rationality. Yet first and foremost he was a heretic; he used this faked Shroud to express his contempt for orthodox Christianity and to provide a lasting joke. In the process he also invented photography.

Leonardo da Vinci; is his the face of the man on the Turin Shroud? As it can only be appreciated in negative, did he also invent photography?

The face is, so the story goes, a self-portrait – perhaps part-painted and partly alchemically imprinted, or *photographed*. He superimposed the facial wounds over it using a kind of screen printing technique, and the head of the man on the Shroud still seems curiously detached from the body. There would indeed seem to be clear similarities between the face of the man on the Shroud (as seen in the photographic negative) and Leonardo's features as seen in the portraits and self-portrait. Other apparent corroborations include the fact that the man of the image is older than Jesus is commonly supposed to have been at the time of his death – possibly in his late forties. Modern research does indeed indicate that this was likely – but in 1492 Leonardo was also the right age at fifty.

Tantalising though such research is, the true identity of the man on the Shroud remains elusive.

In April 1989 an enterprising journalist managed to elicit a statement about the Shroud from Pope John Paul II as they flew to Africa on the same plane. He said:

A relic it certainly is ... if it were not it would be impossible to understand the reactions of faith that surround it, and which are now even stronger after the results from the testing. One might call it a scientific counterbalance, the way the reactions show themselves even more strongly.

In a sense a relic is always an object of faith ... if so many people believe so [that it is genuine], their conviction which, let us say, induces them to see the imprint as the actual impression of Jesus's body, cannot be without foundation. The problem with which many find difficulty is that of its origins.

The man on the Shroud may never have existed. The Turin Shroud may be a true miracle, its image imprinted on the medieval cloth through a psycho-kinetic process engendered by the continuing and fervent belief of the faithful. The Shroud should not be dismissed lightly, for whenever it was made (or caused) it may remain a profound mystery.

SEE ALSO *Consensus reality; Cosmic Joker; Experimenter effect; Explanations; Haemography; Images that bleed and weep; Incorruptibility; Limits of science; Moving statues; New Testament miracles; Other dimensions; Paranormal portraits; Psychokinesis; Quantum mechanics and the paranormal; The Resurrection; Sai Baba; Stigmatics; Thoughtography; Timeslips.*

St Veronica exhibits the cloth with which Christ wiped his face, leaving his image on it. The imprinting of faces on surroundings is a phenomenon known outside the Church, but it is best known in a Catholic context.

HAEMOGRAPHY

Although there are several cases of spontaneously forming images on record, there is only one known proponent of haemography – the mysterious formation of lettering and images from the blood of a stigmatic. The Italian Natuzza Evolo (born 1924) continues to demonstrate an enormous range of mystical phenomena, including stigmata and bilocation. Handkerchiefs and religious medallions touched by her in her ecstasies became imprinted with faces – some believe they are of the saints or of Christ himself – or lettering, formed from the blood oozing from the wounds of her stigmata.

Outside of a religious context, recognisable faces have been seen to form as part of a poltergeist attack, as at Bromley in south London in the 1970s. The spontaneous appearance of writing on walls is also a common feature of such disturbances.

Natuzza Evolo's haemographic ability is inexplicable – and well attested – but of relatively minor interest compared to the greater phenomenon of the stigmata. Both phenomena seem to be the result of mind over matter (psychokinesis), triggered by great piety and a total imaginative involvement with the agonies believed to have been suffered by Jesus. The mechanism involved, however, remains a mystery.

SEE ALSO *Black Monk of Pontefract; Enfield poltergeist; Incorruptibility; Matthew Manning; Images that bleed and weep; Moving statues; Paranormal portraits; Psychokinesis; Stigmatics; Turin Shroud; Visions of the Virgin Mary.*

PARANORMAL PORTRAITS

Sometimes clouds or other naturally occurring patterns may form into such a striking portrait of recognisable figures, such as Christ (or how he is traditionally supposed to have looked) that the likeness, or *simulacrum*, is taken to be miraculous. One of the most famous photographs of such an image is that of 'Christ in the snow', which appears from time to time in the tabloid press, always with a slightly different background story. The *Sunday People* first carried it in 1958, claiming that it was a photograph of the Alps taken from an aircraft by a man who felt a strange compulsion to do so. When it was developed, a clear image of Christ's head appeared, formed out of the white snowy patches and the black rock for contrast. The photographer, once an atheist, was said to have become a believer immediately.

Such was the public response to the photograph that the *Sunday People* printed it again the following week, and in 1965. They also used it – 'the most famous picture we have ever printed' – to celebrate their five thousandth issue in 1977.

However, the story of its origins is by no means certain, having become something of a piece of foaflore (friend-of-a-friend folklore). A very similar photograph was sent to Sir Arthur Conan Doyle in 1926 by Miss W. Adair Roberts, who obtained it in Vancouver, Canada. (Whenever this photograph is printed there are hundreds of claims of ownership.) The earliest story tells how it was 'unexpectedly secured in the trenches in France' by a cleric in 1917.

There have been many photographs that seem to show holy figures against natural backgrounds. The Buddhist goddess Kwanyin appeared on a photograph said to have been taken from on board an aircraft in 1975 – although once again there are hundreds of conflicting claims.

Roman Catholic visionaries in particular seem to inspire paranormal photographs. The figure of a heavily draped Christ is seen on prints distributed by Veronica Leuken, the 'Bayside Seeress' of New York, and the face of a beautiful young girl appeared spontaneously on a photograph of the apparition's room at Medjugore, Yugoslavia, while the visionaries were communing with the Virgin.

A form of 'Thoughtography' – the imprinting of mental images by a psychokinetic (PK) process directly on to film – may account for the unexpected pictures of holy figures taken by believers. The 'sudden compulsion' to take a photograph, ostensibly of the sky or a mountain top, may be a hint that the individual's PK ability is about to go into action.

A more complex miracle involving a photograph of the gods took place in India in the 1960s, when Sai Baba, considered by thousands to be a living saint, was witnessed to dig randomly in a sandy beach and reveal a 10-centimetre high statue of the god Vishnu. Then he dug once more, to discover a glossy *photograph* of the Hindu gods, shown standing in two rows. Sai Baba's biographer, Howard Murphet, who saw this take place, said: 'This print, I felt, was not produced by any earthly studio.' (Although the mysterious Turin Shroud certainly was if the supporters of the Leonardo theory are correct.)

A tableau of the Virgin Mary and two saints appeared on the gable end of the church at Knock in Ireland in 1879; its immobility suggests that it may have been a projection – from a magic lantern, the sceptics suggest, or by psychokinesis from the minds of the faithful. Other spontaneously appearing images on walls include the likeness of Dean Liddell of Christ Church, Oxford that appeared on

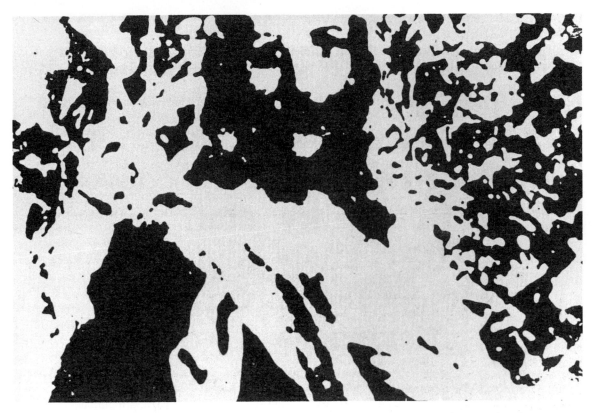

'Christ in the snow', one of the most famous pictures of simulacra, the phenomenon whereby natural scenes or objects seem to take on the face or figure of recognisable characters.

the wall of Christ Church Cathedral a few days after his death in 1923. Building work has since obscured it.

The faces that appeared on the kitchen floor of Maria Gomez Pereira in the Spanish village of Belmez were inexplicable – and, some said, of diabolical, rather than divine, origin. In August 1971 Maria discovered the image of a face emerging from the cement of the kitchen floor. When it persisted for six days, Miguel, the Pereiras' son, smashed it up and cemented over it. In September another face appeared, gradually degenerating, as if through age or infirmity. As the news of the phenomenon spread, the floor was dug up to discover a possible cause. A number of human bones were found, but this was not surprising as the entire street was known to have been built over a graveyard.

As the months progressed, other faces came and went, many of them smaller than the original.

Professor Germasn de Argumosa, a parapsychologist, witnessed the formation of one of the faces: ' . . . the face slowly assumed contours before our astonished eyes . . . I must admit my heart was beating faster than usual.' When world-famous parapsychologist Professor Hans Bender of the Freiburg Institute arrived in Belmez in 1972, he was in no doubt about their authenticity, but noticed how each observer perceived the faces differently.

People interested in the occult flocked to see the faces for themselves, often trying to contact the 'spirit artist' through mediumistic trances. A tape recorder was left running in the otherwise empty room; the sound of many people crying and shouting could be heard when the tape was played back. In 1983 the faces began again in earnest, and have been coming and going ever since.

In the *Journal of the Society for Psychical Research* (SPR) of July 1987, researcher Manfred Cassirer wrote:

In a wider context . . . examples of pictorial idea-plasty may be compared with the phenomenon of 'Direct Writing', of which the earliest alleged instance is to be found in the Bible.

In the Bromley poltergeist case in south London in the 1970s, there was a face formed from two kinds of fertiliser present on the premises, and there was also a perceptible change during the period while it was under my observation. . . . At Bromley we also had Direct Writing and little crosses, one of which appeared in my presence.

The Catholic Church has an ancient tradition of paintings done without human hands (*acheiropoieta*), of which there is a supposed example at the Sancta Sanctorum in the Lateran.

Whatever the source of paranormal images, they seem to induce in their observers a sense of elation, of being in contact with the miraculous. In October 1988 the following story appeared in *Attitudes*, the magazine of the Matthew Manning Centre. It was entitled 'Watch out for miracles'.

When the face of Christ began appearing on the outside wall of a church in Guatemala City, the populace started flocking to the shrine in droves. . . . Before long miraculous cures began to occur. Before much longer something else occurred. During a violent rainstorm, the rain, lashing away at the outer white-washed wall, revealed the kindly face to be not that of the good Lord, but country singer Willie Nelson, whose picture had been covered over by painters. Alas, poor Willie did not seem to have a good way with miracles . . . it's not who you have faith in, but how much you believe.

SEE ALSO *Autosuggestion*; *Case of Ruth*; *Consensus reality*; *Cosmic Joker*; *Fantasy-prone personalities*; *Foaflore*; *Haemography*; *Hallucinations*; *Images that bleed and weep*; *Psychokinesis*; *Sai Baba*; *Thoughtography*; *Tulpas*; *Turin Shroud*; *Visions of the Virgin Mary*.

IMAGES THAT BLEED AND WEEP

Spontaneous stigmata in the flesh of the faithful, miraculous though the phenomenon is, is perhaps more understandable than wooden crucifixes or plaster statues bleeding or weeping. Yet such events continue to be reported.

On 16 March 1960 Mrs Pagora Catsounis of New York noticed that a painting of the Virgin Mary was shedding tears under its glass. The tears vanished before they could collect at the bottom of the frame. Four thousand people visited her home in the first week after the discovery. Then Mrs Catsounis discovered that her aunt also owned a weeping Madonna. Samples of the watery fluid were analysed and discovered not to be human tears, and investigator Raymond Bayless found stains under the eyes of the paintings that could have been dried serum. Significantly, however, he was present when a pilgrim said she saw the painting begin to cry. Others in her group said that they had seen it too – but Bayless maintains that there were no tears, just the immovable stains.

However, many paintings or statues do, apparently, cry real tears and bleed real blood. The plaster statue of Christ that belonged to Mrs Anne Poore of Boothwyn, Pennsylvania, bled from the palms every Friday from 1975. A local priest attested to the miracle, adding that: 'It has bled as long as four hours. I have seen the palms dry, then minutes later have observed droplets of blood welling out of the wounds . . . Incredibly, the blood seldom runs off the statue. Its robes are now encrusted with dried blood.'

Samples of the blood were tested by Dr Joseph Rovito. They were discovered to have an astonishingly low red cell count, indicating extreme age, but to flow with the freshness of new blood. Dr Rovito said: 'It's so old we can't even determine the blood type.' Many Catholics concluded that this was actually the blood of Christ.

American parapsychologist D. Scott Rogo tells the story of the Reverend Robert Lewis, whose grandmother had died before he was ordained. On the great day of his ordination he and a friend were

A bleeding picture of Christ in the church at Mirebeau-en-Poitou, France, in March 1912. Religious pictures often bleed or weep, apparently in response to a crisis in their owners' lives.

Weeping Madonna at Rocca Corneta, Italy. Although religious statues and pictures tend to exhibit this phenomenon most frequently, ordinary family snapshots have been known to 'weep'.

in his house when they saw tears flooding down a photograph of his grandmother, soaking the velvet backing. After they removed the photograph from the frame it dried very slowly, resulting in some marked puffiness around the grandmother's face 'as though the water had originated there and run downwards from the eyes'. Rogo points out that Lewis had often seen his grandmother weep with joy: 'He wanted to share his joy with her . . . so he used his psychic ability to stage the event.'

The quasi-religious phenomenon of crying or bleeding images resembles those associated with poltergeists; both kinds of phenomena seem to arise from the psychological state of the owner of

the paintings, or of the residents of the disturbed houses. The phenomena seem to defuse the personal crisis, although some instances are taken as omens of disaster.

The bronze statue of a Japanese lady owned by Allen Demetrius of Pittsburgh wept on 6 August 1945, the night the atom bomb was dropped on Hiroshima. She also wept ten days before the nuclear accident at Three Mile Island, Pennsylvania. Demetrius has since proposed that the statue be displayed at the United Nations, 'as a warning against war'.

Political upheaval and insurrection was the background to the bleeding images of the Dwan family on 15 August 1920 in Templemore, County Tipperary, Eire. As the nationalists fought the Black and Tans in the civil war, all the statues and religious paintings belonging to Thomas Dwan and his sister-in-law, Mrs Maher, began to bleed simultaneously. Then Mrs Maher's lodger, a pious young man named James Walsh, discovered anomalous pools of water on his bedroom floor. Pilgrims by the thousand flocked to Templemore, and the pools of water became as much a feature of the pilgrimage as the bleeding images. The phenomena lasted for just a month during which time an estimated one million people visited the Dwans' house – and an uneasy peace descended on the area.

The weeping Madonna of Syracuse, Sicily in August 1953 seems to have had a specific use in the life of Mrs Antonietta Janusso, who owned the statue. The newly wed Mrs Janusso found married life difficult; she and her husband were forced to live in poor conditions, and she had a series of mysterious illnesses that made her effectively bedridden. Shortly after she discovered she was pregnant she began to have convulsions, and to be periodically deaf, dumb and blind. Lying in bed, she looked up at the statue on a shelf and saw that it was crying. The news spread, and soon the little bedroom was packed with the curious. Even despite this inconvenience, Mrs Janusso began to feel better; by the time the statue ceased to cry, many days later, she was completely cured.

Miracle it undoubtedly was, but was it of divine origin, as Mrs Janusso herself believed, or had it another paranormal explanation? The exteriorisation of hysterical symptoms has long been thought to induce 'macro-PK' on the surroundings. Just as this sort of projection may explain some cases of poltergeist attacks, Mrs Janusso's 'miracle' served to defuse a personal crisis. While others may join in the awe, the true benefit is bestowed on those who need it most.

SEE ALSO *Enfield poltergeist; Explanations; Haemography; Healing; Hypnosis; Mass hysteria; Moving statues; Paranormal portraits; Psi-mediated instrumental response (PMIR); Psychokinesis; Rosenheim poltergeist; Stigmatics; Turin Shroud; Visions of the Virgin Mary.*

MOVING STATUES

The apparent movement of holy statuary, a phenomenon consistently reported throughout the centuries, reached epidemic proportions in Ireland in 1985. It began with the experience of four children in Asdee, County Kerry. In February they were among thirty schoolchildren who went to pray in St Mary's Church; there they saw the large statues of Jesus and the Virgin Mary beckoning and their eyes moving. The children spread the news and the church was quickly packed to capacity; soon American pilgrims were among the worshippers.

Within weeks there were similar reports from over forty other sites in Ireland, the most dramatic being at Balinspittle in County Cork and at Carns in County Sligo. At Balinspittle there were rumours of holy images that bled and wept, and a 150-kilogram statue of the Virgin that stood at a roadside shrine was seen to move, as if rocking on its heels. In two months over two hundred thousand people flocked to the site, many seeing the statue move in some way. Some people claim to have seen the face of Christ superimposed upon that of the Virgin, and on 31 July many viewers thought they saw an image of Christ on an Irish television report on the shrine. Technicians examined the video but found nothing unusual. On 31 October – Hallowe'en – worshippers at the Balinspittle shrine were appalled to witness three youths axe the statue, shouting: 'You stupid fools, worshipping a statue!'

At Carns in September four schoolgirls saw the Virgin Mary in a vision, which was followed by appearances of St Bernadette (herself one of the most famous Catholic visionaries) and of a crucifix in the sky. These visions were also seen by others. Within days the area became a shrine for an estimated twenty thousand people.

However, the wave of miracles now began to change significantly in tone. At Mitchelstown in County Cork, children began to scream and cry: they had seen 'shocking things', such as the face of Jesus turning into that of a demon. The atmosphere in the church became cold and frightening and some of the altar boys collapsed. A local woman, Mrs Eileen Graham, said it was as if the children had been 'tuned to something'. She told reporters that another (anonymous) woman had seen the Devil in a vision at the shrine a full six weeks before any other visions had been reported there. Mrs Graham herself had seen 'the face of an old woman in a nun's habit. ... Then I saw Our Lady's face and half of it growing old. There was a huge big bag under her left eye. Then there was a tear running down her face. I cried.'

The clergy cautioned against pious overreaction, while assuring non-believers that 'the people who see these things are in no way abnormal or hysterical'. ('Hysteria' is regarded by the Church as the ultimate insult.) Irish bishops were said to discuss the phenomena, but – perhaps deliberately – never came to any agreement. A spokesman said: 'I can say that the Church moves much more slowly in these matters than do the statues.'

Psychiatrist Professor Anthony Clare said: 'So many people reading so much significance into such banal events ... suggests a very deep need indeed for simple reassurance.' If, however, the statues had really moved as described, the events could hardly have been 'banal', and heavenly intervention may be considered more than 'simple reassurance'. But did they really move?

Visiting reporters established the ease with which an optical illusion of movement can be induced by shifting the gaze very slightly from the brightly lit statue (especially the head, which often has an illuminated halo) to the background darkness. Many forms of folk and ritual magic involve staring at a candlelit mirror, or into a candle flame, until the face of a future spouse, one's Guardian Angel or a demon may appear. In a similar way, focusing on a brightly lit object in an atmosphere of devotion tires the eyes and heightens susceptibility to illusion. In highly motivated groups, a form of mass hysteria – itself, however, a label rather than an explanation – may reinforce the visions.

It is also significant that the Asdee miracle came the day after the children had seen a film about the life of the Italian stigmatic Padre Pio, and that news of the 'Dance of the Sun' at Medjugore had just been publicised in the Irish press. The Balinspittle shrine, which was modelled on that at Lourdes, had been dedicated in 1954, a designated Marian year.

But it may be that the statues did move – through the grace of the Virgin or through some psychokinetic interaction between the statues and the devout.

SEE ALSO *Autosuggestion; Case of Ruth; Consensus reality; Cosmic Joker; The Devil; Explanations; Entity enigma; Fantasy-prone personalities; Haemography; Hallucination; Hysteria; Images that bleed and weep; Incorruptibility; Mass hysteria; Psychokinesis; Stigmatics; Turin Shroud; Visions of the Virgin Mary.*

STIGMATICS

St Paul wrote: ' ... let no man trouble me, for I bear in my body the marks of the Lord Jesus' (Galatians 6:17), which is widely taken as a reference to his stigmata, the mysterious spontaneous wounds that correspond to those believed to have been suffered by Christ. Stigmata may consist of anything from simple reddening of the skin over the sites of the traditional wounds – the head that bore the crown of thorns, the side pierced by the lance, the scourged back, and the holes where the nails were believed to have been hammered through the hands and feet.

Besides St Paul's single, oblique reference, the first known stigmatic was St Francis of Assisi, stigmatised after a vision in 1224. A winged seraph appeared to him; as he struggled to rise to his feet he was smitten with the pain and physical appearance of the stigmata. His biographer, Thomas Celano, wrote of these wounds:

His hands and feet seemed pierced in the midst by nails, the heads of the nails appearing in the inner part of the hands and in the upper part of the feet, and their points over against them. ... Moreover, his right side, as if it had been pierced with a lance, was overlaid with a scar, and often shed forth blood so that his tunic and drawers were ... sprinkled with sacred blood.

The nail-like protrusions of sinew made walking difficult for the saint and were: 'marvellously

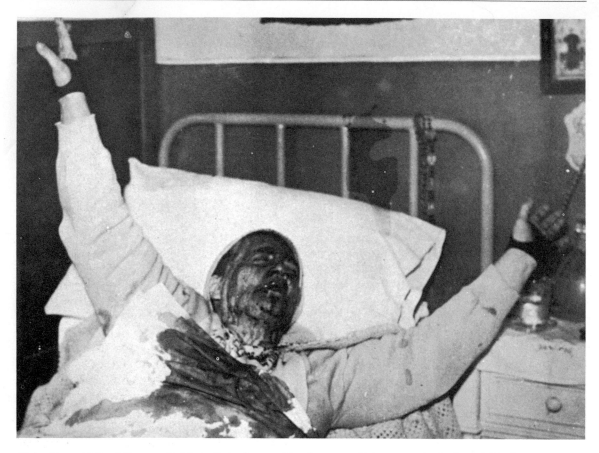

Sister Elena Aiello of Cosenza, Calabria, Italy, in one of her frequent religious ecstasies during which she was stigmatised with the wounds of Christ. Stigmata seem to be created by the fervently religious imagination, for the hand wounds tend to be in the palms, yet Jesus would have been nailed to the cross through the wrists – as seen on the controversial Turin Shroud.

wrought by the power of God ... implanted in the flesh in such wise that if they were pressed in on either side they straightway, as if they were one piece of sinew, projected on the other'.

News of the saint's bizarre affliction spread, and soon stigmata became common enough for it to be an acknowledged phenomenon associated with the devout. In 1894 Dr Imbert-Gourbeyre listed 321 known cases; but Father Herbert Thurston, the Church's authority on physical phenomena, suggested in the 1950s that there had been many more cases throughout history.

By far the highest proportion of stigmatics are women, and of the men only St Francis was fully stigmatised. In more recent times great publicity surrounded Padre Pio, the Capuchin friar whose agonising wounds came upon him during a retreat in 1915 and only left him on his death in 1968. Although he sought privacy, his fame spread and he himself became an object of veneration.

Some stigmata were borne internally, only becoming visible after death. St Catherine of Siena suffered agony for five years until her death in 1380, when the wounds became visible spontaneously. They were especially obvious when her body was 'translated' (dismembered to be used as relics).

Sister Maria Villani, a Neapolitan Dominican nun, believed that she had been pierced in the side and heart by 'a fiery spear of love' during an ecstasy. When she died aged eighty-six, in the late seventeenth century, her body appeared dark and shrivelled, but after death she became radiant and youthful. When the surgeon performing the autopsy plunged his scalpel into her chest, a great plume of smoke and intense heat burst out. He was repeatedly burned before he managed to remove the heart, which was witnessed to bear a scar such as might have been made by a spear: 'the lips of the wound', wrote the sister's biographer, 'are hard and seared, just as happens when the cautery is used, to remind us, no doubt, that it was made with a spear of fire.'

Undoubtedly the most famous female stigmatic of the twentieth century was the Bavarian ecstatic Teresa Neumann, who suffered the 'agonies of Christ' every Friday from 1926 – when a host of mysterious illnesses abruptly disappeared, to be replaced by the stigmata – to the day of her death in 1962. Wounds in her head, hands, feet and side appeared spontaneously every Friday and often gushed up to half a litre of blood during the day. She would lose consciousness – giving investigators the opportunity to probe the wounds and establish the authenticity of her ecstatic state – and often nail-like protuberances in the wounds, similar to those of St Francis, were clearly visible. Perhaps more astonishing than the stigmata were the associated phenomena; Teresa stopped eating and

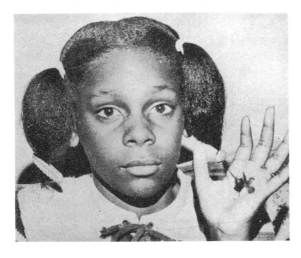

The only known black, Protestant, stigmatic, Cloretta Robertson of Oakland, California. At the age of eight she was mysteriously stigmatised on and off during the week before Easter 1972. Although investigated by a team of psychiatrists and doctors, they found nothing to account for the phenomenon.

drinking thirty-five years before her death (nothing except the communion wafer passed her lips during this time), and her digestive tract shrivelled in the 1930s. During her ecstasies she also spoke in 'tongues'; on several occasions her utterances were proved to be Aramaic, the language spoken by Christ.

Another modern stigmatic who spoke – and wrote – Aramaic while entranced was the illiterate Teresa Musco, a poor Italian seamstress who died in 1976. She received the stigmata during a vision in 1969, and predicted – accurately as it proved – that she would die aged thirty-three, believed to be the same age as Christ. Although she was fully stigmatised with all five wounds, only her hands were completely pierced. Associated miracles included holy statues that wept blood in her presence, and the lack of rigor mortis in her body for one week after her death – although it was later to decompose normally.

Sceptics usually fall back on accusations of fraud, alleging that the stigmatics surreptitiously inflicted the wounds on themselves, but this has never been proved in a single case. More likely, but less susceptible to investigation, is the idea of subconscious, psychokinetic 'fraud'. There may be cogent sociological and psychological reasons for stigmatism; almost every known stigmatic has chosen, or had thrust upon them, circumstances of obscurity, chastity and poverty. Yet according to British sceptic Eric Dingwall, the real characteristics of certain apparently humble and saintly stigmatics are suppressed exhibitionism and sexual deviancy, which causes traumatic conflict with the religious rules they live by. Writing of St Mary Magdalen de' Pazzi, who was stigmatised in 1585, he said she was a 'classic example of the ascetic female flagellant and masochistic exhibitionist with a sadistic streak'. Certainly that particular saint's self-flagellation, and the vigour with which she beat her nuns, attests to some sort of sexual, rather than godly, satisfaction.

Hypnotic suggestion has succeeded in reproducing a noticeable reddening of the subject's skin on the palms of the 'stigmatics's' hands. But if there is a psychosomatic cause for the most dramatic stigmata then it will have to be investigated further than a modern hypnotic trance permits.

Perhaps more significant is the similarity between stigmata and some physical phenomena associated with poltergeists. Eleonore Zugun, a Hungarian poltergeist victim of the 1920s, suffered from invisible attacks in which her skin came up in red weals, apparent bite marks and even raised lettering. She believed her attacker to have been a devil. No doubt the Catholic Church would have agreed – it makes a clear distinction between the miraculous powers of God and those of the Devil, who seeks to deceive in order to destroy.

In almost every recorded case, stigmatics have been devout Catholics from poor backgrounds. Cloretta Robertson may have been poor, but in every other way the ten-year-old differed from the pattern. She was stigmatised in the palms for nineteen days over Easter in 1972 and was investigated thoroughly by two psychiatrists, whose report appeared in the American journal *General Psychiatry* in May 1974. What was remarkable was not the fact that blood spontaneously oozed through her palms, nor that she was the only known black stigmatic – but that she was not Catholic, nor even a particularly devout Christian.

Cloretta's may have been the ultimate subconscious attention-seeking, but if so it failed, for in order for the stigmatic to become truly famous he or she must appeal to the imagination of the faithful. Manifesting abilities of the flock – but outside it – she was merely at best a psychiatric freak, or at worst a pawn of the Devil.

Together with the greater miracle of incorruptibility the phenomenon of stigmata may reveal the hand of God, or it may underline the extent of our ignorance about the powers of the human psyche.

SEE ALSO *Consensus reality; Cosmic Joker; The Devil; Entity enigma; Fantasy-prone personalities; Fireproof people; Uri Geller; Haemography; Healing; Hypnosis; Images that bleed and weep; Incorruptibility; Nina Kulagina; Moving statues; Paranormal portraits; Philip experiment; Psychokinesis; The Resurrection; Rosenheim poltergeist; Shamanism; Speaking in tongues; Suspended animation; Tulpas; Turin Shroud; UFO paradox; Visions of the Virgin Mary.*

VISIONS OF THE VIRGIN MARY

Since the beginning of the twentieth century there have been nearly three hundred reported visions of the Virgin Mary that have met with the approval of the Church. There have been countless others, each of which provokes a local, or even international, cult that ensures a measure of fame. Of the visions in the past 150 years, the most famous are those that took place at Lourdes in France and at Fatima in Portugal, although the present visions of the Virgin at Medjugore in Yugoslavia have already attracted more than ten million pilgrims in under ten years.

Writer-researcher Hilary Evans has noted the ubiquity of the visionaries' poverty; their humble circumstances may, as the visions proclaim, enable them to see the Holy Mother, whereas the rich and educated cannot. On the other hand, the frustrations endured by the poor and pious may conjure up the ultimate figure to comfort them and give them status in the eyes of the world.

Whatever the cause of the visions, they seemed to be concentrated in France during the nineteenth century. In 1846 in La Salette, a village near Grenoble, eleven-year-old Maximin Giraud and fifteen-year-old Melanie Calvat were tending a herd of cows when they saw a weeping woman standing in a dried-up river bed. They were frightened but she invited them to come closer, for: 'I have come to tell you great news.' She wore white and yellow and seemed 'brighter than the sun, but not to be compared with it'. She prophesied illness and famine due to the failure of the crops, and entrusted them with secrets, some of which were passed on to Pope Pius IX in 1850. At first the children were punished for lying but the dried-up stream where the Lady had stood flowed with water the next day, and very soon after the vision the Irish potato famine began.

In 1888 thirteen-year-old Jean Bernard was collecting firewood around the village of Vallensages, near St Etienne in central France, when he saw a *'grande dame'* standing with her foot on a lizard. The vision was wearing gorgeous raiment with a

Girls in ecstasy during a vision of the Virgin Mary at Garabandal, Spain, in the summer of 1961. The Virgin tends to appear to female children who are usually poor and uneducated. This may prove more about the fantasy life of the visionaries than the predilection of the Virgin for the 'meek of the Earth'.

golden crown on her head. She requested that he kill the lizard, which he did. Then she disappeared only to return to the same spot six days later. By this time Jean had told his family about the vision, and they accompanied him – but only he saw the lady. He asked the Virgin (for he was in no doubt about her identity) to cure a thirteen-year-old girl who had been deaf since birth. The girl began to hear, and news of the miracle spread. (The girl herself eventually became a nun.)

The Virgin appeared to Jean on a total of twenty occasions, coming to him twice a week at a set time. She urged the villagers to attend more Masses and repent of their wicked ways, or, she said, she could no longer restrain the wrathful hand of her son.

By the time of her eleventh appearance, Jean felt the need to ascertain her identity by using two traditional tests for apparitions. He said to the vision: 'If you are the mother of the Lord, step forward. If you are the Devil, step back.' The lady stepped forward. He then threw holy water at her, but she merely smiled – a demon would have disappeared peremptorily.

On her final appearance at least eight hundred people waited to watch Jean become entranced.

He asked her to create a sacred spring – Hilary Evans calls this 'another standard folklore item' – but she did not do so. The Church never recognised Jean's visions, but he was granted an education by the local clergy and eventually became a priest. He died, his visions largely forgotten, in 1932.

But it was the encounter of the little shepherdess, Bernadette Soubirous, with a visionary lady in 1858 at Masabielle near Lourdes, that caught the imagination of Church and laymen alike. Bernadette's life had been one of utter deprivation; she had been sent away to work when her family had been housed in the local jail. The fourteen-year-old girl was known to be deeply pious. The local priest had been overheard discussing the visions of La Salette, adding that if the Virgin were to appear at Lourdes she might well appear to Bernadette.

While out tending her sheep, Bernadette was startled to see a radiant being standing in a tree. She described the vision as 'a girl in white, no bigger than myself', and gave loving detail of its attire. However, the shepherdess had her doubts about its intentions – at one point she ran home for holy water to throw at 'this thing', but the vision remained unmoved by such doubt.

The apparition was to return several times, but it was only when prompted by the local priest, a fanatical Mariologist, that Bernadette asked the lady who she was. She replied: 'I am the Immaculate Conception' – a phrase that the visionary did not immediately, or consciously, understand. The doctrine of the Immaculate Conception was only four years old at the time of Bernadette's vision, and was causing heated controversy within the Church.

A stream miraculously sprang up near the grotto where 'this thing' had first appeared, and soon those who drank of it or bathed in it were reporting miraculous cures. Bernadette entered a local convent, where life was made hard for her by a Mother Superior who disbelieved her visions. The girl was allowed out to see the new statue that had been erected at the grotto in honour of the vision. At first she murmured that it was very nice, but finally admitted that it bore little resemblance to what she had seen. Instead of the young girl the statue represented a standard version of the Virgin Mary. Bernadette died of a tubercular knee in 1879; her corpse was discovered to be incorruptible and she was canonised.

In the year of her death a tableau of the Virgin, St John the Evangelist and St Joseph was seen on the gable end of the church at Knock in County Mayo, Eire. The flat, two-dimensional quality of the vision has led to the suggestion that it was simply a lantern-slide projection, a deliberate fake. However, the shrine at Knock is now a world-famous site of pilgrimage and has been visited by Pope John Paul.

A year later the Virgin visited Wales. At the end of August 1880 four boys, aged between nine and fifteen, saw her float through a bush, hands raised as if in blessing, in the grounds of Llanthony Abbey. The vision was seen twice more; on the final occasion it appeared to four people whose impromptu singing of *Ave Maria* was interrupted by an upheaval in the surrounding mountains, which seemed to bulge with light. At its centre stood, they said, 'a most Majestic Heavenly Form' which glided towards 'the Holy bush' (wild rhubarb). The vision disappeared rapidly, but there were some reports of healing connected with leaves from the bush.

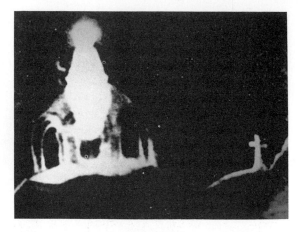

Almost the only known photograph of a vision. The Virgin Mary appears over the Coptic Church of St Mary, Zeitoun, Cairo, Egypt, in 1968, where she stayed visible for ten days, sometimes changing position slightly. The vision seems curiously static as if it were some kind of holograph – but who or what had the facilities to create such a unique mass hallucination?

In 1917 three Portuguese peasant children – Jacinta dos Santos aged six, her brother Francisco Marto aged eight, and Lucia aged nine – were tending their flocks when the apparition of a boy told them to pray. They were later to call him an 'angel'. He appeared several times before the more famous and dramatic events took place at Fatima. The three children saw a flash of lightning, but no rain fell. Instead they had a vision of a beautiful girl, aged about eighteen, who said she had come from Heaven and would return to them on the 13th of every month for six months.

As the news of the vision spread, the children were accompanied by increasing numbers of the faithful and the curious whenever the young girl visited them. On 13 October 1917 there were an estimated seventy thousand people gathered at Fatima when the celebrated 'Dance of the Sun' took place. The sun seemed to swivel, emitting coloured rays and an intense heat. Those who looked into the sun did so without damaging their eyes – a phenomenon repeated during the visions at Medjugore in the 1980s.

The Lady entrusted the children, particularly Lucia, with secrets, which were passed to the Vatican. The Pope is believed to have opened the sealed document in either 1942 or 1960, and to have collapsed with horror. They are believed to be prophecies of appalling global disaster that should have been revealed to the world years ago.

In 1932 and 1933 the Virgin appeared to five deprived children at Beauraing, Belgium, after they had played in the local Lourdes grotto. They had thirty-three visions, and although a detailed contemporary investigation was carried out, the Church remained unconvinced of their authenticity. Yet at their height, the Belgian visions attracted over thirty thousand people.

Starting in 1961, four eleven- and twelve-year-old Spanish girls saw the Virgin two thousand times in four years. As at Fatima, the Virgin only appeared after the children had been 'called' by an angel. The visionaries of Garandabal would enter profound ecstatic trances, sometimes falling backwards in perfect synchronisation, and were found to be impervious to pain while entranced, as Bernadette had been. The Virgin appeared to them with angels, and sometimes with 'the eye of God'. She told of a global warning, which one of the girls, Conchita (now living in the USA), will give, followed by the abrupt conversion of the USSR to Christianity and a 'permanent supernatural sign which will remain until the end of time'. Those who do not then repent must suffer the consequences.

In 1968 the Virgin Mary appeared for all to see – over a Coptic Orthodox church at Zeitoun in Cairo. She was first seen by Muslim workmen who were convinced it was a nun about to throw herself off the roof, and ran to fetch a ladder. The vision moved away from them, but remained over the church for ten days, attracting vast crowds and being photographed. In April 1986 her reappearance over the church of St Demiana in Cairo caused a flurry of other phenomena, such as a flood of light during an extensive power failure. The vision manifested frequently during that year, sometimes accompanied by a dove, or with the infant Jesus in her arms. Her appearance coincided with worsening relations between the Coptic Christians and Muslim fundamentalists in the area.

The contemporary visions in Yugoslavia can also be seen in a political, as well as a religious, context. The state is officially atheist and intolerant of religion, but the charismatic events at Medjugore have made the place a centre of pilgrimage. Commercial considerations also put some pressure on the authorities to accept the events, although not until all those involved had been threatened, and one priest given eighteen months' hard labour, for championing the cause.

The visions began in June 1981 when six children, aged between eleven and sixteen, saw the Virgin on a hill. She called herself the Queen of Peace; the children called her 'Gospa', the Lady. She brought the familiar exhortation to repent, urging in particular fasting and prayer, besides prophesying disasters if the world ignored her pleas. Ivanka, Vicka, Mirjana, Jakov and Ivan saw the Lady every day, sometimes twice a day, for years, although Mirjana and Ivanka ceased having daily visions shortly after the first year, and the Lady only appeared to them afterwards on their birthdays. They are ordinary children in every way, and their ecstasies have been rigorously tested; when entranced they are impervious to pain, even ignoring a nylon thread being brushed across their eyeballs.

Several miracle cures have been hailed as a result of pilgrimage to Medjugore, including that of a woman in an extreme stage of multiple sclerosis. Incontinent, blind and lame, she was helped up the hill to the church where the children have their visions. During the Mass she realised she could see – and ran to tell a friend. All her other symptoms disappeared immediately.

On several occasions the 'Dance of the Sun', similar to that seen at Fatima, has been witnessed by thousands. Base metals appear to become gold during the visions, and photographs have been taken of a beautiful woman's face among the clouds, and of a paranormal cross in the sky.

Perhaps the most astonishing aspect of the Madonna of Medjugore, however, is her ecumenical tolerance. She has told the visionaries the name of the most pious person in the locality – a woman who is a Muslim.

The Virgin of these visions may be taken as an exteriorisation of the archetypal feminine principle that appears to comfort, counsel and warn. Similar hallucinations are common outside a religious context.

Hilary Evans, in his *Gods; Spirits; Cosmic Guardians* (1988), cites the case of the late researcher Rosalind Heywood, who took mescalin for an experiment. She saw a vision that she knew to be 'the Divine Mother', who had come to give 'a glimpse of what love was: infinitely far from possessive doting, quite unsentimental, yet warm and comforting – and above all personal. That was the Divine Mother's attitude to all and everything. She was literally in love with the whole universe.'

On hearing of her vision, proponents of various schools of thought – Jungian, Freudian and so on – tried to explain it away using their own interpretations. Rosalind Heywood wrote: 'That enraged me at first. Then I saw that it was very funny. What label the experts choose to give this product of my model psychosis seems of no importance at all. . . . I know that, whatever she was, she represented all that I could possibly grasp of perfection.'

SEE ALSO *Autosuggestion; Case of Ruth; Cosmic Joker; Entity enigma; Fairies; Hallucinations; Healing; Hypnosis; Images that bleed and weep; Incorruptibility; Jung and the paranormal; Katie King; Moving statues; Paranormal portraits; Propensity for psi; Psychokinesis; Sex and psi; Shamanism; Stigmatics; UFO paradox.*

INCORRUPTIBILITY

St Cyril of Jerusalem, writing in the fourth century, said: 'Even when the Soul is gone, power and virtue remain in the bodies of the saints because of the righteous souls which have dwelt in them.' The phenomenon of incorruptibility – the failure of a corpse to decompose – is one of the greatest and least understood miracles most commonly connected with the Church.

Many phenomena are associated with incorruptibility. There is absence of putrefaction, absence of rigor mortis, and a fragrance ('the odour of sanctity') that is emitted from the body. Sometimes bleeding occurs from wounds or stigmata. In rare cases there may be some form of ritualised movement, such as hands raised, then lowered, in bless-

ing; and the body may feel warm long after death. The long-forgotten burial place of the saint may be revealed in a dream; sometimes strange lights attend the burial or dance over the grave; long-dead saints may exude a fragrant, clear oil that contains healing properties; relics of the saint's body may also prove to heal the faithful.

No one knows for certain how many incorruptible saints there are. Only two historians have deemed the subject worthy of study: Father Herbert Thurston, who in the late nineteenth century wrote extensively on the physical phenomena associated with the devout; and American Joan Cruz, whose *The Incorruptibles*, which listed 102 known cases, was published in 1977. The phenomenon may, however, be considerably more widespread; hundreds of incorruptibles may lie unremarked in their graves.

Several incorruptibles were early English saints; St Ethelreda, who died of cancer in AD 679 at Ely, was found, sixteen years later, to be miraculously preserved. The Venerable Bede wrote in his *Ecclesiastical History*:

And when so many years after her bones were to be taken out of the grave, a pavilion being spread over it, all the congregation of brothers were on the one side and of sisters on the other, and the abbess, with a few, being gone to take

Bernadette Soubirous lies totally uncorrupted by the grave over a hundred years after her death. At her exhumation it was seen that the tumour on her knee had disappeared, resulting in a slight shortening of the leg.

up and wash the bones, on a sudden we heard the abbess within loudly cry out. ... Not long after they called me in, opening the door of the pavilion, where I found the body of the holy virgin taken out of the grave and laid on a bed, as if it had been asleep.

Although a doctor had removed a tumour from the saint's jaw just three days before her death, on her exhumation it was noticed that there was only 'an extraordinarily slender scar' at the site of the operation.

A similar smoothing away of scars after death happened to Bernadette's body. She had died in 1879 of a tumour on one knee – after her exhumation some years later it was discovered that the tumour had disappeared, resulting in a slight shortening of the leg. Today she looks as if she sleeps; only a thin layer of wax covers her face to prevent discoloration (although the mask-maker took the opportunity to improve on nature – he straightened her nose and thinned the peasant girl's eyebrows).

Even a death that would seem to hasten decomposition may result in incorruptibility. St Teresa Margaret, who died in 1770 of gangrene, would appear to have been partially putrefied even before her death, yet just two days later her body had become radiantly beautiful, and instead of the stench of her illness and death a persistent fragrance emanated from her. Today she lies in a glass coffin in Florence, a little blackened and dried, but perfectly preserved.

Other bodies are found to be miraculously whole and fresh despite the unpromising conditions in which they were buried. St Charbel Makhlouf, who died in Annaya, Lebanon in 1898, was buried in a virtual mudbath without a coffin. Strange lights were seen over this place and the grave was opened two months later. The holy man was discovered to be perfectly preserved, although his clothes had rotted away. Washed and dressed, the body was placed in a coffin in the chapel of the St Maroun monastery, where it began to ooze what appeared to be fresh blood to such an extent that the clothing had to be changed several times a week. Fragments of the blood-soaked cloth were found to have healing properties. In 1927 the body was placed in a zinc-lined coffin, together with reports from many witnesses, including doctors, on the incorruptibility and its associated phenomena.

Yet in 1950 pilgrims drew the attention of the authorities to a strange liquid oozing through the wall of the shrine. The coffin was opened; the zinc lining had corroded badly but the saint was intact, lying in eight centimetres of clear fluid. Since then the coffin has been opened annually – each time there is no change and the oil is drained away and distributed among the faithful, who believe it to cure many ills.

Records show that incorruptibility is not a monopoly of the Church. The body of a young wife, Julia Buccola Petta, was exhumed in 1927, six years after her death, and discovered to be perfectly preserved. A photograph of her incorrupt body is on the plaque that now marks her grave in Mount Carmel Cemetery, Hillside, Illinois. In 1977 the body of two-year-old Nadja Mattei, who had died in 1965, was exhumed and found to be incorrupt. Her mother claimed that she had dreamed repeatedly that the child begged to be taken from her grave.

Several cases of apparent incorruptibility have proved, on investigation, to be the result of natural preservation due to saponification (where the body tissue turns to a soapy mass, giving the illusion of perfect preservation), or to embalming through peculiar conditions of the air, soil or background radiation found in some tombs or caves. Such possibilities are acknowledged, however, by those who investigate cases of incorruptibility. The true nature of the phenomenon remains a mystery, perhaps transcending natural laws and entering the realms of the mystical. As Joan Cruz wrote: 'For those of us who have loved and admired certain of the saints, it is a comfort of sorts to know that they are not just somewhere in the great realms beyond, but that their actual bodies, which will one day be made glorious, are still present among us.'

SEE ALSO *Consensus reality*; *Explanations*; *Healing*; *Inspiration in dreams*; *Katie King*; *Life after death*; *Limits of science*; *Carmine Mirabelli*; *The Resurrection*; *Stigmatics*; *Turin Shroud*; *Vampires*; *Visions of the Virgin Mary*; *Zombies*.

CHURCH OF JESUS CHRIST OF LATTER DAY SAINTS (MORMONS)

Today 5.4 million members of the Church of Jesus Christ of Latter Day Saints, commonly known as the Mormons, believe that theirs is the only Christian Church authorised by God. According to their tenets, the original Church of the first century died out with the last of the Apostles, and was only restored to the Earth in 1827 through the agency of the 'prophet' Joseph Smith.

Smith was a farm boy from Palmyra, New York, said to be deeply confused by conflicting claims made during a local religious revival. He prayed for guidance and was rewarded by a vision of God and Jesus, who told him that his mission was to restore the lost – and only – Church to the Earth. An angel also entrusted him with translating the hieroglyphics on gold and brass plates found in a nearby hill, Cumorrah. They became the *Book of Mormon* – the history of Israelites who had migrated to the New World in 600 BC written by Mormon, an ancient American prophet – which for Mormons has equal authority with the Bible (the history of the Israelites in the Old World). As soon as they had been translated, the plates were taken away by the angel, although three witnesses, besides Smith himself, attested to having seen them.

Two other lesser holy books were to come later. In the *Doctrine and Covenants* Smith and his successor set their authoritarian seal on the fledgling church; while *The Pearl of Great Price* was said to be miraculously translated from an ancient Egyptian papyrus, divinely guided to Smith.

Very rapidly Joseph Smith became 'President, Prophet, Seer and Revelator' of the Church of Jesus Christ of Latter Day Saints – a 'Saint' simply meaning a member of the Church – which detractors called 'the Mormons'. Hundreds flocked to join him, many of them making the hazardous sea journey from Europe. For most, the Prophet's revelations came as a shock – although it was relatively easy to obey the new dietary rules (known as the Word of Wisdom) of abstinence from alcohol, tobacco, tea and coffee, the law of tithing and of polygamy proved a severe test of faith.

The Mormon camp at Nauvoo, Illinois, aroused strong feelings among the locals. In 1848 Smith and his brother Hiram were taken into custody – for their own protection, it was said – and were murdered by a mob with painted faces. It was unthinkable that the newly restored Church should be leaderless, and Smith, it was believed, had chosen a worthy successor.

Brigham Young soon earned himself the nickname of 'The New Moses', both among the Saints and, grudgingly, among outsiders. He was a natural leader, driven by an inner vision that the faithful found compelling, and he was tough – some said merciless. Nevertheless he led his wagon train of Saints westward across America, always trusting to divine guidance. Indians and outlaws attacked them; hunger and disease were constant companions; and schisms split the sect more than once. Young fell ill with a mysterious sickness and they became stuck in the most unpromising of places – a hill overlooking miles of salt flats, in the remote Midwest. Then Young appeared, suddenly cured, to announce his latest revelation: 'This is the place!'

The Saints toiled against almost overwhelming odds to make God's promise come true – that 'the desert shall blossom as a rose'. But one more miracle was to occur during Young's supremacy. Their first, fragile harvest was attacked by a horde of locusts, but Young prayed and an enormous flock of seagulls arrived to eat up the locusts, even though they were nearly a thousand kilometres from the sea. The Saints could get on with building Salt Lake City.

Young, following Smith's commandment, insisted that plural marriage was God's will. Later apologists explain that women outnumbered the men to such an extent that polygamy was the only 'decent' way to maintain their self-contained society, but sinister rumours abounded about Mormons stealing women and about Mormon-funded secret societies spreading over the American continent and into Europe. Even the official abolition of polygamy in 1890 in the state of Utah, and throughout the Church, did nothing to stop the rumours. Today, stories still circulate about plural marriage being secretly encouraged by the Church in Salt Lake City.

An active worldwide missionary campaign ensured that membership grew; but until recently no blacks were allowed to join the priesthood (all Mormon males over the age of twelve are expected to become priests). Officially the colour bar existed because a black skin was believed to be the biblical 'mark of Cain'; although it still has that pedigree, blacks may join and become church elders now.

As Christ's Latter Day Church, it teaches New Testament principles – baptism by immersion, healing, speaking in tongues – although only the first is confidently practised. Members are expected to keep the dietary rules encapsulated in the Word of Wisdom, pay a tenth of their income to the Church, and attend the many services and social functions it holds. An interview with the local bishop (to establish the member's worthiness) precedes a visit to the 'Temple', where sacred and secret rites – sceptics point to their remarkable similarity with those of the Freemasons – 'seal' wives to husbands, children to parents, and the dead to the living, 'for time and all eternity'.

Latter Day Saints believe that the dead will be given a chance to hear the (Mormon) Gospel, and because it is only possible to be baptised by immersion in the physical world, they will be offered the chance to be baptised by proxy. Baptism for the dead is a major part of the Temple ritual, and the necessity to know the names of as many of their ancestors as possible has ensured that the Saints have the most far-reaching genealogical library in the world.

Although proselytising in the 1960s encouraged widespread prejudice against them, the Saints, with their emphasis on self-help and clean living and their belief in a God whose blessings may just as easily be material as spiritual, have since become easily assimilated into most Western societies. Yet in 1985 a document was acquired by the Church leaders that was to prove – literally – explosive. It purported to be a letter written by Martin Harris, one of the three witnesses to the incident of the discovery of the gold plates in 1827, to a newspaper editor (who later became a Saint). Dated 1830, the letter predated Smith's official account of the discovery of the plates by eight years, and told how he had them not through angelic guidance, but through 'money digging' using a 'seer stone'. It quotes the first Latter Day Saint as saying about his discovery: 'I . . . only just got it because of the enchantment. An old spirit told me to dig up the gold but when I take it up the next morning the spirit transfigured himself from a white salamander in the bottom of the hole and struck me 3 times.' There was no mention of an angel or of the all-important First Vision.

Anything connected with the occult is anathema to the Latter Day Saints; outside the Temple even ritual is frowned upon as being too like 'the Scarlet Woman' – the Roman Catholic Church – and the paranormal is seen as the work of the Devil. The news of the Salamander Letter produced waves of disbelief, shock and heart-searching among the faithful. Many overseas members have still not heard of it, despite the furore caused by three car bombings in Salt Lake City connected with the sale of the documents in 1985. Yet they were fakes; the significant point is that the church leaders had not only believed them genuine, but had expected to find them. Somewhere, such letters really exist.

Today the church is affluent and fundamentalist. It is undergoing a puritanical purging. Women, whose role is that of wives and mothers, are discouraged from seeking a career and from intellectual questioning. Yet for many it is an attractive religion – the missionaries' basic question of: 'Have you ever wondered where you came from, why you're here and where you're going?' summing up the seekers' archetypal quest.

The scandal of the Salamander Letters, however, still threatens to blow up into enormous proportions. As Jan Shipps, the leading non-Mormon historian of the Latter Day Saints, says: 'It forces the Church hierarchy and the Mormon in the street to confront the fact that the Mormon story as they believe it is not the way it was. It proves that magic and occult practices were present at the outset of this important religious movement.'

SEE ALSO *Angels*; *Apports*; *Cosmic Joker*; *The Devil*; *Entity enigma*; *Fairies*; *Fox sisters*; *Healing*; *New Testament miracles*; *Old Testament miracles*; *Ritual magic*; *Speaking in tongues*; *UFO paradox*; *Visions of the Virgin Mary*; *Witchcraft*.

BUDDHISM

Uniquely among the major religions Buddhism makes no claim to divine revelation. Rather it is the teachings of a human being, Gautama Siddhartha, who, through his own efforts, awoke to the law of life within himself.

Born in 563 BC into a princely Indian family, Siddhartha renounced his luxurious life to carry out religious austerities and solve the fundamental problems of human existence: birth, sickness, old age and death. For six years he travelled around India seeking out philosophies and ascetic disciplines, but could not find the answers he sought. Then, aged thirty-five, he sat under the Bodhi tree at a site now called Bodhgaya and entered meditation. It was under this tree that he obtained supreme enlightenment and became a Buddha or Enlightened One.

The Buddha had awakened to the law of life that permeates the universe and all things in it. He understood that the universe is a living entity and experienced the dynamic, eternal truth of the interrelation of all things, the formation and disintegration of everything in perfect harmony with the rhythm of cosmic life.

Buddhists believe there is no separation between body and mind, spiritual and material, latent and manifest; that they are each the inseparable half of the perfect whole. An example of this is illness, whose symptoms are seen as manifestations of disease made in the heart or mind.

A similar Buddhist principle is that of the oneness of life and its environment. From the Buddhist point of view the environment is not static, but reflects the changing life conditions of the individual. In other words, the same environment can be perceived in a myriad different ways by the same person depending on his or her life state.

After the Buddha's death at the reputed age of eighty, the Buddhist Order split into two. The Theravada, or Hinayana (meaning Small Vehicle), became almost exclusively monastic. The Mahayana (Greater Vehicle) maintained that enlightenment towards which everyone, monk or layman, could aspire. There are many schools of Buddhism, but the underlying principles are the same. Tantric Buddhism combines magical and mystical elements to gain enlightenment, the most important ritual implements being the *vajra* (shaped like a pronged thunderbolt, a male symbol representing the Absolute and concentrated power), and the *ghanta* (a bell-shaped female symbol, representing the receiver). Some forms of Tibetan Buddhism use visualisation techniques to gain enlightenment, often conjuring up the image of a pure, princely figure holding sacred objects.

The Zen school, also based on meditation, teaches that enlightenment is reached by breaking through the normal limitations of thought and reasoning. One technique used by the Zen masters is the *koan* – a puzzle that is impossible to solve by reason; for example: 'What was your face before you were born?' Nichiren Daishonin, the thirteenth-century Japanese priest revered by his followers throughout the world as the True Buddha of the Latter Day of the Law, taught that every human being possesses Buddhahood, and that the way to activate it is by chanting Nam-myoho-renge-kyo to the Gohonzon, a specially inscribed mandala representing the highest life state. As he wrote to a disciple in 1255:

> If you wish to free yourself from the sufferings of birth and death you have endured through eternity and attain supreme enlightenment in this lifetime, you must awaken to the mystic truth which has always been within your life. This truth is Myoho-renge-kyo. Chanting Myoho-renge-kyo will therefore enable you to grasp the mystic truth within you.

The basic Buddhist teachings are contained within the Four Noble Truths, and are Dukka – suffering; Samudaya – suffering arising from craving and desire; Nirodha – cessation of suffering; and Magga – the practice that leads to cessation of desire, and known as the Noble Eightfold Path. This, in turn, consists of eight modes of being: right view, right thought, right speech, right action, right mode of life, right effort, right mindfulness and right concentration. Nirvana is a state beyond existence and non-existence, achieved when all desire is extinguished.

SEE ALSO *Formative causation; Hallucinations; Healing; Holism; Karma; Left and right brain; Quantum mechanics and the paranormal; Reincarnation; Ritual magic.*

II Secrets of the Mind

**Precognitive dreams ● Inspiration in dreams ● Prophecy and prediction ● Astrology ● Divination ●
Jung and the paranormal ● Akashic records ● Prodigies ● Lightning calculators ● Tulpas ●
Doppelgängers ● Thoughtography ● Cottingley fairies ● Fantasy-prone personalities ● Case of Ruth
● Hallucinations ● Creative visualisation ● Hysteria ● Mass hysteria ● Mesmerism ● Hypnosis ●
Autosuggestion ● Ouija board and planchette ● Fireproof people ● Suspended animation ● Shamanism
● Possession ● Multiple personality ● Hypnotic regression ● Hypnotherapy**

When Ted Serios produced his 'thoughtographs'
– photographs of thoughts – in the 1960s, some
people were not amazed. Among them were members of esoteric societies and occultists, who acknowledge the tangible power of the imagination,
and whose lives revolve around rituals for shaping
and controlling the creatures of their minds.

To say that something is 'all in the mind' or 'just
imagination' is effectively to dismiss it, yet pheno-
menologists know that such an attitude is profoundly mistaken. Phantasms of the living,
doubles or doppelgängers, may create wonder and
confusion, as did Emélie Sagée's doppelgänger
when it could be seen at the same time as the real
young woman. When her employers dispensed
with her services she let it be known that she had
lost nineteen other posts because of her ideoplastic
idiosyncrasy. (And how many times, one wonders,
had her double been taken for either herself, or
a ghost? How many other people we meet are literally not what they seem?)

A high proportion of the Western population
actively seeks to dispense with reality as much as
possible. According to a major American research
programme, fantasy-prone personalities sometimes spend up to 90 per cent of their time recon-
structing reality in their minds, to their greater
satisfaction – just as two young girls faked photographs of fairies out of frustration that no one else
could see the little creatures that they saw all the
time around the stream at Cottingley in Yorkshire.

The hoax was only incidental to the point at issue,
yet many commentators are satisfied with the confession alone.

When we see creatures that are not visible to
others, and that are not to be found in any natural
history textbook, it may be said that we are hallucinating. Again, this term tends to be used dismis-
sively, as if all those who hallucinate are frauds
or subnormal, or both. Yet there is evidence that
some people who hallucinate are actually demonstrating a unique form of creativity. One such was
'Ruth', the American woman living in London
whose pioneering psychiatrist helped her to confront and control her terrifying hallucinations.
Now rid of the nightmarish aspect of her mental
creations, she amuses herself by hallucinating
friends to while away the time when she is bored.
But more significantly, it was discovered that on
at least one occasion Ruth's hallucinations were
seen by someone else.

Sympathetic studies into the nature of hallucinations have rediscovered what mystics and occultists have long believed: that many hallucinations
show a disturbing similarity to the evil – or benign
– spirits that in the annals of demonology sought
to possess, or influence, the afflicted. The concept
of possession is showing signs of a renaissance
among some enlightened doctors and psychiatrists, who find it a useful concept in the treatment
of such provocative disorders as multiple personality.

The controversial practice of hypnotic regression – where the subject is put into a hypnotic trance in order to relive past incarnations – has also raised many questions about the creative potential of the mind. The subject frequently calls upon deeply buried, but normally acquired, knowledge with which to create a plausible 'past life'. Sometimes he appears to be possessed by the spirit of the historical person he claims to be describing; at other times he displays what may be truly paranormal knowledge. From such fragmentary studies one can conclude that the human psyche is something of a magpie – collecting and collating facts, fantasies and personalities from all levels of being and from past, present and, (arguably), future states of consciousness.

With this half-submerged ability to use snippets of information from other dimensions, we are all born fortune-tellers. Some, with a superior ability to poach from the future, are better at it than the rest of us, and can prophesy and predict, reading the cards or the runes with a degree of confidence and accuracy that sceptics find disconcerting. Some forms of divination have the built-in aid of archetypal pictures (as in the Tarot), or whole traditions and a ponderous science, as in astrology. There are enormous problems for left-brained rationalists in such systems, and they tend to reject them out of hand. Yet these systems work – at subtle, intuitive, and practical levels – and have much to offer modern man if he will only enquire within.

So ingrained is the sceptic's contempt for the 'fairy stories' surrounding altered states of consciousness that he will ignore even the best-authenticated cases of mind over matter, such as those of firewalking, suspended animation and the anaesthetic properties of hypnosis. (In the latter case ordinary people were denied pain-free operations for decades because the Establishment refused to experiment with hypnosis.)

Often our minds behave as if they belong to someone else – the meanings of our dreams are impenetrable, yet we created them at another level of being. Extraordinary abilities are hidden within our psyche, and profound anxieties and complexes lurk in its depths. All of these may be explored for our ultimate benefit, through hypnosis or the technique of creative visualisation – a gentle wander through an inner journey that illuminates the secrets of the mind.

PRECOGNITIVE DREAMS

The people of the ancient world drew on their dreams for insight and advice, believing they were divinely inspired. While besieging the city of Tyre in Phoenicia in 332 BC, Alexander the Great dreamt of a satyr dancing on a shield. Aristander, his dream interpreter, saw it as an ingenious pun: *satyros* (Greek for satyr) could equally well be interpreted as *sa Tyros* – 'Tyre is yours'. The campaign, which had not been promising, continued and was won by Alexander.

Sigmund Freud and other psychoanalysts have recognised the ability of the dreaming mind to use puns – coded messages that attempt to speak directly to our subconscious minds. Dreams may also centre around the enactment of a well-known phrase or saying, rather like the parlour game known as charades. One newly promoted publishing executive lacked self-confidence about advertising her own project. She dreamt of an admiring board of directors, one of whom held out a beautiful baby to her. On waking, the phrase 'It's your baby' rang in her ears, giving her confidence to argue her case. There was no opposition, and the project won praise and distinction for her. 'It could have been wish-fulfilment, of course,' she said later, 'but I woke with such confidence that the dream, no matter what its roots, had served its purpose.' Yet the phrase 'It's your baby' would have had only one, entirely different, meaning for anyone from another time, such as a Victorian woman or anyone without a knowledge of modern American slang.

The most famous premonitory dreams are those that concern disasters or tragedies. Before a slag heap engulfed the village school and its pupils at Aberfan in Wales in 1966 there were many dreams and premonitions of doom in that village. One little girl dreamt that she went to school but there was

The Archduke Franz Ferdinand and his wife leaving the Town Hall, Sarajevo, on 28 June 1914, a few minutes before they were shot dead. The night before, a friend of theirs dreamt they had written him a note telling him of their assassination.

nothing there, 'just a big black hole. I was frightened, and cried.' Dismissing this as 'just a bad dream' her parents sent her off to school, where she died. Unfortunately all the Aberfan premonitions, like many others warning of disaster, were reported only after the event and therefore, genuine as they may have been, have no veridical value for the psychical researcher.

J. W. Dunne, the engineer whose interest in dreams led to the publication of his classic *An Experiment With Time* (1927), recorded all his dreams, often discussing them with his sister. In 1913 he dreamt of a high railway embankment, knowing with full certainty that it was a place just north of the Forth Bridge in Scotland. He 'saw' a train going north fall over the embankment, with several carriages crashing to the bottom of the slope, followed by boulders. He tried to 'get' the date of the disaster, but succeeded only in having the vague feeling that it was March or April. On

14 April 1914 the *Flying Scotsman* fell on to the golf links from the parapet 25 kilometres north of the Forth Bridge.

In the same year a Balkan bishop, Monseigneur Joseph de Lanyi, had a nightmare in which he saw Archduke Franz Ferdinand (of the Austro-Hungarian Empire) and his wife shot at point-blank range as they sat in their car. He also dreamt that he had found on his study table a black-edged letter bearing their arms, which read: 'Your Eminence . . . my wife and I have been victims of a political crime at Sarajevo. We commend ourselves to your prayers. Sarajevo, 28 June 1914, 4 a.m.' The next day the bishop heard of the assassination of the Archduke and his wife at Sarajevo, which triggered the First World War.

Not all premonitory dreams are concerned with warnings about dire events to come; some work directly for the dreamer's material benefit. For twelve years John Godley became 'the bookies' nightmare', dreaming winners of the next day's races. After his first few successes he ensured that his predictions were recorded and witnessed before the event, thus providing some of the most outstanding evidence of precognitive dreams – yet, perhaps because they concerned the vulgar world of gambling, or were not about tragedies, they have been largely ignored by psychical researchers. After twelve years his mysterious and lucrative gift abruptly left him.

In recent years several premonitions bureaux have been set up; they require details of any vivid dreams that appear to be about future events, in advance of those events. So far, their files have proved inconclusive. The tendency, however, for such bodies to deal exclusively with tragedies may miss the point. The evidence is that millions of ordinary people regularly dream about all manner of future events, sad, tragic, happy and quite trivial. In the last analysis, dreams may be intended only for the dreamer.

SEE ALSO *Akashic records; Astrology; Creative visualisation; Divination; Inspiration in dreams; Jung and the paranormal; Other dimensions; Parapsychology; Prophecy and prediction; Society for Psychical Research; Time; Timeslips.*

INSPIRATION IN DREAMS

In 1863 the German chemist August Kekulé was confronted by the problem of the chemical structure of the aromatic compounds, particularly how the hydrogen and carbon atoms in benzene linked together. He fell into a doze and 'saw' the benzene molecule as a snake that formed into a circle and swallowed its own tail. On waking, Kekulé realised that the carbon atoms must form a ring – which proved to be correct.

James Watt, inventor of the steam engine, also dreamt how to make lead shot by dropping molten lead into water from a great height. The actual dream image was one of falling rain, but Watt was obviously so perfectly in touch with his subconscious that he interpreted it exactly.

Louis Agassiz, the nineteenth-century Swiss palaeontologist, repeatedly dreamt the structure of a fossil fish that eluded him in his waking state. Twice the details of the dream faded before he could note them down, but on the third night he kept a notebook by his bed. Looking at his notes in the cold light of day he doubted that they made sense; put to the test, however, they fitted perfectly.

Several writers dream entire plots of novels; Charles Dickens frequently found his characters parading before his dozing mind fully formed. Samuel Taylor Coleridge dreamt the epic poem *Kubla Khan* in one (possibly opium-induced) dream, copying most of it down from memory the following morning. He was interrupted by a 'person from Porlock', however, and forgot the ending.

More recently Angus Laverny, expert on Rubik's inventions for the London toyshop, Hamley's, dreamt the solution to Rubik's Clock, which has a hundred billion permutations, eight weeks after seeing it at a toy fair in 1988. He can now solve the problem posed by the clock in eighteen seconds.

The common advice to 'sleep on' a problem seems to be profitable; the evidence is that most problems – of Nobel prize-winners or the man in the street – can be solved by using dreams, the royal road to the unconscious.

SEE ALSO *Autosuggestion; Creative visualisation; Doppelgängers; Fantasy-prone personalities; Formative*

Charles Dickens claimed that the plots of his novels and his characters came to him fully formed while he dozed.

causation; Left and right brain; Possession; Precognition in dreams; Prophecy and prediction; Psychic music, art and literature; Shamanism; Society for Psychical Research; Thoughtography; Tulpas.

PROPHECY AND PREDICTION

Three of history's major seers have foretold that the end of the world will come in the last years of the twentieth century. The fifteenth-century Yorkshire prophetess Mother Shipton (real name Ursula Sontheil) allegedly put it in 1991; the sixteenth-century French doctor and astrologer Nostradamus saw the end in 1999, while the Irish prophet of the twelfth century, St Malaki, placed it just before the year 2000.

Mother Shipton had a wide reputation as a witch, which was reinforced by her sinister appearance. She fell foul of Cardinal Wolsey, who set off to Yorkshire intent on having her burnt; however the seeress said that he should 'see York but never enter it'. He paused fifteen kilometres out of that city, where he was arrested for treason, and died on the journey back to London. It also seems that Mother Shipton correctly described the Great Fire of London. The end times prophecy attributed to her, however, was written under her name by a Victorian, Charles Hindley of Brighton, who only 'prophesied' events that had already taken place. When his one future prophecy – that the world would end in 1881 – failed to come true, the landlord of the public house near Mother Shipton's birthplace in Knaresborough took the matter into his own hands and changed the date to 1991.

Michel de Nostradame, more popularly known as Nostradamus, began his remarkable career as a prophet with a detailed description of the death of Henri II, which came about just four years afterwards. Nostradamus, writing in rhyming quatrains, said that 'in a cage of gold he shall pierce his eyes'. The king's golden visor was pierced by a lance during a joust. The prophet died in 1556,

Nostradamus, the sixteenth-century seer, whose enigmatic verses are taken by many as accurate prophecies.

but his fame spread and today his writings continue to be studied by millions eager to interpret the somewhat jumbled and obscure quatrains as descriptions of events in our own time. Certainly it seems that the 'emperor [who] will be born near Italy who will cost the Empire dear' refers to Napoleon, who was born in Corsica, and the 'Hifter' or 'Hister' who will cross the Rhine in tanks is commonly taken to be Hitler. However, his apparent prophecy about the sinking of the Californian seaboard in an earthquake in May 1988 failed to come true, so perhaps we can breathe again in 1999 when, as he says: 'In 1999 and seven months the Great King of Terror shall come from the skies' and the world, beginning with the 'city of the seven hills', will be destroyed.

St Malaki made highly specialised prophecies about the popes, using for their names Latin codes such as *De rure Albo* (from the country of Albion), a clear reference to the only British Pope, Nicholas Brakespeare or Adrian IV. The twelfth-century saint foresaw the reign of all the popes in the right order, including John XXIII, whom he called

'Pastor and Mariner' – this pope was the patriarch of Venice, a sea-going community. The present pope, John Paul II, he calls 'From the toil of the Sun', the meaning of which is not yet apparent, but the significant point is that he lists him as second from the last of all the popes. The last, as the first, will be called Peter of Rome, and he will 'feed the sheep among great tribulation' around the year 2000.

Attempts have been made to see into the future using hypnosis. Given the evidence, however, hypnotic progression seems even less likely to fit the facts than hypnotic regression seems to describe authentic previous lives; however, there are several cases where the subject has described a severely depopulated world trying to carry on normally in the face of uncontrollable plagues. Nuclear wars are relatively seldom mentioned.

In 1985 Margot Grey's important book *Return From Death* was published; it described several Near Death Experiences (NDEs) and how they changed the lives of those who have had them. Many of these people reported that during the experience they had received a personal and global vision of the future. These intimate prophecies, especially those that concern the imminent (but unexpected) deaths of loved ones, usually come true. The global visions, in general terms, tend to describe plagues, economic disasters and climatic upheavals that will devastate large areas of the world. Most of them predicted large-scale earthquakes, tidal waves and volcanic eruptions in 1988. That year saw the dangers of the 'greenhouse

Will the end of the world look like this? Prophets of doom tend to place the last days in the 1990s.

effect' and the stripping of the ozone layer as a reality, together with abnormally widespread flooding in many parts of the world, and the devastation of part of Armenia by a massive earthquake. Yet it may be that visionaries are vouchsafed a kind of Ghost of Christmas Yet To Come scenario, where the worst is shown, which need not come to pass. Judging by the horrors outlined by the likes of Nostradamus, one may fervently hope that this is so.

SEE ALSO *Astrology; Cosmic Joker; Divination; End times cults; Holism; Hypnotic regression; Near death experience; Precognitive dreams; Timeslips.*

ASTROLOGY

Mankind has been making astronomical observations for more than eleven thousand years. Solon, the Greek statesman, observed that astronomical calculations must have been made nine thousand years before his time; while notches carved on reindeer bones and mammoths' tusks indicate that the phases of the moon were being recorded around 25,000 BC.

Early man evolved myths about the sun and moon – creating a fiery, masculine deity and receptive, feminine earth mother. Natural forces were seen to determine the welfare of people, and priests and shamans gradually learned to predict the cycles of both sun and moon. By 2872 BC Sargon of Agade was using astrologer-priests to predict the future – although modern astrologers would not always recognise their methods.

In those days gods, planets and all living things were believed to be inextricably linked. Every individual was part of the entire cosmos, from which there was no separation – a primitive echo of theories which are now gaining credence once more in the fields of modern physics and biology, such as in Dr Rupert Sheldrake's theory of formative causation. Egyptian pharaohs, Babylonian kings and the rulers of Chaldea were all considered to be living representatives of the Sun God on earth, and were

Egyptian mummy case depicting the zodiac. Over the centuries astrology has come to be seen as an enormously useful system of psychological archetypes.

closely involved with astrology. Indeed, Rameses II (*c.* 1300–1236 BC) established the four cardinal points of the modern zodiac – Aries, Libra, Cancer and Capricorn.

The establishing of accurate calendars coincided with the identification of a belt of fixed stars against which sun, moon and other planets moved – now known by their Greek name, the zodiac. Between 700 BC and 400 BC Babylonian calendars combined a map of the zodiac with symbolic animals, mythical beings and gods; the oldest known Babylonian horoscope dates from 409 BC. They further divided the year into twelve months, the cycle of night and day into twenty-four hours, and the degrees of the circle, the basis of every horoscope, into 360 degrees.

By 280 BC, when a school of astrology was founded on the Greek island of Kos by Berosos,

astrology was firmly established and respected as both art and science. The Greek word *horoscopos* means 'I watch that which is rising', and originally referred just to the ascendant – that is, the point of the zodiac rising over the horizon at the exact moment of birth.

Probably the greatest, and certainly most influential, of all Greek astrologers was Claudius Ptolemaius (*c.* AD 100–178), better known as Ptolemy. His *magnum opus*, the *Tetrabiblos*, is a set of four astrological textbooks combining the accumulated wisdom of the Egyptians, Babylonians and Chaldeans, with the numerology of Pythagoras and Plato's theories about the four elements. He also gives the first 'house system' – that is, the twelve divisions of the horoscope into thirty-degree sections, each corresponding to a stage or part of an individual's life. Ptolemy's work was so comprehensive that his rules, meanings and methods of prediction continued to be used until the Renaissance.

Following Ptolemy's death, astrology mirrored the decline of the great classical civilisations, and was fiercely attacked by the early Christian Church – most notably by St Augustine. Despite numerous biblical references – including the dramatic astrological prediction about the birth of Jesus Christ by the Magi – it became a debased superstition associated with evil spirits, paganism and witchcraft.

Astrology was then primarily preserved by Islamic astronomer-astrologers in the advanced Arabic cultures of North Africa and the Eastern Mediterranean. Albumasur, sometimes known as Abu Maaschar (AD 805–85) wrote the *Introductorium in Astronomiam*. This was translated and circulated via Spain to Europe during the early Middle Ages, where it proved to be a major influence in the revival of astrology and astronomy.

The new European universities also aided the resurgence of astrology by including it in their curricula. In 1125 the University of Bologna founded a special chair of astrology, while from 1250 the subject was also taught at Cambridge (founded in 1225). Throughout the Renaissance astrology won further acceptance and power, for several popes supported and encouraged such studies. Sixtus IV, Julius II and his successor, Leo X, all relied upon astrological advice. Pope Paul III even had the hours for his Consistory fixed by astrologers.

Meanwhile, in England, Queen Elizabeth I consulted her court astrologer-magician, the mysterious Dr John Dee, every day at one stage during her reign. Across the Channel one of the most famous seers of all time, Nostradamus, advised the widowed French queen, Catherine de' Medici. His predictions seem to have been a combination of astrology, necromancy and clairvoyance. Later master astrologer (and Rosicrucian), William Lilly (1602–81), cunningly hedged his bets and advised both Cavaliers and Roundheads during the English Civil War. Lilly was a master of horary astrology – that is, the art of interpreting a chart drawn for the exact moment a question is posed – and his rules and interpretations are still referred to today. His greatest claim to fame was the accurate prediction of the Great Fire of London of 1666, fourteen years before it happened.

A heady mixture of astrology and the separate occult arts of alchemy, numerology and magical ritual characterised the astrologers of the Renaissance. While it added depth and breadth to the public's understanding and was fresh and inventive, it also contributed to astrology's fall from grace.

The discoveries of noted astronomer-astrologers – in particular Copernicus, Kepler and Isaac Newton – fuelled a mechanistic, logical and scientific approach that gradually pervaded both arts and sciences. However, each of these men (all of them members of at least one hermetical secret society) had also delved seriously into astrology – which was still usually studied in conjunction with astronomy. Indeed, Newton retained a personal belief in astrology throughout his scientific career; and Kepler said: 'Astrology derives from experience which can be denied only by people who have not examined it.' But the spirit of the times was against anything that smacked of mysticism; with the dawn of the Age of Reason astrology had once more descended to the level of jumbled, inaccurate thinking and superstition.

In 1781 Uranus, planet of revolution and change, was discovered. This was the first of what are called the outer planets – the remaining two being mysterious Neptune (1846) and, most recently, Pluto, Lord of the Underworld (1930). The original seven planets – Sun, Moon, Mercury, Venus, Mars, Saturn and Jupiter – are known as the personal planets of the horoscope, which affect personality and individual destiny; while the slow-moving outer planets are believed to influence whole generations in a more impersonal way. Much controversy and heated astrological discussion has surrounded these modern discoveries, and while the meanings attributed to Uranus and Neptune are now more or less stable, there is still some disagreement about Pluto's exact significance.

Perhaps two of the newly discovered planets had a hand in the revival of astrology, for by the nineteenth century attitudes towards occult sciences (Neptune) were undergoing a major revolution (Uranus). The establishment of a popular astrological press was spearheaded by Richard James Morrison, who used the pseudonym 'Zadkiel' and Robert Cross Smith ('Raphael'). And when, in 1875, Helena Blavatsky (1831–91) founded the mystical-spiritual organisation known as the Theosophical Society serious, scholarly astrology was once again in the ascendant. Alan Leo (1860–1917) was the best-known professional to emerge from this movement; his textbooks are still used today. Charles Carter (1887–1968), who in 1922 became President of the Theosophical Society, taught himself from Leo's shilling manuals. He is one of the most noted British astrologers of the twentieth century, and himself wrote a number of excellent textbooks.

In many ways the nineteenth-century 'occult revival' prepared the ground for astrology's modern development. Sun-sign columns are found in virtually every popular newspaper and magazine – although this merely scratches the surface of a highly complex and subtle subject and should never be taken completely seriously. Besides popular astrology, there has also been considerable in-depth investigation into the accuracy and validity of this ancient art.

The eminent psychologist C. G. Jung conducted a number of astrological experiments that convinced him of its inherent reality. And the London- and Zurich-based Centre for Psychological Astrology, founded by two psychologist-astrologers – Dr Liz Greene and Howard Sasportas – continues to explore a combination of psychology and astrological symbolism in its seminars and publications.

Further interesting research has been undertaken by various scientists investigating mysterious cyclic patterns that affect both human beings and animals. Cosmobiologist Reinhold Ebertin, son of an astrologer, has done a great deal of work in this field. English astrologer John Addey has spent more than thirty years analysing the harmonics of cosmic periods – revealing significant wave patterns that reflect a harmony with planetary movements. Certain patterns seem to correspond unfailingly with particular professions, or susceptibilities to disease.

French researcher Michel Gauquelin was originally a confirmed sceptic, yet intrigued by cosmic cycles and their effect upon life on Earth. His subsequent investigations into correspondences between an individual's planetary positions at birth and eventual profession have completely changed his mind, and added considerable statistical weight to arguments in favour of astrology. Most recently Dr Percy Seymour, principal lecturer in astronomy at Plymouth Polytechnic, has developed a controversial theory that draws on various scientific disciplines to present a new and persuasive view of astrology.

SEE ALSO *Aleister Crowley; Biorhythms; CSICOP; John Dee; Divination; Fate; Formative causation; Holism; Jung and the paranormal; Left and right brain; Michel Gauquelin and the Mars effect; Prophecy and prediction; Ritual magic; Sunspots.*

British scryer Bette Palmer, who has achieved remarkable success in seeing the future through the use of a crystal ball. Interestingly, she developed this talent after training as a healer with a Canterbury-based group, the Foundation for Global Unity. They believe that all paranormal abilities can be learnt, and used positively for the good of mankind.

DIVINATION

Divination today may be divided into three broad categories: character analysis, fortune-telling and oracles. Since character reading is less concerned with psychic ability, and more with a finely honed gift for observation, it is more a product of the supernormal than of the paranormal. Yet most professional readings contain an element of character analysis partly to gain trust and establish the right atmosphere and, in some cases, as a kind of padding.

Fortune-telling, soothsaying or clairvoyance relies upon the abilities of the seer to interpret a given set of symbols – cards, bones, tea leaves or whatever – and combine this with an intangible mixture of telepathy, intuition and imagination. The Runes, *I Ching*, Tarot and ordinary playing cards use formal sets of unchanging symbols, each with their own previously designated meaning – frequently subtle, and always affected by the proximity of other symbols. Random images, such as those perceived among tea leaves, form a basic structure that is then coloured by intuition, knowledge of the querent (client), and freewheeling mental association. The basic difference is that little intuition is required to extract an answer from the oracles, while other symbolic methods demand both knowledge and, arguably, psychic abilities on the part of the interpreter, or diviner. Palmistry and its companions, phrenology and physiognomy, seek symbolic messages in the body itself. Lines on the palm, the position of bumps on the skull, or the shape of face and features have meanings from which an analysis of character, health and future potential can be made.

Oracles such as the *I Ching* and the Runes, are generally consulted by the seeker on his or her own behalf. Traditionally, an official fortune-teller would manipulate the oracle and pronounce on the results, but this is rarely done nowadays. In addition, oracles such as the *I Ching* already contain written advice and so are one step removed from methods requiring study and some degree of psychic sensitivity to achieve results.

'Know thyself' were the words carved above the entrance to the famous Delphic oracle, and this is what all forms of divination are really about. Consulting an oracle should, ideally, direct an individual's attention to the forces shaping his destiny and present him with a selection of possible choices. Decisions resulting from a consultation are therefore the ultimate responsibility of the querent's own inner motivation – which, hopefully, the oracle has elucidated.

The *I Ching* or *Book of Changes*, one of the most famous oracles, is an extremely ancient, many-layered text, uniting the fundamental beliefs of Confucian and Taoist philosophies. China's oldest history book, the *Shu Ching*, says that prophecy was held in such high esteem by the ancient governments of China that even the Emperor's opinion was discarded in its favour. Chinese seers were used by every section of society for generations; their main tool was the *I Ching*.

A legendary Chinese sage, Fu Shi, is believed to have created the original *I Ching* over 4500 years ago. It is based on eight trigrams, or collections of three horizontal lines, each of which stands for aspects of nature, personality and society. The lines themselves are either yin – broken, receptive and feminine; or yang – solid, masculine and assertive in nature. These represent the two universal forces, each useless without the other.

The initial work was then extended by King Wen, founder of the Chou dynasty (1150–249 BC) while he was being held prisoner for seven years. He assembled the sixty-four hexagrams (combinations of six lines) and wrote accompanying commentaries, known as the Judgements. His son, the Duke of Chou, continued this work after his father's death, adding commentaries on each of the six lines of the hexagrams, plus commentaries on the Judgements. The great Confucius and his disciples then wrote what are called the Ten Wings – a collection of interpretative notes and comments which form part of the *Book of Changes* recognised today. Legend states that Confucius devoted so much time to studying the *I Ching* that three times he wore out the leather thongs binding his copy.

In ancient times tortoise shells and yarrow stalks were used for consulting the oracle, and yarrow stalks remain one method for obtaining a relevant hexagram today. However, eighteen different manipulations are required for the yarrow stalk method, and coins became widely used between 403 and 221 BC. Tossing three coins six times is now the most popular, and practical, method in use.

As with all forms of divination, a ritualised approach is considered essential if one is to gain a meaningful answer. Traditional instructions specify the burning of incense through which the coins used for divination must be passed. The seeker is advised to clarify the question in his mind, deciding beforehand why he needs an answer. Thought and ritual action then create the right atmosphere for consulting the oracle, contacting the unconscious or communing with the higher self.

Disagreements over what the *Book of Changes* is for, and how it should be used, are almost as old as the book itself. Some say that it is primarily a book of wisdom containing the seeds of the great Chinese philosophies. Others approach the book as a living being which, if consulted in the proper manner, will accurately reveal the future as well as provide practical guidance on how to behave in any situation. But perhaps it is both. Jung, in his foreword to the Richard Wilhelm translation, writes: 'If the meaning of the *Book of Changes* were easy to grasp, the work would need no foreword. . . . For more than thirty years I have interested myself in this oracle technique, or method of exploring the unconscious, for it has seemed to me of uncommon significance.'

The Runes, recently 'rediscovered', are a Western oracle of great antiquity and uncertain origins. Norse mythology says that they are the gift of the god Odin, who hung for nine nights upon the Yggdrasil, or World Tree. Wounded by his own blade, and without food or drink, he eventually grew faint and dizzy. But just before he fell he saw the Runes, and 'with a roaring cry' snatched them up and tumbled into the abyss. When he was resurrected from this dark night of the soul, he found himself reborn with both wisdom and well-being – thanks to the Runes.

Runic symbols are actually also words and letters of the alphabet. They are thought to be a combination of pictorial Bronze Age (*c.* 1300 BC) symbolic carvings and later, alphabetic scripts. The word 'rune' stems from the Gothic *runa*, 'a secret thing, a mystery', and they were formerly held to be powerful magical tools that were used for both divination and casting spells.

There are three groups of eight Runes, known as *aettir* and named after the Norse gods Freyr, Hagal and Tyr. These are based on the German runic alphabet, or *futhark*. Three and eight were considered sacred, magical numbers.

Runes have been found carved on huge stone monuments, Viking ships, amulets and weapons. According to the Roman historian, Tacitus, they were sometimes created by cutting a branch from a fruit-bearing tree which was then divided into small parts, marked with runic signs, and scattered at random on to a white cloth. These were then interpreted by a priest.

Runes were also carved or painted on to flat pebbles or discs of some kind, and kept in a little pouch. In medieval times the Rune master or mistress would actually have worn this pouch as part of his or her ritual regalia. These individuals wielded great power over ordinary people, and were even consulted about navigation as well as the more usual concerns such as birth, death, crops and fertility. As far as is known, Runes were last in regular use in medieval Iceland. They are now gaining popularity once more, and modern interpretations of their meanings are available in specialist bookshops.

Cartomancy, or the art of reading the cards, is a simple and popular method of divination. Ordinary playing cards are often used; these are thought to have derived from the Tarot, but lack its rich symbolism.

The Tarot pack consists of seventy-eight cards. There are fifty-six unnumbered cards, known as the Minor Arcana, which are divided into four suits: Cups, Wands (also called Rods or Staves), Pentacles (or Coins) and Swords. The remaining twenty-two cards, or Major Arcana, consist of numbered pictorial cards beginning with O, the Fool, and ending with XXI, the World. The Minor Arcana clearly resembles a modern deck of playing cards. Possibly the name 'playing' cards was originally coined to highlight the difference between ordinary cards and the Major Arcana; indeed Tarrochi, an Italian card game, is still played with the Minor Arcana deck.

There are many theories about the origins of Tarot cards. One story says that they are derived from the writings of the legendary mystic Hermes Trismegistus, councillor of Osiris, king of ancient Egypt. Another suggests that gypsies – a word sometimes held to be a corruption of the word Egyptians – are thought to have carried the cards with them as they wandered the Earth, eventually introducing them to western Europe.

Further speculation centres on the ancient city of Fez (now in Morocco), which, following the destruction of the great library at Alexandria in the seventh century, became a centre for thinkers and philosophers from all over the known world. Since they all spoke different languages they might have decided to create a symbolic pictorial language which encapsulated universal knowledge and spiritual truths. Armed with these pictures, mystics and sages would then have been able to communicate freely with one another on important subjects. In addition, correspondences with both the Hebrew alphabet and the ancient Jewish occult system known as the Kabbala are often suggested, plus links with astrology, numerology, gnosticism and ritual magic.

The facts concerning Tarot cards are slender. The earliest existing cards – seventeen in number – date from 1392, and are kept in the Bibliothèque Nationale in Paris. The first full deck still in existence

'The Sun', one of the Major Arcana cards in a traditional Tarot pack. Each card depicts a potent symbol that interacts with the unconscious mind.

than an apparently innocent deck of cards? Even so, by the late fifteenth century it was being condemned as 'the Devil's picturebook'.

Additional circumstantial evidence for this theory is provided by the Renaissance habit of using *ars memorativa*, or pictorial memory-aids. This idea, adopted and adapted from ancient Greece, was originally intended as an aid to meditation. *Ars memorativa* became an integral part of the whole Renaissance occult movement, and are found on talismans and amulets of the period.

The images of the Major Arcana are indeed powerful, and sometimes disturbing; whatever their true source, when properly used they are widely believed to be capable of unlocking often inaccessible parts of the mind. Meditation, or contemplation of these cards – usually in sequence – may be used to achieve an altered state of consciousness.

Some Jungian psychologists, such as Dr Liz Greene, have linked the images of the Tarot to the archetypal figures and patterns of human life. In *The Mythic Tarot* by Juliet Sharman-Burke and Liz Greene (1986) the authors argue that

> the archetypal nature of the images strikes hidden, unconscious chords in the card-reader, and reflects hitherto unknown knowledge or insight in relation to the client's situation – thus apparently revealing things which could not possibly, in any rational way, be discoverable. This is why 'clairvoyant' or 'psychic' powers are not a prerequisite for a sensitive card-reader, but rather, an awareness of the archetypal patterns . . . at work in life reflected by the images on the cards.

Palmistry, or cheiromancy, is the art of analysing the symbols provided by the shape of the hand, and the lines upon it, to produce a description of character, talents and probable chronology of major life events. Some of this knowledge may be revealed through telepathy between palmist and querent, and arguably some kind of psychometry (gaining information by holding an object) similar to techniques used in psychic diagnosis.

Since the brain and hands are linked by the nervous system, there may be some biological basis for these ancient beliefs and teachings. Indeed,

was painted about thirty years later by an Italian artist, Bonifacio Bembo. These are known as the Visconti deck after the family name of the Duke of Milan, who commissioned them. There is no concrete evidence to suggest that the Tarot existed before the 1300s.

However, most scholars and commentators agree that the Tarot is a kind of book containing esoteric teachings in visual form. The Middle Ages were a dangerous time for non-Christians – so what better way to record and pass on secret knowledge both lines and ridges on the palms do reveal hereditary characteristics. Interesting research conducted by scientists at the University of London has shown that at least thirty congenital disorders correspond to particular patterns on the palms; these patterns are sometimes in evidence before any other recognisable symptoms.

The historical roots of palmistry are difficult to trace. The Chinese system is reputed to be over two thousand years old, and is based upon five elements which are also found in traditional Chinese medicine: Fire, Earth, Water, Metal and Wood. The Chinese further divide the hand into eight 'palaces', corresponding to the eight basic trigrams of the *I Ching*. These links are not surprising, for in ancient China so-called fortune-tellers and medical practitioners underwent very similar training, and were sometimes one and the same person. The Chinese have always set great store by both physiognomy (face reading) and palmistry, maintaining that all ill health is caused by an imbalance in the five basic elements.

The Western tradition is estimated to be about one thousand years old, and is heavily influenced by astrology; traditionally, hands are ruled by the four elements (Fire, Earth, Air and Water) and the seven original planets (Sun, Moon, Mercury, Venus, Mars, Saturn and Jupiter). Since Uranus, Neptune and Pluto were not discovered until relatively recently, they have never been incorporated into modern systems. These planetary energies are thought to manifest as personality traits and impulses that are chronicled in the palms, thus reflecting both character and destiny. However, twentieth-century palmists have abandoned the planets in all but name, preferring a quasi-scientific or psychological approach.

SEE ALSO *Astrology; Biorhythms; Creative visualisation; Aleister Crowley; John Dee; End times cults; Fate; Formative causation; Inspiration in dreams; Jung and the paranormal; Left and right brain; Prophecy and prediction; Ritual magic; Shamanism; Sunspots.*

JUNG AND THE PARANORMAL

Carl Gustav Jung (1875–1961) was originally a colleague of Sigmund Freud, but by 1913 had come to reject and rethink much of what he had learned as a student. In addition to establishing a personal, richly symbolic system of psychoanalysis he was also deeply concerned with the spiritual nature of mankind.

This interest went far beyond intellectual philosophy; Jung recorded numerous personal experiences of telepathy, waking visions, prophetic dreams and even psychokinesis, which suggests that he possessed considerable psychic abilities. He divided the psyche into three parts: the conscious, personal unconscious and collective unconscious. Although he never entirely rejected Freud's belief in the significance of sexuality, Jung's theories of synchronicity, archetypes and the collective unconscious were in many respects closer to ancient occult teachings than those of modern psychology. Indeed, writing in *Memories, Dreams, Reflections* he says: 'The collective unconscious is common to us all; it is the foundation of what the ancients called "the sympathy of all things".'

In 1913 Jung was increasingly disturbed by

Carl Gustav Jung (seated, right), *the psychoanalyst who challenged Sigmund Freud* (seated, left) *to recognise the significance of religion and the paranormal in man's psychological make-up.*

visions, and felt the stirrings of unconscious fears. When he explored these images they seemed to be connected to the outbreak of war, in August 1914. Within the personal unconscious dwells what he called 'the Shadow' – a primitive part of every human psyche. Jung maintained that nations too have group minds, composed in the same way; he believed that the Second World War was a manifestation of the German shadow. Occultists, such as Dion Fortune, were similarly convinced that the First World War corresponded to some great struggle between national forces of good (represented, in Britain, by King Arthur) and evil (the Germanic god of war, Wotan).

In 1920, the year Jung established his basic analytical structure, he also saw a ghost. He had rented a house in the English countryside, and over a period of weeks was troubled by the characteristic phenomena of a malevolent haunting; nasty smells, knocks, and dripping, rustling noises. This culminated in a night-time visitation – he awoke to find half a woman's head lying on the pillow next to him. Eventually Jung discovered that other tenants had left because of the ghost, which seemed to guard its property jealously.

In 1952 he collaborated with the Nobel Prize-winning physicist Wolfgang Pauli in an attempt to define meaningful coincidence, or what they termed 'synchronicity'. This 'acausal connecting principle', they believed, operated beyond the already established laws of physics, transcending straightforward linear cause and effect. Strange collections of coincidences might be simply ascribed to chance. But, as Jung wrote in his *Synchronicity* (1972), 'the more they multiply and the greater and more exact the correspondence is, the more their probability sinks and their unthinkability increases, until they can no longer be regarded as pure chance but, for lack of a causal explanation, have to be thought of as meaningful arrangements'.

His controversial astrological experiment with more than four hundred couples, and his subsequent interest in astrology, was inspired by this theory of synchronicity. With the help of a statistician he analysed the couples' horoscopes, looking for evidence of traditional astrological indications of compatibility in love. The horoscopes of married couples did indeed reveal a significant tendency

for the woman's moon to conjunct the man's natal sun (1:1500 due to chance). Jung did not consider these experiments conclusive, but continued to be deeply interested in astrology and to believe in its principles.

Jung's fascination with the *I Ching*, astrology and dreams demonstrates his involvement with the paranormal. His work in these fields echoes esoteric teachings on the macrocosm as reflected in the microcosm of mankind – 'as above, so below' – yet it is much more accessible.

SEE ALSO *Astrology; Divination; Entity enigma; Fate; Formative causation; Michel Gauquelin and the Mars effect; Ghosts; Inspiration in dreams; Left and right brain; Lexilinking; Library angel; Life imitates art; Precognition in dreams; Prophecy and prediction; Ritual magic; Telepathy; UFOs.*

AKASHIC RECORDS

Occultists and Theosophists believe that there exists on another plane of consciousness a store of records of every deed, thought, event and intention the human race has ever experienced, and that the information stored on these Akashic records can be tapped by psychics, mediums and clairvoyants. First proposed by German Anthroposophist Rudolf Steiner, this astral databank has allegedly been consulted by such sensitives as 'the sleeping prophet', Edgar Cayce.

This somewhat simplistic idea has given rise to much amusement. A reader of the weekly magazine series *The Unexplained* wanted to know where to buy the Akashic records, and some contributors to the *Fortean Times* have referred to them as the 'Trashkashic records' and an 'etheric cesspool', remarking that: 'Obviously there is no quality control in Heaven!'

However, there is a clear connection between this occult version of a universal, time-transcending databank and the Jungian collective unconscious. The 'Super-ESP' beloved of parapsychologists, which refers to an invisible databank consulted by the minds of the living, is frequently less satisfying an explanation, and considerably more tortuous, than that of the Akashic records.

SEE ALSO *ESP; Explanations; Formative causation; Inspiration in dreams; Jung and the paranormal; Karma; Left and right brain; Parapsychology; Precognition in dreams; Prophecy and prediction.*

PRODIGIES

Wolfgang Amadeus Mozart wrote his earliest compositions when he was just five and gave his first dazzling public performance as a pianist the same year. William James Sidis, the American genius, was studying advanced mathematics at three and in 1909, aged eleven, lectured to the Harvard Mathematical Association on fourth-dimensional bodies. Unlike Mozart, who went on to bring his talent to full fruition, Sidis retreated from relentless, cruel media attention into early anonymity.

A child prodigy is one of those miracles of nature that always evoke wonder and awe in the rest of mankind. Whether or not these precocious talents develop to enrich the collective heritage of human achievement or burn out prematurely, the intriguing question of how to explain the phenomenon remains. Many educated theories have been put forward, including the relentless cramming of infant brains, a photographic memory, an obsession with a single talent and, more recently, the discovery that prodigies seem to use the right hemisphere of the brain more frequently than other children.

But none of these theories is entirely satisfactory. They do not, for example, explain the extraordinary case of the Infant of Lübeck, Christian Friedrich Heiner. By the age of one Christian knew basic mathematics and all the main events in the Bible. At three he was fluent in Latin and French, and so renowned for his knowledge of world history that the King of Denmark summoned him for an audience. This amazing child died in 1724 at the age of four, after predicting his own death. Neither

Autistic artist Stephen Wiltshire demonstrates his remarkable gift. He can draw the most detailed building after a cursory inspection – and meets an extraordinarily high standard of draughtsmanship.

do the theories explain Kim Ung-Young, born in 1961 in Korea, who was reading and writing at seven months, speaking fluent English and German at four and solving integral calculus problems on Japanese television a year later. Nor do they explain either the baffling phenomenon of severely retarded children who, although institutionalised, possess one shining talent. Of these children, known collectively as the Foolish Wise Ones or idiots savants, some are lightning calculators, others brilliant pianists or artists.

One such is Stephen Wiltshire, who was featured in the BBC television documentary *The Foolish Wise Ones* in February 1987. Stephen had been autistic since birth, with a very low IQ and no verbal capabilities in his first years. But as a child he soon exhibited an extraordinary talent for draughtsmanship, drawing even the most elaborate buildings that he had seen just once in incredible detail, although as if from a mirror image. Given a test for the programme of drawing the gothic St Pancras station in London, he did so after just twenty minutes of observation, although for much of that time he appeared not to be very interested in it. Yet the finished drawing was almost perfect – down to the crane in the background.

Eminent artist and architect Sir Hugh Casson is profoundly impressed by Stephen's work, saying:

To watch him draw is an extraordinary experience. Where he starts on the paper seems capricious and to him unimportant. He may begin at the top, the bottom or the middle, with the pavement, the roofline or a window. From the first mark, the pencil moves as quickly and surely as a sewing machine – the line spinning from the pencil point like embroidery.

One psychologist put forward the theory that most people, including children, bring to the task of drawing a whole host of expectations, memories, beliefs and so on, which effectively puts up barriers against uninhibited excellence. But children like Stephen have to draw what they see, for their minds do not have such barriers. This theory does not explain, however, why, of all autistic children who have ever been presented with drawing materials, very few have exhibited such genius.

Only the doctrine of reincarnation seems able to offer a totally plausible explanation; it allows that a talent can remanifest – not only as a seed of potential, but as an intact and mature force in the infant mind of its new incarnation. The nineteenth-century French novelist Balzac wrote: 'Laden with the result of their past, and in possession of the capacities they have developed in the course of their evolution . . . men are philosophers or mathematicians, artists or savants, from the very cradle. The endless legacy of the past to the present is the secret source of human genius.'

SEE ALSO *Children and psi; Formative causation; Inspiration in dreams; Karma; Left and right brain; Multiple personality; Possession; Psychic music, art and literature; Reincarnation; Shamanism.*

LIGHTNING CALCULATORS

George Parker Bidder, born in 1806, was six years old when his extraordinary ability for mental computations manifested. Soon afterwards, his father was exhibiting his prowess at fairs up and down the country. Queen Victoria came to hear of him and invited him to Windsor Castle. The question she had prepared was: 'How long would it take a snail, creeping at the rate of eight feet (2.4 metres) a day, to travel from Land's End to Faraid Head – a distance of 838 miles (1349 km)?' The child paused for a second, then gave the correct answer. 553,080 days. George Bidder was highly intelligent and went on to become an excellent engineer and founder of the Electrical Telegraph Company.

By contrast, other lightning calculators have been so stupid that it made their one strange talent even more bizarre. Jedediah Buxton (1702–72), for example, appeared to be of less than average intelligence and remained illiterate all his life. Nevertheless, he could compute calculations of enormous complexity and was able to calculate while working or talking, and could handle two problems at once without confusion.

It may be that some idiosyncratic reading and writing abilities are allied phenomena. Oscar Wilde could master the intricacies of the plot of a novel in three minutes, and could talk about other subjects while he read facing pages simultaneously. Similarly, Branwell Brontë, brother of the literary sisters, could write two letters on different subjects with both hands at the same time.

Dr E. W. Scripture made an in-depth study of lightning calculators, finding certain characteristics possessed by them all. These common denominators are a prodigious memory; rapid recall; a love of arithmetical computations, tricks and short cuts; and a good visual memory. Then in 1903 the psychical researcher Frederic Myers put forward the theory that lightning calculators make dominant use of the right hemisphere of the brain.

A rare clue to the mechanics of the lightning calculator was given by one of them to a writer in the 1970s, who said that he saw the problem written out on a mental blackboard. As he looked, the answer appeared – and he merely read it out, the whole operation taking just a split second from beginning to end. Others have mentioned that they 'see' the *whole* problem and answer at the same time; if asked to give the stages of the solution, they rarely know where to begin.

However, the fact that a few precocious individuals can perform feats of computation that makes electronic calculators appear lumbering is still a largely unexplained phenomenon.

SEE ALSO *ESP; Inspiration in dreams; Left and right brain; Coral Polge; Prodigies; Psychic music, art and*

TULPAS

Tulpas are the deliberately projected thoughtforms of the magical adept or magus; they assume solidity and autonomy in direct ratio to the vividness and persistence of their creator's imagination. To the adept, thought or fantasy actually binds with 'mind stuff' to create an ideoplastic creature that impinges on everyday reality. Most creatures of the imagination fade away almost as soon as they are created, but if accompanied by particularly strong emotions, or if repeatedly conjured up, they take on a permanency and are seen 'out there' by others.

The French explorer Madame Alexandra David-Neel was a Buddhist convert whose religious disciplines enabled her, while in the remote mountains of Tibet in the 1920s, to create an animated thoughtform or tulpa. After shutting herself away in *tsams* (meditation in seclusion) she followed the prescribed rites for visualising and animating a tulpa. She concentrated on the image of a jolly, fat Buddhist monk; within a few months he had acquired a solidity that no longer required so much concentration on her part. After a few more weeks, however, the tulpa underwent a change. He became leaner and more sinister-looking – and began to escape Madame David-Neel's control. He was seen by others, who took him for a real monk. She only succeeded in dissolving him into nothingness after six months of concentration; he had become a 'day nightmare'.

The occultist Dion Fortune (real name Violet Firth) discovered a wolf beside her in bed after she had been thinking about the wolf-monster of Norse mythology, Fenrir. As a practising occultist she realised she had to take control immediately. Digging it in the ribs, she said: 'If you can't behave yourself you will have to go on the floor.' The creature seemed to fade into the wall – only to be glimpsed

Madame Alexandra David-Neel who took to the Tibetan mountains on a spiritual quest. She experimented successfully with creating thoughtforms, or tulpas, *one of which was taken to be a living man by others.*

by others in the house that night. Dion Fortune destroyed the tulpa by visualising a thread joining it to her, through which she withdrew its life force. The creature appeared to dissolve into a shapeless grey mass, then disappeared.

The ability of the human psyche to project doppelgängers, or doubles of a human being, is well documented, but it is only recently, with the investigation into the case of Ruth, the creation of the fake ghost Philip, and the ability of some sensitives to project 'thoughtographs' that the tangible proof of mental creativity is beginning to be recorded. It will not be a simple matter to explain it.

SEE ALSO *Angels; Apports; Boggle threshold; Buddhism; Case of Ruth; Children and psi; Consensus reality; Cosmic Joker; Cottingley fairies; Creative visualisation; The Devil; Doppelgängers; Dragons; Entity enigma; Fairies; Fantasy-prone personalities; Ghosts; Hallucinations; Hypnosis; Hypnotic regression; Images that bleed and weep; Katie King; Left and right brain; Loch Ness monster; Mysterious appearances; Other dimensions; Paranormal portraits; Philip experiment; Psychokinesis; Ritual magic; Seance-room phenomena; SORRAT; Stigmatics; Thoughtography; UFO paradox; Vampires; Visions of the Virgin Mary; Werewolves; Witchcraft.*

DOPPELGÄNGERS

A doppelgänger – human double – emerges from Poe's William Wilson.

There are many cases on record of a living human being spontaneously seeing the double, or doppelgänger (the German *Doppelgänger*, means 'of himself'). The categories of doppelgänger and phantasms of the living frequently overlap, but generally the double is perceived by its original, and the phantasm by others. The German poet and dramatist Goethe (1749–1832) saw himself wearing 'clothes such as I had never worn' one afternoon while out riding. The vision of himself soon vanished, but eight years later he found himself at the same place, wearing the clothes that his double had worn – by accident.

A stranger case was that of the French-born schoolteacher Emélie Sagée, whose double could be seen by staff and pupils of the Livonian school where she worked while she conducted her class. On one occasion in the early nineteenth century, no fewer than thirteen of the girls saw two Mademoiselle Sagées standing at the blackboard, and the entire school – forty-two people – saw her simultaneously in the garden and in the school. When the double manifested, Emélie felt suddenly fatigued; when it faded away she revived. On one occasion it appeared when she was thinking that she ought to be elsewhere, supervising the girls.

Two of the pupils dared to try and touch the double, and

> They did feel a slight resistance, which they likened to that which a fabric of fine muslin or crêpe would offer to the touch. One of the two then passed close in front of the armchair, and actually through a portion of the figure.

Emélie was asked to leave her post because of the unsettling effect of her doppelgänger on the school. She then revealed that she had lost nineteen other jobs due to the same cause.

In this, as in many – but not all – cases, the double appears to draw strength to manifest from its human original, inviting comparison with the fatigue reported by the Misses Moberley and Jourdain before their Versailles 'adventure', and with that experienced by materialisation mediums after their trance. One man reported that his double appeared just before a bad attack of migraine, raising questions as to whether the double caused the migraine, or vice versa. There are several similar cases where living people have been mistaken for ghosts or crisis apparitions, warning of disaster. Occasionally the double seems to serve a purpose; cases are known of it advising its original on the right course of action. There are, however, cases where the double has become malevolent and attacked the original; in one case the doppelgänger attempted to stab the real woman to death.

Certain psychological states may be inferred about those who commonly have such experiences, but perhaps of more significance, however, is the inference that many of the people we see or meet may not be the entities they seem.

SEE ALSO *Boggle threshold; Case of Ruth; Consensus reality; Cosmic Joker; Creative visualisation; Entity enigma; Fantasy-prone personalities; Ghosts; Hallucinations; Katie King; Multiple personality; Mysterious appearances; Philip experiment; Society for Psychical Research; SORRAT; Thoughtography; Timeslips; Tulpas; Visions of the Virgin Mary.*

THOUGHTOGRAPHY

Since the invention of photography there have been many claims that photographs showed paranormal 'extras', which were allegedly recognised as images of the dead. At the turn of the century spirit photography thrived, but many practitioners were proven frauds, their photographs being simply double exposures.

In the 1960s, however, Dr Jule Eisenbud, associate professor of psychiatry at the University of Colorado Medical School, discovered that an unemployed alcoholic bellhop, Ted Serios, could project his thoughts directly on to photographic film. Eisenbud set him carefully controlled experiments in which he was to concentrate on certain target images and project them on to virgin film. Certain significant factors emerged from the many 'hits'; the images seemed to be 'thoughtographed'

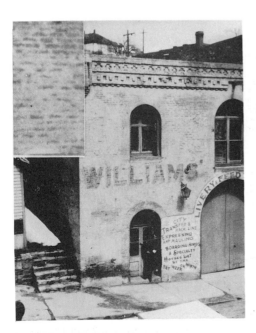

Ted Serios's 'thoughtograph' (right) *in response to the set target* (left). *Note the difference in façade and the extra sign on the left of the side door in Ted's version.*

from a strange angle, high in the air, and to show marked differences from the real target locations – for example, a building might be thoughtographed as having a pebble-dashed façade instead of the plain brick of the real building.

Serios also produced completely black or completely white frames in the middle of a blank roll of film, or produced thoughtographs showing the researchers wearing clothes they did not possess or sitting in places where they were not. His habit of placing what he called his 'gismo' over the lens of a camera naturally drew accusations of fraud. But independent observers discovered this to be merely a short, hollow tube made of cardboard with nothing hidden in it. An unreliable subject because of his drinking habits, Serios lost interest in the experiments in the early 1970s.

At roughly the same time Walter and Mary Jo Uphoff were investigating the thoughtographic abilities of Japanese psychic Masuaki Kiyota, with similarly thought-provoking results. The earlier Japanese sensitive Tenshin Takeuchi, investigated by Dr Fukurai, had managed to project a whole sentence from a book besides three specific Japanese characters, on request, onto photographic film.

Thoughtography seems to add credence to the ancient occultists' belief that thought can be made 'real' enough to impinge on the physical world – the stronger or longer the thought, the more vivid its impact. Perhaps specially gifted psychics are permanently in a suitable state of mind to produce impressive thoughtographs and it may be that the 'spirit photographs' beloved of early Spiritualists, when not fraudulent, were actually thoughtographs, created by the mind of the sitter or photographer, or both.

SEE ALSO *American Society for Psychical Research; Case of Ruth; Consensus reality; Cosmic Joker; Cottingley fairies; Creative visualisation; Fantasy-prone personalities; Uri Geller; Ghosts; Hallucinations; Images that bleed and weep; Katie King; Nina Kulagina; Left and right brain; Loch Ness monster; Metal bending; Moving statues; Other dimensions; Eusapia Palladino; Paranormal portraits; Parapsychology; Philip experiment; Psychokinesis; Quantum mechanics and the paranormal; Ritual magic; SORRAT; Timeslips; Tulpas; UFO paradox; Vampires; Visions of the Virgin Mary; Werewolves.*

COTTINGLEY FAIRIES

Between 1917 and 1921 teenager Elsie Wright and her eleven-year-old cousin Frances Griffiths took two batches of photographs of fairies around the 'beck' (stream) at Cottingley in Yorkshire. Encouraged by Elsie's mother Polly, a keen Theosophist and believer in fairy life, the girls allowed the photographs to be seen by a few neighbours. It was only when Polly mentioned them at a local Theosophical meeting, however, that their fame began to spread.

Within months, leading Theosophist and expert on fairy lore Edward L. Gardner was in possession of sharpened prints of the photographs – and very soon Sir Arthur Conan Doyle became involved in the story. His book *The Coming of the Fairies* was due to be published that year, and he was keen to use the Cottingley photographs in his promotional tours.

Gardner and, later, medium Geoffrey Hodson, visited the girls and found them impressive witnesses. However, further attempts to take fairy photographs, under the men's supervision, were not successful. Sir Oliver Lodge, senior member of the Society for Psychical Research, had no hesitation in pronouncing the pictures frauds, and the publication *Truth* proclaimed: 'What is wanted is not a knowledge of occult phenomena but a knowledge of children.'

Over the years Frances and Elsie maintained a solemn silence about their fairy photographs, while sporadic attempts were made to prove them frauds. American conjurer and a founder member of CSICOP, James 'the Amazing' Randi, even had the prints computer-enhanced by technicians at NASA during the 1970s; when nothing incriminating could be found, he fell back on the 'invisible thread' explanation. He failed to suggest where two young girls in the provinces in the early twentieth century could have laid their hands on such a useful item.

However, Randi did suggest that the fairy figures bore a suggestive resemblance to illustrations in the 1914 *Princess Mary's Gift Book*, as did researcher Fred Gettings and television presenter Austin

The Cottingley fairies – photographs faked by cousins Elsie Wright and Frances Griffiths in the 1900s in west Yorkshire. They perpetrated the hoax because they found it impossible to take photographs of the fairies they saw.

Mitchell at roughly the same time. As always, the responses of the ladies were ambiguous.

In 1983 retired sociology lecturer and psychical researcher Joe Cooper elicited a confession: the photographs were indeed fakes, made simply by propping up cut-outs (based on the *Gift Book* illustrations) in the grass with hat pins. Although a tape of the confession was first sent to the weekly publication *The Unexplained*, the story was picked up by several national newspapers, including *The Times*. Unfortunately all of them, except for *The Unexplained*, missed the point of the confession.

Joe Cooper was chosen as confessor, not merely because he had befriended the old ladies, but because he himself believes in fairies – and the photographs were faked because the girls had tried, and failed, to take photographs of the fairies that they saw frequently. Frances said: 'I became so used to them that unless they did something unusual I just ignored them.'

Elsie was the more reluctant to talk about their escapade, although she made it clear that she did not have a very positive memory of seeing fairies. Looking at an old photograph of herself, Hodson and Frances, she was to say: 'Look at that – fed up with fairies!'

Frances told Joe Cooper that: 'I'd rather we were thought of as solemn-faced comediennes', as she continued to nurse the long-standing joke. But towards the end of her life, in the mid-1980s, she was to see at least one other manifestation of the fairy life she had sought to capture on camera sixty years before.

SEE ALSO *Angels; Case of Ruth; Children and psi; Consensus reality; Cosmic Joker; Cryptozoology; CSICOP; The Devil; Entity enigma; Explanations; Fairies; Fantasy-prone personalities; Hallucinations; Philip experiment; Sex and psi; Society for Psychical Research; Thoughtography; Tulpas; Visions of the Virgin Mary.*

FANTASY-PRONE PERSONALITIES

It is estimated that about 4 per cent of the Western population are 'fantasy-prone'; that is, happiest when living in a world of their own imagination, while being normal in every other respect. Such people – mainly women – retain the common childhood ability to conjure up imaginary playmates, surroundings and scenarios, and are reluctant to accept the 'real' world as it is.

In a major experiment carried out by Drs Sheryl C. Wilson and Theodore Barber of Cushing Hospital, Framingham, Massachusetts, twenty-seven female fantasy-prone subjects were tested together with a control group of twenty-five 'normal' women. With an average age of twenty-eight, all except two of the fantasy women were graduates, and all led normal lives.

The twenty-seven subjects proved to be unusually receptive to creative visualisation, hypnotic suggestion and psychic abilities, which included healing at a distance, telepathy, out-of-the-body experiences (OOBEs) and mediumistic trances. Thirteen of the women admitted to having had at least one phantom pregnancy, with severe associated symptoms. The subjects also showed higher than usual abilities to control their autonomic bodily functions, being able, for example, to slow their heart rate at will.

All of the fantasy-prone women spoke of regular hypnopompic and hypnagogic visions – vivid hallucinations during the period of falling asleep and waking. (They were relieved to learn that these conditions are surprisingly common.)

Asked what percentage of each day they spent fantasising, some replied that it would be easier to calculate what percentage was spent not doing so. Eleven of the women estimated that they fantasised for over 90 per cent of each day, but some were careful to point out that they deliberately controlled their ability to do so while driving.

One woman recalled her perplexity when told that Santa Claus did not exist; why should adults want to invent him when the world she saw was full of such magical creatures as fairies and tree spirits? This anecdote recalls, almost verbatim, the reasons given for the faked Cottingley fairy photographs, which were devised, one of the perpetrators confessed, because of their frustration at not being able to capture on film the fairies they often saw.

Fantasy-prone people are, however, more than interesting psychological anomalies. The case of Ruth, whose hallucinations once impinged upon the reality of someone else, points to the profound significance of such creativity.

For centuries magical adepts have claimed to conjure up spirits to carry out their commands – and to create deliberate thoughtforms, or 'tulpas', which may be taken as real by others. Some of these creations may be mythical, such as griffins or gnomes, while some may be winged humans, such as the 'mothmen' or 'birdwomen' often recorded in the *Fortean Times*. The Loch Ness monster and the yeti may or may not exist, but there are enough believers to manipulate reality so that they do, on some ideoplastic plane.

Imagination and artistic and creative ability reside – or flow through – the right hemisphere of the brain, which is favoured by most women over the analytical, mechanical left half. The West is a markedly left-brained society, unlike the East with its emphasis on instinct and its respect for paranormal powers. The perfectly balanced society would have equal respect for rational thinking and communion with spirits, but such a society is unlikely to exist in the near future.

SEE ALSO *Bigfoots, almas and yeti; Case of Ruth; Consensus reality; Cosmic Joker; Cottingley fairies; Creative visualisation; Entity enigma; Fairies; Formative causation; Eileen Garrett; Healing; Hypnosis; Inspiration in dreams; Left and right brain; Lightning calculators; Loch Ness monster; Near death experience; Out-of-the-body experiences; Philip experiment; Precognition in dreams; Remote viewing; Ritual magic; Shamanism; SORRAT; Telepathy; Thoughtography; Tulpas.*

CASE OF RUTH

In the 1970s, Ruth, an American woman living in London, became the patient of her fellow countryman Dr Morton Schatzman, who in 1971 set up the Arbours Crisis Centre for psychiatric cases. At first Ruth confessed only to a profound sense of disorientation and agoraphobia. Continued therapy, however, revealed that her real problem was the persistent hallucination of her father, which was making her life a nightmare.

Utterly 'real' in every sense to her, he was neither seen nor sensed by anyone else. 'I can count his teeth,' she told Schatzman. 'I can smell him.' The hallucination was particularly unwelcome because her father had sexually molested her when she was a child. He was no ghost, however, for at the time of the hallucination he was alive in the USA.

The psychiatrist was fascinated by this case, because in every way other than the hallucinations Ruth behaved and thought rationally. In his expert opinion there was nothing psychotic or pathological about her personality.

He suggested she try to confront the hallucination, rather than succumb to its terrorisation. Although not an easy process, Ruth finally managed to treat it with some degree of disdain – for example, when it appeared while she was taking a bath she merely asked it to hand her a towel. That was the breakthrough; soon Ruth could summon and dismiss the hallucination at will.

However, Schatzman discovered that Ruth's capacity to create three-dimensional figures was unusual to a degree. She could, for example, hallucinate Schatzman himself at another point in the room, while the real doctor took notes. She could 'see' a room grow dim or light at will (but she could not read the titles of books on the shelf when she hallucinated the room 'light').

Her strange ability took on a new meaning for her when she deliberately hallucinated a double of her husband, who was away on business. They made love – reportedly a particularly satisfying encounter.

Now in command of her life once more, Ruth took a trip to the USA and visited her father. During this time she hallucinated her husband sitting in her car – and her father also saw it. On another occasion her husband saw Ruth's projected double sitting on the sofa, while the real Ruth remained elsewhere. Generally, however, her mental creations did not impinge on the reality of others.

Neurophysiological tests carried out on Ruth while she was hallucinating gave all the indications that she was confronting a 'something' that was real to her in visual and spatial terms. The doctor who conducted these tests said: 'You've produced the appearance of a real person.'

Schatzman believes that Ruth is not mad, but that she is extremely creative – to such an extent that she can reorder reality, which occasionally can impinge on other people.

Ruth now manipulates her talent; boring car journeys can be relieved by hallucinating a friend as a passenger, or she can summon up her husband to keep her company. Occultists have long believed that such mentally projected 'thoughtforms' can be experienced by others. Werewolves, for example, are allegedly created and unleashed by master magicians. Long periods of isolation, fasting and prayer could perhaps have triggered off a similar process for the saints, producing visions of the Virgin, or of Heaven and Hell.

In parapsychology, the work of Dr Jule Eisenbud with Ted Serios shows that some rare people can project their thoughts directly on to photographic film. Other psychics have also shown themselves to be competent 'thoughtographers'.

Theoretical physics shows that there is no such thing as objective reality – everything that is observed is changed by the fact of the observer. In practical terms a pliable reality is bad news for the infant discipline of parapsychology. Perhaps of all the phenomena explored by researchers only the experimenter effect can be proven.

SEE ALSO *Angels; Autosuggestion; Boggle threshold; Children and psi; Consensus reality; Cottingley fairies; Creative visualisation; The Devil; Doppelgängers; Entity enigma; Experimenter effect; Fairies; Fantasy-prone personalities; Haemography; Hallucinations; Hysteria; Images that bleed and weep; Katie King; Left and right brain; Men in Black; Parapsychology; Philip experiment; Quantum mechanics and the paranormal; The Resurrection; Ritual magic; Sex and psi; SORRAT;*

Stigmatics; Thoughtography; Tulpas; UFO paradox; Visions of the Virgin Mary; Werewolves; Witchcraft.

HALLUCINATIONS

A standard dictionary definition of a hallucination is 'the illusion of seeing or hearing something when no such thing is present'. To 'see things' – or worse, to be caught talking to non-existent things – is in Western society the mark of the mentally unstable.

But if the Society for Psychical Research's massive *Census of Hallucinations* was a representative survey, it showed that one in ten of the population of Edwardian Britain had experienced some form of hallucination – perceived, and even interacted with, something or someone when no such thing or person was present. It may be that those who were willing to communicate with the SPR had a predisposition to hallucinate, but there are no data on that point.

Hallucinations may be visual, auditory or even olfactory – or a persuasive intermixture. Many people who are plagued by hallucinations are schizophrenic, and the affliction is more or less constant. Some, like novelist Evelyn Waugh, go through a phase of hallucinating; his took the form of voices discussing him in increasingly derogatory terms. At first he believed them to be real, but he came to know and fear them as insubstantial – yet, as he said on television in the 1960s: 'It wasn't at all like losing one's reason. One's reason was working hard, but on the wrong premises.'

Most sufferers from hallucinations eventually find themselves in institutions for the mentally sick, drugged into quiescence. Few psychiatrists actively attempt to understand the hallucinations of their patients, but one such is Dr Wilson Van Dusen, formerly of the Mendocino State Hospital in California, who spent sixteen years treating the hallucinations of his patients as realities, 'for that is what they are to the patient'. He published his findings in *The Presence of Other Worlds* (1974), in a chapter entitled 'The Presence of Spirits in Madness'.

He found that all the sufferers felt as if they were in touch with beings from other planes or dimensions; every one of the patients he studied objected to the term 'hallucination'. There appeared to be two types of being contacting the patients – a Higher and a Lower, although the Lower seemed to predominate. These intruders of the mind

are similar to drunken bums ... They suggest lewd acts and scold the patient for considering them ... they brag that they will produce some disaster on the morrow and then claim credit for one in the daily paper ... They invade every nook and cranny of privacy, work on every weakness and belief, claim awesome powers, make promises, and then undermine the patient's will....

Writer Colin Wilson describes these Lower Orders as being like 'bored children with nothing better to do ... basically tormentors'. They bring nightmare into daily life; one man saw a soldier appear to call him to help his country, but he noticed that the soldier's insignia was subtly wrong and he hit the man, who disappeared. The patient hurt his hand quite badly against the wall.

At this point, disturbing similarities between the Lower Order hallucinatory beings and the elementals who toy with our sanity through the ouija board or in poltergeist attacks begin to emerge. There may even be links between these creatures and the demons of old. Even some of the alleged visions of the Virgin and other religious figures, or many of the abducting ufonauts of today, seem to fit into this frightening jigsaw.

Yet the Higher Order hallucinations are gentle, loving and good for the soul. One of Van Dusen's patients experienced a hallucination of a beautiful woman who 'showed a knowledge of religion and myth far beyond the patient's comprehension'. Although aware of the non-real aspects of the encounter, the patient had the sense of being made a better person because of it. In another culture he might have been venerated as a visionary or a saint, a Chosen One.

Van Dusen became fascinated by the writings of the Swedish mystic Emanuel Swedenborg (1689–1772). He concluded that: 'All of Swedenborg's observations on the effect of evil spirits entering themselves in need of psychiatric aid. The late Doris Stokes, for example, was clairaudient – she heard voices which she believed came from discarnate spirits. Mrs Stokes believed that in passing on their messages to the living she was performing a service, and there were thousands who agreed with her.

SEE ALSO *Angels; Case of Ruth; Consensus reality; Cosmic Joker; Cottingley fairies; The Devil; Doppelgängers; Entity enigma; Fairies; Fantasy-prone personalities; Ghosts; Images that bleed and weep; Katie King; Left and right brain; Moving statues; Multiple personality; Near death experience; New Testament miracles; Ouija board and planchette; Philip experiment; Possession; Propensity for psi; Psychic music, art and literature; Remote viewing; Ritual magic; Shamanism; Doris Stokes; Thoughtography; Timeslips; Tulpas; UFO paradox; Vampires; Visions of the Virgin Mary; Werewolves; Witchcraft; Zombies.*

Emanuel Swedenborg, the Swedish mystic whose description of angelic and hellish spirits have been proved to match with the hallucinatory experiences of schizophrenics.

man's consciousness conform to my finding.'

At the Wrekin Trust's 1988 conference on reincarnation several doctors and psychiatrists confessed to how they came reluctantly to believe that many of their patients were, in the classic sense, possessed. One doctor said: 'I have every reason to believe that there are good and evil spirits waiting to influence us or even take us over. The evil tend to mimic the good for a while, but the Bible is right – "by their fruits ye shall know them".'

Many hallucinations can, however, be directly ascribed to fatigue, to the hypnopompic or hypnagogic states, or to other psychosomatic conditions. (One man's doppelgänger appeared during a migraine attack.) Yet even here the nature of the hallucinations may be inexplicable in any symbolic or psychological terms, and imply a temporary contact with other levels of being.

Some people hear voices or see figures that are not perceived by others, yet they do not consider

CREATIVE VISUALISATION

The human mind has almost unlimited powers of creativity; both a great painting and a great thought begin as a concept seen as a whole in 'the mind's eye'. To become conscious of this process of creative visualisation is the first step towards harnessing its extraordinary power, whose secrets have been jealously guarded by magical adepts through the centuries.

Mental creations can, depending upon the single-mindedness with which they are called into being, impinge on the reality of others. The adept conjures up thoughtforms or tulpas that achieve a degree of ideoplastic solidity and are, it is claimed, perceived as real by others. Werewolves, vampires and other legendary monsters may be deliberate magical creations. Encounters with fairies, demons, angels, the Virgin Mary and ufonauts may be part of a similar process, whereby a culturally determined belief is externalised as a vision. Similarly, hallucinations of menacing entities may be – as shown in the case of Ruth – ultimately controllable and malleable.

Dr Brian Roet, Australian hypnotherapist based in London, whose work with creative visualisation has uncovered rich seams of hidden meaning.

Ordinary people can learn to utilise the extraordinary creative powers of the mind through the modern therapeutic technique known as 'creative visualisation', which refers to the viewing of internal pictures in the mind. It is a simple, sensitive and effective way of communicating with the unconscious. These pictures occur naturally in dreams, daydreams and fantasies and have a wide application in psychotherapy.

It has been suggested that there is a continuous internal picture-show projected beyond conscious awareness. One can enter this 'movie house of the mind' and utilise these films in many positive ways. Imagining a successful outcome to some situation – seeing a future picture of the desired outcome – may well influence activities in a positive way to secure this result.

One form that these pictures may take is an internal journey into the unknown. The visualiser is led through a variety of encounters with frightening challenges. Often he comes face to face with monsters, dragons, waterfalls, tunnels and caves – just as classical heroes travelled the world overcoming powerful enemies. In therapy the visualiser confronts such challenges, and in the process automatically overcomes problems 'on the surface' in his real world. There is no need for translation or interpretation of the visions, as they are already metaphorically linked with reality.

The theory involved with this form of creative visualisation suggests parallel worlds in the mind. By confronting the fears in the fantasy world the adjoining worlds of the personality gain in strength.

To achieve benefits from creative visualisation one initially needs the non-interfering support of a therapist or friend who guides from the outside, using 'clean language' – words that will not imply or suggest any imagery. The visualiser sits quietly and comfortably, with eyes closed, allowing himself to drift into a daydream trance state by focusing on any internal pictures that may occur. The direction of the journey may be determined by 'going into' a feeling and imagining what it looks like from the inside.

The monsters, dragons and devils commonly encountered on such journeys are initially terrifying, but – almost inevitably – change into sensitive and powerful allies if the visualiser approaches them as a friend. These internal pictures are spontaneous, not directed by the conscious mind, and apparently random; yet they are as real to the viewer as the waking state.

SEE ALSO *Angels; Buddhism; Case of Ruth; Cottingley fairies; The Devil; Doppelgängers; Dragons; Fairies; Fantasy-prone personalities; Formative causation; Ghosts; Healing; Hypnosis; Hypnotherapy; Left and right brain; Loch Ness monster; Other dimensions; Paranormal portraits; Philip experiment; Ritual magic; Telepathy; Thoughtography; Timeslips; Tulpas; UFO paradox; UFOs; Vampires; Visions of the Virgin Mary; Werewolves; Witchcraft.*

Harry Secombe, Peter Sellers and Michael Bentine – The Goons – sharing a joke. Uncontrollable laughter is the one acceptable form of hysteria.

HYSTERIA

Hysteria has had so confused a history that the term has now no consistent meaning, and its symptoms are misunderstood. It is usually traced back to ancient Greece, where it was observed that diviners and sibyls often went into convulsions while entering the trances in which they exercised their extrasensory oracular powers. With the spread of rationalism, however, confidence in divination dwindled, and the convulsions and loss of control tended to be regarded as a behavioural disorder. Men were not supposed to lose control; only women, it came to be assumed, were susceptible. And with the development of what came later to be called organicism, the symptoms were attri-

buted to a disorder of the uterus; hence 'hysteria', from the Greek *hustera*, womb.

'Going into hysterics' is still used in this sense – but it is no longer regarded either as a disorder of the uterus, or confined only to women – an assumption demolished by the father of English medicine, Thomas Sydenham, in the seventeenth century. Sydenham also pointed out, however, that hysteria had taken a different guise, largely unrecognised, in which it was not only widespread – 'of all chronic diseases, unless I err, the commonest' – but was rarely diagnosed. Hysteria, he warned, could mimic other disorders so successfully that even the most expert of physicians might be deceived.

Clinically, this type of hysteria represents what Sir James Paget a century ago labelled 'neuromimesis'. It can occur in bizarre forms, such as *pseudo-*

cyesis – false pregnancy – in which women have been reported as undergoing the entire cycle from morning sickness to labour pains; or *couvade*, where the father has the labour pains. Hysteria can imitate actual blindness, or deafness, so effectively that everybody concerned is deceived.

In this form it is often associated with the wishes or whims of the patients: a form of unconscious malingering, designed to extricate them from difficult situations or to win them sympathy. Understandably, this has given hysteria a bad name; humiliating to the patient, irritating to the doctors (who have to go through endless tests to eliminate the possibility of a physical or chemical cause, in case their suspicion that hysteria is responsible is unfounded) and uncomfortable for psychiatrists, aware as they are that there is no known remedy.

Hysteria should not be dismissed simply as a nuisance, however. Paget insisted that he had found it 'among the very good, the very wise, and the most accomplished' of his patients, it was as if the symptoms provided them with a way of breaking out of the constraints that their lives, for various reasons, imposed on them. In *Creative Malady* (1974) Sir George Pickering took up this theme, showing how individuals as different as Charles Darwin, Florence Nightingale and Marcel Proust had exploited illness – manufactured it, in a sense – to allow them to escape the distractions that otherwise would have prevented them from fulfilling their destinies.

An even more striking example of the potential value of hysteria has since been provided by Norman Cousins, in his *Anatomy of an Illness* (1979). Told he was dying of a blood disorder for which there was no remedy, he cured himself by laughter – watching comedy films and television programmes. Hysterical laughter is the only variety of hysteria that is unreservedly welcome; but the use Cousins made of it suggests that the entire subject could benefit from a reappraisal.

SEE ALSO *Autosuggestion; Fantasy-prone personalities; Healing; Hypnosis; Left and right brain; Mass hysteria; Miracles of St Médard; Shamanism; Stigmatics; Visions of the Virgin Mary; Witchcraft.*

MASS HYSTERIA

Outbreaks of mass hysteria have been reported in every era, from all parts of the world. Originally they appear to have been induced by shamans, as a form of tribal therapy. With the help of drumming and dancing, members of the tribe would throw off conscious restraints, liberate instinct and feel the better for the experience – much as we still do after enjoyable occasions in a theatre or a cinema, when an audience becomes convulsed with laughter. The Dionysian revels in classical times were on the same pattern.

In the late Middle Ages, however, with the spread through Europe of the dancing mania in which men and women were suddenly swept away into wild communal gyrations, the feeling tended to be that they were in the grip of communal diabolic possession. This was reinforced when reports of outbreaks in institutions claimed that the people involved appeared to have supernatural powers – as at Loudun in France, in the 1630s, when the possessed nuns sometimes displayed clairvoyant powers. Still more remarkable evidence, in that it was well attested, was Carré de Montgéron's account of the way in which the *convulsionnaires* at the churchyard of St Médard a century later, were able to withstand fierce heat, and submit to violence, without sustaining any ill effects.

Subsequently mass hysteria has manifested itself in three main ways. It has been seen in revivalist religious meetings of the kind that John Wesley held, his belief being that the convulsions and other symptoms indicated possession by the Holy Spirit; in sporadic outbreaks in schools, hospitals and workplaces; and in crowd behaviour.

In *The Crowd* (1896), Gustave Le Bon advanced the theory that people can be carried away, when they are together in sufficient numbers, partly because the relative anonymity allows them to behave out of character, but also by a form of contagion, resembling the effect of hypnotism. Taking up this point, a number of writers have since suggested that this may be a throwback to the way in which ants in their anthills and starlings in their flocks appear to lose any individual identity. It is as if their actions are regulated by a group mind. (More modern research indicates a link between group hysteria and pheromones, subliminally detectable scents that modify or provoke otherwise unexplained behaviour.)

As most orthodox scientists have declined to accept the existence of mind except as a product of brain, this group mind hypothesis has found little favour. When outbreaks occur, every possible physical explanation for the symptoms – usually malaise, headache, nausea, constriction of the throat, trembling, lassitude and occasionally convulsions – is usually suggested. Leaks of poisonous gas, boiler fumes, the effect of chemical sprays and food poisoning are the usual candidates; only when they are ruled out is the possibility of hysterical contagion considered.

It is not a popular diagnosis. Outbreaks are most commonly reported from schools, and parents tend to be furious at the slur – as they think of it – on their children. In workplaces managements will be readier to blame the air conditioning system rather than risk offending their employees. The most embarrassing place of all is hospitals, where it tends to be attributed to an elusive virus.

The embarrassment has arisen because, on several occasions, the 'virus' has struck down doctors and nurses rather than patients. This has made it difficult to make the explanation sound convincing, for why should the virus be so selective? But the convention is that hospital staffs are not hysteria-prone and consequently any clinical alternative, however implausible, will have to do.

That teenagers at pop concerts can become hysterical is accepted, and for a time it caused concern. Now, it is soccer crowds that are the worry,

Mass hysteria at a pop concert. Easy to recognise, it is almost impossible to explain.

particularly since it has been found that mass hooliganism is being deliberately aroused by cabals who have found that they can stir fans up to mob violence. But the refusal to accept the possibility of extra-sensory communication acting to provide the dynamic has prevented researchers from examining the evidence for psychic contagion. Such research that has been done to try to explain the mystery of the way starlings fly in flocks has concentrated on trying to explain it 'rationally' – with conspicuous lack of success.

SEE ALSO *Cosmic Joker; ESP; Explanations; Fantasy-prone personalities; Formative causation; Hypnosis; Hysteria; Jinxes; Miracles of St Médard; Moving statues; Possession; Shamanism; Speaking in tongues; Telepathy; Traumas and psi; Twins; Visions of the Virgin Mary; Witchcraft.*

MESMERISM

In its original form, Mesmerism was derived from different and apparently unrelated sources; but all of them derived from shamanism. As one of their healing methods, shamans would put a sick member of the tribe into a trance with the help of music and drumming; convulsions would be induced, sometimes accompanied by possession; eventually the patient would collapse into a coma, from which he would wake up cured – if all went well.

In early civilisations the procedure came to be modified, but 'strokers' continued to practise running their hands down the patient's body, without actually touching it, to induce the trance, convulsions and the cure. Exorcists also worked on the same principle, although their main concern was to drive the demons, who were assumed to be in possession, out of their victim.

By the eighteenth century 'stroking' had come to be identified with magnetism – presumably because of the resemblance to the process by which an iron bar can be magnetised. Studying the work of Newton, the young Austrian physician Franz Mesmer had an inspiration. If the moon was

Franz Mesmer supervises a lady undergoing treatment in his magnetised tub.

responsible for tides, why should there not also be a biological tie-up, analogous to gravity and magnetism – a force acting through a 'fluid', invisible but permeating everything (as gravity does), and influencing all living creatures? It was a concept similar to the one that explorers were to find in tribal communities which accepted the existence of *mana*. This is a form of action at a distance, used, it was assumed, by the gods for their purposes, but capable of being tapped by shamans and sorcerers for good or evil.

Mesmer proceeded to practise 'animal magnetism', as he called it, with varied fortunes but eventually, in the early 1780s, with success; he and his method became the craze in Paris. The report of the investigating committees appointed at the request of Louis XVI in 1784 rejected the idea of animal magnetism, but accepted that the method – putting patients into trances, with convulsions – could be very effective because of its effect on the patients' imaginations. Precisely because of this, they argued, it was dangerous; particularly for women, as in their trances they might shed their inhibitions.

Mesmer retreated to Switzerland, where he continued to practise in obscurity. Although a few of his followers (*'magnétiseurs'*) continued to follow his method (as they do to this day), Mesmerism took a different course – largely on account of the research of one of his disciples, Count Chastenet de Puysegur.

It was not necessary, Puysegur found, to induce convulsions: the coma stage could be brought on quietly. But it was an unexpected type of coma, resembling sleepwalking; those who were in it came to be described as *somnambules*. Not merely did they walk, and talk; they appeared to become different individuals, sometimes much more intelligent than their normal selves. A few displayed 'higher phenomena', such as clairvoyance. One of Puysegur's patients even responded to his unspoken instructions, stopping in mid-sentence when given the mental order: 'Stop!'

The French Revolution drove the Mesmerists underground, but they emerged again under Napoleon, and by the 1820s animal magnetism was flourishing in many parts of Europe. Investigators were finding that Puysegur's method worked, and that they could produce similar results. A further investigation by the French Academy of Sciences actually produced a favourable report in 1831, but this aroused the wrath of the medical establishment in France, and was soon overturned. Even demonstrations of painless surgery were rejected as fraudulent. This was not the result of the mesmeric trance, doctors claimed, but of the ability of the patient to pretend not to feel anything, for which he would doubtless be well remunerated.

In Britain, the main interest of the 1840s centred in the ability of some mesmerised subjects to develop second sight – or even 'second taste'. Such distinguished scientists as the polar explorer William Scoresby and the biologist Alfred Russel Wallace were among those who satisfied themselves as to the ability of some of their subjects to describe what they were tasting, even when they were out of sight and hearing. One of Scoresby's subjects could actually tell him not only that he was eating a biscuit, but also what type of biscuit it was.

Most scientists, however, remained sceptical; and in the 1840s James Braid presented his rival theory of hypnotism to account for the way in which the trances were induced. The introduction of anaesthetics means that the chief potential advantage for medicine was removed, and the entry of Spiritualism, with table-turning and mediumship, took over the paranormal aspects of Mesmerism. In so far as the concept lives on – as when we speak of being mesmerised by something

or somebody – it is generally thought of as little different from being hypnotised. The theory of animal magnetism is assumed to be totally discredited.

This, however, is misleading. There is a great deal of evidence for the existence of some force – *mana*, animal magnetism, psychokinesis, however it may be described – which exists, but has yet to be explained (as, indeed, gravity and magnetism have yet to be explained). And a study of the evidence that the early Mesmerists provided is sufficient to demonstrate that it should not be rejected out of hand.

The consequence of that rejection from the 1780s to the 1840s was in fact a tragedy; it meant that hundreds of thousands of people had to suffer the agony of amputations and other forms of surgery without the relief of pain that the mesmeric trance could provide. Eventually, in the 1880s, scientists and surgeons had to admit that they had been wrong, that the mesmeric/hypnotic trance state existed, and could provide pain-free operations. But although the evidence for 'higher phenomena' was as strong, it continued to be unacceptable – and is to this day.

SEE ALSO *Electric people; ESP; Explanations; Fantasy-prone personalities; Fox sisters; Valentine Greatrakes; Healing; Hypnosis; Hypnotherapy; Hysteria; Limits of science; Mass hysteria; Miracles of St Médard; Out-of-the-body experiences; Possession; Psychokinesis; Remote viewing; Shamanism; Telepathy; Traumas and psi.*

HYPNOSIS

James Braid coined the term 'hypnosis' in 1843 to rescue the mesmeric trance condition from the occult associations of 'animal magnetism'. The trance, he insisted, was induced, not with the help of a fluid from outer space, but through the subject's neurophysiological reaction to the hypnotist's promptings. The increased sensibility of subjects, including what had been put down to clairvoyance, was simply the result of hyperacuity of the senses in the trance state.

When Braid died in 1850 he had still failed to convince the medical profession of the reality of the hypnotic trance, let alone of the fact that it could be exploited to treat patients for a variety of common disorders. It was left to A. A. Liébeault, a French country doctor, and Professor Hippolyte Berheim of Nancy, to provide such convincing demonstrations of the therapeutic effects of simple suggestion under hypnosis that – quite suddenly, in the 1880s – doctors throughout Europe began to try it, and to find that it worked. At the same time Jean-Martin Charcot persuaded scientists, as well as some doctors, to accept hypnosis by assuring them it was a form of induced hysteria, which only hysterical patients developed. With animal magnetism discarded, and with the hypnotic trance categorised as a mental disorder, the trance condition could at last be accepted as genuine.

In the early 1880s battle was joined between Bernheim, who insisted that anybody could be hypnotised, and Charcot; and it quickly became clear that Charcot had been wrong. Reports of experiments began to proliferate, some concerned with the use of suggestion under hypnosis to treat disorders, but many describing the variety of phenomena that could be induced, such as the effects of post-hypnotic suggestion. Told to put on a hat, half an hour after the trance ended, a subject would duly put on a hat without knowing why, often making elaborate, implausible excuses for the action. And the 'higher phenomena' of Mesmerism, as they had been known, were often encountered (including second sight and 'second taste' where the patient can taste what the doctor put in his mouth while out of sight).

The last years of the century saw materialism at its most dominant in science; and materialists dismissed the 'higher phenomena' as spurious. Doctors, too, realised that hypnotherapy could present a threat; if it worked, it could be practised readily enough by men and women who had no medical qualifications.

The public, too, remained doubtful. Hypnotists, the fear was, might enjoy the power Svengali wielded in George du Maurier's novel *Trilby*, published in 1895. Occasionally court cases appeared to confirm that hypnotists could seduce their subjects, or make them commit crimes. And although

a commission of inquiry set up by the British Medical Association confirmed in 1891 that Bernheim's claims for hypnotherapy were justified, the report was shelved.

By that time psychologists, too, were growing wary of hypnosis. For a few years, it was the chief talking point at their international conferences, but by the turn of the century it had ceased to command attention. As the leading psychologist of the time, Pierre Janet, was to recall, 'No one doubted the acknowledged power of suggestion. It was simply no longer discussed.'

From this time on until the 1970s the chief practitioners of hypnosis were to be found in theatres and clubs, where they invited volunteers from the audience to come up on stage to be placed in a trance, and then put them through a variety of humiliating performances. Told they were cats, they would go down on all fours and make lapping noises; told they were drunk, they would lurch around the stage.

Serious research into hypnosis was conducted by a few individuals; a small minority of doctors practised it; a rather larger minority of dentists used it to supplement, and sometimes to supplant, their efforts to spare patients pain. But the prevailing dogma in the medical profession – that organic disorders could be successfully treated only by physical methods, drugs and surgery – blocked hypnotherapy; and the dominance of behaviourism in psychology, particularly in the United States, meant that conventional psychologists either ignored hypnosis or conducted research merely to squeeze it into the prevailing mould.

One consequence has been a protracted controversy over whether hypnosis is, or is not, a 'state'. As the behaviourists made no distinction between consciousness and trance, they were unable to accept that hypnosis existed in its own right; they argued that it was simply a different display of consciousness, like day-dreaming. Even when behaviourism began to fall out of favour, psychologists continued to follow the same line and thereby excuse themselves from investigation of, say, 'second taste'.

For a while it looked as if hypnotism might acquire respectability through being used to help in police investigations. Among the findings of the investigators a century ago was that under hypnosis some people remember details which they have forgotten, or perhaps were not aware of, at the time; and this has proved useful in cases where a witness who has seen a crime committed has been able when hypnotised to give additional details.

Such has been the prejudice against hypnotism, however, that in the summer of 1988 the British Home Office issued guidelines to Chief Constables saying that there was no proof that information obtained in this way could not be obtained in any other way; consequently, 'We do not think it is a practical weapon for the police to use against crime.' This was not, however, a directive; and a few weeks later the newspapers reported that a man wanted for kidnapping, rape and murder had been caught, thanks to the description that a boy, one of his intended victims, had been able to give to the police under hypnosis of the car in which he had been abducted. So exact was the information that the police were able to trace the car, and on checking found it was the one that had been in use at the time of the murder. When arrested, the man confessed; and subsequently received a life sentence.

On the evidence, the hypnotic (or mesmeric) trance is a 'state' in the same sense that sleep is – or, more to the point, sleepwalking. It is a throwback to human life before consciousness and judgement took over, allowing the liberation of faculties and powers largely lost since then. It can be used for dubious purposes; but its potential for health, and its value as a memory-arousal technique, would make its exploitation desirable even without fresh confirmation of the 'higher phenomena', if conventional scientists continue to reject them.

SEE ALSO *Autosuggestion; Creative visualisation; ESP; Fantasy-prone personalities; Formative causation; Healing; Hypnotherapy; Hypnotic regression; Hysteria; Limits of science; Mass hysteria; Mesmerism; Multiple personality; Possession; Shamanism; Telepathy.*

AUTOSUGGESTION

The power of suggestion has been universally recognised for centuries. 'I think, therefore I am' carries a powerful message to mankind, indicating that positive thought will create positive outcomes – and vice versa. Autosuggestion refers to a form of internal dialogue in which suggestions are made in an altered state of mind. The basis of this belief is that the unconscious mind will respond maximally to the directions reported by a specific routine.

An early example of autosuggestion came from Emile Coué, the nineteenth-century lecturer who had his followers repeat rapidly, morning and night, 'Every day in every way I'm getting better and better.' Accompanying this ritual they fingered a knotted rope, moving from knot to knot with each recital. This simple technique brought about major changes for the better.

Self-hypnosis utilises autosuggestion by directing oneself to go into a trance state and repeating positive remarks for specific personal goals. It has been shown that these techniques have a far better result than similar phrases repeated in the conscious state. Autogenic training uses similar principles to direct one's attention to different parts of the body to facilitate awareness.

Autosuggestive techniques are used to boost confidence, overcome fear, heal physical conditions, improve the immune system and create well-being. The two components involved are being in an altered state of consciousness and directing yourself with simple, rhythmic and repetitive sayings. Many of the problems from which we suffer are related to negative suggestions learnt in childhood, that are continuously reinforced by negative autosuggestion for the rest of our lives.

The meditative state occurs in self-hypnosis, daydreaming, before sleep and on awakening and in meditations. These are the most suitable times for repeating positive phrases. Much Eastern chanting creates the necessary altered state for autosuggestion; brainwashing also depends on similar techniques.

Some examples of phrases used in autosuggestion are: I will be more relaxed and assertive; I am my own person and will accept myself as I am; I am able to say 'no' if that is best for me; I will respect my feelings and respond to them.

Autosuggestion does not need to be logical or analysed by the conscious mind. It is only necessary to have the specific directions instilled in the unconscious mind to have them effectively bring about the desired result.

SEE ALSO *Creative visualisation; Fantasy-prone personalities; Hypnosis; Hypnotherapy; Left and right brain; Ritual magic; Suspended animation; Witchcraft.*

OUIJA BOARD AND PLANCHETTE

A planchette session. Similar to the ouija board, the idea is to communicate with other beings, usually believed to be discarnate. In most cases, however, the users find themselves in touch with the less savoury aspects of their own subconscious minds.

Many people have experimented with the parlour game involving a ouija board (the name is taken from the French and German words for 'yes'). It is a polished board with the letters of the alphabet and the words YES and NO inscribed on it in a circle, in the middle of which is a pointer on which a group can rest their fingertips lightly. A more common version of this game is glass rolling or sliding, in which home-made alphabet cards are arranged on a polished surface and the participants rest their fingertips on the edge of an upturned glass that serves as a pointer. Questions are put – usually beginning with the time-honoured 'Is there anybody there?' – and usually the pointer, or glass, moves around the alphabet, spelling out a message.

A less common version, which was very popular with the Victorians, is the planchette. This is a small wooden device standing on rollers or wheels and which carries a pencil, point downwards. The planchette is placed on a sheet of paper and the participant puts his or her fingertips on it. After a while the pencil may begin to write, ostensibly giving messages from spirits. The planchette has the advantage that it can be used by one person, whereas glass rolling or the ouija board will only work for the solo participant in exceptional circumstances.

A natural extension of this is automatic writing, in which the experimenter holds a pen or pencil very lightly, point touching paper. After a while the pen may write, apparently of its own accord, although its output may well consist of gibberish or doodles. However, some very impressive collections of apparently paranormal writings have been produced through the planchette or automatic writing, such as the prose and poetry of 'Patience Worth' that used the mediumship of Mrs Pearl Curran in the 1930s.

Some years ago a famous board-game company produced a ouija board that they marketed as a game. Such was the public outcry in both the USA and Britain that the game was withdrawn. It was seen as an open invitation to 'dabble in the occult', with all the dangers that such a situation implies – obsession, mental instability, depression, poltergeist outbreaks and even possession by evil spirits and suicide. Children and teenagers were thought to be especially vulnerable.

Certainly it seems that in a group of people all manner of subconscious emotions may play a part in causing ostensibly paranormal phenomena to accompany the movement of the glass or pointer. There are many cases of objects flying about, poltergeist-style, in the room where the game is being played, terrifying all the participants. In an atmosphere heavy with vague expectancy that something 'occult' and horrifying may happen, it probably will.

Yet it is possible to view the 'game' scientifically and to treat it in the light-hearted manner recommended by those groups who have had great success in inducing macro-PK, such as the Philip and SORRAT groups. Often it is possible to direct the glass or pointer to spell out certain messages just by willing it to do so silently. Sometimes it is not even necessary to touch it, although others in the group should keep their fingers on the pointer. Clearly, such an experiment is a subconscious battle of minds – in that respect it does seem like many other board games, even chess!

Problems arise, however, when other entities appear to take control of the proceedings; usually their communications bear a strong resemblance to graffiti in their vulgarity or obscenity. Sometimes they spell out messages of hate – which may come from the minds of the group – but occasionally details are given about the entity's life on Earth that are later discovered to be accurate. Psychologists and parapsychologists tend to relate such experiences to the maelstrom of emotions released by the expectancy of the group – or ascribe the veridical details given to the ubiquitous cryptomnesia or Super-ESP theories.

Occultists and Spiritualists are more certain of their ground. Both agree that Earthbound spirits, often not aware they are dead, roam around confusedly trying to make contact with the living. Both also agree that there are many lower types of spirit or elemental that have never been incarnated in human bodies and that seek to cause mischief by masquerading as spirits of the dead, and even by possessing the bodies of those that lay themselves open to the occult without sufficient knowledge or preparation. (Both occultists and Spiritualists, however, believe that they have no need to worry on this score.) Aleister Crowley, no friend of Spiritualists, warned that they

> deliberately invite all and sundry spirits, demons, shells of the dead, all the excrement and filth of the earth and hell, to squirt their slime over them. This invitation is readily accepted unless a clean man be present with an aura good enough to frighten the foul denizens of the pit ... They are more contagious than Syphilis, and more deadly and disgusting ... shun them as you need not mere lepers!

While Crowley had no fear of laying himself open to anything except charges of hypocrisy, it may well be inadvisable for those of credulous and suggestible frame of mind to play with the ouija board or planchette.

SEE ALSO *Angels; Autosuggestion; Kenneth Batcheldor; Cosmic Joker; Aleister Crowley; The Devil; Entity enigma; Fairies; Life after death; Matthew Manning; Parapsychology; Philip experiment; Possession; Psychic music, art and literature; Ritual magic; Shamanism; SORRAT; Witchcraft.*

FIREPROOF PEOPLE

The Old Testament tells how King Nebuchadnezzar threw Shadrach, Meshach and Abednego into the fiery furnace – whence they emerged unscathed, due to the protection of the Lord. Fireproof people are not quite so rare as this story suggests, however.

Traditionally, blacksmiths have been considered 'Masters of Fire' and some of them became legends of incombustibility. The aptly named Nathan Coker of Easton, Maryland frequently demonstrated his unusual immunity; on one occasion he was witnessed to pull off his boots and put a white-hot shovel on the soles of his feet, as a witness said '. . . and kept it there until the shovel became black. He also used molten lead as if it were a mouthwash – all his feats of incombustibility he treated nonchalantly. "It don't burn," he said.

''Since I was a little boy, I've never been afraid to handle fire.'''

Coker seemed in a normal state of consciousness while performing his extraordinary feats, but he was in the minority among fire handlers. Individuals who are impervious to flames and heat are usually in some sort of altered state of consciousness, such as trance, auto-hypnosis or the elevated state of the fakir whose prodigious feats of mind over matter are legend. Bernadette Soubirous, while communicating with the vision of the Virgin Mary, was observed to hold her hand in the flame of a candle for over fifteen minutes without mark or hurt; a woman being tortured with electrodes by the Gestapo escaped the agony by inducing an out-of-the-body experience.

One of the greatest Spiritualist mediums, D. D. Home, specialised in levitation and in handling live coals. He could also confer his incombustibility temporarily on others, often handing them white-hot embers in a borrowed handkerchief, yet neither flesh nor cloth was even scorched. The medium believed himself to be empowered by the spirits of the dead – it may have been the power of this belief that brought about the significant shift of consciousness needed in order to accomplish this feat.

The most dramatic feats of incombustibility have often been associated with equally dramatic trance or 'hysteric' states. Marie Souet, one of the adherents of the St Médard cult of the 1730s in Paris, was witnessed by the sceptical magistrate Carré de Montgéron to become rigid with convulsions (a common manifestation of the cult), then to lie, wearing only a linen shift, suspended over a fire for thirty-five minutes. The flames that actually lapped around her body did not do damage to either herself or the shift. Similarly, St Catherine of Siena often fell into ecstatic trances, lying across an open fire, and remained unhurt.

Many primitive cultures practise firewalking – the ritual of crossing fiery or white-hot pits without so much as a hair of their head or any part of their apparel (even such highly flammable material as grass reeds or rushes) being scorched. Many Hindu or Shinto cultures use the fire-trench walk as a test, and proof, of their spiritual powers. Visiting Europeans have discovered that they, too, can emerge unharmed from the fire, if led across it by a holy man. One Western firewalker said of his Indian experience: 'The idea is that the sadhu takes on all the pain to himself and then negates it by will-power. The stones are genuinely hot, the bodies of the walkers untreated by any artificial preparation. There seems to be no rational explanation . . .'

In the 1980s the 'coal stroll' became fashionable among New Age seekers, particularly in California. It represents the individual's deepest fear that must be confronted and overcome; those who succeed feel 'born again'.

There have been several organised firewalks advertised in London. For about £50 one can learn to achieve the right state of mind to walk over the hot pit and emerge unblemished. Although techniques vary, they are generally based on autosuggestion, sometimes requiring the firewalker to chant a phrase, such as 'cool, wet grass', before

A sure sign of great discipline; fakirs and holy men have long subjected themselves to feats of suspended animation in order to develop their spiritual nature.

and during the walk. The preparation often consists of group discussion about the nature of fear and how to confront it, which may last for some hours before the walk is attempted. One such coal stroll was attended by Professor John Taylor of London University – a sceptic – who suggested that at no point were the soles of the feet in contact with the coals for long enough to scorch. While the majority of the group were not burnt (Taylor among them), some of the participants were.

Another London firewalk was attended by Dr Brian Roet, a hypnotherapist who took part for personal, rather than professional, reasons. The preparatory ritual in this case consisted of a long discussion about private fears, which were written on a piece of paper and burnt in the flames. Each participant chose a log and threw it in the fire, then the group stood around it, singing songs and holding hands. Dr Roet was among the first to walk:

> It felt like walking on thistles, but I felt no heat and wasn't burnt. A couple of people had been hanging back, getting to the edge of the pit then changing their minds while the rest of us walked. At the very end of the session one of them did walk – and was very badly burned. If he had been among the first I wouldn't have done it. I just believed that they wouldn't have let us attempt it if there was a chance of being hurt.

This incident seems to reinforce the theory that some form of auto-hypnotism is involved, but it fails to explain why, in some well-attested cases, a firewalker's shoes were burnt off but he remained untouched by heat or flame. When Dr W. T. Brigham of the British Museum underwent a firewalk on the island of Kona in the South Seas the locals told him to remove his boots beforehand, for they would not be protected magically as would he. He protested and was allowed to walk some 45 metres across the trench with the magical adepts. They all laughed uproariously as his boots burnt off, leaving the rest of his clothes and his body unscathed.

SEE ALSO *Autosuggestion; Electric people; D. D. Home; Hypnosis; Hysteria; Levitation; Mass hysteria; Miracles of St Médard; Old Testament miracles; Out-of-the-body experiences; Psychokinesis; Ritual magic; Shamanism; Spontaneous human combustion; Suspended animation; Turin Shroud; Visions of the Virgin Mary; Witchcraft.*

Holy men over the centuries have pushed their bodies beyond normal limits. Suspended animation is just one of their astonishing achievements.

SUSPENDED ANIMATION

Certain fakirs, shamans and holy men have long been known to be able to induce a trance in which their bodily functions shut down, and during which they are believed to be in contact with a reality outside time and space. Suspended animation can be induced through drugs or physical and mental exhaustion, and can mimic death so thoroughly that some adepts have mistakenly been buried, while others have ensured that they are buried as part of their mystical ordeal. The aim of many such fakirs is to remain in full control of the four states of consciousness: waking, sleeping, dreaming and catalepsy, which is a biological 'shutdown' deliberately induced to aid meditation.

Some forms of catalepsy are pathological, and have resulted in the nightmare of premature burial – the basis of many, if not all, of the vampire legends. Others, taking the form of a sort of mystical sleep, herald the arrival of magical or paranormal powers, as in the ritual comas assumed by adepts of the ancient mystery schools of Greece and Egypt. Some commentators believe that Lazarus was only symbolically 'raised' as part of an initiatory rite connected with the Essene sect. The so-called 'hysterical catalepsy' also seems to be a significant factor in the stigmatising of the Catholic devout.

It is in cultures with a tradition of extreme physical control that the most spectacular feats of suspended animation have been recorded. In 1974 a jujuman from Togo in West Africa was buried – before a large crowd – in a coffin topped with slabs of concrete and layers of mortar. After a couple of hours a panic-stricken crowd began to beg the authorities to free him, but the jujuman suddenly burst through the concrete and the earth – leaving his nailed coffin intact. He claimed he learnt the 'trick' by meditating for long periods underground.

Ivan Sanderson, author of *More Things* (1969), tells another West African story. A bizarre scene confronted the representative of the British Resident in Calabar, British Cameroons in 1932. Investigating the refusal of some busmen who refused to pay their taxes he found them – whole families and their animals – sitting motionless under more than two metres of water. They appeared to be asleep. That official fled; but the villagers were back to normal when another arrived. Strangely, none of the 'Old Coasters' found anything odd in this story.

Those who practise transcendental meditation (TM) claim that they gain unusual control over their bodily functions, and can slow down their heartbeat or pulse at will. Novice Tibetan monks are often required to demonstrate their discipline by wearing just a thin, soaked shirt in below freezing conditions – and to dry it out with their body heat and suffer no ill-effects. Less arduous is use of the 'mind mirror', a biofeedback device that shows the user the pattern of his or her brainwaves; it seems that once they are actually seen it becomes easier to change them at will, without recourse to a trance or some other altered state of consciousness.

An extraordinary form of physical control was practised by a now extinct Japanese Buddhist cult. Its adherents would begin a fast unto death, aiming to die after four thousand days of semi-fast, followed by complete starvation. Many of them died on the exact day that they had chosen to be installed in their tombs.

The phenomenon of suspended animation is, in its extreme manifestations, one of the most difficult for rationalists to accept, for it implies a control over the borderline area between life and death, and an intimacy with the state known as death that challenges almost every physical law and may be compared to the extraordinary phenomenon of incorruptibility, where dead bodies do not decompose. It appears that the state that is generally considered to be final, at least in its physical form, also has exceptions to the rule.

SEE ALSO *Autosuggestion; Boggle threshold; Creative visualisation; Consensus reality; Electric people; Fantasy-prone personalities; Fireproof people; Foaflore; Hallucinations; Hypnosis; Hysteria; Incorruptibility; Left and right brain; Levitation; Life after death; Limits of science; Near death experience; New Testament miracles; Psychokinesis; The Resurrection; Ritual magic; Seance-room phenomena; Shamanism; Spontaneous human combustion; Stigmatics; Traumas and psi; Vampires; Witchcraft.*

SHAMANISM

Shamanism, Professor Mircea Eliade asserted in his pioneering survey of the subject, is 'one of the archaic techniques of ecstasy – at once mysticism, magic and "religion" in the broadest sense of the term'. He was anxious to demonstrate that it is not simply a primitive form of Spiritualist mediumship; certainly not, as some anthropologists have argued, a form of mental derangement that impressed tribal communities because it gave the impression that the shaman was in communication with the spirits.

In its commonest forms, as reported by the early explorers and missionaries, the shaman-to-be attracted the attention of the tribe as a young man by occasionally going into trances. This would lead to a course of training, often extremely rigorous, with fasting and other forms of deprivation, to discover whether he would be fit for the vocation. Once qualified, the usual procedure was for him to enter into a trance, often accompanied by con-

A Siberian shaman chief pursues an inner journey through trance.

vulsions, in which he would either be possessed by a spirit who would address the tribe through him, or would visit the spirit world and return, coming out of the trance, to tell what he had seen and heard.

Eliade wanted to restrict the term 'shaman' to those who practised in this way, distinguishing them from medicine men and witch doctors who employed other techniques of divination: 'The shaman specialises in a trance during which his soul is believed to leave his body and ascend to the sky or descend to the underworld.' This distinction is now rarely maintained, except by purists; shamanism embraces all manner of tribal seers, whatever methods they use. And a question that Eliade thought was settled remains in dispute: can the shamanic trance state actually bestow the paranormal powers that tribes have believed in, and have been confirmed by some investigators?

In his *Primitive Culture* (1871) Edward Tylor, the leading anthropologist of his time, had no doubt that in their trances shamans sometimes had superhuman powers; and although he doubted they were paranormal, he felt sure that shamanism could not be accounted for by fraud. In *The Golden Bough* (1890), however, James Frazer described it bluntly as spurious. Examining the evidence, Eliade himself was left convinced that shamanism does have a paranormal component. Although research into this question is still in its beginnings, a fairly large number of ethnographic documents have already put the authenticity beyond doubt.

Certainly the accepted basis of shamanism was the ability of the shaman to exploit *mana*, or what is now described as 'psi' – psychic energy. He was expected to have clairvoyant faculties; to be able to foretell what the weather would hold (and perhaps bring rain, to end a drought); to say where game would be more plentiful; and to warn if danger threatened. He was expected to detect sorcery and witchcraft, if some members of the tribe were using them illicitly; and to use his healing powers, often by putting the sick members of the tribe into a therapeutic trance, with the help of rhythm, music and dancing.

The shaman was the precursor of the prophets, as in the Old Testament, and of Homer's seers. In many parts of the world shamanism is still to be found in a variety of forms, such as in Haitian voodoo. It seems that it was originally an evolutionary device, designed to restore faculties that the emergence of consciousness and reasoning capacity had begun to block; but when it came into conflict with Church and State, it usually went underground or degenerated into divination by rote, as in the interpretation of animal entrails.

SEE ALSO *Spiritism; ESP; Ritual magic; Divination; Possession; Miracles of St Médard; Traumas and psi; Left and right brain; Other dimensions; Life after death; Telepathy; Remote viewing; Witchcraft; Fantasy-prone personalities; Healing; Suspended animation; Fireproof people; Old Testament miracles; Curses; Prediction and prophecy; Autosuggestion; Hypnosis; Traumas and psi.*

POSSESSION

At some early stage in the development of man, when tribal communities were forming, they found that a few individuals appeared to be able to obtain information of value by entering a trance. In that condition they often spoke in a different voice, as if they had been temporarily taken over by – or so it was assumed – a spirit. They were possessed.

In early civilisations, possession continued to be attributed to divine intervention, as in the Old Testament and Homer. Because entry into the possessed condition was often accompanied by convulsions, epilepsy was also regarded as the gift of the gods, and called the 'divine disease'. But by the fifth century BC the Hippocratic writings were claiming that possession was no more divine than any other disorder, and this was thereafter the standard rationalist assumption.

Among the Israelites, however, it was coming to be believed that the possessed really were taken over by spirits; and the spirits could be diabolic, working either brazenly or craftily for Satan. Much of Jesus's healing mission was devoted to exorcism – the casting out of devils.

For a time, the early Christians accepted that possession by the Holy Spirit, of the kind that St Paul promised would provide the ability to heal the sick, to prophesy and generally to work miracles, was eminently desirable. But one of its gifts, significantly, was 'discerning of spirits' – detection of those that were diabolic. It was not long before the fact of possession began commonly to be regarded as the Devil's work, particularly if the prophesying did not remain impeccably orthodox. At best, the possessed were treated by exorcism; but they became increasingly likely to suffer persecution as witches or heretics.

As T. K. Oesterreich showed in his *Possession*, first published in 1921, a remarkable feature was the way in which the possessed did not merely speak as if a devil was speaking through them, but acted the part – or parts: sometimes there might be half a dozen devils, each with a different character, so that even the features of the possessed would be seen to change as each took charge.

Often, though, the possession was not complete. In the most notorious (and best documented) of all investigations of possession, dealing with the outbreak at the convent at Loudun in the 1630s, both Sister Jeanne and Father Surin – who came to exorcise her, but himself became possessed – described how they had had the curious experience of watching and listening to themselves, as they mouthed obscenities and blasphemies, unable to stop.

Vanessa Redgrave stars in The Devils, *the story of the mass possession of nuns at St Peter's Church in Loudun, France, in the seventeenth century.*

Possession has since come to be commonly regarded as a symptom of dual or multiple personality. The 'self' is not a unity, the hypothesis goes, but a collection of selves which ordinarily work in unison, or perhaps leave day-to-day management to an executive self. But this does not adequately account for what has become the most familiar form of possession, mediumship, in which the 'control' often seems to be a distinct entity, capable of providing information not available to the mediums when they are not in their trances.

With the collapse of belief in the Devil, too, even among practising Catholics, old-style diabolic possession is less often encountered. But even the Anglican Church still has exorcists among the clergy, and there is one remarkably detailed recent account of how it feels for a Catholic to be possessed: Evelyn Waugh's *The Ordeal of Gilbert Pinfold*. Although he presented it as a novel, he claimed on television it was factual.

The fact that the ordeal was triggered by an unwise combination of alcohol and medicinal drugs has tended to obscure the book's significance as a documentary on possession; but the voices that plagued Waugh behaved very like those that persecuted Surin at Loudun. Psychiatry still has much to learn from case histories of this kind.

There is a significant upsurge in a belief in benevolent possession among adherents of the New Age. It is believed that discarnate spirits may, with permission from the 'host', become 'walk-ins' – take over a living human being with his or her blessing.

SEE ALSO *José Arigo; Autosuggestion; Black Monk of Pontefract; Boggle threshold; Case of Ruth; Consensus reality; Curses; The Devil; Direct voice; Doppelgängers; Ectoplasm; Enfield poltergeist; Entity enigma; Fantasy-prone personalities; Ghosts; Hallucinations; Healing; D. D. Home; Hysteria; Jinxes; Mass hysteria; Men in Black; Carmine Mirabelli; Miracles of St Médard; Multiple personality; New Testament miracles; Ouija board and planchette; Out-of-the-body experiences; Paranormal portraits; Philip experiment; Psychic music, art and literature; Reincarnation; Ritual magic; Seance-room phenomena; Shamanism; SORRAT; Stigmatics, Doris Stokes; Tulpas; UFO paradox; Witchcraft; Chico Xavier.*

MULTIPLE PERSONALITY

The human personality may be seen as consisting of several different parts, each capable, under certain circumstances, of assuming an autonomy. The term 'multiple personality' describes a condition in which one or more of these parts has split off from the rest and appears to displace the 'true' personality. These psychological fragments may not even be in contact with the other parts, and take turns to exhibit a wide range of different behaviour, while the 'host' personality may be only vaguely aware that this is happening.

The most common cause is personal trauma, especially childhood experiences so distressing that the individual has to create 'new parts' in order to survive. The new personalities may need to be beyond conscious contact with the 'host' in order to function effectively, and each has the power to deal with the otherwise intolerable situation. If anger is called for, one of the new parts will be angry; if avoidance is useful, one will be shy; and so on.

Gradually these parts develop a life of their own and can take control of the 'host' at different times, although he or she may not recognise that this is happening. Modern therapy aims to integrate the personalities, using a variety of techniques such as hypnosis and psychotherapy. If successful, the main personality will begin to accept responsibility for his behaviour and find ways of confronting his problems as a single, cohesive person.

There have been cases, however, where such a neat psychological approach fails to meet the facts. The displacing personalities may indicate paranormal knowledge, or claim to be the discarnate spirits of specific people, temporarily possessing the 'host' body. One of the most dramatic cases on record is that of Lurancy Vennum of Watseka, Illinois, who as a thirteen-year-old in 1877 became unconscious after an epileptic fit. She then became possessed by various entities, including the 'control' – Mary Roff, who had died aged eighteen, twelve years before. For nearly a year Lurancy was displaced by Mary; she behaved (according to Mary's family) like the dead girl and exhibited

Publicity still from The Three Faces of Eve, *a classic story of multiple personality. People seem to develop extra personalities in order to survive a personal crisis.*

detailed knowledge of the Roff family's home and habits. Then Mary announced that she had to return to Heaven; Lurancy became herself again.

The research of Dr Ian Stevenson into cases 'suggestive of the reincarnation', carried out since the 1960s, has indicated that apparent cases of memories of past lives, especially among Indian children, may often be due to possession, itself a possible alternative explanation to multiple personality. When the Hindu boy Jasbir Lal Jat 'died' of smallpox in 1954 his body was apparently taken over by the spirit of a Brahmin boy who had just died. Jasbir 'came alive' as this other personality, recognised his home and family and was familiar with everything about the dead boy. It was only after two years that his 'real' personality re-established itself.

It seems that the phenomenon of multiple personality is far more complex, and less susceptible to orthodox treatment, than many modern psychologists like to think.

SEE ALSO *José Arigo; Case of Ruth; Creative visualisation; The Devil; Formative causation; Hypnosis; Karma; Katie King; Left and right brain; Life after death; Near death experience; Possession; Psychic music, art and literature; Reincarnation; The Resurrection; Sai Baba; Shamanism; Doris Stokes; Traumas and psi; Witchcraft.*

HYPNOTIC REGRESSION

Regression to an earlier period in life is an accepted technique in medical hypnosis. The patient is invited to travel back in time, sometimes as far back as early childhood, and encouraged to relive the period in question as if it were the present. In this way the causes of later-life problems can be revealed, and effective therapy carried out through *abreaction*, or re-experiencing a traumatic event that was hitherto suppressed by the conscious mind. Common features of regressions under hypnotic suggestion are the mass of detail that can come to the surface and the dramatic vividness with which an earlier period is relived.

Some hypnotists have taken things a stage further and asked their subjects to go back to before their birth. Subjects have then produced colourful and detailed accounts of a former life. They have provided information they are certain they could not have obtained by normal means; they have convincingly impersonated characters unlike those of their normal selves; and they have responded to the hypnotist's questioning as if really speaking from the past rather than recalling previously learned material.

Accounts of experiments in past-life recall go back to at least 1924, when Colonel A. de Rochas published his book *Les Vies successives (Successive Lives)*. Popular imagination was first seized by the subject in 1956, with the appearance of Morey Bernstein's *The Search for Bridey Murphy*, in which an American woman named Virginia Tighe apparently reverted to a former self in nineteenth-century Ireland. The search came to an end when a newspaper revealed that much of the information produced under hypnosis originated from Mrs

Tighe's childhood in her present life. She had even had a young playmate whose mother was named Bridie (*sic*) Murphy.

Undeterred, other hypnotists embarked on the search for memories of previous lives. Two interesting projects involving several subjects were those of Arnall Bloxham, an antiquarian and amateur hypnotist, and Leonard Wilder, a dental surgeon and member of the British Society of Medical and Dental Hypnotists. The 'Bloxham tapes' received wide publicity in a book and television programme, and offered compelling evidence for the reality of several earlier lives, some of them containing obscure but accurate historical details. The less publicised but considerably more interesting work of Wilder showed the whole subject to be rather more complex than either critics or supporters had supposed. After producing evidence similar to that of Bloxham, he hypnotised some of his subjects a second time after an interval of several years, and found that memories of supposed former lives had altered substantially.

The leading authority on modern reincarnation research is the psychiatrist and parapsychologist Ian Stevenson. He has noted that 'previous-life personalities' appear to consist of 'the subject's current personality, his expectation of what he thinks the hypnotist wants, his fantasies of what he thinks his previous life ought to have been, and also perhaps elements derived paranormally'. Stevenson stresses the great difficulty in proving that information produced during a regression could not have been learned in the subject's present life.

Previous lives elaborated under hypnosis can be of value to psychiatrists seeking to cure psychosomatic problems. Particularly interesting work in this area has been described by psychiatrist Denys Kelsey and his former wife Joan Grant in *Many Lives* (1970). Grant has also written a number of books described by her as 'biographies of previous lives I have known'. Kelsey has become the leading British exponent of the use of past-life regression as therapy for present-life problems. Otherwise inexplicable phobias, for example, are often discovered under hypnosis to have originated in other incarnations. Unearthing them has the effect of ridding the patient of them instantly and completely.

Although accounts of previous lives produced under hypnotic regression are not always what they seem, there may well be an element of genuine past-life recall in some of them.

SEE ALSO *Autosuggestion; Case of Ruth; Cosmic Joker; Creative visualisation; Fantasy-prone personalities; Hallucinations; Hypnosis; Hypnotherapy; Hysteria; Karma; Life after death; Mesmerism; Multiple personality; Near death experience; Possession; Reincarnation; Shamanism; Spiritism; Tulpas.*

HYPNOTHERAPY

Due to the difficulty in defining hypnosis – how it works or what happens in a hypnotic trance – the medical world has shown great reluctance to embrace it wholeheartedly. The pathway from Mesmer to the present has been devious and diverted, involving charlatans, power-hungry therapists and a great deal of misunderstanding. Today there is still some distance to travel before hypnosis assumes its rightful place in the healing arts. The press are prone to report sensational cases where fraudulent persons masquerading as 'hypnotherapists' exploit unfortunate clients morally, financially or even sexually.

There is a vast difference between medical and stage hypnosis. The aim of the latter is to provide entertainment using 'performers' who are deep hypnotic subjects. The hypnotist makes use of group expectation, rapid commanding techniques – and fear – to suggest often humiliating actions to the volunteers. As the stage hypnotist has no knowledge of the performers' past history, psyche or emotional state it may well be that untoward side-effects occur following such performances. In some countries this form of entertainment is illegal for this very reason.

In medical hypnotherapy, on the other hand, the aim of the therapist and patient is to use the hypnotic trance to gain access to positive unconscious resources and in this way to achieve healthy change. The two work together as a team – the patient uses his abilities and motivation, the therapist his support and knowledge, to guide the patient along a suitable pathway.

The trance state is a healing state possessing relaxation, inner calmness, access to forgotten material, positive attitudes and an overcoming of the resistance created by the conscious mind. It is a vehicle for change. Patients report very pleasant experiences when being in a trance. It is as if the logical, analytical part of the mind is reduced, allowing the creative, dreaming, visualising part to become more prominent. Research into right and left brain behaviour shows that hypnosis is a right brain phenomenon, which explains such trance experiences as time distortion, change of sensations, a 'parallel awareness' of being in the consulting room and also elsewhere, such as lying on a beach, and a heightened awareness of fantasy.

One of the most important aspects of hypnosis is that it allows us to do things that are otherwise restricted by the conscious logical mind. This is evident in stage hypnosis, where the performer eats an onion believing it to be an apple, or is able to be rigid with head and feet resting on two chairs. Medical hypnosis releases us physically and mentally from over-protective restraints; this is extremely useful when past experiences are limiting our present lives.

The most common fears and fallacies associated with hypnosis are:
1. The hypnotist will have power and control over me and make me do things I do not wish to do.
2. What happens if I don't come out of the trance?
3. I may discover something terrible in my past which will terrify and torment me.

None of these anxieties is founded in fact. Most people report extreme difficulty in entering a trance if the therapist is not trusted and accepted. With stage hypnosis only volunteers (those with a desire to perform) who are deep hypnotic subjects go into a trance on stage; in medical hypnosis it is essential for a good rapport to exist between hypnotist and patient. If past experiences are recalled, they are used in a therapeutic way to release their effect on the present.

Although hypnotherapy is not the instant panacea, the magic wand that some people hope for, with its aid a multitude of conditions are improved, ranging from the physical to the psychological. Because of its power to relax it is useful for any condition related to stress or tension. In this way it is similar to other meditative states such as yoga and transcendental meditation. Some of the most common problems helped by hypnosis are headaches, insomnia, nervous tension, lack of confidence, skin conditions relating to anxiety, habits such as nail biting, bed-wetting and smoking, chronic pain, bowel conditions associated with inner conflict, phobias and eating disorders. Hypnosis also enables psychotherapy to be carried out in a much calmer, subtler and more rapid way than is possible in the conscious state. Patients in the trance state can face their fears and guilt on a deeper psychological level, and have access to the fantasy world they have created.

The relaxing trance state is beneficial on its own, but the main benefits of hypnosis are achieved by using this state to alter incorrect beliefs. The skilled and supportive therapist provides the relaxed patient with a pathway to better health by overcoming hurdles, altering destructive attitudes, facing fears and releasing guilt.

With the passage of time evidence is mounting to show the massive benefits and minimal side-effects of hypnosis in medicine today. Hopefully it will lose the stigma and fears associated with it and become a more acceptable part of medical practice alongside other forms of complementary medicine.

SEE ALSO *Autosuggestion; Creative visualisation; Formative causation; Healing; Hypnosis; Hypnotic regression; Left and right brain; Mesmerism; Reincarnation.*

III Extraordinary People

John Dee • Aleister Crowley • Fox sisters • D. D. Home • Katie King • Eusapia Palladino • Carmine Mirabelli • Helen Duncan • Eileen Garrett • Nina Kulagina • Uri Geller • Doris Stokes • Chico Xavier • Coral Polge • Valentine Greatrakes • José Arigo • Sai Baba • Matthew Manning

The so-called laws of nature, fractious at the best of times, are at their most insubordinate in the company of mystics, seers and psychics, for whom they might as well not exist. Sometimes people with paranormal talents can control them to some degree; in other cases the strange abilities come upon them without permission and without warning.

Those who seek secret knowledge often find it, with sinister results. John Dee discovered secrets of all sorts, and was said to be both necromancer and spy. Aleister Crowley sought to be the Beast of the New Testament, and merely succeeded in being beastly, yet even he faced other-worldly entities that would have driven a lesser man to death – and he developed a terrifyingly effective way with curses.

Those who communicate with the spirits of the dead – mediums – have always been a breed apart. They exhibit a frightening disregard for consensus reality by producing objects (apports) out of thin air, levitate themselves, and even materialise the dead in bodily form.

Both D. D. Home and the lesser-known Brazilian medium Carmine Mirabelli demonstrated a wide range of amazing effects. Home is still famous for his controversial levitations, his incombustibility, and having survived two decades of mediumship without once being exposed as a fraud. Mirabelli also rose into the air (where he was photographed, hovering), and in his hands solid objects turned into fluid, while the dead were temporarily resurrected through his mediumship (somewhat malodorously, according to some reports).

More pristine, but said to come from the same other-worldly plane, was the full-form materialisation of 'Katie King', whose appearance at seances began in the 1860s and continued until 1974 (as far as is known). Unfortunately Katie was involved with the young London medium Florence Cook, who later, it is said, confessed to being a fraud, and who was probably at the centre of a squalid sexual intrigue involving the scientist who investigated the materialisation. Yet the claims and counter-claims made for this too, too solid spirit were so outrageous that perhaps they should be taken seriously, and Katie's exuberant, death-defying character means that she appears in this section in her own right.

Both Mirabelli and Home had been convinced by the reality of the spirits from whom they believed their abilities came. But one of the most striking psychic talents of the twentieth century belonged to Eileen Garrett, whose extraordinary clairvoyance could not, she felt, be ascribed with total conviction to any one source. Her 'spirit controls' may have been an externalisation of fragments of her personality, or they may indeed have been separate entities.

Psychics with no known belief system to support their work include Uri Geller and the Russian Nina Kulagina, who recently sued a magazine that claimed she was a fraud – and won. Nina has been extensively researched by Soviet scientists, and discovered to have powers that appear to equal those of the legendary Home.

Nina has also shown that she can influence living creatures, although stopping a frog's heart on demand may strike some as extremely sinister in its implications. Easier to approve, but not necessarily to understand, are the talents of the great healers, some of whom have other paranormal talents.

José Arigo, 'surgeon with the rusty knife', performed apparently brutal operations on conscious people with total confidence. No pain or fear was felt by the patient, and the operations were almost always successful. Although José was put in prison for practising medicine illegally, his jailer let him out in order to carry on healing! Valentine Greatrakes tempted Providence by practising healing during the witchcraft hysteria of the seventeenth century, and today Matthew Manning has been banned from healing in West Germany. Yet despite such restrictions, he continues to teach people how to heal themselves, and has literally been a lifeline for many people who had been given up by the medical profession. It is significant that he became a healer after he acknowledged the futility of causing poltergeist attacks, indulging in automatic art and bending spoons.

JOHN DEE

The most famous English magus, John Dee was born in 1527 when the Sun was in Cancer and Sagittarius in the ascendant – traditionally a perfect astrological combination for a career in the occult. At the age of fifteen he went up to Cambridge, and as an acknowledgement of his scholarship, was created Greek Under-Reader and a fellow of the newest Cambridge college, Trinity, where he was rumoured to be engaged in the black arts.

Such a great scholar was in demand as visiting lecturer at all the great European universities, and Dee used every opportunity to discuss the fine points of theology, navigation, astronomy, astrology, mathematics – and ritual magic – with his academic colleagues. But it was for his astrological knowledge that Dee became famous, and it was to put him in great personal danger.

In 1553 Princess Elizabeth was under house arrest on the orders of her Roman Catholic sister, 'Bloody Mary'. The Princess summoned Dee to cast the Queen's horoscope; but Mary heard of this 'plot' against her and threw the astrologer into jail. It seemed almost as if Dee led a charmed life, for at a time when Protestants were being horribly tortured and burnt at the stake, he, as one who was believed to consort with devils, survived. Perhaps a mere sorcerer was small fry compared to the heretics of the Reformation – or perhaps his rumoured connections with the Order of the Rosy Cross ensured him friends in high places.

In 1558 Elizabeth became Queen; Dee was appointed as her astrologer and – although the evidence is elusive – he was probably also engaged as a spy. But this period was of great significance for Dee the magus, for he began to work with mediums, the better to communicate with angels.

Dr John Dee, Elizabethan occultist, and his accomplice, Edward Kelly, raise a corpse in order to interrogate it about the future. Necromancy was only part of Dee's bizarre repertoire.

The first medium was unsatisfactory and Dee rid himself of the man after just a few months, but the next, Edward Kelley, was a practised occultist with a practical knowledge of alchemy, ritual magic and necromancy. It was to be a long and disturbing partnership.

Kelley used a variety of techniques, including a 'shewstone' – something similar to a crystal ball – in which he saw the Archangel Uriel. The angel gave him instructions for making a protective talisman, an essential tool for one engaged in the perilous business of communicating with angels who might not be all they claimed to be. (Joseph Smith, founder of the Mormon Church, claimed to translate the *Book of Mormon* by means of the mysterious Urim and Thummim, which seemed to have similar properties to a 'shewstone'.)

Over the next seven years Dee meticulously recorded his conversations with the angels, who taught him the Enochian language and angelic magical rites. Many of his notes are, perhaps deliberately, obscure, while others are cyphers or concern fine points of angelic syntax and grammar. Some, however, come straight to the point: on 5 May 1583 the Archangel Uriel presented Kelley with a vision of many ships on the sea and of a woman being beheaded by 'a black man'. There seems little doubt that these were predictions of the attempted invasion by the Spanish Armada in 1588, and the death of Mary Queen of Scots in 1587 (the 'black man' no doubt referring to the executioner in his hood).

Dee and Kelley and their families travelled widely throughout Europe at the angels' behest, finally arriving at Cracow in Poland in 1587. During a seance on 17 April it emerged that the angels urged the two men to engage in wife-swapping. Dee balked at this, wondering whether or not devils were masquerading as angels, but, as the recommendation was more in the nature of a command, it was obeyed. However, it marked the end of the Dee–Kelley partnership. Dee was so shattered by this unexpected turn of events that – it is said – he renounced magic for ever, returning to England, where he died in 1608. Kelley, always something of a semi-criminal, died in a Dutch jail in 1595.

The Enochian language and the apparent communication of angels may have been illusory, but it is certain that they were not deliberate fabrications by Dee and Kelley. In some respects the language is reminiscent of Hélène Smith's 'Martian', a language that she spoke and wrote fluently, and which she earnestly believed was given to her by the inhabitants of the red planet. Yet, on analysis, its structure and grammar were similar to the percipient's native French.

Dee and other adepts sought angelic wisdom, just as others seek that of fairies or spirits or ufonauts – and many are rewarded, up to a point, when the whole elaborately constructed belief system is confronted by a ludicrous, dangerous or unacceptable demand from the controlling entity. The old saying that 'those whom the gods love they must first destroy' aptly describes the fate of many such seekers.

SEE ALSO *Angels*; *Astrology*; *Church of Jesus Christ of Latter Day Saints (Mormons)*; *Cosmic Joker*; *Aleister Crowley*; *The Devil*; *Divination*; *Entity enigma*; *Fairies*, *Ritual magic*; *Speaking in tongues*; *UFOs*.

ALEISTER CROWLEY

Possibly the most notable – and certainly the most notorious – of modern magical adepts, Aleister Crowley was born in 1875, the son of a fanatically religious but wealthy brewer. When his family's influence drew him to the New Testament the young Crowley found himself particularly fascinated by the arcane mysteries of the Revelation of St John, in which he discovered, among much else, 'the Beast whose number is 666'. He believed he was literally reading about himself, and welcomed the status instantly.

Crowley was to become the subject of sensational reports in the popular British press – they dubbed him 'the Wickedest man in the World', and ascribed the wildest possible sins to him. The fact that he established his own temple in Sicily for what were rumoured to be unspeakable rites, and that he called himself 'The Great Beast 666', made wonderful headline material, especially when accompanied by a photograph that showed him looking literally diabolical, with deep-set, piercing eyes under a completely bald head. In fact Crowley, who had a highly developed sense of the theatrical, deliberately fostered this image.

For most of his adult life Crowley earned a reputation as a fearless mountaineer, a talented poet and cynical pornographer. His life is, however, best understood in the context of the revival of esoteric studies that took place in Europe in the nineteenth century and was much influenced by the writings of the French occultist known as Eliphas Lévi.

At the end of the nineteenth century the main British manifestation of the esoteric revival was the society known as the Hermetic Order of the Golden Dawn, which was to boast, among others, such famous names as Irish poet W. B. Yeats and the author of *Dracula*, Bram Stoker. Crowley joined it as a young man, taking on the ritual name of Perdurabo ('I shall endure'), perhaps the first of his many assumed names and titles.

The leader of the Golden Dawn at that time was the magician MacGregor Mathers, whose studied flamboyance was no match for Crowley's. Perdurabo set out to supplant him, but was expelled from the order.

The urge to have power, to harbour great ambitions, seems to be a common characteristic of all magical adepts. The supremacy that Crowley sought in the occult world did not reside simply in the knowledge of ritual magic (or 'magick', as Crowley preferred to call it) or of the Kabbala, but in some personal, special revelation such as Mathers claimed to have had from Higher Powers. Crowley now set out in search of such a revelation – and found it in Egypt, during what became known as 'the Cairo working' in 1904, when, according to his own account, his Holy Guardian angel came to him and dictated what became known as *The Book of the Law*.

Two main strands run through this work and through Crowley's activities for the rest of his life. The first is an occult theory of history, according to which mankind has lived through two great aeons: that of Isis, the prehistoric age of the dominance of Woman; and that of Osiris, the age of the dominance of the male principle and of the great religions – Judaism, Buddhism, Christianity and Islam. Crowley claimed that it had been revealed to him that the present aeon was the commencement of that of Horus, the Child, which was also the age of Thelema, self-will, whose central commandment would be 'Do what thou wilt', the words he painted on the door of the temple he founded at Cefalù in Sicily, and which were seized upon by the popular press. (However, the whole quotation was: 'Do what thou wilt is the whole of the law, love under law, love under will.')

Things went badly wrong for Crowley in Sicily, although he found time to amuse himself by shocking visitors by offering them 'love cakes' made of excrement. His use of drugs to heighten awareness (but to which he was certainly addicted), his flagrant use of sex in his rituals, and the mysterious death of one of his magickal brothers led to Crowley being expelled from Sicily by the authorities.

Sex was central to Crowley's magickal practice, and the idea of harnessing sexual energy to invoke Higher Powers remained one of his basic principles. This concept, probably as old as mankind itself, and certainly found in the Tantric mysteries of oriental religion, was put into enthusiastic practice by Crowley himself, in both heterosexual and homosexual forms.

Having failed to dominate the Golden Dawn, but having succeeded, in his own mind at least, in becoming the leading magician of his age, Crowley created his own order, in which he was 'the Beast' and his mistress 'the Scarlet Woman'. He thus followed several precedents in finding in the scriptures a prophecy of the consummation of his own career, as summed up in his most famous work, *Magick in Theory and Practice*. Crowley wrote: 'I am the Beast, I am the word of the Aeon. I spend my soul in blazing torrents that roar into Night, steams that with molten tongues hiss as they lick. I am a hell of a Holy Guru.'

At the end of his life Crowley lived in lodgings in Hastings, Sussex, addicted to alcohol and heroin. His final act, in 1947, was to curse the doctor who refused to give him more heroin – the man died, as predicted, less than twenty-four hours after the magician. Crowley's last words were: 'I am perplexed.'

SEE ALSO *Creative visualisation; Curses; Great Beast 666; Prophecy and prediction; Ritual Magic; Sex and psi.*

FOX SISTERS

Although people had been communing with the spirits of the dead since the beginning of time, it was only in the 1840s that the movement known as Spiritualism began.

Three months after the Fox family had moved into their cottage in Hydesville, New York in 1848, anomalous rapping sounds began to disturb the two girls, Margaretta, aged fifteen, and Kate, aged eleven. The house already had a reputation for being haunted, but the disturbances began in earnest with the arrival of the Foxes.

On the night of Friday, 30 March 1848, Kate entered into a dialogue with the ghostly noises, snapping her fingers in response to the raps. 'Mr Splitfoot, do as I do,' she said, clapping her hands. The same number of raps echoed through the house. Then Margaretta joined in; soon their father was interrogating the invisible presence. When he asked if it were human there was no reply, but his question, 'Is it a spirit? If it is, make two raps', was answered in the affirmative, with the code that was to become widespread among Spiritualists seeking to commune with the spirit world.

This particular spirit, in answer to further questions, rapped out that 'he' had been a destitute pedlar who had been murdered on that spot some years before. Contemporary critics of the Fox family were to point to the lack of evidence for this story, but fifty years later demolition of a wall in their old family home revealed the bones of a man.

Very soon the Fox girls became quite fearless in their brisk dealings with the next world, and their fame spread. Within a year of their first 'conversation' with the dead pedlar they were invited to give a demonstration of their powers before an audience in Rochester. A huge success, it was fol-lowed by what amounted to a promotional tour for the new Spiritualist movement, in which they were joined by an older sister, Leah, who also proved to be a talented 'medium'.

The girls claimed that the raps travelled with them, insisting at every opportunity: 'You have been chosen to go before the world to convince the sceptical of the great truth of immortality.' The world, however, was not entirely convinced and feelings ran high. The girls were attacked in print as impostors and tools of the Devil, and physically assaulted.

In the summer of 1850 they reached New York, where they became an overnight sensation. One reporter wrote of their demonstrations: 'We saw none that we could suspect of collusion. . . . We came away utterly disbelieving in all supernatural agency, and at the same time unable to say how any human means could be used without detection.' The Editor of the *Tribune*, Horace Greeley, was convinced that they were genuine and became their staunch – and influential – ally.

By this time the girls had rivals. A host of 'mediums' had sprung up on both sides of the Atlantic; they manifested a wide range of phenomena including automatic writing, the apportation of objects and 'direct voice' trance, in which the dead were believed to speak – more or less in their earthly voices – through the medium.

Nevertheless, the Fox sisters' rise to fame continued, especially when Kate submitted herself to scientific scrutiny during a visit to England. William (later Sir William) Crookes, was fascinated by the raps and thuds that arose spontaneously whenever the medium rested her hand on a wall or piece of furniture. The sounds, described by Crookes as 'a triple pulsation, sometimes loud enough to be heard several rooms off', continued to be heard when Kate was enclosed in a wire cage or suspended on a swing from the ceiling, or 'when she had fallen fainting on a sofa'. Within months Crookes was to conduct an impressive investigation into the mediumship of D. D. Home, and shortly after that – and much more controversially – into that of materialisation medium Florence Cook.

Leah, who had not been involved in the original communications with 'Mr Splitfoot', was the first of the sisters to become a professional medium and co-operated in several experiments. Investigators were convinced that 'the medium has no more power over the sounds than the investigators have'. This declaration of belief, however, came too late to diffuse the effect of a shattering statement from one Mrs Norman Culver, a relation by marriage of the sisters. She swore that the girls were frauds and that Kate had shown her how to produce the raps by 'cracking' her toes. 'Catherine told me to warm my feet,' she said, ' . . . she sometimes had to warm her feet three or four times in the course of an evening. . . . I have sometimes produced 150 raps in succession.'

On 21 October 1888 Margaretta (now Mrs Kane) and Kate (now Mrs Jencken) called a meeting in New York's Academy of Music. To a packed hall, Margaretta said: 'I am here tonight as one of the founders of Spiritualism to denounce it as an absolute falsehood from beginning to end, as the flimsiest of superstitions, the most wicked blasphemy known to the world.' In the electric silence that followed, Mrs Kane stood motionlessly in her stockinged feet, while raps were heard apparently coming from all over the hall. 'It's all a trick!' Mrs Kane shrieked repeatedly, to confused applause.

This was not, however, the end of Spiritualism, nor – strangely – even the death knell of the sisters' career. Within a year they had retracted their confession; Margaretta blamed it on the pressure put on them by others, notably her sister Leah and 'persons high in the Catholic Church' (of which she became a member).

Letters to her from her husband, which she published after his death, show clearly that he believed she was involved in deliberate fraud. In one letter he wrote: 'Oh, Maggie, are you never tired of this weary, weary sameness of continual deceit?' and in another he advised: 'So avoid "spirits". I cannot bear to think of you as engaged in a course of wickedness and deception.' Both took to drink and drugs and both were early widows, living out their lives maintaining the truth of their retraction.

The arrival of 'Mr Splitfoot', and their apparent power over him seems to indicate that they were at the centre of an authentic poltergeist attack, especially considering their pubescence – frequently a trigger for such manifestations. But, as their fame spread, it seems they became victims of their own public relations, and of a society ripe for signs and wonders. (Even the area in which they lived had a history of other-worldliness – Joseph Smith, founder of the Mormons, had reputedly had his visions not far away – in Palmyra, less than twenty years before.)

Most serious psychical researchers dismiss the case of the Fox sisters as bringing the whole world of the paranormal into disrepute. Thousands of Spiritualists, however, still revere their name.

SEE ALSO *Apports; Automatic writing; Church of Jesus Christ of Latter Day Saints (Mormons); Enfield poltergeist; Ghosts; D. D. Home; Katie King; Life after death; Eusapia Palladino; Parapsychology; Seance-room phenomena; Spiritism; SORRAT.*

D. D. HOME

Born in 1833 in Scotland, Daniel Dunglas Home (pronounced 'Hume') was brought up by an aunt in America, where his psychic gifts soon became apparent, blossoming with the coming of Spiritualism in the 1850s. Apart from the more common seance-room phenomena such as materialising human arms or hands, and making musical instruments appear and play without human aid, Home specialised in levitation – of objects, and of himself.

Within a few months of his first public levitation in Connecticut, Home was lionised on both sides of the Atlantic. The darling of High Society, he gave demonstrations of his powers before the court of Napoleon III, where Prince Metternich schemed to expose him as a fraud; the plot came to nothing and Home's reputation was, if anything, enhanced.

In 1855 he dined with Elizabeth and Robert Browning; the after-dinner phenomena so favoured the hostess that Robert Browning became hostile to the medium. Years later his satirical poem 'Mr Sludge The Medium', clearly aimed at Home, did some damage to Spiritualism. But Home's lack of judgement in taking money off Mrs Jane Lyons, an elderly widow, did more harm: he was charged with extortion. The judge found Mrs Lyons guilty of perjury, but ordered Home to pay back the money, saying: 'For as I hold Spiritualism to be a delusion, I must necessarily hold the plaintiff to be the victim of delusion.'

Yet, on the whole, Home's career soared successfully. He performed his astonishing feats in houses he had never visited before – sometimes at a moment's notice, on his own (in other words, without accomplices), and without any form of apparatus. Yet more astonishing was his ability to confer his phenomena temporarily on others.

Even sceptics found that, in Home's presence, they could be levitated and, like him, could become incombustible. Home frequently thrust both hands, sometimes even his face, into white-hot coals without burning or marking himself. Blazing cinders taken from the fire in hankerchiefs could be given to guests to hold for minutes at a time, without either themselves or the handkerchiefs being affected. Sometimes Home's body would lengthen as he levitated; the investigators who held his trunk as he rose felt a rippling sensation as he elongated, often as much as 20 centimetres.

A convinced Spiritualist, Home believed that his phenomena were produced by spirits of the dead to prove their continued existence. He spoke of being lifted up by them, 'though', he added, 'should I have fallen from the ceiling of some rooms in which I have been raised, I could not have escaped serious injury'.

On one particular occasion, if he had fallen he would surely have been killed. On a winter's night in the Victoria district of London, Home levitated, floated out of a third-storey window over the street – then floated back in through the next window. Naturally such a feat remains controversial; the three witnesses were Captain Charles Wynne, his cousin Lord Adare and the Master of Lindsay – all of them his friends and followers. (Home, whose sexuality was ambiguous, is believed to have had a homosexual affair with Adare.) Yet while it is true that they could have simply lied about the event, Home's more public feats had assured him a devoted enough following. Sceptics hint at hypnosis of the witnesses, and some even propose that the tubercular and fragile Home used a rope to swing from one window to the next.

Whatever the truth of the matter, at least two distinguished scientists were persuaded of his psychic gifts. In Russia Alexander von Boutlerow conducted highly successful experiments into his psychokinetic powers, and in England Sir William Crookes spent some months investigating the medium. Home actively encouraged Crookes to be sceptical, saying: 'Now, William, I want you to act as if I was a recognised conjurer, and was going to cheat you and play all the tricks I could. ... Don't consider my feelings. I shall not be offended.'

Crookes saw no reason why psychic abilities should not register on scientific measuring devices. He devised, among other experiments, one that tested Home's ability to cause an accordion to play unaided. The instrument was secured in a specially designed copper cage, and Home was permitted to touch it only at the opposite end to the keyboard. Yet the accordion – proved to be mechanically normal – continued to play. (One of its favourite tunes was 'Home Sweet Home'.) Years later Crookes wrote that these experiments 'appear conclusively to establish the existence of a new force, in some unknown manner connected with the human organisation, which ... may be called the Psychic Force'.

Home's heyday was between 1850 and 1860; soon after that his health, and his psychic powers, began to fail. With his second wife, the daughter of Alexander von Boutlerow, he went to live in a warmer European climate. He gave an occasional seance for friends, and wrote his autobiography, *Lights and Shadows of Spiritualism*, in which he attacked sceptics and charlatans with equal scorn. He died in 1886.

An elusive character, Home must nevertheless be treated with some respect even in a more sophisticated age. From the many eye-witness accounts of his feats it would seem that he was indeed an extraordinary psychic, although the source of his abilities may well have been different from the spirits he himself believed were responsible.

SEE ALSO *Apports; Boggle threshold; Consensus reality; Fireproof people; Katie King; Nina Kulagina; Levitation; Carmine Mirabelli; Eusapia Palladino; Psychokinesis; Seance-room phenomena; Sex and psi; Spiritism.*

KATIE KING

First appearing in the stage act of alleged Spiritualists Ira and William Davenport in America in the 1860s, the materialised spirit known as 'Katie King' grew to prominence when she and her medium were investigated by British scientist William (later Sir William) Crookes in 1874.

Seventeen-year-old Florence Cook, a teacher from the East End of London had, it was claimed, been the focus of much spirit activity for some years. When the spirits threw her in the air and ripped off her clothes before an adolescent audience, Florence lost her job. Shortly after this she and her sister began to hold regular 'home circles' (invitation only), and the full-form materialisation of Katie King soon became an integral part of the proceedings.

Katie King claimed to have been one Annie Owen Morgan, long-dead daughter of Henry Owen Morgan, an ex-pirate who became Governor-General of Jamaica in the eighteenth century. She confessed to having been a thief and murderess, but her mission on earth was to persuade the living of the reality of the spirit world.

Customarily, twenty minutes after Florence Cook retired, entranced, behind her seance-room curtain, Katie would appear, dressed in a white veil and shroud, and walk among the sitters. Often she demonstrated her tangibility by sitting on men's laps or inviting them to touch her. On one occasion the marked resemblance between spirit and medium provoked an attack – one Mr Volkman tried to seize Katie, but lost his grip when other sitters, outraged at his behaviour, fought him off. The spirit disappeared behind the curtain, and a few minutes later investigation showed Miss Cook, somewhat dishevelled, lying behind the curtain.

Volkman certainly had an axe to grind; shortly after this incident he married Miss Cook's great rival, Mrs Guppy, but enough doubt had been created to worry the Cook girl's benefactor, a rich widower called Blackburn. While he dithered about continuing their retainer, Florence offered her talents for investigation to William Crookes, who

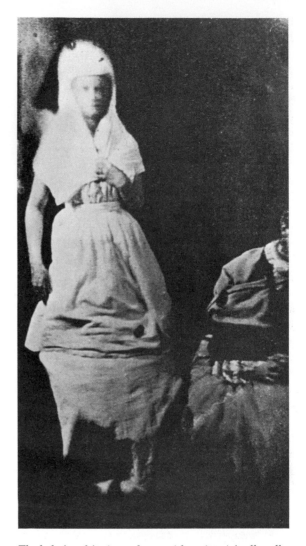

The lady in white (seen here with a sitter) *is allegedly the full-form materialisation of 'Katie King', a long-dead pirate's daughter who was permitted to manifest as living proof of life after death through the mediumship of young Florence Cook in the 1870s. The story seems ridiculous, yet the medium and the materialisation were taken in by the eminent London scientist William Crookes for the purpose of 'investigation'. But most commentators today believe Florence and Katie were one and the same, and that the medium and Crookes used the alleged mediumship as a cover for their sexual intrigue. Even so, Katie King will not lie down: in 1974 she was claimed to have materialised at a seance in Rome, this time without being aided and abetted by Florence Cook.*

had just completed a series of thorough experiments into the paranormal abilities of D. D. Home.

For three months in 1874 Crookes became obsessed with Katie/Florence; regular seances were conducted at his London home, where Miss Cook lived during that time. He took over forty photographs of Katie and Florence, and several of himself, arm-in-arm with the spirit materialisation. On at least one occasion he invited another young medium, Mary Showers, to join in the research by materialising her own spirit, 'Florence Maple'; both mediums and both spirits – Crookes claimed – strolled around the house together. Mary Showers later confessed to being a fraud.

Coinciding with Katie's call to return whence she came was Miss Cook's confession that she had been secretly married for three months to a mariner called Corner. Her collaboration with Crookes at an end, Mrs Corner gave subsequent seances where she materialised a dancing spirit called Marie – who was proved beyond doubt to be the medium in her underwear. She retired to the life of a middle-class housewife; in later years she was to confess to having seduced Crookes and persuaded him to parade her 'Katie King' seances as authentic. Crookes never renounced his interest in psychical research, although he did not conduct any more formal experiments in the subject, and his positive comments on the subject of many years later were taken to refer to his work with Home.

Although the Cook case seems to have been clearly fraudulent, a spirit materialisation calling itself 'Katie King' appeared during one of Fulvio Rendhell's seances in Rome in 1974, and by an infrared camera technique was photographed materialising and dematerialising. This spirit did not resemble Florence Cook, but the 'Katie' of a hundred years before had confided to a sitter that she had been 'much prettier' than Miss Cook in life.

Most parapsychologists, and some Spiritualists, today dismiss the Cook–Crookes collaboration as a squalid sexual intrigue, fortunately only a temporary aberration on the part of the great scientist. But some writers, notably Brian Inglis, and many Spiritualists, maintain that Florence Cook was genuinely gifted and that Katie King was indeed briefly resurrected through her mediumship.

E. W. Cox, a contemporary of Crookes, said in reference to the case: 'If facts, their importance cannot be exaggerated – if frauds, their wickedness cannot be exceeded.'

SEE ALSO *Boggle threshold*; *Cosmic Joker*; *Doppelgängers*; *Helen Duncan*; *Ectoplasm*; *Entity enigma*; *Ghosts*; *D. D. Home*; *The Resurrection*; *Seance-room phenomena*; *Sex and psi*; *Tulpas*.

EUSAPIA PALLADINO

Eusapia Palladino was the most outstanding physical-effects medium in the history of psychical research. No other individual has been so thoroughly investigated over such a long period, or has provided more consistent evidence for the reality of the whole range of seance-room phenomena. She was studied for more than twenty years by at least fifty scientists from Italy, France, Poland, Russia, England and the USA.

Her childhood was not a happy one. Her mother died shortly after Eusapia's birth in 1854, and her father was murdered when she was twelve. Perhaps significantly, her mediumship emerged the following year at an informal home seance in Naples in which she revealed a remarkable talent for causing furniture to move towards her and rise into the air.

Her gifts came to the attention of a local academic, Professor Ercole Chiaia, some twenty years later. But for Chiaia the world might never have heard of Eusapia; in 1888 he appealed publicly for scientists to study her, in a letter to the eminent criminologist (and extreme sceptic) Professor Cesare Lombroso.

In 1891 Lombroso did so, and in a series of sittings he and his five colleagues were fully satisfied that the phenomena they had witnessed were genuine. The following year a seven-man commission of distinguished academics from several fields was set up under Professor Schiaparelli, director of Milan University. Seventeen sittings were held and a positive report was issued.

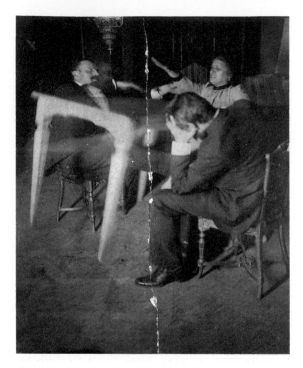

The Neapolitan medium Eusapia Palladino raises a table through her psychic powers during a seance in 1903 in London. Infra-red photography seemed to show objects being levitated by ectoplasmic 'pseudopods' or levers, normally invisible to the naked eye.

Before long Eusapia was an international star of the psychical research circuit. Scientists from as far as St Petersburg came to Naples to see her in action; she in turn travelled to Rome, Genoa, Palermo, Paris, Turin, Warsaw and Cambridge. Her international career ended with a visit to the USA in 1909.

Professor Enrico Morselli, who studied her closely over a long period in his Genoa laboratory, compiled a list of thirty-nine varieties of phenomena that he had observed. These ranged from raps on tables, levitation of the table itself and attraction of distant objects towards her, to just about everything else ever reported to have taken place at a seance: alterations of weight, sudden drops in air temperature, direct writing, the appearance of faces in dishes of clay (some with eyes and mouths open) and the materialisation of human-looking limbs.

One of the most outstanding investigations into her powers was carried out by a team based at the Institut Général Psychologique in Paris that included Pierre and Marie Curie, Henri Bergson and Charles Richet (all future Nobel Prize winners) and Arsène d'Arsonval. The forty-three sittings held between 1905 and 1908 are of special interest both for the instrumental methods used, and for the tightness of the controls imposed. In addition to her usual feats Eusapia managed to discharge an electroscope and to increase the weight on a scale by 7 kilos, in both cases without physical contact.

The 1908 investigation in Naples by three members of the Society for Psychical Research is regarded as one of the most important in the field of physical mediumship. The Hon. Everard Feilding, Hereward Carrington and Wortley Baggally were seasoned and highly sceptical field workers with abundant experience of fake mediums. Their 260-page report in the *Proceedings* of the SPR (Vol. 23 1909) is a classic. It lists a total of 470 incidents observed under conditions that made any kind of cheating improbable.

Eusapia did appear to 'cheat' on occasions when controls were lax. However, careful investigators such as Morselli, Flammarion and Carrington noted that such actions were involuntary reflexes of her trance state and did not imply deliberate intent to deceive. Indeed, Eusapia regularly urged her investigators not to give her the chance to cheat. A distinguished American magician, Howard Thurston, testified in a detailed report that the phenomena he witnessed could not be explained in terms of conjuring.

SEE ALSO *American Society for Psychical Research; Ectoplasm; Levitation; Mediums; Paranormal portraits; Seance-room phenomena; Society for Psychical Research.*

CARMINE MIRABELLI

In 1911 twenty-three-year-old Carmine Mirabelli was dismissed from his job as a shoe-shop assistant because the shoe boxes kept flying around. As a direct result Mirabelli was confined for nineteen days in an asylum. Two doctors observed him closely, concluding that he was neither ill nor normal, but that he possessed 'the result of the radiation of nervous forces that we all have, but that he has in extraordinary excess'.

He was able to cause objects to move and apparently liquefy, rise into the air or wriggle like a worm. He produced volumes of automatic writing in thirty languages, was telepathic and clairvoyant, and was often reported to travel instantaneously, by teleportation. His most dramatic feats included levitating himself 2.5 metres from the ground (this was photographed), and gradually materialising the dead in solid form. Only a few researchers found Mirabelli of sufficient interest to investigate him during his lifetime. He died in 1951 as a result of being hit by a car.

In 1973 – over twenty years after his death – the Brazilian Institute for Psychobiophysical Research (IBPP) appointed a team to compile a dossier on Mirabelli. Its members included writer-researcher Guy Lyon Playfair, who has done much to make Mirabelli's name known in Britain.

Mirabelli's sons, although sometimes highly critical of Spiritism, were adamant that their father had caused extraordinary things to happen 'almost every day, any time and any place'. Their mother had been resigned to finding herself coping with the results of a poltergeist attack; the family were united in denying that he had cheated or that he had had any motive for doing so.

Yet Theodore Besterman of the Society for Psychical Research had no hesitation in denouncing Mirabelli as a fraud, although he had himself once witnessed examples of apparent psychokinesis in his presence, and also seen the medium write a 1700-word automatic script in just under an hour, and in French – a language Mirabelli had never learned. (He had also produced intelligible automatic writing in Japanese, Hebrew and Arabic.) The moving of objects Besterman ascribed to the use of 'hidden threads', although the other members of the team never found any and he failed to explain exactly how they could have produced such a variety of phenomena. However, Hans Driesch of the SPR and May C. Walker of the American SPR had found the medium 'most impressive', and Guy Lyon Playfair's researches found nothing

to indicate that Mirabelli had cheated or had any cause to cheat.

SEE ALSO *Boggle threshold*; *Enfield poltergeist*; *ESP*; *Fox sisters*; *D. D. Home*; *Katie King*; *Nina Kulagina*; *Levitation*; *Eusapia Palladino*; *Psychic music, art and literature*; *Psychokinesis*; *The Resurrection*; *Society for Psychical Research*; *Spiritism*; *Telepathy*; *Chico Xavier*.

HELEN DUNCAN

One of the most controversial materialisation mediums of the twentieth century was – and still is – the late Helen Duncan. She was the last woman to be prosecuted under the 1735 Witchcraft Act.

Born in 1898 in Scotland and married in 1918, she rose to fame among devout Spiritualists in Scotland and England in the 1930s and 1940s. At her seances, ectoplasm poured from her entranced form and took on the shape of the dead, who were clearly recognised by the 'sitters'.

In 1933 a policewoman grabbed 'Peggy', Mrs Duncan's child spirit guide, and claimed she was nothing more than a cleverly lit undervest. The case was heard at Edinburgh; Mrs Duncan was convicted of fraud and fined £10.

During the Second World War Mrs Duncan settled in Portsmouth, giving seances for the bereaved. In 1943 a sailor materialised at one of her seances, claiming to have gone down with HMS *Barham*. At the time the news of this ship's fate was classified information – it was only made public knowledge three months after the seance. Mrs Duncan's supporters assert that the government of the day believed her work posed a threat to national security, and it was for this reason alone that they arrested her.

In 1944 she was charged at Portsmouth under the Vagrancy Act, but when the case was transferred to the Old Bailey she was charged under the Witchcraft Act. Dubbed 'the trial of the century', Rex *v.* Duncan drew the crowds. Accused of regurgitating butter muslin that masqueraded as ectoplasm, Mrs Duncan had her doctor produce a signed statement, together with an X-ray, to the effect that her stomach was normal – and therefore incapable of such feats.

Several witnesses declared on oath that she was a genuine materialisation medium. They repeatedly pointed out that, although she weighed 140 kilos, one of her spirit guides was the tall, thin Albert Stewart, and that both of them had been seen simultaneously. The famous journalist

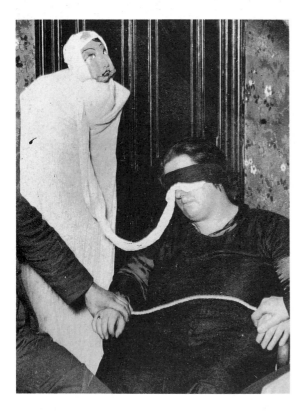

The most blatant fake 'spirit materialisation' – or so it seems. The 'control', known as Peggy, of Mrs Helen Duncan was nevertheless widely believed to be genuine. Mrs Duncan was the last person to be prosecuted under the Witchcraft Act of 1735, and served nine months in Holloway Prison in 1944 after being found guilty of fraud. After her release, she was seized during another seance by the police and died shortly afterwards. Deemed by the Spiritualist faithful to be a martyr, Mrs Duncan remains the subject of great controversy. It is claimed that she has appeared in the 1980s, in her discarnate state, as a materialisation at the seances of Midlands' medium Rita Goold.

Hannen Swaffer, a convinced Spiritualist, was called as a witness for the defence and was contemptuous of allegations that the ectoplasm was butter muslin. The chief reporter of the *Scotsman*, J. W. Herries, declared he had witnessed Mrs Duncan materialise the late Sir Arthur Conan Doyle (himself a champion of Spiritualism towards the end of his life).

Mrs Duncan and three 'accomplices' were, however, found guilty. The medium was sentenced to nine months' imprisonment, which she served in Holloway Prison.

Deemed a martyr to the cause by fellow Spiritualists, Mrs Duncan was subsequently welcomed back to the seance circuit, although some said her powers were diminished. The Spiritualists' National Union withdrew her membership, but her friends were loyal.

As a direct result of the furore caused by the court case in 1944, the Witchcraft Act was replaced in 1951 by the Fraudulent Mediums Act. The first person whom the police intended to prosecute under this Act was Mrs Duncan. At a seance in Nottingham in 1956 the entranced medium was seized, lights flashed in her face, and the room searched for incriminating 'props'. Nothing was found.

Mrs Duncan, however, was found to have suffered major burns on her stomach and was in shock. Spiritualists believe that interfering with an entranced medium causes the ectoplasm to withdraw so rapidly into the medium's body that it results in physical and mental injury. Six weeks after the police raid Mrs Duncan was dead, her martyrdom assured.

Existing photographs of her materialisations show a doll-like 'Peggy' and extrusions that look remarkably like inflated rubber gloves. But there were many who were convinced by her powers. In the 1980s investigators from the Society for Psychical Research witnessed the apparent full-form materialisation of Mrs Duncan during a seance given by Midlands medium Rita Goold. The deceased medium appeared – in the near-darkness – to be as large as in life and to have an authentic east Scottish accent.

To this day the case of Helen Duncan provokes enormous controversy.

SEE ALSO *Cosmic Joker*; *Ectoplasm*; *Fox sisters*; *Katie King*; *Carmine Mirabelli*; *Eusapia Palladino*; *Seance-room phenomena*; *Tulpas*; *Witchcraft*.

EILEEN GARRETT

Eileen Garrett was born in County Meath, Ireland on 17 March 1893. Within two weeks of her birth she was orphaned by the separate suicides of her mother and Spanish-born father, apparently due to the strain of sectarian strife.

Eileen's upbringing was left to an aunt and uncle; shortly after her uncle's death she saw him standing in front of her, 'looking young, erect and strong'. The apparition predicted, accurately, that she would study in London – her clairvoyant powers were to be developed by the founder of the College of Psychic Studies, Hewat Mackenzie.

By the mid-1920s, her precognitions had become almost daily events. They included apparitions of her wounded husband in the trenches of the First World War, and in 1928 visions of the R101 airship disaster – which she followed up with post mortem communications from its dead captain. To many people these seances provide the most impressive evidence for survival on record.

Although she had only a rudimentary education, her gifts, intelligence and integrity endeared her to such luminaries as Conan Doyle, George Bernard Shaw and C. G. Jung, whose theory of the collective unconscious appealed to her. She wrote:

> To prove the existence of spirit intellectually has been left to religion and to sentiment, but neither clearly defines a way to an afterlife acceptable to the measuring rule of science. I live in a world filled with phenomena of a transcendental nature, which does not seem to allow itself to be put aside, but acts continually as a guiding force. . . . I suspect that this field, discredited by those who do not experience its nature, belongs to the inner workings of what we call mind, as yet to be explored.

Eileen gave some weight to the idea of a superconscious, a global memory bank that contained everything that has happened or that is to come. This idea is akin to the Akashic records of the Theosophists, and similar in theme to the morphogenetic field of Dr Rupert Sheldrake.

The medium had two spirit controls – Uvani, an

'The thinking person's medium', Eileen Garrett, being overshadowed by her 'control', Abdul Latif. Mrs Garrett was always aware of the need to doubt the true nature of her 'spirit guides', believing them to be possibly split-off aspects of her own personality.

Indian soldier from many centuries ago, and Abdul Latif, a twelfth-century physician from the court of Saladin. Eileen's attitude towards them was ambivalent. She wrote in her autobiography *Many Voices* (1968): 'I have maintained a respectful attitude towards them. I have never been able wholly to accept them as spiritual dwellers on the threshold which they seem to believe they are.'

In 1931 she was the guest of the American Society for Psychical Research (ASPR), and gave sittings in New York and universities throughout the USA. On one occasion she was asked to give her clairvoyant impressions about unknown objects sealed in numbered envelopes. The artefacts included a Babylonian clay tablet – not only did Eileen describe it perfectly, but she also gave a detailed description, down to two small scars, of the secretary who had packed it. Psychologist Lawrence LeShan, who masterminded the experiment, was amazed. He said that Eileen's description so matched the woman that she could have been 'picked out of a line-up of ten thousand'.

Eileen's sittings traced many missing persons, and impressed many a sceptic with the reality of the afterlife. Tough film director Cecil B. de Mille was reduced to tears by her accurate description of his dead mother, who she said was standing by his side. Even when she was anaesthetised, her spirit controls continued to speak through her; the medical staff clearly heard commands given in Hindustani.

During her middle years she opened a tea-room, and ran a workers' hostel and the literary magazine *Tomorrow*. In 1951 she founded the Parapsychological Foundation in New York, where her quest for understanding of psychic phenomena is continued by her daughter.

At the time of her death in 1970, at Le Piol in France, Eileen Garrett perhaps knew few of the answers to the questions that had so perplexed her – about the nature of the mind, and of human survival of bodily death. But she had asked the questions and inspired many others to do the same, and had herself been an inspiration.

SEE ALSO *American Society for Psychical Research; Case of Ruth; Consensus reality; Fantasy-prone personalities; Formative causation; Jung and the paranormal; Left and right brain; Multiple personality; Possession; Shamanism.*

NINA KULAGINA

In 1968 the Soviet press first wrote about the psychokinetic (PK) abilities of a forty-year-old housewife and mother of three from Leningrad. Nina Kulagina, who is also known by her maiden name of Nina Mikhailovna, could reportedly move objects without touching them, or 'without the

Soviet psychic extraordinary, Nina Kulagina, moves a matchbox without touching it. Madame Kulagina sued a Russian magazine for libel when they claimed her powers were fraudulent – and won.

mediation of muscular exertion', as was written later in the *Great Soviet Encyclopaedia*. The objects included a compass needle, matches, cigarettes empty matchboxes and other wooden, metal and plastic items. Nina's apparent psychokinetic abilities attracted the attention of numerous Soviet and Western researchers, though at first the scientific community was more than sceptical and suspected tricks and sleight of hand. No other Soviet psychic has been tested as extensively and thoroughly.

Between 1968 and 1978 she demonstrated, on many occasions and under controlled conditions, the movement of objects weighing up to 380 grams – doing so at distances of up to 2 metres, without touching the objects or using any other known physical means. She could move single objects in specific directions, or several objects at once – all in the same direction or each in a different direction. At times selective movement of one object from the group was possible, either spontaneously or at the experimenter's request.

By focusing her gaze on one pan of a set of laboratory scales, Nina could make it move down even when a load of up to 30 grams was placed on the other pan. Mental concentration enabled her to divide an air bubble that was contained in a glass tube with water, and move the two parts to opposite ends of the tube. She lifted objects weighing up to 30 grams and suspended them in the air; and she produced movement of objects in a partial vacuum, in water and through various shields (flat and three-dimensional, open and closed) made of paper, wood, ordinary and lead glass, transparent plastic, ceramics, sheet lead, aluminium, thin sheet copper, steel and other materials.

In some experiments, Nina produced a remote influence on various physical and chemical detectors. Under her influence, liquid crystals changed colour and luminescent crystals – which normally need to be stimulated by cathode rays, electric fields or other means – began to glow in darkness. Two substances that normally begin to react at $70\,^{\circ}C$ did so at room temperature. When a scintillation detector was placed near the target objects at the moment of the experiment, the readings were one-third of those expected from average ordinary background activity.

By mentally 'drawing' images on photographic paper placed in a black envelope, Nina produced photographs in the shape of an imperfect cross, circle, square and star. She was also able to expose photographic film shielded by lead sheets 1.5 millimetres thick, and by ebonite 20 millimetres thick.

In several experiments Nina demonstrated apparent PK influence upon biological systems. At the experimenter's request, she tried to suppress the vital functions of white mice. A few movements of her hands rendered the mice motionless, as if dead; but as soon as she removed her hands, they returned to normal. Her influence on an isolated frog's heart was observed under laboratory conditions. The heart was placed in a physiological solution with electrodes attached to it to record its activity, which normally would have continued for thirty to forty minutes and could then have been reactivated by electrostimulation. Forty seconds after Nina began her influence the heart stopped, and electrostimulation was unable to reactivate it.

From 1978 to 1984 Nina's phenomena were studied by physicists from the Institute of Precise Mechanics and Optics in Leningrad, the Research Institute of Radio-Engineering and Electronics and the Baumann Higher School of Technology in Moscow. According to their report, published in 1984,

Nina's hands generated enormously strong electromagnetic and acoustic fields – far exceeding the strength of the Earth's magnetic field, which in turn is ten thousand to ten million times greater than that of an ordinary human being. In carefully controlled conditions, a laser beam was observed to decrease noticeably in intensity under Nina's influence. Numerous researchers noted that Nina produced PK effects while in a state of great stress, accompanied by considerable increase in heart rate, blood pressure and blood sugar level and by weight loss.

In the late 1970s, Yuri Kobzarev of the USSR Academy of Sciences Research Institute of Radio-Engineering and Electronics wrote: 'I have become convinced that the phenomena demonstrated by N. Kulagina . . . are in no way tricks but essentially manifestations of unusual human capabilities. This conviction of mine, based on the results of experiments specially set up, is shared by many people, among them professors and academicians.'

In 1986 a journalist named Strelkov referred in the magazine *Chelovek i Zakon (Man and Law)* to earlier articles by another journalist, Vladimir Lvov, and accused Nina Kulagina of fraud. She subsequently sued the magazine and won, and in May 1988 the magazine published a retraction of its statements about her. This is the first occasion on which a psychic has sued a Soviet publication for libel and won.

SEE ALSO *Uri Geller; Healing; D. D. Home; History of Soviet psi; Matthew Manning; Carmine Mirabelli; Parapsychology; Propensity for psi; Psychokinesis; Soviet psi today; Thoughtography; Traumas and psi.*

URI GELLER

One of the most controversial personalities of his time, Uri Geller was born in Tel Aviv in 1946. Following the separation of his parents, he spent a short time at a kibbutz and then went with his mother to Cyprus, where he attended the Terra Santa College in Nicosia. He returned to Israel to

'Psychic superstar' Uri Geller demonstrates his gift for metalbending from his home in Reading, Berkshire, in 1985. Geller has always maintained that almost anyone can learn to develop psychokinetic powers – but, as the Bible says, children are by far the most open to 'miraculous' abilities ('Be ye as a little child . . .').

Cyprus school have given accounts of similar feats.

On leaving the army in 1968, Geller soon became known for his spontaneous displays of telepathy at parties, and in October 1969 he gave his first public performance. His professional debut followed a few months later. His basic repertoire was to bend metal objects, chiefly cutlery and keys, and to demonstrate telepathy with members of the audience. This repertoire remained essentially unaltered over the following two decades. Israel's magicians promptly denounced him as a fraud – a clever conjurer pretending to be psychic. The first 'exposure' of many appeared in October 1970 in the popular weekly *Haolam Hazeh*. Despite the allegations, Geller went on to become one of the highest paid entertainers in the country.

In August 1971, author and medical researcher Dr Andrija Puharich flew to Israel to investigate him. He became convinced, after a series of informal tests, that Geller was able to demonstrate both telepathy and psychokinesis (PK). The American researcher also held a number of hypnosis sessions during which Geller appeared to be in contact with extraterrestrial intelligences. These are described in Puharich's book *Uri* (1974).

With the help of astronaut Edgar Mitchell, Puharich arranged for Geller to visit the USA in 1972 to undergo a series of laboratory tests at the former Stanford Research Institute (now SRI International) under the supervision of physicists Harold Puthoff and Russell Targ. These and several subsequent scientific tests were reported in Charles Panati's *The Geller Papers* (1976), which also includes the positive findings of four stage magicians.

Visiting Britain in 1973, Geller became an overnight sensation after appearing on radio and television; a further attempt to debunk him by *Time* magazine in March that year had little effect. Tours of western Europe followed, and the publication of Puharich's book increased international Gellermania, as did the appearance in 1975 of Geller's *My Story*.

Gellermania ceased as suddenly as it had started and from 1976 to 1985 relatively little was heard from him. However, he was far from inactive. A meeting with the late Sir Val Duncan, chief executive of the Rio Tinto-Zinc Corporation, introduced him to multinational big business, and it was at Sir Val's urging that Geller began to develop his talents to

fight in the Six Day War of 1967, and was wounded in both arms during a gun battle in Jerusalem. At a rehabilitation centre he met his future wife Hanna Shtrang whose brother Shimshon ('Shipi') was to play an important part in making Geller's a household name around the world.

Geller showed unusual abilities at an early age, as several who knew him well have testified. His godmother, Mrs Susan Korn, remembers a spoon bending in the palm of Uri's hand when he was four or five, at which age he could also apparently read her mind. A former fellow member of the kibbutz has described Geller's ability to make the hands of his watch move without visible contact with the knob, while both teachers and pupils from his

Graphic description of the cosmic vision of the
Rosicrucians, a powerful semi-secret occult group
whose influence has extended from its inception –
which was possibly in the thirteenth century, much
earlier than has generally been thought. Among
their notable adepts were Dr John Dee,
Nostradamus, Leonardo da Vinci, Sir Isaac Newton
and William Lilly. The order of the Rosy Cross, like
all other hermetic societies, believes it knows the
secrets of the universe, both visible and invisible,
manifest and in the making, of the microcosm and
macrocosm. Their rituals were concerned with
bringing the Word into physical being, as in the
practice of alchemy.

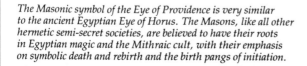

The Masonic symbol of the Eye of Providence is very similar
to the ancient Egyptian Eye of Horus. The Masons, like all other
hermetic semi-secret societies, are believed to have their roots
in Egyptian magic and the Mithraic cult, with their emphasis
on symbolic death and rebirth and the birth pangs of initiation.

Necromancers successfully invoke a spirit, for which they seem
remarkably unprepared. Necromancers were more often
supposed to exhume corpses and temporarily animate them in
order to discover what the future may hold, a practice
frequently ascribed to modern satanists.

A young Iranian dervish sticks a skewer through his cheek at the height of his self-induced trance. The power of the mind over pain is legendary; trances induced by rhythmic dancing, chanting, special breathing techniques or meditation are all equally effective not only against physical pain, but other manifestations of bodily trauma, such as bleeding and scarring. It seems strange that in the sophisticated West the sick are expected to suffer the trauma of operations and the side effects of drugs when these techniques have been proved over the centuries.

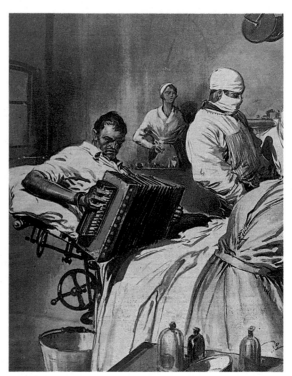

Eighteenth-century caricature of Franz Anton Mesmer, showing an obvious prejudice against his theory of 'animal magnetism'. Mesmer had shown that certain gestures, known as 'magnetic passes', could induce apparent convulsions or collapse in the patient, after which they were healed of their mental, emotional and physical ills, and may even have developed some psychic abilities in the process. Although Mesmerism and hypnotism are different, both of them act as triggers for a self-healing potential, and therefore neither can be easily dismissed.

In 1934 piano accordian player Guglienano Bonfoco had his leg amputated without anaesthetic at his own request. He played his instrument throughout the operation, which acted as a powerful focus for his mind; even in the face of terrible physical agony, the mind can allow itself to be distracted enough for the patient to feel little. It has been proved time and again that hypnosis is a potent anaesthetic; operations ranging from simple dentistry to major surgery can be conducted with the patient fully conscious throughout, if he or she has been hypnotised first. Sceptics, when faced with the evidence, have had to fall back on the line that the patients must have been bribed to show no pain.

Ahmed Hussain walks over burning coals at Carshalton, England, in 1937. Firewalking seems to depend on a light trance, although there are cases on record where the physical effects seem to depend on something considerably stranger – one European who took part in a firewalk in the South Seas had his boots burnt off, but his feet remained unscorched. The local holy man said that this was because his boots had not been magically blessed, but his feet had.

Stage hypnosis – instant command technique and dramatic change in behaviour of the subject. Frequently he or she is made to perform humiliating acts to the amusement of the audience. Yet hypnosis is an extremely valuable tool in therapy for all manner of ills. In the hands of a skilled operator it is highly ethical, never humiliating, and has no adverse side effects.

Jesus resurrects Lazarus, one of the raisings from the dead mentioned in the New Testament. Yet there is evidence that Jesus was an adept of the Essene mystery school, whose rites included many symbolic deaths and rebirths as initiations. This account may refer to such a rite – a symbolic, rather than an actual resurrection.

St Veronica shows the cloth used to wipe the face of the suffering Jesus, which, according to legend, became imprinted with his image. Other examples of haemography include the Turin Shroud, but this phenomenon is by no means reserved for Christian 'miracles'. The Fortean Times *regularly carries accounts of mysterious images that are found on anything from walls to tortillas.*

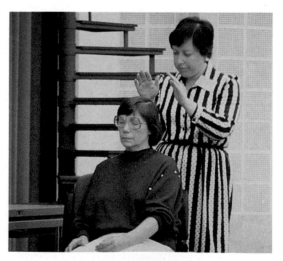

Larissa Vilenskaya demonstrates the healing force at a conference in Basel in 1984. Although a few people are born natural healers, it seems that most can learn how to tap into the healing power. Although healers can never guarantee a certain outcome, their work never has ill side effects, and usually confers a profound sense of tranquillity.

help locate oil and precious minerals. Understandably, few details of such activities were publicised, although at least two mining executives have publicly admitted to having made use of his services. In his second autobiographical work, *The Geller Effect* (1986), Geller describes other services performed for assorted businessmen, and for law enforcement and intelligence agencies in a number of countries.

By 1985, when Geller and his family came to live in Britain, he was a millionaire. Though he continued to arouse heated controversy he was never conclusively shown to be fraudulent, and the mass of testimony in his favour far outweighs the allegations against him. Several of these, though widely repeated, have been proved untrue. The records of the Beersheba court at which he is supposed to have been convicted for fraud show that he never appeared there; a denunciation by a former business associate has been fully retracted; and the former editor of *Haolam Hazeh* has admitted that articles attacking Geller may have been pure fiction.

Geller has been neither debunked nor definitively proved to possess genuine psychic abilities. To the frustration of parapsychologists, he has refused to take part in controlled experiments that might settle the question once and for all. He remains an enigma, and a remarkably resilient survivor. He deserves credit for bringing ostensibly genuine psychic phenomena into the homes of millions through his radio and television appearances, and for encouraging many people to undertake serious research into border areas of science.

David Berglas, one of Britain's leading stage magicians and a Geller-watcher for fifteen years has said

> If he is a genuine psychic and genuinely does what he claims to do by the methods he claims to use, then he is the only person in the world who can do it. He is the only one to have demonstrated consistently. He is a phenomenon, and we must respect that. If on the other hand he is a magician or a trickster or a con-man, he is also phenomenal – the best there is. So, whichever way you want to look at him, we must respect him as one or the other.

SEE ALSO *CSICOP*; *Limits of science*; *Metal bending*; *Parapsychology*; *Psychokinesis*; *Telepathy*.

DORIS STOKES

Until her death in 1987, Doris Fisher Stokes was the best-known British medium of her day and a 'psychic superstar' across the world, especially in Australia and New Zealand. As a child she had seen a body being carried out of a neighbouring house, but was puzzled by the fact that walking by its side was the man whose corpse it was. Her mother was disturbed by Doris's strange abilities, but her father, a natural psychic, encouraged her. It was only after his death and her marriage, just before the Second World War, that she began to develop her talents fully, although, after a hilarious experience at a 'development circle', she gave up any idea of formal training as a medium.

Doris was clairaudient; she heard, rather than saw, discarnate spirits. Those who had been 'on the other side' for a while came through strongly to her, whereas the newly dead sounded faint and confused. As in life, bombastic personalities tried to drown more timid souls, but Doris knew all their tricks and proved to be a kind but firm mistress of ceremonies. She never went into a trance, or used dimmed lights or other bizarre effects. She would address the invisible in the same neighbourly way as she talked to the audience – and time and again she scored direct 'hits', providing accurate and often detailed information about the sitters and the voices in her ear.

Sceptics were frequently – and instantly – converted. At a demonstration given by Doris in the early 1980s to launch her book *More Voices in My Ear*, a journalist who had been vociferous about the 'nonsense' of Spiritualism was reduced to tears by a message that Doris said was from the girl's discarnate twin. Although the medium could have made enquiries about her audience, there was no prearranged seating plan – and Doris's memory was none too sharp. The information given to the journalist was typical of messages that came through Doris, consisting of trivial details about the colour of the curtains in the living room or worries about the health of a pet. It was as if she were reading the minds of the sitters – or as if the dead were indeed reporting back to her.

She was not, however, afraid to mention more important matters. One depressed widower was told that his wife warned against the overdose he was planning for that night. An aborted child told its mother she was forgiven for its death.

Towards the end of her life Doris played to packed houses in several countries. One of her favourite venues was London's Dominion Theatre, a huge place normally used for musicals. Perhaps she overstretched herself; certainly her health was not good. But whatever the cause her performances laid her open to charges of collusion with members of the audience, and even to exploiting the bereaved.

Yet Doris Stokes was one of the few mediums who had ever admitted cheating. As a young woman she had listened to the conversations of the sitters before the demonstration she was about to give, and incorporated the names she had heard into her 'messages'. However, her spirit guide Ramononov told her she must apologise to those whom she had cheated and confess what she had done, or there would be no more genuine information from the other side. Doris claimed that she was never tempted to give false information again.

Parapsychologists see mental mediumship as a mixture of telepathy between the living and 'super-ESP', an access to a pool of information akin to the collective unconscious. Doris found such tortuous explanations amusing. 'They just talk to me, love, and I pass the messages on,' she said.

SEE ALSO *CSICOP*; *ESP*; *Explanations*; *Eileen Garrett*; *Parapsychology*; *Society for Psychical Research*; *Telepathy*.

CHICO XAVIER

Francisco Candido Xavier was born in 1910 in the small town of Pedro Leopoldo in the interior of Brazil. His childhood was not a happy one – his mother died when he was five and he was brought up by his godmother, who regularly beat him and

sent him out to work when he was eight. His formal education was minimal, ending at thirteen. After working as a kitchen hand and shop assistant and in a textile plant he obtained a low-level job at the local branch of the Agriculture Ministry, where he remained until his retirement in 1961.

However, this was not the typical life of a poor Brazilian who never made good. 'Chico' Xavier is a household name throughout his country and its most prolific author – in fact the second most prolific writer in Portuguese to date, with nearly four hundred books to his credit; or, as he has repeatedly insisted, to the credit of the several hundred discarnate authors who transmit their works through his mediumship.

Chico's unusual talents first showed themselves at school, where he regularly felt the presence of spirits helping him with his essays. He became a practising Spiritualist medium in 1917, specialising in what the Brazilians called psychography. (This is considered to be spirit-inspired, unlike automatic writing which is regarded as merely the expression of the subconscious mind of the writer.)

His first book appeared in 1932 and caused a literary sensation. Entitled *Parnaso de Além-Túmulo (Parnassus of Beyond the Grave)*, it contained 259 poems signed by almost every major name in Brazilian and Portuguese poetry – fifty-six in all. The distinguished academician Humberto de Campos declared after a careful study of the poems that 'their authors show the same characteristics of inspiration and expression that identified them on this planet'. Campos died soon afterwards, whereupon he promptly joined Chico's growing team of spirit authors – much to the dismay of his widow, who sued for her share of author's rights. She lost her case at a widely publicised trial in 1944 which only served to increase Chico's fame and the sales of his books.

These include fiction, poetry, children's stories and a wide range of historical, religious and scientific works. In addition, Chico has regularly produced messages from recently deceased people, often containing a wealth of personal detail. His whole literary output has been produced in public, most of it at his weekly sessions in Pedro Leopoldo and Uberaba, where he went to live permanently in 1959. When he writes, he turns his head away from the paper and shields his eyes with his left hand, while his right hand moves at such speed that an assistant has to remove each completed sheet of paper. His handwriting is large and clear, and no corrections or alterations are made before publication. Chico has not only declined to take credit for his writing, but has also refused any form of payment. All profits go to Spiritualist charities.

Chico's most popular work after *Parnaso* (still in print over fifty years after its first publication) is the nine-volume novel *Nosso Lar* (*Our Home*), attributed to 'the spirit of André Luiz'. The narrator, a doctor, opens with his own death and arrival in 'the next world'. Of special interest are the many passages in which the processes of death and rebirth, and the interactions between the two worlds, are described in language that is often highly technical.

No normal explanation for Chico's prodigious literary output has been produced. His works are notable not only for their wide range, but also for their quality as imaginative writing that is both entertaining and instructive. No medium in any country has produced a comparable body of evidence for the reality of spirit communication, nor such a variety of well-written and enjoyable books. SEE ALSO *Life after death*; *Left and right brain*; *Carmine Mirabelli*; *Psychic music, art and literature*; *Spiritism*.

CORAL POLGE

Coral Polge, wife of British Spiritualist healer Tom Johanson, does not claim to see spirits or hear their voices, nor do the spirits guide her hands as in classic automatic art. She does, however, receive vivid mental impressions of discarnate people, whom she sketches in charcoal or pencil. Sometimes the visual impressions are accompanied by other sensory feelings – 'Doesn't he stink!' she exclaimed while drawing an old man – 'All that whisky and ''baccy''.' (Both portrait and accompanying details were confirmed by two ladies in the audience; he was their dead grandfather.)

Coral Polge's psychic impression of a communicator came through as this drawing, recognised by a member of the audience as his grandmother. A photograph of her is remarkably similar to Polge's drawing.

British medium Coral Polge, who draws the impressions she receives of discarnate people. Her portraits are detailed, and time and time again are totally accepted by 'sitters' who recognise them.

Miss Polge attended Harrow Art School, but detested portraiture, preferring textile design. A medium told her she had a great future in psychic art; in 1950 she led her first Spiritualist circle and since then has produced over forty thousand detailed portraits of the dead.

She finds it difficult to produce portraits to order, and draws whoever can 'come through', although most of her drawings have some significance for members of her audience. At one meeting in 1987, in the London headquarters of the Spiritualist Association of Great Britain, she drew eight portraits; all except one were 'claimed'. Eventually one woman felt compelled to take it home; the next day she recognised it as an exact line drawing of her boyfriend as he had looked years before as a child film actor – and who was still alive.

Although, to many, Coral Polge's work provides proof of survival, it may also be a form of ESP – the images and impressions coming to her through some kind of telepathy with the sitters. Whatever the mechanics of her extraordinary gift, Coral Polge is one of the most impressive mediums working today.

SEE ALSO *Creative visualisation; ESP; Images that bleed and weep; Matthew Manning; Paranormal portraits; Psychic music, art and literature; Telepathy; Chico Xavier.*

VALENTINE GREATRAKES

Born on 14 February 1629, and brought up as a wealthy Protestant in Lismore, Ireland, Valentine Greatrakes was to become the greatest healer of his day. His fame was all the more remarkable because he specialised in curing scrofula – commonly known as 'the King's Evil' – which could, it was believed, be cured only by the monarch's touch. Therefore, not only was his gift potentially treasonable, but in an age hysterically paranoid about the black arts, he laid himself open to charges of witchcraft.

His early days were notable only for the ease with which he was acceptable to both the Cromwellians and, after the Restoration, the Monarchists. He was thirty-four when he first felt what he described as 'an impulse or strange persuasion' to heal the sick, although he was loath to act upon it for some while, and his wife dismissed the impulse as 'idle imagination'. Nevertheless, she encouraged him to try to heal some of the local poor, especially those suffering from scrofula, then a widespread disease which could literally eat away face and body, and the symptoms of which could be revolting.

Greatrakes was naturally squeamish, but when he felt the impulse to heal he touched open sores with equanimity. One of his first patients showed dramatic signs of improvement within a few days of being healed and was completely cured within a month.

The healer began to treat those afflicted with ague (malaria), and extended his work to all the sick.

As his fame spread, the authorities summoned him; the Dean of Lismore forbade him to practise his gift, but Greatrakes ignored the command. Perhaps because of his high social standing he was able to continue his work unimpeded.

He believed that his powers came from God and flowed through his hands – which were, according to contemporary reports, 'the largest, heaviest and softest . . . of any man of his time'. He would lay his hands upon the afflicted part of the body and smooth over other parts with a stroking movement, giving rise to his nickname of 'The Stroker'. His touch commonly made the skin feel first cold and numb, then healthy and warm.

He refused to accept money or gifts for his healing and made himself open to scientific scrutiny; although some patients were not healed by him and the illness of others returned after a while, many were proved conclusively to be cured. He travelled to England, where his fame had preceded him, and impressed even the sceptics with his honesty and integrity. He never made false claims or rashly raised the hopes of the sick, but neverthe-less succeeded in curing many of their long-standing afflictions.

About five years after he felt his 'impulse' to heal, his gift left him and he retired to live out his life as an Irish country gentleman, becoming the High Sheriff of Waterford. Cynics point out that this withdrawal coincided with the execution of nine people in the Midlands who could allegedly cure epilepsy; they were hanged as witches. Yet over the centuries many mediums, psychics and healers have discovered that their powers – undoubtedly genuine at the outset – gradually waned. Many resorted to trickery in order to keep up appearances; it says much for Greatrakes that he did not.

He never knew how his gift worked, but, believing that it was divinely inspired, suspected that some form of exorcism was involved, some release of the inner conflict that had brought about the disease.

SEE ALSO *José Arigo*; *Autosuggestion*; *Healing*; *Matthew Manning*; *Mesmerism*; *Witchcraft*.

Valentine Greatrakes – 'the Stroker' – a seventeenth-century healer who specialised in curing those afflicted with scrofula.

JOSÉ ARIGO

José Arigo's entry into psychic surgery was dramatic. He was suddenly compelled to rush into the room where a neighbour lay dying of cancer of the uterus; he plunged a knife into her, twisting it brutally, then reached in to draw out the tumour. He collapsed and could not remember the operation, but the woman recovered. The local doctor testified that the object Arigo had thrown in the sink was indeed a human tumour.

After this he opened a primitive clinic in his native Congon Las do Campo, Brazil; he would accept neither money nor gifts for his work, and saw an average of three hundred people a day. During the 1950s and early 1960s the authorities turned a blind eye to his unorthodox activities, for the public were very much on his side, but in 1965 he was arrested for practising medicine illegally and sentenced to eighteen months' imprisonment – although he was regularly let out to heal the sick!

The Roman Catholic Judge Filippe Immesi went to see Arigo perform his legendary operations for himself; a woman with cataracts in both eyes was cured by Arigo unceremoniously plunging nail scissors into her eyes and removing the cataracts. After he had said a prayer some mysterious liquid appeared on a piece of cotton wool, with which he wiped her eyes. He had used neither anaesthetic nor antiseptic – yet she felt no pain or fear, and was completely cured. There were no after-effects or infection.

American researcher Andrija Puharich (who was to promote the talents of Uri Geller some years later) visited Arigo's 'surgery' and had a benign tumour removed from his arm in just five seconds. Filmed by a camera crew, Arigo slit open Puharich's arm with an unsterilised penknife, pressed on the tumour, which popped out, and wiped the knife on his shirt. Puharich felt nothing; there was little bleeding and no infection.

Sometimes Arigo merely prescribed drugs for his patients, but many of them were obsolete or even banned, and often he prescribed in dangerous amounts. Yet when the drugs were taken by his patients they made miraculous recoveries, even from the point of death.

Arigo always worked in trance, believing himself to be a channel for the discarnate Dr Adolphus Fritz, who died in 1918. (During the operations Arigo spoke with a distinctly German accent.) When shown a film of his work, Arigo fainted.

In 1970 he began to tell friends that he would die soon; he was killed in a car crash in January 1971, taking the secret of his miracle cures to the grave with him. Yet it is unlikely that he knew how they worked – to him it was simply God working through him.

SEE ALSO *Valentine Greatrakes*; *Healing*; *Matthew Manning*; *Carmine Mirabelli*; *Miracles of St Médard*; *Psychic surgery*; *Spiritism*; *Chico Xavier*.

Sai Baba, believed by many to be a living Hindu saint, who has been seen to raise the dead.

SAI BABA

Satyanarayana Raju was born on 23 November 1926, and is believed to be the reincarnation of Sai Baba, a Hindu holy man who had died in 1918. The new Sai Baba exhibited a gift for the miraculous early in life, regularly appearing to pluck sweets and flowers out of the air. When sceptics demanded that he prove his extraordinary identity he threw down a bunch of jasmine flowers, which as they fell spelt out 'Sai Baba'; and on a visit to the holy man's town of Shirdi, Satya recognised his followers.

Since 1939 Sai Baba has performed miracles that match any chronicled in the New Testament. Wearing a tight-sleeved shift, he will pluck so many objects out of thin air that he jokes about the 'Sai Stores'; most frequent are quantities of 'vibhuti', or holy ash, which has produced miracle cures when eaten, and religious medallions. Sai Baba has often produced crucifixes for Christians among his followers – at least one of them showed Christ with a broken nose, as does the Turin Shroud. (He reveres Christ as a master who taught peace and sacrificed himself for the world.)

He produces 'personalised' medals, with names and birth dates on them, and on several occasions has been witnessed to lead others to a stretch of sand where he will draw up objects, such as statuettes or even paranormally produced photographs of the gods, as if charming a snake. Lucas Ralli, of the Sathya Sai Baba Council of the United Kingdom says:

> ... my wife and I have ... witnessed dozens of the 'miracles' performed right under our noses. I have two rings which he materialized for me. At our last interview he materialized food (Indian sweetmeats) for the twenty-five people who were in the interview room. It was delicious and still warm (from wherever it had come!).

Dozens of people have been cured of serious illnesses by eating the holy ash, or by touching Sai Baba, or by merely being in his presence. On at least one occasion he has raised a dead man, who was already stinking with putrefaction, dark and cold. The sick man had gone to Sai Baba, who apparently laughed at him; the man's wife implored him to help. Sai Baba replied: 'Everything will be all right.' But the man – apparently – died, and again Sai Baba laughed. He eventually visited the house of mourning and stayed for a short while with the corpse. The holy man called the family in – and the dead man was sitting up and smiling.

Yet Sai Baba refers to all his miracles, whether raising the dead or apparently transmuting the base metal of holy medallions into gold (something that was also seen to occur in the 1980s at Medjugore during the visions of the Virgin), as 'small items'. His real purpose in this incarnation, he believes, is to bring peace and help avert global disaster. He promises to return in the twenty-first century as Prema Sai to further this cause, but there are those who believe that he is already a living avatar, a Hindu saint.

SEE ALSO *Apports*; *Healing*; *Miracles of the New Testament*; *Paranormal portraits*; *Psychokinesis*; *Reincarnation*; *Turin Shroud*; *Visions of the Virgin Mary*.

MATTHEW MANNING

Undoubtedly one of the most remarkable of modern British psychics is Matthew Manning, now a healer of international status. Born in 1955, he had a childhood relatively free from paranormal activity, although today he admits that his earliest memories concern objects spontaneously moving around him. It was only in 1967, when his father found a Georgian silver tankard inexplicably in the middle of the dining room floor, that Matthew became the focus for some of the most persistent and provocative poltergeist activity on record.

For twelve weeks objects regularly appeared to move by themselves in the Mannings' Cambridgeshire home. Matthew's architect father Derek was in no doubt that something paranormal was happening and Dr A. R. G. Owen, a Fellow of Trinity College, Cambridge, and also an experienced psychical researcher, was called in to investigate.

After a brief respite the activity resumed – with a vengeance. Matthew was thrown out of bed, and the bedclothes after him; that night the dining room 'looked as if a bomb had hit it'; lights turned themselves on and scribbled writing appeared on walls, including the phrase: 'Matthew beware'. Matthew noticed that the phenomena divided roughly into three groups:

> ... the first was purely disruptive and annoying, the second was concerned with symmetry and balance (where strange assortments of objects were found uncomfortably balanced on each other), and the third was a demonstration of noisy and boisterous movement, designed it seemed, to attract spectators.

All this happened during the Easter holidays of 1971; on Matthew's return to boarding school it seemed as if the poltergeist had gone with him.

Objects flew about and the beds were found piled up; one boy who was discovered to be faking some of the effects in order to have Matthew blamed was plagued by genuine phenomena for days afterwards. Although many of the boys were frightened by the poltergeist, and some were sceptical (not having witnessed it personally), most of them found it amusing – something that Matthew, with hindsight, believes saved him from worse attacks.

Dr Owen wrote to Matthew's beleaguered headmaster:

> I investigated a minor outbreak of poltergeist phenomena at Mr. Manning's home a few years back. I believed that they were not due to trickery, but real phenomena. . . . These events, though rare, do occur more often than is supposed. . . . They are due to unusual physical forces which people sometimes develop without being aware of. . . .

At this time Matthew discovered other psychic gifts, which undoubtedly diffused some of the disruptive energy. He had out-of-the-body experiences (OOBEs), and found he had a natural talent for automatic drawing, painting and writing – all of which phenomena are believed by Spiritualists to be manifestations of the spirits of the dead.

Today Matthew is extremely cautious about ascribing these phenomena to any particular source. Many of them, he feels, came from his unconscious mind, but some seem to have come from somewhere 'outside' – particularly the writing in Russian and Arabic and perhaps notes apparently signed by post-war Labour minister Stafford Cripps (of whom Matthew had never consciously heard) and by philosopher Bertrand Russell (Matthew thought his name was 'Bertram'). When he allowed his hand to be drawn towards the paintbox extraordinary works of art ensued, in wildly different styles – such as those of Dürer, Beardsley and Picasso, many of which were signed as such.

The automatic art may have stopped the disruptive poltergeist energy, but Matthew's psychic field was widening. While at home for a weekend he deliberately tried to 'project' himself into the past; he held a conversation with Henrietta Webbe, who had lived in the house in the seventeenth century, and subsequently visited it as it had been in her

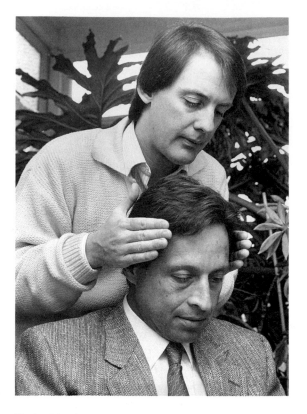

Healer Matthew Manning at work. He believes that almost anyone can learn to be a healer.

day. But the most complex timeslip involved the autocratic Robert Webbe, the first owner of the house, who seemed to inhabit a twilight world, sometimes knowing he was dead, but sometimes convinced that Matthew and his family were interlopers in the seventeenth-century house.

Gradually Matthew and Robert Webbe developed a poignant relationship through automatic writing and, occasionally, Webbe even showed himself as he was in life. On one occasion over three hundred signatures – apparently of the seventeenth-century local villagers – materialised on Matthew's bedroom wall while no one was in the room.

In 1973, when Israeli psychic Uri Geller began to make an impact on British television, Matthew discovered that he, too, could bend metal, leading to his being dubbed 'Britain's answer to Uri Geller'. However, the life of an international psychic super star was not for Matthew, who began to attract attention for his ability to influence living matter.

Working with a variety of scientists in the United States, Matthew proved that he could, for example, influence the electrical skin resistance of human beings by using his own method of concentration, visualisation and a kind of 'channelling' of some outside power. But the most significant of the American experiments were those conducted with professors Fred Lorenz and Loring Chapman in California, where it was shown that Matthew could transmit 'states of arousal or sedation', and that his brainwave patterns matched that of the subject completely.

Matthew showed Dr John Kmetz in San Antonio that, by laying his hands on or over a flask containing cancer cells, he could influence their rate of degeneration dramatically; on one occasion he increased their destruction, compared to that of a control sample, by 1200 per cent. Yet it was at this point that Matthew lost faith in scientists, for the more spectacular the result, the less likely they were to be convinced by it and the more likely they were to accuse him – and each other – of fraud.

In the late 1970s Matthew went off on the 'hippy trail' to India, where he failed to find a guru but instead had a life-changing mystical experience of the interconnectedness of all things. He came back determined to become a healer.

Since then he has built up an international reputation as a healer, although he is wary of labels. 'I give people permission to heal themselves,' he says. For about half a week he sees patients at the Matthew Manning Centre at Bury St Edmunds in Suffolk; the rest of the time he travels, passing on what he has learnt to others in healing workshops and through lectures. He compares learning to be a healer to learning to play the piano: 'I may be the equivalent of a concert pianist,' he says, 'but I can teach almost anyone to pick out a simple tune.'

He sees his work as improving the quality of living and, in some cases, helping people to die without pain or fear. But miracles do happen; one man who had suffered agonising and immobilising cluster headaches for over a year was completely cured by Matthew in less than a week. Faith appears to have little to do with it; sceptics, young children and animals respond equally well.

The medical profession have shown a grudging respect for his work, and invited him to speak to the Royal College of Surgeons because 'people are voting with their feet ... we have to know what people like Matthew Manning are doing'. Matthew recommends his patients to accept all available forms of therapy, orthodox or complementary. His greatest criticism of the medical establishment is that they tend to have a negative attitude that reinforces the patient's illness; much of his work is spent trying to reverse that attitude.

His aim now is to reach as many people as possible, especially the young, with his idea of global healing, which is based on unconditional love for all things. Although he began his healing career as an agnostic, he is now convinced that true healing comes from elsewhere, from 'the boys and girls upstairs'.

SEE ALSO *José Arigo*; *Creative visualisation*; *Uri Geller*; *Ghosts*; *Valentine Greatrakes*; *Healing*; *Metal bending*; *Out-of-the-body experiences*; *Philip experiment*; *Psychic music, art and literature*; *Timeslips*.

IV The Unpredictable World

Charles Fort ● Cosmic Joker ● Life imitates art ● Lexilinking ● Library angel ● Sentient machinery ● Fate ● Twins ● Curses ● Jinxes ● Spontaneous human combustion ● Mysterious disappearances ● Mysterious appearances ● Devil's footprints ● *Mary Celeste* **● Fishfalls ● Cryptozoology ● Bigfoots, almas and yeti ● Loch Ness monster ● Lake monsters ● Foaflore ● Werewolves ● Dragons ● Phantom hitch-hiker ● Explanations**

If the world is truly unpredictable then it is random and chaotic, and the so-called 'laws of nature' or even man's labelling of phenomena are redundant. But human beings seek to impose order on chaos, and if an event cannot be explained, then at least it may be labelled. In these small ways do we seek to tame the universe.

Occasionally, however, a true iconoclast arises whose thinking is so original, and whose condemnation of the accepted view of the world so utter, that he must be either a saint or a heretic. Charles Fort, 'father of anomalistics', was a quiet, bookish man whose idiosyncratic writings have provided a new view of reality for the twentieth century. Yet the great bulk of his work consisted of no more than facts – reports of anomalous phenomena – which, because they were rejected by the scientific establishment, he called 'damned data'. By their very nature, 'Fortean' phenomena are unlikely to be replicable and therefore escape the attentions of investigators, but these rogue facts of human existence provide researchers with an exciting and profoundly disturbing view of the real world . . .

In 1974 American Jack Angel sat watching television and had half an arm burnt off from within, and eleven years later Londoner Paul Hayes burst into flames as he walked through the streets at night. Both were survivors of the strangest fire – spontaneous human combustion – but many others perish in a similarly mysterious manner, in heat that is estimated at over 1650°C (3000°F) yet does not burn clothes or ignite nearby petrol, and that leaves a part of the body untouched. No one knows how many people die in this terrible way, for only one brave coroner has ever stated a death to be due to 'spontaneous combustion'. 'Death by misadventure' may be the verdict that obscures many SHC fatalities.

There appears to be no reason for the selection of the fire's victims, although attempts have been made to link the deaths to alcoholism (but some of the victims are babies), post-menopausal depression (but some of the victims are men) and karmic resonance (there is no data on this point). Some types of anomalous happenings do, however, seem to have only too much of a pattern.

When people of the same name share the same fate, or when jinxes harry families throughout the generations, there does seem to be a behind-the-scenes malevolent force, which may be called the Cosmic Joker. This childish jester, or implacable fate, once hurled a uniquely formed 'ice bomb' at the feet of a specialist in ice formations; rained eggs down on a school called Keep Hatch; and makes things seem as though they belong to Looking Glass Land, where nothing is as it appears. Here, just when life seems to revert to the rational, ordered world we think we know, it is immediately

Charles Fort, 1874–1932, the American 'father of anomalies', collector of 'damned data' – facts of experience that are rejected by the scientific establishment as being 'impossible'.

Cover of an issue of Britain's Fortean Times, *named after Charles Fort.*

upset again. When the elderly ladies who once perpetrated the Cottingley fairy hoax admitted their guilt no one was very surprised, yet there was a very surprising rider: the fairies had been faked because the women said they had often tried to photograph them but failed. Most reporters and commentators only noted the confession, not the reason for the hoax.

Charles Fort coined the term 'teleportation' for the (suggested) method by which objects, animals and people are moved paranormally from place to place. History is littered with cases of mysterious disappearances – such as that of the crew of the *Mary Celeste* – and equally abrupt appearances. Similarly the fish and frogs that regularly fall on an astonished world must come from somewhere by some means, and not, as the so-called 'experts' are fond of suggesting, via a tornado or whirlwind. If meteorological phenomena could be found that scoop up one particular species of rare frog and nothing else, then they deserve a mention here in any case.

The world is full of weird creatures, not all of them as archetypal as dragons or the Loch Ness monster. Some of them may be our everyday companions, such as a car, a telephone or a word processor – for such machines are beginning to reveal a disturbing sentience, and not all of their reaction to their owners are the stuff of human kindness.

CHARLES FORT

Charles Hoy Fort, iconoclastic philosopher and father of anomalistics, was born in 1874 in New York State, where he died in 1932. A fanatical researcher, by the age of twenty-three he had accumulated twenty-five thousand notes on the apparent infallibility of science. Dissatisfied, he destroyed them and collected more, also writing two books entitled *X* and *Y*. The first suggested that Martians had colonised the Earth, and the second that a strange civilisation lived at the North Pole. Neither of these ideas was entirely serious. No publisher would take the books and they, too, were burnt.

A legacy enabled Fort to devote the rest of his life to research; he spent some months in the British Museum Library, but most of his energies centred around collecting and collating newspaper clippings of extraordinary incidents from around the world. The many reported phenomena that interested him included: spontaneous human combustion; unexplained 'falls' (showers) of fish, frogs, coloured sands and periwinkles; mysterious appearances and disappearances of people and objects; and out-of-place objects and animals. Fort coined the term 'teleportation' to describe the mysterious, and often apparently instantaneous, disappearance of an object or person from one location and its materialisation elsewhere. The term is now commonly used by science fiction writers and parapsychologists.

He published four books: *The Book of the Damned* (1919); *New Lands* (1923); *Lo!* (1931) and *Wild Talents* (1932). It was the first that was to make a lasting impact. 'The damned' were, according to Fort's philosophy, facts that refused to fit scientific models or find conventional explanations. He mistrusted dogmatic explanations, saying: 'One measures a circle beginning anywhere.' Fort's written style is complex; his views provocative – and deliberately contradictory. 'As with all clowns,' he wrote, 'underlying buffoonery is the desire to be taken seriously.' Of his many thought-provoking statements, 'I think we're property' has probably had the most impact. He mused: '. . . once upon a time, this earth was No-Man's Land, that other worlds explored and colonized here, and fought among themselves for possession, but now it's owned by something, all others warned off'.

A constant source of amusement to Fort was the tortuous explanations proffered by 'experts' – usually scientists – to account for weird phenomena. He repeated that science itself was not his enemy, but he was opposed to the dogmatic assertions of scientists and their readiness to attribute fraud to those connected with strange happenings.

In 1931 the eminent writer Theodore Dreiser and another novelist, Tiffany Thayer, organised the inaugural meeting of the Fortean Society, although Fort himself declined its presidency. Initially a success, the society became the platform for increasingly bizarre ideas and it, together with its magazine, *Doubt*, died with Thayer in 1959. However, with the coming of the flying saucers in 1947 and a surge of interest in anomalistics, Fort's ideas became increasingly relevant. Today Fortean periodicals include the *Journal of the International Fortean Organisation, Pursuit*, published by the Society for Investigation of the Unexplained, and the British-based *Fortean Times*.

Fort's belief in the interconnectedness of strange phenomena was way ahead of his time and remains even further beyond the paradigms of the scientific establishment. Few accepted researchers dare acknowledge Fort's overview or his direct challenge to the limits of 'natural laws' although Jung's ideal of the collective unconscious, and Rupert Sheldrake's theory of formative causation, are compatible with such an approach.

SEE ALSO *Apports; Balls of light; Bigfoots, almas and yeti; Black Monk of Pontefract; Boggle threshold; Cosmic Joker; Cryptozoology; CSICOP; Curses; Entity enigma; Explanations; Fishfalls; Formative causation; Jinxes; Jung and divination; Lake monsters; Life imitates art; Lightning calculators; Miracles of St Médard; Mysterious appearances; Mysterious disappearances; Paranormal portraits; Parapsychology; Prodigies; Seance-room phenomena; Society for Psychical Research; SORRAT; Spontaneous Human Combustion; Crop field circles; UFO paradox; Vampires; Werewolves; Witchcraft.*

COSMIC JOKER

The idea of the Trickster, the archetypal destroyer of men's fortunes and souls, is present in many ancient cultures. Often indistinguishable from the Devil, he amuses himself by changing shape and form and toying with human fate. Charles Fort

One aspect of the Cosmic Joker – the Great God Pan, from whom the word 'panic' is derived.

wrote: 'We are being played with', and suggested that the controller of the revels was a cruel, bored child, a Cosmic Joker who uses us as pawns in his game. Certainly many examples of fate or synchronicity seem to attest to the malign influence of some organising intelligence.

Some researchers see the hand of the Joker in parapsychology, where the crucial video film of a poltergeist's activities is blank or mysteriously damaged. Recording equipment frequently malfunctions during ghost hunts, for example; it could be a side-effect of an electromagnetic disturbance caused by, or causing, the phenomenon – or it could be the perversity of the joker. The unreliability of most paranormal phenomena – the fickleness of their choice of subjects and the difficulty in replicating them to order – may well be something inherent in the nature of the paranormal. This may

itself be a 'joke' – for the experimenter effect ensures that paranormal phenomena perform for believers and not for sceptics.

Another aspect of the Joker's trickery is the apparently deliberate destruction of certain human beings through some form of continued harassment. Roy C. Sullivan, American park ranger, was struck by lightning seven times – each time more severely than before. He shot himself after the eighth bolt struck him.

Reputations are also the Joker's targets. Witnesses of UFOs are frequently sober, respectable citizens. The alien crew may give them some object, such as a pancake, said to be extraterrestrial in origin. It may mysteriously vanish before it can be investigated, or analysis may reveal that it is disappointingly mundane. Such a trick also finds its way into all manifestations of the entity enigma; the angel Moroni gave Mormon leader Joseph Smith the gold and brass plates which, after their hieroglyphics had been translated with angelic help, became known as the *Book of Mormon*. Unfortunately the angel took the plates away before they could be displayed to the world. In this way fairy gold traditionally vanishes leaving its owner poorer than before, both materially and in the eyes of the world. Similarly, will o' the wisps and mermaids lure the unwary to their doom. The hand of the Joker may be seen in the vexed world of psychical research, where the most blatant-seeming frauds may hide authentic phenomena. The case of Katie King and the materialisations of Helen Duncan appear on the surface to be obvious fakes, yet both ladies have their supporters – not merely among the lunatic fringe – and may not be dismissed lightly. Objective research is further complicated when apparent phenomena may be a mixture of the genuine and the fraudulent; Eusapia Palladino cheerfully admitted to cheating when entranced, and many a talented psychic has been known to eke out waning powers by sleight of hand.

The Joker creates false confessions that muddy the already murky waters of psychical research. The Fox sisters confessed to being frauds, yet the phenomena recorded during their early days appear to be genuine. The old ladies who, in their youth, claimed to have photographed fairies at Cottingley in Yorkshire, confessed to faking the pictures – yet the reason they did so was typical of the Joker's influence. They said they had not been able to photograph the fairies they had seen, so they perpetrated a hoax.

Confusion and despair may be seen to attract the Joker, who adds to them. There are cases of would-be suicides being overtaken by the unexplained phenomenon of spontaneous human combustion, as if the extreme emotions involved generated the fire, or as if they cried out to be crowned by an even more terrible fate.

Many UFO cults show another aspect of the Joker. The contactee around whom the quasireligious organisation revolves is often given predictions about global or local events which prove to be true. Having gained a devoted following, however, the leader is vouchsafed a prophecy of the end of the world; the cult is required to sell its property and camp on hilltops to await their salvation in the shape of alien spaceships. The deadline passes and the aliens do not appear.

It may seem whimsical to presuppose the existence of the Cosmic Joker, even as an archetype, but history attests his power, especially among those who 'tempt providence'. After all, Goliath was believed to be unbeatable and the *Titanic* unsinkable . . . .

SEE ALSO *Angels; Church of Jesus Christ of Latter Day Saints (Mormons); Cottingley fairies; CSICOP; Curses; The Devil; Helen Duncan; Entity enigma; Experimenter effect; Explanations; Fairies; Charles Fort; Jinxes; Katie King; Lexilinking; Library angel; Life imitates art; Mysterious appearances; Mysterious disappearances; Eusapia Palladino; Spontaneous human combustion; UFO paradox; Visions of the Virgin Mary.*

LIFE IMITATES ART

Forteans have long noted the propensity for life to imitate art, rather than vice versa. Some cases of this phenomenon are particularly striking, giving added credence to Charles Fort's idea that 'we are being played with' by a Cosmic Joker.

The actor originally cast to play John Lennon in the BBC documentary *A Day in the Life* was dismissed when Yoko Ono discovered his real name was Mark Chapman, the name of Lennon's assassin. Chapman had, in fact, changed his name to Lindsay in the year Lennon was murdered.

In 1966 writer Pearl Binder and two friends sketched out the opening of a novel together. Ms Binder proposed that it should be set in the near future, when the population explosion would mean that there were refugee camps in Hyde Park. A professor whom they called 'Horvath-Nadoly' would be one of those camping out there. A few days later the writers discovered that a foreign tramp had been found wandering in Hyde Park. His name was Horvath-Nadoly. Ms Binder said 'We felt we had invented this tramp, and in the process brought him to life, and a pretty awful life.'

Just one of film producer Irwin Allen's disaster movies that had an uncanny knack of heralding real tragedies. This film was premiered at the same time as a major fire broke out in a tower block in Brazil.

In 1979 the star of the film *Les Chiens*, about the dangers of keeping German shepherd dogs, was badly savaged by one outside a restaurant; an actress who was up for the lead in a play called *Hammer* was beaten to death by the playwright with a sledgehammer; while film producer Irwin Allen seems to have an unfortunate affinity with fate. As the *Fortean Times* listed: 'When his *Poseidon Adventure* opened, the *Queen Elizabeth* capsized. When his *Towering Inferno* premièred, three skyscrapers caught fire in Brazil. And his film about a volcanic eruption – *When Time Ran Out* – coincided with the Mount St Helens eruption.'

Sometimes the phenomenon of life following art ensures personal harassment, with the unwitting victim coming under suspicion from the authorities. In the lead-up to the D-Day landings, top-secret codewords were given as clues in *Daily Telegraph* crosswords. The authorities interrogated the man who had set the *Telegraph* crosswords for twenty years – schoolmaster Leonard Dawes – but eventually they had to admit that he was innocent and the extraordinary connection was 'just a coincidence'.

Concurrently with the actual events, the story of the kidnapping and brainwashing of heiress Patricia Hearst was told in detail by James Rusk in his novel *Black Abductor*. The writer was seized by the FBI but he knew nothing about the real-life abduction, believing sincerely that he had written complete fiction.

In 1979 a child drowned in the pond of Julie Christie's farmhouse. Six years before, the actress had starred in the film *Don't Look Now*, playing the mother of a drowned child. The police constable who gave evidence was called Frank Podmore, the same name as one of the early members of the Society for Psychical Research – who had been found drowned in a pond.

SEE ALSO *Autosuggestion; Cosmic Joker; Curses; Foaflore; Charles Fort; Jinxes; Karma; Lexilinking; Ritual magic; Witchcraft.*

LEXILINKING

One aspect of coincidence that implies the 'stage management' of a Cosmic Joker is that of lexilinking – the striking synchronisation of words, especially names. A simple example is the case of John Stott, who crashed his car in the south of England in 1985. The incident was investigated by WPC Tina Stott and recorded by desk sergeant Walter Stott.

The lexilinks can be complicated, involving other strands of synchronicity: in 1970 Eric Jansen, a Dutchman working in Yorkshire, took his English girlfriend for a weekend to the Lake District. He was homesick and spent much of the journey talking about Holland. On the way to Keswick a driver stopped to ask Jansen the way – he was Dutch, and his name was Eric Jansen. The only hotel open over the winter boasted a waitress from Jansen's home town; the only other guests were a Dutch family, one of whom was called Eric Jansen. Did all these people come together in this remote spot simply to alleviate one man's homesickness, or was there some karmic thread pulling them together, however briefly?

Magical adepts believe that to know the name of something is to have power over it; certainly similar names seem to trigger similar destinies in some cases. A famous example is the striking similarity of the doom of two ships – the *Titan* and the *Titanic*. The first was the brainchild of Morgan Robertson, whose novel of 1898, *The Wreck of the Titan*, or *Futility*, foreshadowed in bizarre detail the fate of the second in 1912. Professor Ian Stevenson, an American parapsychologist, believes that the events in the novel show the author's unconscious foreknowledge of the sinking of the *Titanic*. He notes:

> I think we can consider the correspondence either exact or impressive on the following ten points: name of ship; myth of unsinkability; collision with iceberg; sinking in month of April; displacement tonnage; length of ship; speed of ship at impact; number of propellers; number of lifeboats; enormous loss of life.

Yet a corollary to this lexilink had a fortunate outcome. Only months after the *Titanic* sank, a tramp steamer was ploughing through the foggy Atlantic with only a young boy on watch. It came into his mind that it had been thereabouts that the *Titanic* had met its doom, and he was suddenly terrified by the thought of the name of his ship – the *Titanian*. Panic-stricken, he sounded the warning. The ship stopped, just in time: a huge iceberg loomed out of the fog directly in their path. The *Titanian* was saved.

The fact remains that not all Eric Jansens or ships with the same name share the same fate; obviously other factors bring the synchronicity into play. It may be that certain names are linked through a kind of habit, a re-enactment of fate through a form of morphic resonance – or it may be that the Cosmic Joker merely enjoys playing with words.

SEE ALSO *Boggle threshold; Cosmic Joker; Curses; Fate; Formative causation; Charles Fort; Jinxes; Karma; Library angel; Life imitates art; Ritual magic.*

LIBRARY ANGEL

The Jungian 'acausal connecting principle' that theoretically creates coincidences is so well known to writers and researchers that it has earned itself the title of 'the library angel' (a term coined by writer Colin Wilson). Urgently needed and elusive reference material is found under the most unpromising circumstances, or the right book may actually fall open at the right page at the student's feet, if his or her need is great enough. The library angel tends to function best when a deadline approaches, suggesting that it is called into being in a similar way to the eleventh-hour syndrome, or that it may be generated by the psi-mediated instrumental response, both of which appear to be due to the workings of the individual's unconscious mind.

Instances of the library angel at work may be complex. American psychologist Dr Lawrence LeShan had a mysterious brush with this kind of synchronicity in 1967. He was having lunch with Dr Nina Ridenour to discuss the draft of his book on mysticism when she advised him to read Byng's *The Vision of Asia*. Almost immediately he searched for the book in two eminent libraries, but without success. On his way home he took an unaccustomed route and found a book lying on the ground. It was *The Vision of Asia* by L. A. Cranmer-Byng. LeShan telephoned Dr Ridenour, saying: 'I have a funny story to tell you about the book you recommended.'

'Which book?' she replied. On being reminded of *The Vision of Asia*, Dr Ridenour was adamant: 'I have never heard of it!'

SEE ALSO *ESP; Fate; Eleventh-hour syndrome; Inspiration in dreams; Left and right brain; Psi-mediated instrumental response; Remote viewing; Telepathy.*

Images of the Devil mostly stem from early Christian ideas. He was, they believed, originally Lucifer, Son of the Morning, whose rebellion against God had him flung out of Heaven. Thereafter he lurked on the earth, seeking to pervert the ways of God and lead men into temptation. At the time of the witchcraft hysteria he was perceived as a monstrous goat, which is often reflected in the design of modern Tarot packs (left), or a great vampire bat (centre). He is sometimes still expressed as a dragon, who is – as in the biblical Book of Revelations – conquered by that other great archangel, St Michael (right). Today he is generally thought of as the archetypal image of man's baser desires rather than as a personification of evil. Yet there are some who believe that this weaker concept in itself is a measure of his influence over men.

The Mowing Devil, from a 1678 woodcut – an early version of the crop field circle?

Although angels appeared in the Old Testament merely as 'messengers' from God, it was only in the nineteenth century that they became large, sexless, winged creatures whose function seemed to be sentimental, rather than informative. Stone angels adorn tombstones (above left and above right) and dead babies were commonly supposed to become smaller versions with cute little wings (left). Yet if angels exist as some form of personalised channel of other-worldly information, these days they are more likely to look like ufonauts, or even the man in the street (opposite).

Fairies have a long history of guileful dealings with mankind. They take many shapes (left), often seducing men and leading them, literally, astray into a fairy kingdom in which ten of their years may be a hundred of ours. Elves (right) and gnomes, creatures of the woodland and underground, have often sought to waylay mankind for their own ends. Fairy gold is notoriously elusive, and fairy promises always deceptive, yet fairies remain ever entrancing and just out of our reach.

The Kennedy family, a singularly successful dynasty in terms of worldly achievements, was also, it seems, doomed to a series of inexplicable tragedies. Not only were President John F. Kennedy and his brother Senator Robert Kennedy killed by assassins, but other members of the family fell prey to accident and illness to an unusual extent. Were they in some way jinxed by fate?

Lord Carnarvon discovers the tomb of the boy king, Tutankhamun, in the Valley of the Kings in 1923. Legend has it that the curse put on the tomb by the ancient Egyptian priests fell with full force upon the archaeologist whose death, shortly after the opening of the tomb, remains largely unexplained. Other accidents and deaths associated with those who were connected with the tomb have been reported, although not everyone involved in mounting its exhibitions have been struck down.

SENTIENT MACHINERY

There is a growing body of evidence to indicate that machines may temporarily show signs of intelligence, or 'behave' in ways that reveal a distinct psychokinetic relationship with human beings. In 1978 seventy-five-year-old Lloyd B. Wihide from Keymar, Maryland was pinned to the ground by a 300 kilogram tractor wheel. The pain was agonising, and he pleaded for instant death, saying: 'Please God, release me.' At that moment the tractor moved forward – uphill. Rescuers commented that a dozen men could not have moved the tractor off the man. Coincidence may be ruled out, as heavy machines do not move uphill when left to their own devices. Wihide was in no doubt that his deliverance was due to divine intervention, whereas parapsychologists might invoke the phenomenon of psi-mediated instrumental response (PMIR) where machinery reacts psychokinetically to the urgent needs of human beings.

Some machines are intended to show intelligence, or at least to be efficient at mimicking human thought processes, yet even these can be interfered with through PK. Israeli psychic Uri Geller has on separate occasions erased computer discs, stopped a computer tape and wiped out a pattern on a magnetic program card by the power of his mind alone. Sceptics search for rational explanations, but apart from collusion and fraud there remains only the

The ancient enemies of BBC Television's Dr Who, the Daleks, are seen gathering their powers for another assault on all decent lifeforms. But can machines take on an autonomy? Can our telephones, televisions and computers develop a life of their own?

conclusion that the electromagnetic force generated by Geller's mind is more powerful than that of the computers.

Experiments have been designed to explore the relationship between man and machine. In 1950 the mathematician Turing devised a method of determining whether or not machines can think, an update of 'the imitation game'. A woman (a man in the original game) and a machine are placed in separate rooms, connected via a printer with a person whose task it is to ask questions of each and to analyse the responses in order to work out which is the woman. If the machine manages to convince the examiner that it is a living, breathing woman, it will have shown intelligence – in other words it will have made that leap of perception of what it feels like to be a woman rather than just trotting out preprogrammed responses. This perception requires a sense of cause and effect, of lateral thinking, rather than a conditioned response.

The argument generally given for machines being unable to achieve this flash of intuition is that they are soulless automata functioning homogeneously rather than creatures split into mind and body. This invisible, intangible mind or soul, this ghost in the machine, separates man from computers and makes him an intelligent being. At a neural level, however, the human brain and the computer function alike, though the human is more likely to show emotion – to get excited or bored by mathematical problems, for instance – than a computer.

A computer designed by scientists at Imperial College, University of London, to imitate the human brain seems to have decided to go on strike rather than get bored. The 'neural net' was composed of a large number of interconnected electronic cells – like a human brain in concept – and was designed to help throw light on how babies learn to communicate. One theory which the machine was testing is that babies babble nonsense until they get a response from their parents telling them that they have hit on something worth storing and repeating. The machine had picked up a crude vocabulary, but then the problems arose. Michael Gera, one of the scientists, said: 'The task basically wasn't taxing enough and it just decided not to do it. In human terms, it had an attack of boredom.'

A less cut and dried case of a computer with a mind of its own was reported in the *Daily Mail* on 26 May 1988. Staff at a Stockport office contacted *Personal Computer* magazine, who video recorded their rogue computer for three months. The Amstrad, which had previously moaned and generated spurious characters, was shown to crackle, light up and then start flashing words on the screen. The video also showed that it was not plugged in.

IBM scientists at the Yorktown Heights laboratory in the USA, however, blame this sort of phenomenon on cosmic rays. The diminishing size of computer circuits and their increasing sensitivity to low-power signals make them more vulnerable to interference from outer space. These 'cosmic glitches' and the more localised phenomenon of 'electronic fog' are responsible for other, until recently unexplained, phenomena. Robots in Japan have killed ten times in the last nine years, and in six cases stray electromagnetic waves – from antennae, personal computers and arcade games, among other sources – are suspected.

In the early 1980s Ken Webster, a British teacher, suffered a poltergeist attack in his northern cottage. During the course of the disturbance mysterious messages appeared on the screen of his word processor and corresponding files were found to have been opened for them. This correspondence was revealed to be the work of several discarnates, including a group from the future – truly ghosts in the machine?

There is also the possibility of long-distance interference from the machines themselves. Proponents of psychokinesis claim that the human mind can influence events at a distance, consciously or otherwise: poltergeist activity generally stems from prepubescent children quite unconscious of the havoc they wreak. There is no reason why machines should not have the same abilities.

Charles Benson, an Irishman living in Norwich, was telephoning a friend in London when, according to *Weekend* of 7–13 March 1984, a crossed line linked him with his brother in Australia. They had lost contact shortly after leaving Ireland in 1921, and each had presumed the other dead. The odds given for this were the standard to one offered for any out-of-the-ordinary event. It conjures up the science fiction image of a sentient telephone network connecting one not with the person one was trying to call, but with the person one should have been calling.

Recent Fortean Foaflore includes the tale of a radio beacon, stolen from a North Sea oil rig and hidden in a wardrobe. It started transmitting 'Mayday' calls which were picked up by foreign satellites, and was only discovered after a major land and sea search. Perhaps it just wanted to be found.

Humans have always personified their tools and imagined some life force to live in them. The concept of sentient machinery, at least for the present, seems to lie more in our endowing machines with faculties that mirror or mimic our own minds – or even have a life/consciousness of their own – than in reality. But this may not necessarily remain so. Humanity's development has taken place over thousands of years, and is limited by genetic factors. Computers are only in their infancy; there is no limit to the capacity that machines can reach, so no limit on artificial 'brain' size in the future. Until then, though, sentient machinery is more a human reflection on reality than evidence of complex machine behavioural psychology.

SEE ALSO *Eleventh-hour syndrome; Foaflore; Formative causation; Library angel; Philip experiment; Psi-mediated instrumental response; Psychokinesis; SORRAT; Telephone calls from the dead.*

FATE

Fate is generally taken to mean a destiny against which we are powerless, and it recurs as a potent factor in many areas of the paranormal. In prediction one casts runes or horoscopes, traditionally to learn one's fate – in the latter it seems dependent upon a predestined path set in motion at the moment of birth. In prophecy one sees a future of global and religious significance, laid out as if already a fact. Christians believe that the coming of Christ was clearly prophesied in the Old Testa-

ment, and that it fulfilled its promise down to the last detail. Modern end times cults take the biblical prophecy of the battle of Armageddon literally.

Genetic predispositions obviously account for much of our 'fate', but it hardly seems an adequate explanation for the parallel lives of identical twins who have been separated at birth and reared in different cultures. Some even marry people with the same names, have the same hobbies and pets, suffer redundancies and receive windfalls at the same time. It seems that the link between identical twins extends beyond the mundane in a kind of morphogenetic capsule.

The lives and violent deaths of Presidents Lincoln and Kennedy have been found to show no fewer than seventeen marked synchronicities, given here in full:

1. Lincoln was elected president in 1860 and Kennedy in 1960.
2. Both men were involved in civil rights.
3. Both were assassinated on a Friday and in the presence of their wives.
4. Both were shot in the head, from behind.
5. Both their successors were called Johnson, were Southern Democrats and in the Senate.

Howard Carter removing the consecrating oils that had been poured over the innermost coffin of the boy king, Tutankhamun. Merely an academic investigation to him, it was nevertheless seen as an act of desecration, and the tragedies that soon befell Carter's party were widely believed to be the work of an ancient curse.

The lives and deaths of Presidents Abraham Lincoln and John F. Kennedy seem horrifyingly linked, even down to the number of letters in the names of their respective assassins, and the fact that Lincoln's secretary was called Kennedy, and Kennedy's secretary was called Lincoln. Is there, after all, a Cosmic Joker who amuses himself by aligning our destinies with those of others?

6. Andrew Johnson was born in 1808 and Lyndon B. Johnson in 1908.

7. The assassins, John Wilkes Booth and Lee Harvey Oswald, were born in 1839 and 1939 respectively.

8. Booth and Oswald were both Southerners favouring unpopular ideas.

9. Lincoln was killed in Ford's Theater, Kennedy in a Ford automobile.

10. Both Presidents had a son die while they were in the White House.

11. Lincoln's secretary, whose first name was John, advised him not to go to the theatre. Kennedy's secretary, whose name was Lincoln, advised against the trip to Dallas.

12. Booth shot Lincoln in a theatre and ran to a warehouse. Oswald shot Kennedy from a warehouse and ran to a theatre.

13. The names Lincoln and Kennedy each contain seven letters.

14. The names John Wilkes Booth and Lee Harvey Oswald each contain fifteen letters.

15. Both assassins were killed before coming to trial.

16. The names Andrew Johnson and Lyndon Johnson each contain thirteen letters.

17. The first public proposal that Lincoln be a Presidential candidate endorsed a John Kennedy as his running mate.

Academic discussion of synchronicity inevitably includes the theory that apparent links are imposed on a random universe by the observer, oneself. But when the hand of fate deals the cards it is difficult to escape the notion of divine retribution, or the malign influence of the Cosmic Joker.

TWINS

Twins are of two distinct types: fraternal or dizygotic twins, formed from two fertilised eggs (zygotes) at the same time; and identical or monozygotic twins, formed from the cleavage of a single fertilised egg. Fraternal twins are normally no more alike than siblings born years apart, and may be different sexes. Identical twins are always of the same sex and, having the same gene pattern, resemble each other – especially in the early stages of life – in great detail, although, curiously enough, not to the extent of having matching fingerprints.

That twins of both types manifest telepathic links, for example, in having an impulse to telephone each other or to express spontaneously the same thought at the same time – is commonplace. Even more mysterious, however, is their occasional, and well-documented ability to experience pain or distress simultaneously.

In one case, in July 1948, Alice Lambe was sitting quietly at home in Springfield, Illinois, when she was thrown off her chair by an enormous unseen blow on the left side of her body. It was accompanied by a sharp pain and followed by a feeling of shock. At that precise moment, 110 kilometres away, her identical twin, Dianne, was thrown across the carriage as the train she was travelling in was derailed. Later it was found that she had

Three hundred pairs of twins, many of whom had been separated since birth, met for The Frost Programme *on British television in January 1968. Many of the separated twins had led astonishingly parallel lives, even to the extent of marrying women with the same names and wearing the same number of rings on the same fingers. Genetic programming cannot explain such synchronicities, but perhaps the old idea of an inescapable Fate can do so.*

two fractured ribs and severe concussion. When her sister complained of severe pain for some days after the incident she was X-rayed and found to have fractured two ribs in the same place as Dianne.

In another, tragic, case, reported in the Australian magazine *Truth* by Mrs Joyce Crominski, one of her identical twin sisters, Peg, died on the way to hospital as the result of a car accident in which the steering wheel penetrated her chest. At the moment of the accident her twin, Helen, awoke, screaming in her bed at home. When she indicated a severe pain in her chest her parents called an ambulance, but she too died on the way to hospital.

Identical twins, and especially those reared apart, have been much studied for the light they shed on the relative effects of genetic inheritance and environmental factors. But twin studies, especially those conducted by Professor Tom Bouchard at the University of Minnesota, have also thrown up much more mysterious data.

One of the most famous cases is that of the identical 'Jim' twins, born in 1939 in Piqua, Ohio, and put out to adoption when they were four weeks old. Ernest and Sarah Springer took one of the boys and named him Jim. They believed that his twin had died at birth, but the other boy had in fact survived, and was adopted by Jess and Lucille Lewis who also chose for him the name Jim.

Jim Lewis always knew intuitively that he had an identical twin brother, and in 1979 he set out to find him. With the help of the court that had arranged their adoption the two men, now aged thirty-nine, met at last in Jim Springer's home in Dayton, Ohio. Their rapport was instant, but the coincidences in their lives that emerged as they talked are truly astonishing. Here are just some of them:

1. Both had married women called Linda, and then divorced and married women called Betty.
2. Lewis had named his first son James Alan; Springer called his James Allan.
3. Both had dogs they named Troy.
4. Both had worked for a hamburger chain and in filling stations; both had been part-time deputy sheriffs.
5. Both drove Chevrolets, drank the same beer and chain-smoked the same brand of cigarettes.
6. Both took their families on holiday to the same small beach near St Petersburg, Florida.
7. Both bit their fingernails to the quick.
8. Both put on 4 kilos in weight when in their teens and both lost it later.
9. Both like doing woodwork in their basement workshops, enjoy stock-car racing and dislike baseball.
10. Both have had vasectomies.
11. Both had had minor heart attacks and suffered from migraines and haemorrhoids.

The case of the 'Jim' twins is remarkable, but by no means unique. Mrs Bridget Harrison of Leicester and Mrs Dorothy Lowe of Burnley, Lancashire, are also twins who met in 1979 for the first time since their birth in 1943. Their lives showed many correspondences like those of the 'Jims' – both stopped piano lessons at the same stage; both had cats called Tiger; one named her son Richard Andrew, the other Andrew Richard, to give but a few of many examples. But the most striking correspondence was that both had kept a diary for one year only – 1960. Both chose the same make and colour of book for the purpose, and the days they filled in and the days they left blank matched exactly. When they met Professor Bouchard at Minneapolis airport in 1979 he noticed that both wore seven rings, with two bracelets on one wrist and a watch and bracelet on the other.

These, and many other examples of separated identical twins collected by Professor Bouchard and others, seem to indicate something far less straightforward than the possible genetic determination of behavioural choices. If identical twins break their legs, or have their handbags stolen, at the same time in different locations (both recorded cases), if they choose the same names for their children or their pets, is that the result of their genes? Or is it rather that twin studies have merely revealed patterns of synchronicity that affect all our lives?

SEE ALSO *Cosmic Joker; Curses; Fate; Formative causation; Charles Fort; Lexilinking; Life imitates art.*

CURSES

Curses are generally associated with primitive cultures or rural witchcraft, yet the mechanism that seems to be behind them is an integral part of Western culture. Any doctor, for example, who declares to a patient that he, the sufferer, has a certain number of months to live is pronouncing a curse – literally a death sentence. Many patients obediently die on the given 'deadline'. Similarly, most ritual curses require the victim to know they have been laid against him. His will becomes paralysed and he dies. Even sceptics have been adversely affected by curses, indicating that, on some atavistic level, sophisticated people too have little or no defence against them.

In 1971 Robert Heinl, a retired colonel in the US Marine Corps, co-wrote with his wife a book about the Haitian dictator Papa Doc Duvalier. Duvalier's widow ritually cursed the book, much to the amusement of the Heinls – but things began to go badly wrong for them. The manuscript was lost, turning up, when it was too late, in a locked room in the publishers' offices. A copy of the manuscript was despatched to the printers, where the binding machine immediately broke down. A journalist from the *Washington Post* who was due to interview the authors fell violently ill with appendicitis. Colonel Heinl hurt his leg on a lecture platform, then he was badly bitten by a dog. Finally, in 1979, the Heinls went on holiday to St Barthelémy, an island near Haiti; the colonel dropped dead. Mrs Heinl said: 'There is a belief that the closer you get to Haiti, the more powerful the magic becomes.' Voodoo, the magic of Haiti, is notorious for its efficacy; perhaps the Heinls, who knew a great deal about it, were subconsciously believers and obligingly fulfilled Madame Duvalier's curse?

Curses made by those about to die seem to have heightened power. One of the alleged Salem witches, standing on the scaffold, told her persecutor that he would 'drink blood' – he was to die of a haemorrhage, choking on his blood.

Inanimate objects are often associated with curses. The skull, said to be that of a North African woman, that was rescued from the sunken payship of the Spanish Armada off the coast of Scotland had dramatic effects on those who touched it. It was recovered in 1950 by Royal Navy diver Lieutenant Commander 'Buster' Crabbe, who was to go missing – presumed dead – under mysterious circumstances some time later. The skull became the property of the Western Isles Hotel, Tobermory, where the barman accidentally knocked it to the ground. That day he fell and cracked his own skull. In 1970 the new owner of the hotel, Richard Forrester, tried to drill a hole in the skull so it could be hung as a grisly *objet d'art* in the bar. The bit on his electric drill bent at an angle of 45 degrees as soon as it entered the skull, and Forrester suffered immobilising head pains for two days. Anyone else who touched the skull immediately developed agonising pains in the head.

Stones taken from traditional holy sites exert a powerful destructive influence on their owners. In 1977 the Loffert family from New York State, on holiday in Hawaii, took some stones from the Mauna Loa volcano despite warnings from the locals that this would anger the goddess Pele. Shortly after the Lofferts returned home the volcano erupted, and an extraordinary series of disasters plagued the family. These events continued even after the stones had been returned to the island – it transpired that one of the family had secretly kept three. When these also had been returned, the curse seemed to lift.

Not everyone ignores warnings of curses; in 1981 town councillors in King's Lynn, Norfolk, refused to move an eighteenth-century stone landmark, even though it was unsafe and a target for vandals. It bore the Latin inscription: 'Whoever shall remove or have removed this monument let him die the last of his line.' One wonders what befell the vandals who desecrated it.

Those who disturb tombs are notoriously open to inexplicable doom. Shakespeare's resting place is protected by a curse in verse, but the most famous tomb curse is that of the Egyptian boy king Tutankhamun. In 1923 British archaeologists Howard Carter and Lord Carnarvon discovered the tomb, with all its golden treasures unplundered, after years of searching for it. The Egyptian workers believed that this success was due to Carter's purchase of a pet canary; shortly after the momentous discovery a visiting American archaeologist, James Brested, heard a loud, 'almost human' cry from behind Carter's residence. The canary had been killed by a king cobra – the symbol of the boy king – and this was widely taken as a sign that the dead pharaoh was avenging himself for the desecration of his tomb. Brested, despite his Western cynicism, wrote of the bird's death: 'There was almost universal concern that something terrible would happen.' Within weeks Lord Carnarvon fell prey to the infection resulting from an insect bite; he died of pneumonia, aged fifty-three. At precisely the same time as his death, all the lights in Cairo inexplicably went out – and back home, Carnarvon's dog howled and fell dead.

'The mummy's curse' has been a popular target for sceptics and debunkers, but apparently its baleful influence continues. In 1979 George LaBrash suffered a stroke while guarding the pharaoh's mask while it was on exhibition in San Francisco. He, at least, believed his illness to be the direct result of contact with the curse, for he sued the authorities for disability pay on the grounds that the stroke was a 'job-related injury'. He lost the case. But, as sceptics delight in pointing out, hundreds of people have survived transporting, guarding or maintaining the treasures of Tutankhamun, and thousands have viewed them without ensuing disaster.

Some intended victims of curses have survived them, such as Lance Sieveking, journalist and father of *Fortean Times* Co-Editor Paul Sieveking. In 1928 he met the magickal adept Aleister Crowley, who cast his horoscope for him. A number of the predictions came true, but Crowley's afterthought did not. He had written: 'By the way, you will oblige me personally by dying at the age of forty-five.' Sieveking senior, then thirty-two, lived another forty-three years.

There are many who believe that the ability to override even the most terrifying curse, or the propensity to suffer from one, depends upon an individual's karmic inheritance – perhaps upon his previous relationship with the person who put the curse on him. All those who believe in karma and reincarnation, however, agree that one must never wish ill on anyone, for the curse will rebound many times over, either in this life or in future incarnations.

Folklorist Margaret Bruce of County Durham in the north of England believes that the traditional method of cursing by sticking pins in a doll representing the victim is merely a childish way of saying 'I hate', and has little real power. However, sympathetic magic has a history of powerful results, even though many magicians, as occultist Dion Fortune said, are protected from any psychic backlash by their own ineptitude.

Hate is destructive, and it can be demonstrated to be tangible, like all emotions, in a simple exercise designed to awaken the intuitive side of the brain. One person, standing several feet away from his partner, thinks of someone he hates or loves, without saying which emotion he is feeling. The partner walks slowly towards him, eyes closed and palms open, and stops when he feels something different 'in the air'. Very powerful thoughts of hate can virtually knock someone over; certainly they can literally stop an individual in his tracks. But the negative emotions of hate and jealousy have been proved to cause a host of physical and psychosomatic ills in the 'sender'; it seems that hate is literally a poison and a contagion.

SEE ALSO *Autosuggestion; Creative visualisation; Aleister Crowley; Fate; Jinxes; Karma; Life imitates art; Mass hysteria; Possession; Reincarnation; Ritual magic; Sentient machinery; Tulpas; Witchcraft.*

JINXES

Whereas a curse is a conscious attempt by one individual to harm another, a jinx is an inexplicable run of bad luck that runs in families, attacks the same person repeatedly or seems to recur in a certain location. The family of United States President John F. Kennedy and the Guinness brewing dynasty both suffer from jinxes, curious mixtures of unforeseeable tragedies and – especially in the case of the Guinness family – suicides and scandals.

The American Kennedy family who provided the tragic President of the 1960s – and many more instances of apparent family jinx.

There often seems to be prescient malice in the patterning effect seen in jinxes. The Marquis of Chaumont loathed Tuesday so intensely that he had the word deleted from all his books and newspapers. For seventy-nine years he was ill every Tuesday, dying in 1780 – on a Tuesday. Psychologists suggest that the alleged 'jinx' in this case arose from the Marquis's pathological phobia about Tuesdays; autosuggestion made it a self-fulfilling prophecy.

No such explanation fits the doom that befell Roy C. Sullivan, a forest ranger in Shenandoah National Park, Virginia, who was struck by lightning five times with increasing severity. After his retirement – with the hope that a less open-air lifestyle would reduce the likelihood of being struck – Mr Sullivan was hit a further three times. The last time he was so badly burned that a witness thought at first that he was a charred log. However, he survived – and shot himself.

Sometimes ill luck seems to cling to 'carriers' who do not themselves suffer from it. The classic example is that of 'Typhoid Mary', a cook in New York in 1906 – wherever she went people went down with the dread disease. Although free of it herself, she was kept in hospital. When the epidemic died down she changed her name and, five years later, took a job as a cook in a maternity hospital. Twenty-five people contracted typhoid, two fatally.

There are several cases on record of nursemaids whose charges suffered terrible accidents or died mysteriously. Eighteen-year-old Christine Fallings of Florida left behind four dead children and three who narrowly escaped fate while in her care. Christine was never accused of causing the tragedies, which involved organic illnesses, such as meningitis, spontaneously attacking her charges. Perhaps significantly, Christine was an epileptic – some of the children also suffered inexplicably from convulsions. The unhappy nursemaid told a newspaper: 'Sometimes I wonder if I don't have some kind of spell over me when I get around young 'uns.'

Cases have been reported of unconscious arsonists, around whom fires break out, which are reminiscent of some aspects of poltergeist outbreaks. Similarly, there are increasing numbers of people whose very presence apparently causes electrical equipment, especially computers, to malfunction. Such examples of 'jinxes' may be the result of a psychokinetic interaction between man and machine, but does not explain Roy C. Sullivan's fateful relationship with lightning, nor the terrible end of the British man who, having had most of his face burnt off in an accident, died from AIDS – contracted from a transfusion of infected blood given him during a skin graft operation.

Accident black spots may not always be the result of poor road building. In the 1980s a stretch of road between Gracious Lane Bridge and Chipstead flyover near Sevenoaks in Kent saw nine deaths as a result of 'carbon copy' accidents, in which the drivers had inexplicably swerved across the central reservation. Mrs Babs Davidson, however, did not succumb to the jinx and lived to tell a tale that is highly suggestive. She was driving along the road in roughly the same place where the other accidents had happened when she saw an unfamiliar road mistily branching off to the right, which she felt 'a tremendous compulsion to take ... [I] forced myself to go on. I was very relieved when I found I had done the right thing ... ' The existence of a ghost road that lures travellers to their doom recalls traditional stories about goblins or will o' the wisps, elementals whose chief delight lies in deceiving mankind. Forteans often refer to this personified mischief as the Cosmic Joker.

It may be, however, that the secret of ill luck lies in the creation of a habit; succeeding generations of a dynasty who once suffered a great disaster are more likely to repeat the tragedy than others because it has become part of their morphogenetic field. According to Dr Rupert Sheldrake's theory of formative causation, once a group, or species, has done something – to behave, or even evolve, in a certain way – then future members

of that group find it easier to do the same. Jinxes may be an aspect of this far-ranging formation of habits.

SEE ALSO *Autosuggestion; Cosmic Joker; Curses; Electric people; Experimenter effect; Fate; Foaflore; Formative causation; Charles Fort; Ghosts; Karma; Lexilinking; Life imitates art;* Mary Celeste; *Psi-mediated instrumental response; Psychokinesis; Sentient machinery.*

SPONTANEOUS HUMAN COMBUSTION (SHC)

The phenomenon of spontaneous human combustion (SHC) is commonly believed to be merely a literary creation by Charles Dickens, who used it as a device to kill off the villain Krook in *Bleak House.* Dickens based all the details of this grisly death on carefully researched reports of real cases, but even so a casual reader may believe – and hope – that if the phenomenon is real, it is nevertheless rare. The evidence, however, points in the other direction.

The phenomenon appears to follow a pattern: typically, only part of the victim, such as a foot, is found whole, while the rest of the body is reduced to ash or even a viscous, foul-smelling oily substance. Sometimes the victim's clothing is only slightly scorched; occasionally the body is found burnt away inside clothes that are untouched by the fire. Similarly, the surroundings, although they may include highly flammable substances such as petrol or foam-filled cushions, show only minimal signs of contact with fire or great heat. Clearly SHC behaves like no ordinary fire, and death by SHC is no ordinary end.

A classic case is that of Mrs Mary Reeser of St Petersburg, Florida in 1951. The sixty-seven-year-old widow, who lived alone, had presumably retired to bed as usual on the night of 1 July. In the early hours of the next morning a neighbour, Mrs Carpenter, smelled burning which she believed originated with a faulty water pump. She turned it off and went back to bed. At 8 a.m. a telegraph boy arrived with a message for Mrs Reeser, who would not answer her doorbell. Waves of heat were being emitted from the door, and the doorknob itself was too hot to touch. With the help of two workmen Mrs Carpenter broke into the apartment and, as the police report was to read:

> Within a blackened circle about four feet in diameter were a number of coiled seat-springs and the remains of a human body [which] consisted of a charred liver attached to a piece of backbone, a skull shrunk to the size of a baseball, a foot encased in a black satin slipper but burned down to just above the ankle, and a small pile of blackened ashes.

The 'overstuffed easy chair' in which Mrs Reeser had been sitting had been burnt down to its

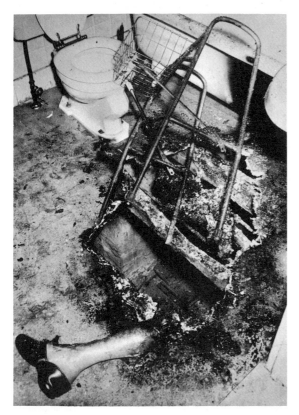

The remains of Dr John Thomas Bentley, a possible victim of spontaneous human combustion in Pennsylvania, 1966. Victims of SHC become a sludge of viscous soot – except for one limb, usually a foot. Fire does not usually behave so selectively.

springs, but apart from electrical fittings that had melted with the heat there were no other signs of fire in the apartment. The widow's destruction was so complete that at first the witnesses believed she was not in the building.

By a nice piece of synchronicity, a leading fire-death specialist, Dr Wilton Krogman, was on vacation in the area and was called in. He stated:

> I cannot conceive of such complete cremation without more burning of the apartment itself. In fact the apartment and everything in it should have been consumed. Never have I seen a human skull shrunk by intense heat. The opposite has always been true; the skulls have either abnormally swollen or have virtually exploded into hundreds of pieces ... I regard it as the most amazing thing I have ever seen. As I review it, the short hairs on my neck bristle with vague fear. Were I living in the Middle Ages, I'd mutter something about black magic.

As news of this strange death spread, suggestions as to how it came about flooded in. One of the most ingenious, which the authorities took seriously for some time, was that the widow had been kidnapped by enemies, taken elsewhere and murdered. Her body had then supposedly been cremated in some kind of super-heated furnace, the remains taken back to the apartment, the chair burnt and electrical fixtures melted – presumably the finishing touch was to heat the doorknob. Other people fell back on the idea of napalm or an 'atomic pill' – whatever that may be.

The conspiracy theorists became excited when the FBI were called in, but disappointingly the CIA were not involved and no Men in Black had been reported in the neighbourhood. Mrs Reeser's death remains a mystery.

In Britain every year 1–2 per cent of all fire deaths are officially listed as 'cause unknown'. It may be reasonable to assume that a high proportion (if not all) of these are the results of SHC. Yet this is only part of the picture; many fire deaths are given the verdict of 'death by misadventure', which satisfies the coroner's sense of propriety. There has been only one (known) case that was officially described as; 'death by spontaneous combustion'; the death of eighty-nine-year-old Mrs Margaret Hogan of Dublin in 1970. The coroner, Dr P. J. Bofin, stated:

> There is no doubt that the woman died from burning. The circumstances . . . are unusual, and would conform to what is called spontaneous combustion . . . it's simply a term carried on in forensic literature to describe a set of circumstances in which a person is burned to death without an obvious source of fire. . . .

Mrs Hogan had been reduced to a heap of ash, yet there had been no fire in the room. Dr Gavin Thurston, coroner for West London, stated the official, sceptics' case when he said: 'No such phenomenon as spontaneous combustion exists, or has ever existed.'

Usually the explanations given for such mysterious deaths are that the victim was sitting near a fire, somehow caught alight and went up in a flash. Yet no known source of heat, including that of crematorium furnaces, can reduce a human being to ash or liquid, leaving at least part of one limb intact and not burning down the house in the process. Bodies take up to seven hours to become a mixture of bone and coarse ash in crematorium furnaces; it is estimated that heat in excess of 1648°C (3000°F) may liquefy a body, but there would be no guarantee that it would not also liquefy the house.

In 1989 a British television documentary sought to explain away SHC once and for all. Cases of apparent SHC were reconstructed, showing how a body may indeed be partially consumed by a ceiling-high fireball in a confined space. Yet all of these cases required a source of heat – and in at least some of them there was no such thing.

Many cases of apparent SHC involve elderly people living alone, although the phenomenon is not confined to this social group. In 1973 the corpse of Mrs Sam Satlow burst into flames as it lay in a chapel of rest in Hoquiam, Oregon and was consumed to the hips. Her coffin was charred, but intact. The doors had been locked.

In January 1939 eleven-month-old Peter Seaton had been put to bed alone. A visitor to the house heard his terrible screams and ran to his aid. He said: 'It seemed as if I had opened the door of a furnace. There was a mass of flames, which shot out, burning my face and flinging me back across the hall. It was humanly impossible to get Peter out.' The *Daily Telegraph* confidently ascribed Peter's death to SHC; the coroner did not.

There have been survivors of SHC. In 1805 Professor James Hamilton, of the University of Nashville, Tennessee was walking home when he felt a stinging sensation in his left calf. Looking down, he was astonished to see a blue flame about 15 centimetres long shooting out of his leg. He clapped his hand over it, starving it of oxygen, and it 'went out'. The wound took longer than usual to heal and left a yellowish deposit on the inside of his trouser leg – which had not even been charred by the protruding flame.

Modern survivors include Jack Angel, who had his right arm burnt off as he sat watching television in 1974. The medics were perplexed because the fire had come from *within* Mr Angel. In 1985 nineteen-year-old Paul Hayes of east London was walking home in the early hours of the morning when his back burst into flames. He said: 'I thought I could hear my brains bubbling . . . I tried to run, stupidly thinking I could race ahead of the flames . . . I thought I was dying . . . ' Then, as suddenly as it had begun, the 'attack' ceased and the badly burnt young man managed to crawl to the London Hospital, where it was remarked that it looked as if the fire had started *within* him. His shirt, which had been – oddly – shredded by the fire, had not been consumed by it. And in 1977 eighteen-year-old Sally Flack of Saltdean, Sussex, was travelling on a bus when her trousers began to smoulder. By slapping them vigorously she put out the fire. The *Fortean Times* added: 'Brighton Council refused to recognise her claim for compensation.'

Sally's case may incline sceptics to the belief that a stray cigarette was the culprit; this was one of the 'explanations' put forward in the tragic case of Jackie Fitzsimmons, who died of mysterious burns in January 1985. The young cookery student had finished a practical examination and was walking down a corridor in the College of Further Education at Widnes in Cheshire when her back caught fire. On her arrival at hospital she was discovered to have 13 per cent burns on her back, and was not considered to be very ill. The police interviewed her two days later and found her in good spirits. Two weeks later she died, officially of 'lung-shock'.

By then the CID had been brought in and the local police had taken the extraordinary step of asking two members of the Association for the Scientific Study of Anomalous Phenomena (ASSAP) to attend the inquest.

Fire experts from the respected Shirley Institute in Manchester prepared a report in which they described how it was impossible for the cookery jacket Jackie had been wearing to have smouldered for a full five minutes after the end of the examination (assuming that she had caught fire by leaning over a burner, for example). The coroner never called the fire experts nor even alluded to their report, which ran to thirty pages. She had died, he concluded, after catching fire by leaning over a burner . . .

Those who believe in SHC put forward a variety of explanations for the phenomenon, ranging from the 'fire from Heaven' theory of instant, or karmic, retribution, to a sort of psychosomatic suicide. It has been remarked that many of the afflicted were depressed or lonely, and several recently widowed. Some victims had actually been attempting to commit suicide when the fire overtook them.

In 1959 Billy Thomas Peterson sat in the driver's seat of a car in his garage in Detroit, waiting to die peacefully from carbon monoxide poisoning. Then the fire came, melting a plastic religious statuette on the dashboard but leaving untouched a full tank of petrol. Billy was still alive, but, according to the local coroner's report:

> His left arm was so badly burned that the skin rolled off. His genitals had been charred to a crisp. His nose, mouth and ears were burned . . . the hairs on his body, his eyebrows and the top of his head were all unsinged. Even through burned flesh hairs protruded unharmed.

He died shortly afterwards, unable to account for the death that overtook his suicide attempt.

In Louisiana in 1952 Glen B. Denney attempted to cut his wrists in the kitchen of his apartment. But somehow he was discovered in the bedroom, a mass of flames – nothing else was burning. The fireman who witnessed the scene said: 'I don't know what caused the fire to burn so hot . . . In all my experience, I never saw anything to beat this.' The coroner decided that Denney had slit his wrists, walked into the bedroom, poured some kerosene over himself and lit it. No oil or kerosene was found or smelt at the scene, and there were no matches.

In 1980 the badly burned body of a man was found in a car near Telford, Shropshire. It was suggested that he had committed suicide by pouring some flammable material over himself and lighting it, but there was negligible damage to the car itself, and no evidence to point to murder.

There are links between anomalous outbreaks of fire and poltergeist activity. In most known cases of inexplicable arson, however, the damage is limited and the fire puts itself out before much harm is done. Yet some poltergeist focuses seem to cause fires to break out wherever they go. In the 1980s an English nanny working in Italy was charged with arson because of the fires that broke out around her. More significantly, she was widely believed to be a witch, a charge that was made publicly in court. Though she was acquitted of both charges – one official, the other unofficial – she had to flee the country.

An aura of witchcraft surrounds the classic case of Grace Pett, who died of SHC in 1744 in Ipswich. Peter Christie, writing in the *Fortean Times* (issue no. 35), reveals that the *Ipswich Times* of the day had carried an article about the case that said:

> The poor old woman had a reputation of being a witch . . . a neighbouring farmer . . . had some of his sheep taken in an odd way, they were supposed to be bewitched, and he was advised to burn one of them. . . . Accordingly, on the very night that this woman was burnt, [the farmer's wife] made their head man bring in a diseased sheep, and make a great fire and burn it to death . . .

The events at the Purdies' farm became such a part of local folklore that they were celebrated in verse, as late as 1875, in 'Grace Pett, A Tale of Witchcraft' by Elizabeth Cotton for the *Suffolk Bibliography*. One verse reads:

> Next day in Her Cottage at Ipswich Found
> All charred to Ashes but Feet and Hands

Grace Pett lies dead on the Unscorched Ground
And the Plague is stayed upon Purdies Lands.

The medical notes of the Grace Pett case contain a significant statement: 'Within the body there is always carried on a gentle combustion, productive of the vital flame.'

Interestingly, many holy people, such as the stigmatic Padre Pio who died in 1968, have been reported as having higher than normal body temperatures, the internal incandescence causing visible haloes. There are some who believe that the image on the Turin Shroud was caused by a sudden burst of intense heat or radiation. It may be that every human being – or indeed, every living creature – has a fire within that only awaits certain circumstances before it bursts forth. But whatever those trigger factors may be, the phenomenon seems to be disturbingly frequent. Despite the difficulty of finding records of cases suggestive of SHC, *Fortean Times* regularly carries stories, culled from local newspapers, that clearly refer to deaths from this kind of fire.

The world-famous insurance company Lloyds of London do not offer special cover against SHC, but a spokesman said that, although 'I've never heard of this phenomenon, which seems very worrying', his firm would 'deem any life insurance policy to cover this eventuality'. If this be comfort.
SEE ALSO *Cosmic Joker; Curses; Electric people; Explanations; Fireproof people; Charles Fort; D. D. Home; Jinxes; Karma; New Testament miracles; Old Testament miracles; The Resurrection; Stigmatics; Turin Shroud; Witchcraft.*

MYSTERIOUS DISAPPEARANCES

There are many cases of sudden or amazing disappearances of people, animals or objects. Since there are also many cases of the anomalous appearance of creatures or objects, this indicates that some kind of cause and effect is in operation.

Many of the alleged disappearances, however, fail to pass scrutiny. In 1809 a British diplomat named Benjamin Bathurst walked round to look at the coach horses outside an inn in Austria – and was never seen again. Soldiers posted in the street saw no one leave; it seemed as if he had vanished into thin air. Yet Bathurst was travelling under an assumed name and had, according to reports, seemed very agitated just before his disappearance. If he were a spy, then the likelihood of his coming to a sudden end was dramatically increased.

On 23 September 1880 David Lang, a farmer of Gallatin, Tennessee, vanished from view as he crossed a field in front of his wife. Two other witnesses saw him disappear. It seemed like a recreation of the Orion Williamson disappearance of 1854 – the foundation for Ambrose Bierce's story, *The Difficulty of Crossing a Field*. But a search of the local records failed to locate a David Lang at Gallatin, nor was one of the witnesses – Judge August Peck – mentioned. Disappointingly, it seems that the story had become foaflore – 'friend-of-a-friend lore', where a dramatic story is repeated until the original is lost completely.

Yet deservedly notorious unexplained disappearances do happen. One of the most famous cases was that of the *Mary Celeste* in 1872 found drifting east of the Azores, her crew gone. Many explanations have been put forward, none of them totally convincing. The ship remains a household name.

Charles Fort coined the word 'teleportation' to describe the paranormal movement of objects through solid matter, and judged this to be a common occurrence. The fish and frogs that regularly fall from clear blue skies must come from somewhere (not to mention the hundreds of other objects and substances, not all of them known to modern man). Many of these fishfalls contain dried or putrefied creatures, as if they had been removed from their natural habitat, then kept suspended until they reach the state in which they fell.

The annals of psychical research contain hundreds of cases of teleportations; objects dematerialise in one place and materialise in another (when they are called 'apports' by Spiritualists). Mediums believe that these are gifts from the spirits, although there are instances of objects disappearing and appearing in a non-Spiritualist setting, such as the Batcheldor experiments. Many objects have been filmed moving through the solid glass wall of the SORRAT minilab.

Quantum mechanics and particle physics suggest that nothing is as it seems, particularly solid objects and even people. Dematerialisation and rematerialisation may not be merely the province of science fiction but may be fact, and common fact at that.

SEE ALSO *Apports; Kenneth Batcheldor; Boggle threshold; Consensus reality; Cosmic Joker; Explanations; Fishfalls; Foaflore; Charles Fort; Mary Celeste; Mysterious appearances; Quantum mechanics and the paranormal; Seance-room phenomena; SORRAT.*

MYSTERIOUS APPEARANCES

According to the archives of folklore and Forteana, people, animals and – more commonly – objects have a disturbing habit of appearing unaccountably from nowhere. Charles Fort wrote of a naked man who was discovered running up and down Chatham High Street, Kent in 1914; he had no idea who he was or where he had come from. No clues were found about the man's identity – his clothes, for example, were never located. He was arrested, interrogated, found to be insane and locked away.

When Fort coined the term 'teleportation' to describe the sudden movement of people and objects from one place to another he suggested that:

an examination of inmates of infirmaries and workhouses and asylums might lead to some marvellous ... disclosures. ... Early in the year 1928 a man did appear in a town in New Jersey, and did tell that he had come from the planet Mars. Wherever he came from, everybody knows where he went, after telling that.

Kaspar Hauser, a mysterious appearance who was assassinated by an equally mysterious appearance.

Medieval legend has it that two green-skinned children appeared at Woolpit in Suffolk. They said they had come from 'St Martin's Land', where it was always twilight. The incident was considered remarkable enough to become local legend, but little more is known about the green children.

Unidentified corpses continue to be found. Between 1974 and 1975, within months of each other, the bodies of three men were found in Dorset. None of them was ever identified.

Two celebrated 'appearing people' were Kaspar Hauser and 'Princess Caraboo'. The former was found wandering in Nuremberg, Germany in 1828, unable to give any account of himself except that he had been kept in a dark room, for as long as he could remember, by an unidentified captor. Hauser was murdered by an assassin who was himself a mystery.

The 'Princess Caraboo' case began in 1817 when

a girl knocked on the door of a cottage near Bristol. Although she spoke no English she managed to indicate that she needed some food. As an interesting vagrant she found herself up before the magistrate, who took her under his wing. She spoke and wrote an unknown language. Various experts were asked to give their opinion of her language; one claimed it was Malay and that she was Princess Caraboo, who had been captured by pirates and escaped, making her way to England. However, one Mrs Willcocks from Devon arrived and alleged that the girl was her daughter, Mary. 'Princess Caraboo' broke down and confessed that this was true – but after being shipped off to America by her putative mother she continued to give exhibitions of her mysterious writing. No one will ever know the truth about the lost girl.

Animals frequently come and go; in recent years an Isle of Wight farmer discovered thirteen calves in his locked cowshed where there had been only twelve the night before. The newcomer was without any identifying mark. The *Fortean Times* reported that a large goldfish disappeared from a pond – to be replaced inexplicably by fourteen small ones.

Spontaneous 'gifts' may be common; part of everyday life that goes unremarked or even unnoticed by a culture unaccustomed to accepting paranormal events. But psychics, Spiritualists and open-minded parapsychologists have always reported teleportations and 'apports' (objects that appear from nowhere during seances). Flowers were favourite apports at the height of the spirit materialisation era, and the deliberately induced seance-room phenomena of researcher Kenneth Batcheldor and others have resulted in the sudden appearance of large objects such as stones. The Missouri-based SORRAT group report the frequent movement of objects through solid floors and walls.

Poltergeist attacks also produce dramatic apports. The case known as the Black Monk of Pontefract began with the sudden 'rain' of a chalk-like substance from a point mid-way in the air. During the investigation of the Enfield poltergeist in 1977 a book disappeared from a bedroom, to be found immediately in a bedroom next door.

The complex history of British psychic Matthew Manning has included examples of almost every known type of spontaneous phenomenon. Manning discovered that his family shared the house with its original seventeenth-century owner, Thomas Webbe, who seemed to exist in a twilight world – sometimes aware he was dead, at others complaining about the Mannings' presence in 'his' house as if he were still alive. As Webbe's relationship with the young psychic developed, the erstwhile owner began to leave objects as gifts on the stairs. These unusual apports included a loaf of bread, which, when analysed, proved to be at least seventy years old, and a letter from an unknown solicitor to an unknown client. In conversation with Matthew Manning, Webbe said he had chosen it as a present because of its curious 'hand' – it was typewritten – something he had never seen before.

SEE ALSO *Apports; Black Monk of Pontefract; Consensus reality; Cosmic Joker; Enfield poltergeist, Entity enigma; Explanations; Fishfalls; Charles Fort; Matthew Manning; Mysterious disappearances; Other dimensions; Philip experiment; Poltergeists; Seance-room phenomena; SORRAT; Timeslips.*

DEVIL'S FOOTPRINTS

The residents of Topsham, Lympstone, Exmouth, Teignmouth and Dawlish in south Devon awoke on Friday, 9 February 1855 to discover a deep fall of snow – and on it, over houses, on high walls, everywhere, there were mysterious footprints. The tracks appeared to have been made by a biped with convex feet or hooves, foot following foot in a single line, without displacing the snow on either side or making any other mark.

Immediately the locals took the tracks to have been made by the Devil's cloven feet, although sceptics suggested, unconvincingly, that they had been made by an otter or badger. Similar tracks had been reported during an Antarctic exploration in 1840 and in Scotland, where they were said to be seen every year and were taken locally to be of supernatural origin.

When the school in the Welsh village of Aberfan (left, seen here 10 years on) was engulfed in a black slag heap in 1966, killing over a hundred children, it became clear that many of the dead had received warnings, often in the form of dreams, which had been ignored by their parents. A common precognitive dream involved an overwhelming feeling of terror and physical oppression, and images such as that of one little girl who said, 'There was a great black pit where the school should have been.' She and her playmates ended their days in the local graveyard (right), her warnings having fallen on unbelieving ears.

Ursula Sontheil, otherwise known as Mother Shipton, is consulted by a client. The seventeenth-century prophetess from north Yorkshire was reputed to have predicted that the end of the world would come in 1981, but it has recently been discovered that this was an invention by a Victorian publican on her behalf. When that year came and went with no terminal upheaval, the verses were amended by some of her modern admirers to read '1991'.

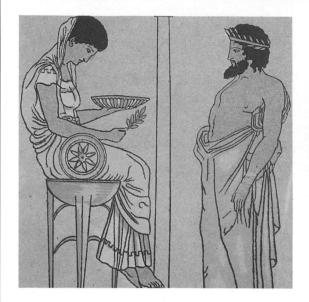

The Delphic Oracle of ancient Greece made obscure
pronouncements that required extensive interpretation.
Nevertheless, it was often very accurate, although rarely
notably reassuring.

A First World War soldier has his fortune told before leaving
for the trenches. It is doubtful whether he would have been
told the truth under the circumstances, for ethical readers
never describe the death or mutilation of their clients, although
they can warn against disaster – a useless line to take in this
case.

Card number O from the Major Arcana of the Tarot pack is
the Fool. Traditional design has him as a young man blithely
stepping off a precipice with his dog at his feet. He is the Holy
Fool, the eternal innocent, who is both wise and foolish, who
leaps empty-handed into the void as part of his grand
initiation, his karmic journey. All Tarot cards have profound
and archetypal meanings that call to the subconscious, but the
Fool begins and ends our journeys, and therefore is of the
utmost significance.

Woodcut portrait of Michel de Nostradame, more commonly
known as Nostradamus, clairvoyant, astrologer, occultist, and
author of the predictive The Centuries, which was first
published in 1555. These rhyming quatrains are widely believed
to predict specific events up until 1999, when the world will
end. Among the events predicted that have already come true
are the abdication of Edward VIII and the rise and fall of Adolf
Hitler. Some of the verses remain obscure. Interestingly, it
seems that Nostradamus was part of an international network
of hermetic occultists who also worked as spies. Another
member of this influential group was Leonardo da Vinci.

The late Doris Stokes, one of the best known and best loved of all Spiritualist mediums in Britain in the 1970s and 1980s. In her heyday she impressed all who met her with her down-to-earth humour and extraordinary psychic gifts. Those who never met her, however, found her work, especially in her last years, open to criticism and suggestion of fraud. One of the most vociferous of these critics was a notable Catholic writer who believes that Mrs Stokes cursed him from beyond the grave for his antagonistic account of her work. Judging by her attitude to critics while alive, however, she would have been more inclined to shrug it off. And there are those today who believe that the discarnate Doris, still communicating, is living proof of her life's work.

Magickal adept Aleister Crowley, who died in 1947, an incorrigible self-publicist who was delighted by the British tabloids' nickname for him as 'The Wickedest Man in the World'. Yet he was certainly much more than an exhibitionist confidence trickster: his knowledge of magickal rituals and the powers of the human mind were extensive and profound, and his scholarship about religious systems and philosophy impressive. Despite his magickal triumphs, he fell prey to drug and alcohol addiction. His last words, uttered in the Hastings boarding house to which he had retired, were 'I am perplexed.' His last act was to curse the doctor who attended him for not permitting him to have an extra supply of heroin. He told the doctor that he would not live more than forty-eight hours after himself. The doctor died on cue.

Uri Geller, seen here in his palatial English home. Since his triumphant explosion on to the international scene as spoonbender extraordinary he has concentrated on working for mining companies as a map dowser – locating potentially profitable areas for them to dig. He is said to have become a multi-millionaire through such successful activities. These days he prefers to be thought of as a showman, although he will never deny his psychic abilities. Rather, he maintains that everyone is a potential psychic, as his innovative experiments in metalbending and telepathy through the media have shown. Whether or not he is always totally genuine, he does seem to be able to bring out the psychic abilities in others, and perhaps it will be for this effect alone that he will be remembered.

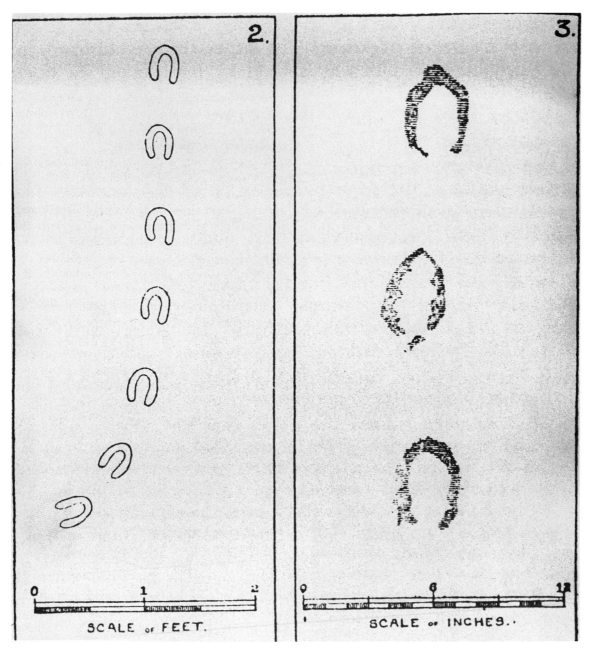

'The Devil's footprints', drawn from life in Devon on 8 February 1855.

In recent years the Romanies have claimed that it was a trick perpetrated by their kin in an attempt to drive away their rivals from the area. According to tallying reports, they claim that it took up to eighteen months to prepare and involved the use of ingenious step ladders and four hundred sets of stilts. The night of 8 February 1855 is still known by the Romanies as 'The Night of Mulo's Walk' – Mulo being the Devil. That such a vast operation was carried out in total silence and invisibility is surely the greatest mystery.

SEE ALSO *Apports; Consensus reality; Cosmic Joker; The*

Devil; Entity enigma; Hallucinations; Mass hysteria; Mysterious appearances; Mysterious disappearances; Other dimensions; Philip experiment; Thoughtography; Tulpas.

MARY CELESTE

It is hard for even the most ardent cynic to deny that the *Mary Celeste* suffered from a jinx. Her career, riddled with misfortunes that centred around the disappearance of her entire crew, was

Mrs Benjamin Briggs and her infant son Arthur were part of the now legendary mass disappearance of crew and passengers from the Mary Celeste, *a sailing ship found deserted and drifting on a calm sea in 1872. Theories about the nature of their disappearance are many, varied, and sometimes extremely bizarre.*

to leave in its wake a series of mysterious tragedies and unexplained deaths.

Originally the *Amazon*, the ship was built in 1860 in Nova Scotia. Shortly afterwards her first skipper fell ill and died. After a fire amidships, two disastrous voyages and a succession of owners, the *Amazon* passed into the hands of J. H. Winchester and Co., a consortium of New York ship owners. By now, she was the *Mary Celeste* .

Her new captain, a devout Christian and competent seaman called Benjamin Spooner Briggs, was to carry a cargo of denatured alcohol from New York to Genoa. Also on the voyage were a crew of seven apparently trustworthy and experienced seamen, Captain Briggs's wife Sarah Elizabeth and their two-year-old daughter. On 7 November 1872 the *Mary Celeste* set sail for Genoa; this was the last time either passengers or crew were ever seen.

On 5 December, a bedraggled sailing ship was sighted in mid-Atlantic by the crew of the *Dei Gratia* bound for Gibraltar. Its skipper, Captain Morehouse, sent first mate Oliver Beveau with two other men to reconnoitre. On boarding the ship they found her totally deserted; her name was *Mary Celeste*.

She had certainly just weathered a storm; yet she was in good condition and there was ample food and fresh water on board. Missing from the ship were the chronometer, sextant, ship's log and a yawl, or small boat. To all appearances, the crew and passengers had abandoned ship in this inadequate vessel, yet their reason for doing so was, and still is, a complete mystery.

At first Morehouse was reluctant to lay claim to the *Mary Celeste* , but eventually he agreed to salvage her. On her arrival in Gibraltar, the mystery ship was placed under the jurisdiction of the Attorney General, Solly Flood, who tried (in vain) to attach blame to Morehouse and his men. Finally cleared of suspicion, they were granted a salvage award of £1700. Some sceptics still allege that Morehouse and Briggs had conspired to set up the 'disappearances' and had planned to split the salvage money. Briggs's continued disappearance, they suggest, might have been the result of dishonour among thieves.

Many more theories have been put forward over the years to account for the bizarre disappearance of those on board the ship. Inevitably these include suggestions of murder, committed by the crew of either the *Mary Celeste* or the *Dei Gratia*. Among various other weird theories are wholesale madness or hallucination caused by eating food contaminated by ergot, a powerful natural hallucinogen; and the possibility that the crew and passengers were eaten by a giant sea monster (presumably with a fondness for navigational apparatus), or abducted by a passing UFO.

One clue may lie in the mysterious death of 1960s' lone yachtsman Donald Crowhurst, who appeared to have jumped overboard to seek a mystical union with God. In his case extreme solitude led to insanity. A form of religious fervour (Briggs was very religious) may have led to an hysterical contagion among those on the *Mary Celeste* – and they may have set off under his direction to a hallucinatory Promised Land.

Possibly the most satisfactory explanation is that the *Mary Celeste* was struck by a tornado at sea. This may have caused the ship's instruments to malfunction temporarily, leading the crew to believe that they were sinking rapidly. Panic set in and they abandoned ship.

Meanwhile, the jinx of the *Mary Celeste* had yet to run its course. She changed hands seventeen times over the next twelve years, frequently catching fire and losing cargoes, sails and even sailors. Eventually her last owner, Gilman C. Parker, deliberately burnt the ship to a cinder – and was promptly taken to court for putting in a false insurance claim. Parker and his associates walked free from the court, but not from the jinx of the *Mary Celeste*. In a short time, Parker went bankrupt and died in poverty; a fellow conspirator committed suicide, and yet another ended his days in a mental institution.

SEE ALSO *Cryptozoology; Curses; Explanations; Hallucinations; Jinxes; Mass hysteria; Mysterious disappearances.*

FISHFALLS

Mysterious rains of strange substances and living creatures are among the most universal and frequent of all Fortean phenomena, and of all rains those composed of fish and frogs are the most common. Fishfalls are regularly reported in the *Fortean Times*, but such phenomena have been observed for far longer than that publication has been in existence.

In February 1859, for example, the residents of Mountain Ash in Wales found live minnows and sticklebacks falling from the sky. They fell, as if predeterminedly, over a long, narrow strip of land. Then ten minutes later there came another rain of these creatures over the same area. One of the fish was sent, alive, to a Dr Gray at the British Museum, who ignored the facts and ascribed the entire event to a hoax. He claimed that two buckets of water containing the creatures had been thrown – ten minutes apart.

In 1666 a shower of fish fell on just one field in Kent, and in 1839 fish fell in a narrow straight line on Calcutta. That same decade saw dried fish fall on two other cities in India, and in 1896 a carp, preserved in a block of ice, fell on Essen, Germany. Other reports tell of putrid and stinking fish, suggesting that the fish had been held long enough – somewhere – to decompose before being dropped.

In 1980 a shower of tiny green frogs fell on Athens. 'Experts' explained that they had been caught up in a whirlwind and then dropped. No whirlwind had been reported, and no debris other than frogs fell.

Charles Fort suggested that the heavens are full of 'horses and barns and elephants and flies and dodoes . . . fishes dried and hard, there a short time; others there long enough to putrefy'. He supposed that we live under a 'Super-Sargasso Sea' which sometimes drops its creatures on the earth during storms – or just on a whim.

SEE ALSO *Cosmic Joker; Explanations; Charles Fort; Jinxes; Mysterious appearances; Mysterious disappearances.*

The heavens may fall . . . 'fishfalls' have been recorded repeatedly from every part of the world.

CRYPTOZOOLOGY

Cryptozoology is the study of the strange, often bizarre creatures reported from around the world and whose existence remains controversial. A number of these, such as the Loch Ness monster and the yeti, are world-famous. There are, however, many others that remain less well publicised but which can be equally authenticated by the reports of eye witnesses and other evidence.

Dr Bernard Heuvelmans, a Belgian zoologist, first used the term 'cryptozoology' in his book *Le Grand Serpent de Mer*, first published in 1965 and perhaps better known under its English title, *In the Wake of Sea Serpents*. Here he documented over five hundred recorded sightings of sea monsters, dating from 1693 to 1965, and attempted to analyse them on a scientific basis.

The use of the word 'zoology' probably reflected the desire of Heuvelmans to rationalise this subject. But the search for unexplained, unidentified life forms is inevitably linked to the paranormal. A common feature associated with sightings of bigfoot, a humanoid reportedly seen in North America, is the appearance of UFOs in the area at the same time. This suggests to some researchers that at least in some cases there is a clear extraterrestrial link. To many modern ufologists it suggests that reality is being manipulated by controlling entities whose aim is psychic control.

The open scepticism of most scientists has handicapped cryptozoological research. Some zoologists display a particular reluctance even to consider the notion that unknown creatures could still remain undetected on the planet. In 1812 the famous zoologist Baron Georges Cuvier, who was convinced that all the large vertebrates had already been discovered, dismissed out of hand explorers' tales of so-called 'black and white' rhinos. But within seven years his pupil Diard had confirmed the existence of the Malayan tapir.

Since then, a further thirty such 'impossible' creatures have been found. They include the Komodo dragon, which is the largest lizard in the world, growing up to 3.2 metres in length and weighing 165 kilos. This was seen by zoologists for the first time in 1912.

Early reports of such creatures are almost inevitably a blend of fact and fiction – Komodo dragons, for example, were first believed to be land crocodiles. But perhaps the most revealing episode of this type occurred in the sixteenth century, as the first Europeans were venturing into Africa. The natives told fearsome tales of humanoid monsters; Pongos were like men, but with hairy bodies. Living in groups, they would attack people, stealing their children, who were never seen again. Being immensely strong, they could not be captured alive – even by ten men.

It is hard to equate this account of pongos, with its paranormal overtones, to what we now recognise as the lowland gorilla – a shy vegetarian. The problem of resolving such tales obviously depends on obtaining definite evidence of the creature's existence. But the fact that a specimen might remain elusive clearly does not mean that the creature cannot actually exist.

Having escaped detection by zoologists for so long means that such apparently mythical creatures are likely to be scarce or localised in their distribution, inhabiting remote and often inaccessible regions. This applies especially in the case of sea monsters, which may lurk in the depths of the oceans where they are difficult to locate, and their existence can only be finally established if they are caught, or if a carcase is washed up on a beach.

Even then accurate identification may not be possible. On 25 April 1977, for example, a Japanese fishing vessel trawling for mackerel off the coast of New Zealand, at a depth of 274 metres, caught a decomposing body, measuring 9.8 metres, and weighing over 1800 kilos. It was clearly the remains of a vertebrate, with a long neck and tail; four fins were also visible – but it did not resemble any known creature. Some experts believed it to be the remains of a pleiosaur, a marine reptile thought

to have become extinct about seventy million years ago, while others pointed to its marked resemblance to a rotting shark. Unfortunately, given its advanced state of decomposition, there was no possibility of a positive identification.

The discovery of a living coelacanth off the coast of South Africa in 1938 had already confirmed that creatures known only from their fossilised remains could still survive in the world's oceans. Almost fifty years later, in 1987, an expedition tracked living coelacanths underwater on the west side of the island of Grand Comoro in the Indian Ocean off Africa's eastern coast. It is here that the only known population of these fish is found. Other, unknown sea creatures could have equally localised habitats.

The cryptozoological puzzles most likely to have paranormal explanations are undoubtedly those involving sightings of giant birds and other winged creatures. There is a certainly no rational explanation for the Jersey Devil, which was reported by many witnesses towards the end of January 1909 in the US state of New Jersey. The creature was said to be the size of a crane, with a head rather like that of a horse. Its four feet were cloven, and it had a long tail and bat-like wings with a span of about 60 centimetres. Some witnesses claimed that the monster glowed red in the dark, while others were certain that it had some more tangible physical presence. A member of a gang of workmen shot and apparently wounded the creature, but it managed to evade capture and disappeared. Later, the Jersey Devil survived electrocution on a railroad track. A witness described how its tail made contact, blowing up over 6 metres of track as a result. But it was seen again, uninjured, in another area later that evening. Then, as suddenly as it had appeared, the Jersey Devil simply vanished. Several later accounts suggest that it may have returned in the 1930s, but these are poorly documented.

There is no universal explanation for reported sightings of mysterious creatures. Some are likely to be hoaxes, or may simply result from incorrect identification of a known species. Others may indeed be encounters with previously unrecognised animals, extraterrestrial entities or even thought-forms, as perhaps was the case with the Jersey Devil.

SEE ALSO *Bigfoots, almas and yeti; Case of Ruth; Consensus reality; Cosmic Joker; Creative visualisation; CSI-COP; Devil's footprints; Entity enigma; Explanations; Foaflore; Charles Fort; Hallucinations; Lake monsters; Limits of science; Loch Ness monster; Mass hysteria; Other dimensions; Thoughtography; Tulpas; UFO paradox; UFOs; Vampires; Werewolves.*

BIGFOOTS, ALMAS AND YETI

Reports of strange humanoid creatures have originated from all continents except Antarctica, but are most prevalent in North America, dating back to 1818. British researchers Janet and Colin Bord, who have carried out extensive studies, have collected evidence of sightings from forty states in the USA and five Canadian provinces. They suggest that there could have been over ten thousand during the past century. The highest density of encounters appears to be in the north-western USA, extending into British Columbia. Here the countryside remains forested, largely undisturbed and sparsely populated.

The native Indian population readily accept the existence of such creatures, which they refer to as sasquatches, although these are now more generally known as bigfoots. Some Indians claim to have established a trading relationship with them, and accept them as part of a small tribe. The putative existence of bigfoots is particularly significant, since North America is a continent apparently devoid of large primates of any kind.

The closest encounter reported with a bigfoot was the sensational story told by Albert Ostman in 1957, thirty-three years after his abduction by a bigfoot family. He described the creatures as taller than humans, being well over 2 metres in height, and weighing about 270 kilos. Ostman escaped without being hurt, and made his way back to civilisation. He claimed that the reason he had kept quiet for so long was that he felt certain no one would believe him.

A frame from a film of Bigfoot taken by Roger Patterson at Bluff Creek, Northern California, on 20 October 1967. Although the creature looks like a man in a bigfoot suit, the film still arouses heated controversy.

The evidence points to bigfoots being inoffensive towards people, although they often exhibit a strong dislike for dogs. This may be related to the particularly unpleasant body odour associated with bigfoots, which many witnesses have described: perhaps the creatures sense that dogs could track them. Alternatively they may associate dogs with wolves or bears, which might attack them in the wilderness.

There is a reasonable amount of evidence to support the physical existence of bigfoot. Various hair samples left at the site of bigfoot encounters have been analysed by experts, who conclude that these did not originate from bears, wolves or people. Nor do they match those of known primates, apart from a slight similarity with gorilla hair.

This evidence is further supported by a sample obtained from the blood left on the surrounds of a window smashed by a bigfoot in Bellingham, Washington State on 14 January 1976. It was tested

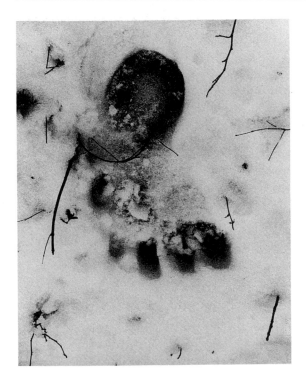

Print in the snow of the 'Bossburg Cripple' – 16½ inches long and deformed – apparently of a hominid creature, found at Bossburg, Washington, in 1969.

by Dr V. Sarich, a physical anthropologist and biochemist working at the University of California, who concluded that it was the blood of a higher primate.

There is also a more sinister aspect to some bigfoot sightings – they may be UFO-related phenomena. A case of this type documented from Roachdale, Indiana in August 1972 began with the appearance of a luminous object in the sky. Sightings of a bigfoot followed, but it appeared never to leave tracks, even when walking through mud, nor did it make any noise.

Local farmers found that dozens of their chickens had been mysteriously mutilated. When they caught up with the creature and tried to shoot it, the men were apparently unable to injure it although firing from close range. Other reports also describe how bullets do not appear to penetrate this particular type of bigfoot, recalling European legends of the werewolf who cannot be killed except by a silver bullet.

If the North American bigfoot is a terrestrial creature, its origins may lie in Asia, from where there have been a number of reports of different humanoid creatures. The yeti of the Himalayan region is the best known, although actual evidence of its existence is scarce. A number of mountaineers have reported finding inexplicable footprints, however, and on occasions they have seen unexplained figures above the snowline. Since the environment there is so hostile, it has been suggested that yetis actually live in high Himalayan forests, and that they venture only occasionally across the snow to search for special lichens which grow on the moraines.

The yeti first achieved widespread notoriety in 1920, when it was introduced to the world's press as *metch kangmi*, translated as the 'Abominable Snowman'. The report emanated from a journalist called Henry Newman, who was serving in the British Army in India. For over seventy years the story of the Abominable Snowman has remained largely unchallenged in Fortean foaflore. But another soldier closely involved at the outset was the late Colonel Stead, who later confided to his son that the yeti was 'a figment of my imagination, old boy. The Tibetans believe in ghosts which they call yetis and so I have invented the Abominable Snowman.' This correspondence has only recently emerged in the journal of the Punjab Frontier Force Association, and was printed in the *Daily Telegraph* on 26 October 1988.

More definite records of similar humanoid creatures can be found from other parts of Asia. There is a report of one being shot during 1925 by an army patrol in the Vanch Mountains of the Soviet Union. It was about 1.7 metres tall and covered in thick hair, which was greyish brown in colour. The soldiers were forced to leave the body under a pile of stones. More recently, ape-like creatures have become the subject of serious scientific study in China during the late 1970s and 1980s. Partial confirmation of their existence was obtained by an expedition organised by the Chinese Academy of Sciences during 1977, although they were unable to capture any one of these creatures. Reddish hair samples suggested that they are primates, and from sightings it was estimated that they are about 2 metres tall. A survey of Zhejiang province in 1980 located a series of nests where the ape-like creatures were believed to rest. The local people knew them well and had to protect their maize crops against these marauders. Again, the creatures were described as having reddish brown hair and walking in an upright fashion.

Debate has centred on the relationships of such creatures with other primates, and on how so many different forms came to exist. They are known under various local names, such as almas, guliavan and kaptars. It seems likely that they are ape-like creatures that may have remained localised and largely protected from evolutionary pressures. If there is a humanoid link, it may well be with a primitive race, possibly descendants of Neanderthal man.

Other suggested links include *Pithecanthropus*, which lived in Asia about three million years ago, and *Gigantopithecus*, a giant ape known to have been widely distributed from India to China, and which survived until at least six hundred thousand years ago – quite recently in geological terms. It is also possible that such creatures could have crossed into North America from Asia via the Bering Strait, before the present land masses separated about twenty thousand years ago, and were the ancestors of bigfoot.

SEE ALSO *Case of Ruth; Consensus reality; Cosmic Joker; Cryptozoology; Dragons; Entity enigma; Foaflore; Ghosts; Lake monsters; Loch Ness monster; Thoughtography; Tulpas; UFO paradox; UFOs; Vampires; Werewolves.*

LOCH NESS MONSTER

Reports of strange creatures in Loch Ness date back to the last century, but it was only in 1933 that the world became aware of the mystery present in the Scottish loch. That November, Hugh Gray, an employee of the British Aluminium Company, saw a large creature in the water. On the shore, close to the small village of Lower Foyers, he took five photographs as the monster broke the

surface about 180 metres away from him. Only one photograph proved satisfactory when the film was developed, but this made world-wide headlines.

No other cryptozoological puzzle has attracted such universal attention. Since 1933 there have been over three thousand recorded sightings, but no truly irrefutable evidence of the creature's existence has been obtained. The nature of the loch itself does not assist investigators, since it is over 200 metres deep in parts, and 35 kilometres long. The water itself is dark and peaty, making underwater photography difficult.

An added dimension to the mystery followed publication of Gray's photograph. A couple who had driven past the loch in July that year came forward to report their encounter with a bizarre monster that had crossed the road from the hillside, and headed – presumably – into the loch. The Spicers described this creature as having a long neck, being greyish in colour and resembling a huge snail – a description which tallied almost exactly with local legends going back many centuries.

The best-known photograph of the monster at the surface of the loch was taken in April of the following year by a London surgeon named Kenneth Wilson. He claimed to have stopped on the road about 60 metres above the loch; then, some 230 metres away, he saw what he believed to be the head of a strange animal emerge from the water. He grabbed his camera, which had a telephoto attachment, and managed to take four pictures before the creature disappeared.

Two photographs proved to be blank when developed by a chemist in Inverness, but the better of the other two, showing a small-headed creature with a long, arched neck apparently coming up for air was bought by the *Daily Mail*. The scientific community remained generally unconvinced by it. Zoologist Dr Maurice Burton claimed that the surgeon had photographed an otter's tail just as the animal was diving underwater.

Reports continued, however, and a group of interested naturalists, including Richard Fitter and the late Peter Scott, established the Loch Ness Phenomena Investigation Bureau in 1962. Two years earlier, researcher Tim Dinsdale obtained ciné film of what he believed to be the monster. This was

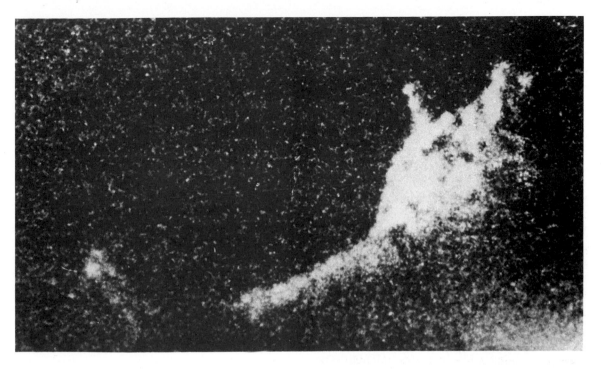

One of the underwater photographs taken in 1975 by a team from the Academy of Applied Science, Boston, Massachusetts, apparently showing the Loch Ness monster quite clearly.

'Nessie' photographed by London surgeon R. K. Wilson on 19 April 1934. Critics point to the lack of background as reference for scale. Those 'waves' could really be ripples.

Sonar boats scanning Loch Ness during Operation Deep Scan in October 1987. No physical monster was found, but the legend remains.

submitted to the Joint Air Reconnaissance Intelligence Centre (JARIC) in January 1966. Their report confirmed that the moving object shown was just over a metre high, with a length of nearly 1.7 metres. They believed it was travelling at about 15 kilometres per hour, and the conclusion was that 'it is probably an animate object'. They ruled out the possibility that the film had recorded a motor boat or submarine.

Another sensational piece of photographic evidence was obtained as part of a sonar sweep of the loch on 8 August 1972. A team headed by Dr Robert Rines, from the Academy of Applied Science in Boston scanned the loch, using a strobe camera that took colour photographs every fifty-five seconds. The sonar record apparently matched that of the strobe photographs, suggesting that a large object had been in sight. Two frames of the film were then passed to the Jet Propulsion Laboratory at Pasadena for computer enhancement. The image appeared to be that of a diamond-shaped flipper, an estimated 2–2.5 metres in length. The flipper seemed to be attached to a rough-skinned body.

Impressive though such evidence seemed at first sight, there were those who doubted its validity. Rikki Razdan and Alan Kielar, senior personnel of an American company which manufactures underwater tracking systems, arrived at the loch in the summer of 1983 to replicate Rines's methods. They found that definitive corroboration of the sonar trace to back the photograph was not possible. The flipper also appears to have been retouched, while the unenhanced originals are no longer available.

A further probe of Loch Ness was undertaken in October 1987. Operation Deepscan was an attempt to scan intensively at least part of the loch using a flotilla of craft. The budget was minuscule, despite much of the equipment and back-up provided by keen sponsors. The leader of the operation, Adrian Shine, had been involved in previous searches and refused to fuel the intensive media interest with rash speculations. No conclusive evidence came to light.

Meanwhile, recent re-analysis of Kenneth Wilson's 1934 photograph, following the discovery of a larger print in the *Daily Mail* archives, suggests that this was a hoax. Researcher Stewart Campbell

has shown that Wilson's stated position when he took his photographs does not coincide with the evidence. In the past the photograph had always been heavily cropped for publication. It is now apparent that the object shown was probably no more than 16 metres from the shore, rather than the distance of 135–180 metres given by Wilson. Nor was a telephoto attachment used, as Wilson had claimed.

These findings are major setbacks to those who believe in the existence of a flesh-and-blood Loch Ness monster. But in this area of Scotland, steeped in the legends of water monsters, the fact that so many people claim to have made sightings means that the possibility cannot be lightly dismissed.

SEE ALSO *Bigfoots, almas and yeti; Case of Ruth; Consensus reality; Cosmic Joker; Charles Fort; Cryptozoology; Lake monsters; Thoughtography; Tulpas; Vampires; Werewolves.*

LAKE MONSTERS

Sightings of lake monsters have long been accumulating around the world, with the highest densities in North America and Africa. During the 1980s much attention has been focused on the search for *mokele-mbembe*, also known as the Congo swamp monster, in the Ubangi-Congo basin in central Africa.

The creature is believed to be a sauropod dinosaur, a small surviving relative of *Brontosaurus*, about 9 metres long, with a long neck and tail. Certainly the vegetation, climate and geology of the area have changed little since the end of the Cretaceous period, about seventy million years ago, when dinosaurs were believed to have become extinct.

Native descriptions of the lifestyle of *mokele-mbembe* have helped to reconcile what had long been a subject of dispute among palaeontologists. One school of thought favoured the hypothesis that sauropods were primarily aquatic, spending most of their time submerged in deep water and

Drawing of the sea monster of Lake Eutopia, Canada. Still waters are widely believed to run very deep indeed, and to hide all manner of weird creatures.

breathing by keeping their heads above water. Unfortunately, the hydrostatic pressure would have made respiration under such circumstances virtually impossible. It then became fashionable to accept sauropods as terrestrial giants which used their long necks to browse on tall plants, rather like giraffes today. Their sheer bulk, however, would have made movement on land exceedingly difficult and slow.

According to the natives of the region, *mokele-mbembe* inhabits rivers and, using its long neck, feeds on the lianas or 'jungle chocolates' which grow on the banks. This would explain the often excessive wear noted on their (alleged) fossilised teeth, since lianas have tough shells. On occasions these creatures may leave the water, but are said not to venture far from it. Local legend has it that *mokele-mbembe* is rare, and may be declining in numbers.

As the ice sheets withdrew at the end of the last Ice Age, a vast network of lakes formed extending from what is now northern Canada south into the United States. These are fertile hunting grounds for monster enthusiasts, with recorded sightings and some photographic evidence available from a number of these lakes. Some of the best known monsters include Igopogo of Lake Manitoba, Ogopogo of Okanagan Lake and Champ of Lake Cham-

plain. In some instances a large number of independent witnesses have been present at the sightings. Igopogo, first recorded in 1908, was seen by twenty people off Manipogo Beach on 22 July 1960. Then three monsters surfaced at the same spot just three weeks later, in front of seventeen people. Igopogo has been estimated to be about 12 metres long, with a humped neck and back.

Even stranger reports of a lake monster come from Lake Elsinore in California. The earliest recorded sighting was in 1884, and subsequent descriptions are similar to those from the Canadian lakes. The creature is said to be snake-like in appearance, about 3.5 metres long and almost 1 metre wide, according to one witness. But the most peculiar fact in this case is that, unlike the more northerly lakes, which in parts can be nearly 250 metres deep, Lake Elsinore has dried up twice in living memory, during 1951 and 1955. No trace of any such creature was seen at these times, which strongly suggests that it cannot be a fish, though it could conceivably be a reptile, amphibian – or even a thoughtform or ghost. What is certain is that the world's lake mysteries cannot be accounted for by any single type of known, material creature.

SEE ALSO *Bigfoots, almas and yeti; Case of Ruth; Consensus reality; Cryptozoology; Dragons; Entity enigma; Loch Ness monster; Thoughtography; Tulpas.*

FOAFLORE

Certain outrageous stories, widely believed as fact, enjoy such universal popularity that they become part of the Forteans' folklore. They are known as 'foaf[friend-of-a-friend]lore', and some of the better-known foaftales include the following.

When 'beehive' hairdos were fashionable in the late 1950s and early 1960s it was common to hear of the death of a friend of a friend whose hair had harboured some kind of bugs that had eaten into her scalp. This seems to be a modern version of late eighteenth-century stories – some of which may well have been true.

A group of friends, including a medical or veterinary student, are eating in an ethnic restaurant. When the meal is nearly over the student discovers that the bones left on his plate are of a cat/rat/dog.

On-the-road foaftales include the famous phantom hitch-hiker story, and several variations of the one about the hitch-hiker who believing he had been invited into a traveller's car, put his hand around the passenger door. However, he was mistaken, and the irate driver drove off – later to discover the hitch-hiker's hand/finger(s) still in the door.

Issue No. 50 of the *Fortean Times* includes the following classic foaftale in its Fishy Yarns section:

A biology student, out fishing with three friends off the coast of Mexico, caught a shark. Cutting it open he discovered his stolen gold Rolex wristwatch on a man's severed arm. Police took fingerprints in a bid to identify the thief.

A student of Forteana is, by definition, prepared to accept a whole host of seemingly outrageous phenomena including fishfalls and startling coincidences. What rouses the suspicions that a particular story may be foaflore is its glib retelling as fact, its sheer popularity and the willingness of the teller to ascribe the happening to someone distantly attached to his or her own circle. Yet one should be wary of dismissing such tales lightly, for foaflore, like folklore, has rich potential for the Fortean and sociologist alike.

SEE ALSO *CSICOP; Explanations; Fate; Fishfalls; Charles Fort; Life imitates art; Phantom hitch-hiker.*

WEREWOLVES

Belief that human beings can change shape and become beasts is very ancient; primitive man would don the skin of a fierce animal for sacred rituals in which he believed himself to take on its characteristics. As time passed, shape-changing became a sign of Devil worship, and were-wolves ('man-wolves'), or were-bears (or whatever the local beast of prey might be) were hunted and destroyed.

Between 1520 and 1630 there were over thirty thousand 'proven' cases of werewolfery in France alone, although perhaps, like the great European witchcraft epidemics, this wave says more about the hunters than the accused. In 1573 a village near Dôle in eastern France was in mortal fear of a marauding werewolf that partially devoured children. When a hunting party came upon the monstrous beast in the act of ripping open a child, they noticed its resemblance to Gilles Garnier, a hermit who lived in the forest. He confessed that he had made a pact with the Devil in one of his forms, who gave him magic ointment that turned him into a ravening beast. Garnier, like most other self-confessed werewolves, was burnt at the stake. One Jean Grenier, however, who boasted of his encounter with a diabolical stranger called the Lord of the Forest, received astonishingly liberal treatment. Even though he had undoubtedly committed hideous crimes and confessed to having used the stranger's wolfskin cloak and ointment to change his shape, he was merely removed to a monastery for the rest of his life.

It seems certain now that many of these murderers were afflicted by lycanthropy, delusional insanity that takes the form of believing oneself to have become a beast, and is often aggravated by the full moon – traditionally the most notorious

The infamous werewolf of Eschenbach, Germany, 1685. Half man, half wolf, such creatures were deemed to have been created through a pact with the Devil.

time for werewolves to strike. The mysterious ointment may well have contained some form of hallucinogen, such as bufotenin, which is secreted by toads and was used by witches to induce sensations of flying. Covered in the ointment and dressed in wolfskin, a lycanthrope would indeed have 'become' a werewolf, having the appetites of the real creature and, if seen from a distance, the shape.

Among the more plausible of the many modern theories put forward about the nature of werewolves involves rabies. Contagious canine rabies, which is communicable to dogs through the bite of wolves and to human beings through the bite of dogs, causes people to snap like maddened dogs and even to run about on all fours. For centuries it was believed that being bitten by a werewolf made the victim a werewolf himself; the connection with rabies is clear, and doubly unfortunate for those accused of werewolfery in less enlightened times.

Yet the phenomenon has such a hold on the

popular imagination that it is hard to believe that its source is merely the pathetic tales of a few diseased peasants running amok. American psychoanalyst Dr Nandor Fodor believes that lycanthropy is a 'psychic mechanism' that can be detected operating through dreams, particularly those featuring transformation, violent bloodshed – and, of course, wolves. Dr Fodor takes the Freudian view that the werewolf is an archetypal symbol of 'sexual sadistic expectations', especially among women with an unconscious masochistic streak.

In his *Man into Wolf* (1951) British anthropologist Dr Robert Eisler made a startling suggestion: that stories of Adolf Hitler biting the carpet in rage indicated 'maniclycanthropic states'. Yet none of the modern theories entirely explains the many cases in which the werewolf has been wounded and traced to the house of a local man where he is seen, back in human form, but wounded in the same place as the monster. Not all our ancestors were blinded by superstition or even by mass hysteria, yet such stories were common in Europe in the sixteenth, seventeenth and eighteenth centuries.

Perhaps there is a clue in the ubiquity of the dark stranger whose magical gifts bring about the shape-changing. Such diabolical figures have been reported throughout history; Men in Black (MIBs) are a standard element in modern UFO encounters. Whatever their context, such beings bring no comfort, but only ultimate disaster for those whom they choose to visit.

SEE ALSO *Angels; Autosuggestion; Case of Ruth; Creative visualisation; The Devil; Doppelgängers; Entity enigma; Fantasy-prone personalities; Hallucinations; Hypnosis; Hysteria; Inspiration in dreams; Mass hysteria; Men in Black; Multiple personality; Possession; Shamanism; Thoughtography; Toad magic; Tulpas; UFOs; Vampires; Witchcraft.*

DRAGONS

Of all creatures of myth and legend, it is the dragon that is accorded a continuing and almost universal awe. An enormous flying reptile, whose very blood and breath are poisonous, it is seen in the West as a demon incarnate. Traditionally, dragons guard treasure and show a predilection for passive maidens, preferably princesses, to be offered as propitiation. A sure way of becoming a legendary hero was to slay the dragon, seize both treasure and princess, and live happily ever after.

Superficially, at least, the symbolism involved in this time-honoured scenario involves Freudian interpretation at its smuggest, although a Jungian might also find familiar elements in the story. However, many versions are not so straightforward. In killing the dragon some heroes also die – the Anglo-Saxon Beowulf attacked the soft underbelly of the 'coiled Worm Grendel', killing both monster and himself in the attempt. In other versions the monster is self-regenerating; the many-headed Hydra was only despatched by Hercules when he had his charioteer burn the stumps of each head as he cut them off.

The Wantley Dragon of South Yorkshire. Creature of myth and legend, literal menace, or monster from the depths of the collective unconscious?

The most famous of all dragon-slayers is St George, believed to have originated from north Africa, whence the story of Perseus rescuing the Ethiopian princess Andromeda from a sea monster came. George's heroic deed is generally accepted as an allegorical allusion to the triumph of the Church over paganism.

Yet symbolism may not account for all dragon stories; the medieval mapmakers' legend 'Here be dragons' may have been the literal truth. Marco Polo's accurate description of a crocodile was given wings by an illustrator who obviously thought them fitting on such an outrageous creature. Yet contestants for the rôle of modern dragon seem pathetic compared to that of myth and legend. The Indonesian Komodo dragon is ugly, lumbering and leathery but does not fly or breathe fire, and the flying lizards of Malaysia glide on webbed wings – but are only 15 centimetres long and unlikely to have posed much of a threat to St George.

The British dragons, more commonly called

'Great Worms', wreaked havoc on the countryside until the seventeenth century, although the best of the stories, such as that of the Lambton Worm, are much earlier. (This Worm was outwitted by an ingenious knight who studded his armour with sharp pieces of metal that severed the monster's heads.) The fact that there are no dragon skeletons, or fossils, littering the landscape can be explained by the fact that dragons, being essentially bags of highly flammable substances, simply self-combust after death.

Many researchers into earth energies believe that the countryside itself is a sort of dragon; sacred sites have been deliberately set out along alignments of powerful earth forces. In Britain many of these lines have come to be associated with St Michael, and so with dragons, for in the Book of Revelation (12:7–9) it is written:

And there was war in heaven; Michael and his angels fought against the dragon; and the dragon fought and his angels,

And prevailed not; neither was their place found any more in heaven.

And the great dragon was cast out, that old serpent, called the Devil, and Satan, which deceiveth the whole world: he was cast out into the earth, and his angels were cast out with him.

The greatest alignment of sacred sites in England begins at St Michael's Mount in Cornwall and runs through several places of ancient power such as the Avebury ring of standing stones. It takes in no fewer than nine places with 'St Michael' in their names, and places with clear dragon associations twelve times. The early Christian missionaries deliberately built their churches on pagan sites as a sign of triumph. It seems more likely that belief built upon belief merely added to whatever 'magical' properties belonged to the land at those locations.

In ancient China geomancers – surveyors using paranormal means – worked out where cities, palaces and so on should be built to gain optimum benefit from the Earth's natural magnetic power. This was seen as being the perfect balance between yin (negative) and yang (positive) currents. Yang areas were sharp-topped mountains inhabited by dragons, and the paths between the peaks were 'dragon paths'. It was necessary to understand the intricacies of geomancy, for to build on an imbalanced site was a grave matter indeed. Indeed, the dragon was such a symbol of power that only the Emperor could depict it with five claws; anyone else who did so was executed.

In most Eastern countries the dragon is seen as a difficult, but potentially beneficial, creature, to be propitiated. Dragons represent the turbulence that is necessary at the start of great work and new undertakings. The Chinese New Year is still celebrated with fire crackers and festive dragons dancing through the streets.

Most people today do not believe in the literal reality of dragons. A surprising number, however, do believe that a great monster lurks in Loch Ness, wilfully elusive though it seems to be. Perhaps dragons would reappear if belief in them were resurrected (although passive princesses, so necessary an accessory in yesteryear, are definitely a thing of the past). The idea of animated thoughtforms, or tulpas, could explain the shadowy existence of such apparently diverse creatures as 'Nessie', the yeti and ufonauts. As scientist Thomas Bearden wrote: 'The collective species unconscious is vastly more powerful than the personal unconscious, and under appropriate conditions it can directly materialise a thoughtform, which may be of an object, or even of a living being.'

Dragons are part of our collective unconscious – almost part of our heritage – and if there is anything in the theory of formative causation it should be relatively easy to create a new generation of dragons through an upsurge of mass belief in them. But perhaps they are much closer to human beings than is generally imagined.

London-based hypnotherapist Dr Brian Roet has discovered that, during their creative visualisation sessions, many of his patients go on an inner journey – and meet a dragon. The dragons are always frightening, but if the patient is encouraged to talk to, or make friends with, the monster, inevitably it is revealed as being small and sad because 'nobody loves me'. 'I meet people who have inner dragons every day,' says Roet, 'but I've never come across one that didn't end up eating out of the patient's hand.'

PHANTOM HITCH-HIKER

One of the great recurring foaflore stories is that of the phantom hitch-hiker. The basic story, which has many variations, is that a motorist picks up a hitch-hiker who sits in the car giving information about him/herself, or uttering local and global prophecies – before vanishing utterly from the vehicle. The shaken driver later discovers that a person answering to that name and description was killed in a car crash on that road on that day some years before.

The tales are current the world over, but as researcher Michael Goss wrote in the *Fortean Times:* 'The localities change, the act doesn't.' Sometimes the hitch-hiker reportedly discusses current affairs – one sweet old lady dressed in expensive clothes (or a nun's habit, depending on the source of the story) on an Interstate Highway between Tacona, Washington and Eugene, Oregon in 1980 warned the driver to repent of his evil ways or he would die in an accident, and predicted another eruption of Mount St Helens. Other ghostly hitch-hikers discuss the holding of American hostages in Iran – before dissolving into thin air.

Goss regards the instances where the hitch-hiker merely hitches a lift, remains silent and disappears as 'closer to the authenticated apparitional encounters on file at the Society for Psychical Research and similar organizations...' He also states that: 'A few ... tales can be instances of apparitional fact imitating ghostly fiction.'

EXPLANATIONS

Charles Fort said: 'There was never an explanation which did not itself require an explanation.' It was a shrewd judgement on the rationalisations of paranormal phenomena by self-appointed scientific 'experts'. Many such explanations are considerably more outrageous than the phenomena they seek to explain away, and many are actually unscientific in their blatant disregard for the facts.

One of the most common explanations for mysterious falls of fish, frogs and other anomalistics, for instance, is that they were 'there in the first place' – but no one had noticed them before. Accusations of hoaxing are also rife: someone must have sprinkled the countryside with tons of periwinkles for a joke, or splashed the same thin strip of land with a bucketful of live minnows twice in ten minutes for a jest. Fort said: 'My own notion is that it is very unsportsmanlike ever to mention fraud. Accept anything. Then explain it your way.'

Sceptics are fond of citing how apparently paranormal phenomena could have been faked, with the idea that if it *could* have been done, it *must* have been done. Even among psychical researchers such an attitude is common – if ectoplasm has once been discovered to be regurgitated butter muslin, then that is what it always is. Such an attitude may be seen as an open invitation to the Cosmic Joker, the archetypal trickster who ensures that nothing – even a fake – is as it seems.

Scepticism is an extreme form of gullibility, which writer Brian Inglis has called 'a mental illness'. Being rational at all costs may, in fact, blind an individual to events in the real world, just as the conditioning of the Maoris blinded them to the approach of the first European ships – they were not part of the Maoris' consensus reality, therefore the vessels were not seen by them. An individual in the last throes of scepticism will accept any rational explanation even if it is utterly ludicrous. When little green frogs fell on Athens in 1980 a tornado was blamed, even though no tornadoes had been reported and only small green frogs fell – no other debris was reported.

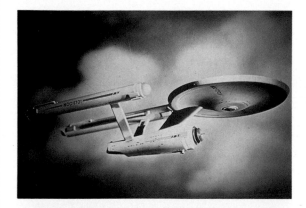

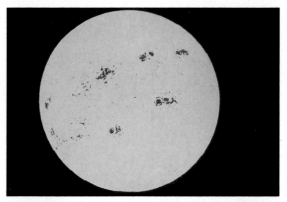

(above left) *In fiction, adventures in outer space are well established. The starship* Enterprise, *captained by Mr Kirk and Mr Spock, has been taking the Good Guys' message to beyond the stars since the 1960s in the* Star Trek *television series and films. In the world of science fact, however, space travel is still largely a dream.*

(opposite) *Dog running under a full moon, the time when, according to folklore, psychic powers are at their strongest. The moon is also believed to regulate physical and emotional rhythms, although modern proponents of biorhythms are undecided about its importance in their various systems. In some tests, the mental, physical and emotional cycles of certain people were discovered to be only days long, while others had greatly extended cycles. Perhaps biorhythms are considerably more individual than any of the current systems allow.*

(above right) *Do sunspots have a radical effect on human behaviour, helping to cause riots, wars and upheavals? There is evidence that solar flares may be considerably more important to us than orthodox scientists believe. The picture shows sunspots on 5 September 1973. Red indicates 'north pole' and blue 'south pole'. Each pair of sunspots has a magnetic line running between them like the lines of force from a horseshoe magnet, stretching up into the sun's atmosphere in an arch.*

Artist's impression of the 'Big Bang' that created the universe, about 15 billion years ago, according to many modern cosmologists. In this picture, the Big Bang is portrayed at a time when giant clouds of gas (white spots) have started condensing into what will later become galaxies. However, the Big Bang theory provokes several questions. What was there before the Big Bang? Is the visible universe the actual extent of the universe or is that merely the extent of our understanding? And in ascribing a date to the beginning of the universe are we being hopelessly medieval, for time is yet another man-made concept with, as modern quantum theory shows, no relevance to the microcosm or macrocosm?

Artist's impression of the earth seen from space, with the moon (left). Are we the only intelligent creatures in the universe? Is the earth alone in its ability to sustain life as we know it? Or is the universe inhabited by life forms that are so different to us that they cannot be monitored by our technology? Are they, essentially, only open to psychic perception?

Dr Jacques Vallée at a UFO symposium in 1980. One of the world's most highly regarded ufologists, he is most concerned with the apparent links between encounters with UFOs and historical accounts of meetings with other-world beings. His researches have led him to suggest that many experiences of UFOs are a curious mixture of 'nuts and bolts' reality and an internal, psychological or psychic experience. In UFOs there may be a temporary merging of different kinds of reality.

'Daylight disc' photographed by Hannah McRoberts in October 1981, north of Kelsey Bay, Vancouver Island, Canada. She was photographing the mountain and neither she nor her companion saw the UFO. Many unexplained objects or figures come to light only when photographs are developed, raising questions about the nature of visible reality. Can a camera be more 'psychic' than a human being, or are we merely so conditioned that we do not notice anomalous phenomena?

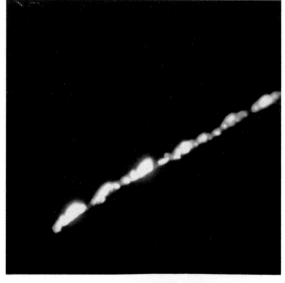

An alleged UFO, but most probably a lenticular cloud, at Phoenix, Arizona. A large proportion of so-called UFOs on investigation become IFOs – Identified Flying Objects. Similarly, flocks of geese seen in unusual lighting conditions, the planet Venus and ordinary aircraft have been mistaken for UFOs. However, just because most UFOs turn out to be naturally occurring phenomena does not necessarily imply that all UFOs can be explained in this way.

Spectacular chain-of-light display seen in the sky over Monserrat, Spain, in 1984. This particular example remains unexplained, but apparently anomalous lights can frequently be ascribed to natural, but rare, geological phenomena. However, many strange lights seem to possess a kind of intelligence, and have been noticed to interact with the observers, and even with the observers' thoughts.

Artist's impression of the 'nuts and bolts' UFO, witnessed landing in April 1966 in Helena, Montana. Many such saucer-shaped craft, with the characteristic portholes and landing gear, have been reported since 1947, when the first 'flying saucers' were seen in America, though there have been few physical signs of such landings.

Publicity badge for the promotion of Whitley Strieber's bestselling Communion (1987), showing the face of an entity allegedly encountered by him. Strieber claimed to have had a series of profoundly disturbing experiences of being kidnapped by aliens. Critics pointed out that as Strieber is, by profession, a writer of fantasy and horror stories, his books may simply be cynical moneyspinning exercises.

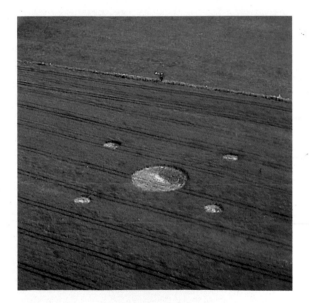

Quintuplet crop field circle observed north-west of Silbury, Wiltshire, in 1989. Although strange circles in fields have been reported over the centuries, the crop field circle phenomenon has only become intense since 1980, when it became a common sight in the south-western counties of England. Theories abound, including the 'upwards vortex' of the scientists, and the 'groaning Gaia' idea of the 'Green' occultists, who think that the circles represent a cry for help from the planet.

Large crop field circle close to an escarpment at Westbury. Unlike the corn in the faked circles, that of the genuine phenomenon continues to grow, even though it lies flat on the ground, twisted either clockwise or anticlockwise. In Japan, the appearance of such circles in or close to paddy-fields was accompanied by a corresponding loss of hundreds of gallons of water from the area.

Since Marilyn Monroe's death in 1962 various mediums have claimed to have been in contact with her, including British 'direct voice' medium Leslie Flint. The discarnate Marilyn has, it is believed, admitted that her death by barbiturate overdose was an accident – yet the most recent research indicates that there was considerable foul play surrounding her last moments.

Angels presenting the souls of the elect to God, from the Breviary of Cardinal Grimani. The ancient Christian idea of heaven and hell, apportioned according to the judgement of the soul, bears little resemblance to the immediate afterlife state as described by those who have had a Near Death Experience (NDE). These people have been clinically dead for a short time and often report a blissful other-worldly experience with no sense of judgement or accusation of sin.

Typically disturbing images of hell: a demon carries off a woman's soul (above) from a fresco in Orvieto Cathedral, and the damned have their eyes scratched out in hell, from a manuscript in the Bodleian (right). Perhaps even more disturbing, however, is the fact that a small percentage of those who report an NDE claim to have actually experienced such terrifying realms. Whereas most NDErs are reluctant to return, those who have had negative NDEs wholeheartedly welcome resuscitation. Most of those who have them appear to be attempted suicides.

The vision of Lama Tsong Khapa, whose vision of the Buddha of Wisdom was accompanied by the pouring out of rays of nectar, causing him to experience great bliss. But some of his companions were unable to share this ecstasy, due to karmic obscurations.

Fort wrote in *The Book of Damned* (1919): 'A great many scientists are good impressionists: they snub the impertinences of detail.' He cites the case of Dr Hahn, who, when he published details of finding fossils in meteorites, was described by a fellow scientist as 'a kind of half insane man, whose imagination has run away with him'. Nevertheless, fossils continued to be found in meteorites.

Astronomers have frequently snubbed the impertinences of detail where sitings of Unidentified Flying Objects are concerned. Favourite explanation for UFOs are misinterpretations of flocks of geese seen in moonlight, or the planet Venus. Occasionally these explanations fit the case, but not every time, yet the 'experts' are satisfied that they have rid the world of another so-called mystery.

The most common explanation is, paradoxically, that there is no such thing. It is the ultra-sceptics' credo that as paranormal phenomena cannot exist they will not waste their time thinking about them, let alone investigating them.

SEE ALSO *Autosuggestion; Boggle threshold; Case of Ruth; Consensus reality; Cosmic Joker; Cottingley fairies; Crop field circles; CSICOP; Helen Duncan; Experimenter effect; Fishfalls; Charles Fort; Katie King; Limits of science; Mass hysteria; Parapsychology; Philip experiment; The Resurrection; Society for Psychical Research; SORRAT; Spontaneous Human Combustion; Turin Shroud; UFO paradox; UFOs.*

V The UFO Enigma

UFOs • UFO classification • Balls of light • Entity enigma • Men in Black • Modern ufology • UFO paradox • Crop field circles

Parapsychology has sometimes been known as the 'Cinderella science', but this term is more appropriately applied to ufology – the study of Unidentified Flying Objects (UFOs), which is generally shunned by academics of all sorts. Yet, ironically, it is in this field that all aspects of the paranormal come together most tantalisingly.

Man has always believed that the gods come from the skies and there have always been gods who fulfil this belief. Things seen in the sky do seem to have a powerful archetypal place in our imaginations, and it may be significant that the creatures who put those things in the sky appear to know this. (When writer Jacques Vallée was asked if the ufonauts could be the ancient gods, he replied cautiously, 'They could certainly make us worship them.')

Although UFOs have been witnessed throughout history, it was only in 1947 that 'flying saucers' were seen in the sky – over Mount Rainer, Washington State, USA, by Kenneth Arnold. Wave after wave of sightings followed, and stories about crashed saucers and government cover-ups proliferated. Then the ufonauts began to contact human beings, explaining that they came from a variety of remote star systems and introducing the contactee to alien ways, even to the extent of having sexual intercourse with him or her. Messages about averting global disaster were passed on, and cult movements grew up around the gospels according to the aliens. More distressingly, hypnotic regression began to reveal that repeated abduction by aliens was common, but that the memory was buried by the abductee until it resurfaced under hypnosis. Often the subject recalled undergoing

some sort of surgical operation at the hands of his captors, and a scar would be discovered on his body that matched the story. Some researchers, such as American Leo Sprinkler, now claim that abductions are so widespread that they organise annual conferences for abductees. Clearly there is something going on that should give us cause for concern, if only to isolate a mass delusion. It does not, however, appear to be that.

The problem with UFOs is that they are essentially paradoxical in nature, combining elements that are both ludicrous and veridical, physical and psychical. 'Nuts and bolts' UFOs leave physical traces, such as scuffed gravel or holes where the craft's landing gear stood. Sometimes the area around the landing site remains as barren as fairy rings for a long time after the visitation, or vegetation in the area may be burnt by the force of the downblast of the UFO as it takes off. Yet the contactee may believe he has dreamt it all – until he sees the evidence for himself.

Sometimes UFOs appear to come and go without contacting, or being seen by, human beings. The perfect flattened circles popularly known as 'Crop field circles' are believed to be the only sign of such a visit, although there are those who believe the phenomenon to be the result of a freak meteorological event, such as a tornado. In terms of hard evidence, both schools of thought are equally valid.

Legends already surround the arrival of the UFOs; witnesses may be visited by the Men in Black (MIB) who appear to be unreal, and issue vague but disturbing threats about discussing the landing with anyone. Even an intense interest in the UFO phenomenon is believed to activate the MIB – one enthusiast claims to have been followed by a man in a black suit who cornered him with the words: 'Can you spare your life?'

Most contactees become changed people as a direct result of their experiences, just as visionaries and mystics are lifted out of one sort of reality and shown another. The similarities between 'classic' apparitions, such as visions of the Virgin Mary, and the encounter experience have been noted by several leading researchers such as John A. Keel, Hilary Evans and Jacques Vallée.

It may be that something 'out there' is playing with us, or is genuinely trying to help us, or that our minds are meeting some other force halfway, each giving the other substance, energy and influence. Whatever the motive, these encounters are succeeding in unsettling and controlling our reality – and as such ought to be the subject of massive co-operation among ufologists and parapsychologists, psychologists, sociologists and his-

torians. But so far only a handful of researchers have seen the significance – and perhaps the danger – of the coming of the UFOs.

UFOs

Reports of mysterious objects in the sky date back to Old Testament times and before. The modern era of the Unidentified Flying Object (a term coined by the United States Air Force in 1953), however, dates back to immediately after the Second World War, at a time of excited speculation about the possibility of space travel and of intelligent life on other planets.

The term 'flying saucer' arose out of the experience of American businessman Kenneth Arnold

George Adamski describes one of his rides on board a UFO to US chat-show host Long John Nebel. But were Adamski's other-world trips just flights of fantasy?

on 24 June 1947. He was flying his own plane in the region of Mount Rainer in Washington State when, in a clear sky, at roughly 3 p.m., he saw what he described as a 'chain of nine peculiar aircraft flying from north to south at approximately 9500 feet elevation'. He was able to observe the strange craft for between two and a half and three minutes; he saw them particularly clearly as they passed in front of Mount Rainer. 'I thought it was very peculiar that I couldn't find their tails but assumed they were some type of jet planes ... when the sun reflected from one or two or three of those units, they appeared to be completely round.' A trained observer, Arnold calculated that the craft had a speed of at least 1200 miles per hour, an astonishing speed for those days. In conversation with a reporter, Arnold described the craft as looking like 'flying saucers'.

As a witness Kenneth Arnold enjoyed, and still enjoys, considerable credibility. He is a cool, rational individual, who could not have been influenced by previous reports of UFOs – because there had been none. He sought rational explanations for what he had seen, and went out of his way to shun publicity; only later did he become a serious researcher into the UFO phenomenon (or a ufologist, as such researchers became known).

Press reports of what Arnold had seen produced a profusion of other sightings – including one by two airline pilots and the first-ever photograph of a 'flying saucer', taken by a US coastguard – within the next ten days. Such was the public furore that the US Air Force set up its own record of sightings, known as Project Blue Book, as early as 1948. This was finally disbanded in 1969 after an official US government enquiry published its findings in the Condon Report, which concluded that 90 per cent of the sightings reported could be attributed to natural phenomena (balloons, meteorites, lenticular clouds and so on), as well as to hoaxes and frauds, and that there was no case for extraterrestrial origins. There were dissenting voices, notably J. Allen Hynek, Professor of Astronomy at Northwestern University, who suggested that a percentage of sightings, albeit small, could not be explained in this way, and that these anomalous reports seemed to support the view that Earth was receiving visitors from outer space.

The most famous abductees of all time, Betty and Barney Hill, discuss the design of the UFO that abducted them in the early 1960s.

Arnold was not, however, the first man on Earth to see the 'flying saucers' – if George Adamski was to be believed. In his *Flying Saucers Have Landed*, which became a bestseller as soon as it was published in 1953, Adamski claimed that he had been seeing – and photographing – them since October 1946. He went further, claiming to be the first human being to enjoy contact with intelligent aliens.

Adamski wrote that his first encounter had taken place on 20 November 1952 near Desert Center, California. The visitor, allegedly from Venus, appeared – in the presence of six other witnesses in what was described as a 'beautiful small craft', which had apparently emerged from a much larger spaceship. 'The beauty of his form', Adamski wrote, 'surpassed anything I had ever seen.'

The Venusian was about 'five foot six inches tall' with long, blond hair and wore a brown uniform of a glossy material with no visible fastenings, seams or pockets. Speaking telepathically, or by means of signs, he told Adamski that others of his people were already living on Earth, disguised as human beings. As in many subsequent reports of contacts with aliens, he announced that his civilisation was concerned about our development of nuclear power and nuclear weapons. Adamski was allowed to see inside his craft, but failed to take a successful photograph of it.

Adamski's account, like most of the hundreds of similar accounts that have followed it, has not been given much credence by serious ufologists. It may be significant that, with growing public awareness of the scientists' view that there is unlikely to be intelligent life on the other planets in our solar system, the alien visitors have tended in recent years to come from further afield than Venus and Mars. However, there remains a residue of cases that cannot so easily be dismissed.

One of these provocative cases was that of a patrolman from Socorro, New Mexico, who in April 1964 reported seeing two people dressed in white near a 200-foot hemispherical object, which then took off with a loud roar, emitting a blue jet flame. Later he saw four deep impressions in the ground where the UFO had stood, and two other impressions where he had seen a ladder leading to a door in its side.

Descriptions of UFO occupants vary widely, some of them clearly influenced by science fiction, but in recent years attention has been focused on one particular type of being. Typically, this is under five feet tall, hairless, with fragile or emaciated limbs, a relatively large, high-domed head, tiny nose and mouth and large, narrow eyes that wrap some way round the head. This is the type of being that features in many reports of abductions of human beings by aliens. On the night of 19 September 1961 Mr and Mrs Barney Hill were driving through New Hampshire when they saw a large, disc-shaped object and felt compelled to stop and walk over to it. Later, under hypnosis by a Boston psychiatrist, they recalled being taken aboard the flying saucer, undressed, and medically examined by a group of such humanoids.

There have been hundreds of similar accounts of abductions, frequently recalled under hypnotic regression, when the subject has no conscious memory of events after first approaching the UFO. In several cases they are associated with mysterious body scars which, under hypnosis, are recalled as being connected with the probing of medical instruments. One possible explanation, favoured by Dr Alvin Lawson and other recent researchers, is that the subjects are actually recalling their birth trauma (although this would not explain the initial UFO sighting). Another explanation is that extraterrestrials are experimenting in genetic engineering, and may even be breeding a new race, a hybrid of *Homo sapiens* and their own. (It has been suggested that such an experiment in the remote past produced the great evolutionary leap between our ape-like ancestors and the far more intelligent *Homo sapiens*.)

The answer to the UFO mystery may lie in outer space – it is highly unlikely that this little planet is the only one to have produced intelligent life. Or it may, as some researchers believe, lie in geological phenomena that we as yet barely understand – perhaps in some form of electromagnetic force. The answer may even lie in the reaches of the human mind, which are just as mysterious and fascinating as anything in the galaxies. The final answer may lie a century, or just a day, away.

Meanwhile, serious organisations such as the British UFO Research Association (BUFORA), are carefully recording and analysing the hundreds of UFO reports that continue to flow in from the public, and are developing increasingly sophisticated techniques for separating the hoaxes and mistaken sightings from genuinely mysterious phenomena. They still, however, have a long way to go before ufology is taken seriously. While parapsychology has finally been awarded its own chair at Edinburgh University, there are few members of the Society for Psychical Research (SPR) who would own up to a serious interest in ufology – eminent researchers Manfred Cassirer and Hilary Evans being notable exceptions.

SEE ALSO *Cosmic Joker; Entity enigma; Fantasy-prone personalities; Charles Fort; Hallucination; Hypnosis; Hypnotic regression; Limits of science; Men in Black; Modern ufology; Other dimensions; Search for extraterrestrial life; Time; Timeslips; UFO classification; UFO paradox.*

Something unexplained – and unnoticed at the time – hangs over this tourist's photograph in 1974.

UFO CLASSIFICATION

Originally developed by the late Professor J. Allen Hynek when he was consultant to Project Blue Book, the following categories are used to classify UFO reports:

1. Nocturnal lights: anomalous lights, often moving erratically or with sudden changes in speed, direction or colour.

2. Daylight discs: the original 'flying saucers' – objects seen in the sky before nightfall. They can be any shape, but usually appear to be made of some kind of metal.

3. Radar visuals: UFOs witnessed simultaneously on radar and visually. Hynek rejected radar-alone 'sightings', as they can be caused by a host of natural factors.

4. Close encounters of the first kind (CE1s): simple sightings of a UFO from close quarters.

5. Close encounters of the second kind (CE2s): a sighting that is accompanied by physical evidence, such as impressions in the soil where the UFO landed, or electrical failure in the neighbourhood of the sighting which returns to normal when the UFO disappears.

6. Close encounters of the third kind (CE3s): by far the best-known category, thanks to the film of the same name on which Hynek worked as consultant to director Steven Spielberg. This category includes contact with aliens and is often not taken seriously even by UFO researchers.

7. Close encounters of the fourth kind (CE4s): contact with, and abduction by, the humanoid occupants of UFOs.

8. Close encounters of the fifth kind (CE5s): not universally accepted by ufologists. This category covers the newly discovered phenomenon of repeated abductions of specially selected humans, who 'bury' the memory of the experience until it is revealed, usually under hypnotic regression. Researcher Leo Sprinkler is at the forefront of highly provocative research into 'repeater abductees'.

SEE ALSO *Balls of light; Entity enigma; Men in Black; Modern ufology; Other dimensions; Search for extraterrestrial life; UFO paradox; UFOs.*

BALLS OF LIGHT

Anomalous balls of light (BOLs) occur in a wide range of contexts, and are usually studied – if at all – as isolated categories. Earth lights, earthquake lights, 'spook' lights, ball lightning, seance-room BOLs, BOL-type UFOs and so on. However, a small, but international, group of researchers, working independently but pooling their findings as Project BOLIDE (Ball of Light International Data Exchange), are accumulating data which not only reveal how little is known about these phenomena, but also raise the possibility that they may not be so distinct as hitherto considered. Underlying many, if not all, may be a core phenomenon with very remarkable attributes.

In Hessdalen, an isolated farming district in central Norway, a flow of observations of luminous objects in the sky have been reported since 1981. Because the sightings recurred, investigators were able to set up observation posts, from which they recorded huge balls of light, moving slowly and silently at low altitude across the terrain.

That the lights have physical existence of a sort is beyond question; they have been photographed on hundreds of occasions, as well as observed instrumentally. But though the local residents reported structured objects, Project Hessdalen's instruments failed to detect anything of the sort: so far as the investigators are concerned, all that was observed were simple luminous phenomena with no discernible shape or structure.

If there is really nothing more to the Hessdalen phenomena than balls of light, this argues strongly in favour of some sort of natural phenomenon. But there is no parallel in our current knowledge for a light that is longer-lasting than any reported earthquake light or ball lightning; which is totally silent; which travels over distances of several kilometres; which has been photographed in front of mountains at no great distance, so that celestial objects seem to be ruled out; and which is far larger and brighter than any known light in nature.

But if there is no parallel for the Hessdalen lights in scientific knowledge, there is in reported experience. American investigator Greg Long – one of BOLIDE's contributors – has been researching the Yakima lights in Washington State over a period of years, documenting characteristics that match in many respects those observed at Hessdalen.

In 1981 Dr Harley Rutledge, a physics professor at Cape Cirardeau, Missouri, published the results of a seven-year investigation of mysterious lights reported in the nearby Piedmont hills. During that period, his instruments and cameras had recorded 178 anomalous objects on 157 occasions. Many were simultaneously observed from separate positions, enabling the investigators to determine the course, distance, speed and movements of the objects, and thus to eliminate all obvious explanations such as aircraft, satellites, meteorites, car headlamps, street lights, refraction effects, mirages and so on.

But there was a further disconcerting dimension to Rutledge's study: on at least thirty-two occasions synchronicity was noted between the movement of the object and the activity of the observers. Somehow, although at a distance of 3 kilometres or more, the objects seemed aware of the observers' actions, and responded to them by modifying their own behaviour.

This would be hard to accept, were it not matched by no less bizarre experiences at Hessdalen, where

Mystery light photographed over Marfa, Texas, in 1986.

project leader Erling Strand established that when a laser beam was directed towards a periodically flashing 'UFO', the flash period was immediately doubled, the original pattern being resumed when the laser was switched off. There is no known phenomenon that behaves in this manner. The implication is that some categories of BOL are capable of something approaching intelligent response, and even something like extrasensory perception (ESP).

The great majority of incidents involving BOLs are simpler, although not necessarily easier to explain. During the Second World War, a Canadian soldier in Belgium saw a glowing globe travelling from the direction of the front line towards Antwerp. It seemed to be about a metre in diameter and looked as though it consisted of cloudy glass with a light inside, giving a soft white glow. It was travelling silently about 13 metres above the ground at a speed of about 50 kilometres per hour. It was not simply drifting with the wind, but was obviously powered and controlled. It was followed by another, which in turn was followed by more – five in all.

Taken in isolation, there is not much that investigators can do to elucidate such a report. The first test, of course, is to try to match it to one or other of the known natural phenomena – ball lightning, plasma associated with power lines, and so on. But often these phenomena are themselves insufficiently understood.

A frequently suggested explanation is the *ignis fatuus*, otherwise known as marsh lights, or will o' the wisp. It is often supposed that this phenomenon occurs when some kind of gas such as methane is generated by the decomposition of organic matter, most often in swampland, and then spontaneously ignites under appropriate natural conditions. But investigator Michael Frizzell has pointed out that 'in the unlikely event that it would assume a basketball-sized shape, such a geometry would provide only enough gas volume to burn for brief seconds, certainly not long enough to account for rapid aerial manoeuvres or lengthy frolics through the woods'. And Curtis Fuller, editor of *Fate*, has challenged the swamp gas theorists 'to produce a little swamp gas under laboratory conditions, ignite it spontaneously, and produce

their own little fireballs that go bouncing merrily along for minutes at a time'.

It is, above all, the *movement* of the light that makes the conventional explanation unsatisfactory. Even if we accept that gas emerging from a swamp might, under certain conditions, be ignited by some natural cause, we could hardly expect it to behave as did the light that a Mr Pike, walking in marshy ground in Queensland, Australia, saw hovering and dancing about 50 metres in front of him. By the time he had approached to within 20 metres, he could see it was a huge glowing ball, hovering about 2.5 metres above the ground. Suddenly it soared to one side. Realising that, if he were to follow, he would be moving into dangerously marshy ground, he halted. The light halted too, 'hesitated' a while, then glided a little closer to him, as though tempting him to follow. Scores of accounts of such 'tempting' behaviour have been recorded.

It is hard not to attribute some degree of purposeful behaviour to the BOL reported in 1938 by three residents of Brunswick, Georgia, who visited an old millpond that local folklore named as haunted by spook lights. They saw a small blue light form near the ground, growing from the size of a tennis ball to that of a football. When it started to move away down the road, they followed it; it was about knee-high above the ground, illuminating the road as it went. They followed it for about half a kilometre to a schoolhouse, where it left the road to travel along one side of the building, after which it rejoined the road and continued on its way. At a fork in the road it 'chose' one route and followed it for another half kilometre, then went over a gate to an abandoned log-house, which it circled, then entered by the only door. After a few minutes it re-emerged and returned the way it had come, at one time passing within less than a metre of the narrator. When it reached the precise point where it had first appeared, it hovered, grew smaller and vanished.

'Spook lights', under various names, are found in many parts of the world. Typical are the Brown Mountain lights in North Carolina, observed since at least 1771 – which rules out car and railway locomotive headlights. Although thousands see these lights every year, descriptions vary: Michael

Frizzell once watched about forty lights for some ninety minutes, though never more than four or five at a time; they appeared at near-ground level, among the trees. After spending several hours on the summit looking in vain for the lights, a local filling station proprietor and a group of companions, were just leaving when a strong light as long as a man's outstretched arm formed a few metres over their heads, emitting a sizzling noise. After hovering motionless for a time, it lengthened and shortened several times in succession. Clearly – quite apart from the fact that there are no swampy areas on Brown Mountain – this is something far more complex than spontaneously igniting marsh gas.

The most commonly suggested explanation for many BOL phenomena is of course ball lightning, despite the fact that it is not known what ball lightning is or what causes it, and although many scientists continue to question whether it exists at all. Ball lightning is most commonly reported as a short-lived (seconds rather than minutes) luminous mass, generally spherical and rarely larger than a half metre in diameter. It is frequently, but not invariably, seen in association with electrical storms; it is liable to explode on contact with objects but often seems to avoid them; sometimes it damages property, but sometimes it passes through solid objects without leaving any trace of its passage.

The thunderstorm connection is apparent in a 1961 case from Australia: a housewife was in her kitchen during such a storm, when she sensed a 'great thing' over her shoulder. She turned and saw a 'fireball' behind her. She ran through the dining room, heading for the stairs, followed by the ball which overtook her in the stairwell and headed upstairs. She followed it into the bedroom where her brothers were still in bed. They heard a violent crash, after which the BOL passed harmlessly through the room and out of the open window.

Occasionally ball lightning 'attacks' humans; yet in France, in 1895, a ball passed through a French farmhouse room, ignoring the two people in it. It passed through the floor (leaving a hole to mark its passage) into the sheepfold below, where it killed five sheep (though with no sign of burn or wound) yet left unharmed the shepherd boy who was with them.

More malevolent-seeming was a French BOL from 1961: a man whose wife was a heavy drinker was woken one morning by his wife's screams. He found her lying on the living-room floor, burning fiercely; his view of her was almost completely obstructed by a luminous sphere. He was severely burned while trying to extinguish the fire, yet the rug on which she was lying was not burned nor was the room damaged. This case seems to suggest a connection with another anomalous phenomenon, that of so-called spontaneous human combustion.

Ball lightning is a very unsatisfactory explanation for any of these cases, nor does it convincingly account for the reports made during the Second World War of what came to be called 'foo fighters'. In one 1944 incident an American bomber crew over Germany reported a big amber BOL that suddenly appeared alongside the B-17, stayed with the plane for about forty-five minutes, then suddenly was gone. Forty-five minutes is way over any known upper limit for the duration of ball lightning, yet the circumstances do not seem appropriate for any other natural phenomenon such as St Elmo's fire.

BOLs also manifest in what seems to be a 'psychic' context. They are frequently reported in seance rooms, but also in less specific circumstances. In 1956 a Mrs Hight was prospecting with her husband in the New Mexico desert. While her husband was away on an exploration trip, she became very ill and felt herself on the verge of death. Then one afternoon a small light appeared in one corner of the cabin; it grew in size and within moments expanded into a large glowing light that changed into a wheel, which whirled through her body. She felt a surge of vitality and well-being: she rose, and realised that the light had completely restored her health.

It is tempting to classify Mrs Hight's experience as the exteriorisation of an interior fantasy, although that would not make it any the less remarkable. But what criteria will enable us to draw a line between her BOL and the 'globe of fire' which on a calm but overcast and wet day in 1843 entered by a chimney into a workshop where about thirty

French hatmakers were working? An old man who suffered from rheumatism was struck and thrown several paces across the room. When he recovered, his rheumatic pains were gone.

It seems improbable that the BOL came to Plancy in order to cure the old man's rheumatism; Mrs Hight's BOL, on the other hand, seems to have visited her cabin for the express purpose of helping her. Does that make her case 'psychic', and the other 'a natural accident'? If so, how do we classify the Egryn lights that appeared during the 1905 religious revival in North Wales, hovering over chapels where a prominent preacher, Mrs Mary Jones, was due to preach? The lights were seen on many separate occasions by dozens of independent witnesses, including sceptical London journalists. The conclusion that the lights were directly associated with Mary Jones seems inescapable; their manifestations seem to have been both controlled and purposeful.

Yet other factors suggest a natural explanation. Lights, seemingly familiar, had been observed in the same area long before Mary Jones's lifetime. Egryn Chapel stands near marshy ground such as might generate will o' the wisp-type BOLs. In addition, Paul Devereux has shown that many of the sightings occur along a prominent geological fault line, which, according to his hypothesis, is capable of generating short-lived luminous effects that could be responsible for many reports of UFOs.

What seems to have been happening in this case, as at Hessdalen and Piedmont, is that a physical BOL phenomenon, either autonomously or under some kind of external direction, was acting in some kind of awareness of human activities. BOLs are, in the strictest application of the term, Unidentified Flying Objects. But just as some BOLs seem to tempt the witness into dangerous terrain, so these BOL cases seem to be inviting us towards the concept of some kind of natural phenomenon at present unknown to science, possessing some degree of autonomous control, and able in some fashion to interact with the human mind.

SEE ALSO *Cosmic Joker; The Devil; Electric people; Eleventh-hour syndrome; Entity enigma; ESP; Fairies; Ghosts; Healing; Modern ufology; Psi-mediated instrumental response; Rosenheim poltergeist; Spontaneous human combustion; Telepathy; Traumas and psi; UFOs; Visions of the Virgin Mary.*

ENTITY ENIGMA

Claims to have encountered other-worldly entities have been made from the earliest times for which records exist. Often a meeting with a divine being has been the starting point of a religious system, and priests have claimed to act under the instruction, often communicated on a face-to-face basis, of deities who manifested to them in human form.

Even today, the best known other-worldly encounters are associated with religious belief. Millions flock annually to Lourdes in southern France, where in 1858 a thirteen-year-old peasant girl, Bernadette Soubirous, is supposed to have encountered the Virgin Mary. She is just one of hundreds of Catholic visionaries, and similar incidents occur in every culture. Whether among primitive tribespeople, or amid the trappings of technical advance, claims are made about meeting either benevolent gods, malevolent devils, or their ministers, angelic or demonic.

Apart from religious figures, most other entities in the past have been folklore creatures – fairies and other forms of 'little people' whose interactions with humans feature in popular traditional cultures throughout the world. More recently the emphasis has been on entities who are literally 'other-worldly' – visiting Earth from other parts of the universe. However, these are not so very different from religious entities, since for many people extraterrestrial Cosmic Guardians and Space Brothers are the equivalent of figures such as Jesus. Indeed, Jesus and other religious figures are quite frequently reported to have been met by witnesses, who claim that they are extraterrestrial beings. On 27 July 1958 George King met the Master Jesus, allegedly a Venusian, at Holdston Down in Devon; while one-time motor-racing journalist Claude Vorilhon (today known as Raël) met him at a garden party on an unnamed planet to which

Jean Seberg as St Joan, patron saint of France. Were her voices from God, as she claimed, or were they much more sinister in origin?

he was invited by his extra-terrestrial contacts. There are, broadly speaking, three ways of accounting for other-worldly entities:

1. They exist, and are what they seem to be.
2. They exist, but are not what they seem to be.
3. They have no material existence, but are some kind of illusion or simulacrum.

Each of these models exists in many versions.

Almost invariably, other-worldly entities are associated with a system of beliefs, and as such they are often considered by those who subscribe to those beliefs – to have physical reality.

Catholic theology, for example, holds that when the Virgin Mary appears to visionaries such as Bernadette, she does so in physical form, for it is accepted Catholic doctrine that she was taken to Heaven in her earthly body.

Difficulties arise when the same entity is described differently by different witnesses. Even granting that Jesus's mother has not aged since her earthly death in the first century AD, one would expect her to appear as a Palestinian woman at least fifty years old. In practice, however, Bernadette described her as 'a young girl, no taller than myself' – and Bernadette was distinctly undersized for her age; to her dying day she maintained that 'she was very young, very young, tiny'.

Other problems arise with other types of otherworldly entity. It is hard, for example, to account for the fact that, although almost every extraterrestrial entity differs from every other, virtually all have certain similarities: like George Adamski's Orthon from Venus, they are more or less human in appearance, and are biologically adapted to our terrestrial climate, gravity, atmospheric content and so on, in defiance of what we would expect to be true of visitors from other worlds.

Many witnesses report physical contact with the entities they encounter. Madeleine Aumont of Dozulé in France, who claimed several meetings with Jesus in 1972, was invited by him to touch his hands ('they were warm like those of a living person') and the wounds he received at the time of his death (she said they felt deep). But objective evidence to support this subjective testimony is wholly lacking. Reports of traces left by entities are comparatively rare and always ambiguous, and neither the religious nor the extraterrestrial entities have ever left any memento of their visit or performed any action that would provide incontrovertible evidence that the visit had taken place physically. Attempts by people who have been taken on board alien spaceships to carry away some souvenir of their experience have invariably been thwarted.

Such considerations explain why there has always been a reluctance, except on the part of the True Believers, to take reports of encounters with other-worldly entities at face value. But while it is very difficult for a witness to prove that his encounter was an objective reality, it is no less difficult for others to prove that it was not. The most they are likely to be able to do is to offer a more probable explanation.

A second school of thought accepts that the entities are real, but that they are not what they seem to be. Even Christian theologians agree that the Devil will often appear in disguise – sometimes even in the form of the Virgin Mary. When

Bernadette had her encounter with Mary at Lourdes, a great many others in the neighbourhood claimed similar encounters. These are generally attributed to deceitful manifestations on Satan's part, hoping to distract attention from the genuine article by causing spurious pseudo-visionary incidents.

Not so very different are beliefs involving amorphous beings who can take on whatever form they choose or may be imposed on them. Theosophical teaching, for example, maintains belief in the existence of a species of beings who may in their non-operational mode have no visible form, but take on whatever form is dictated by circumstances. This is likely to be in response to the witness's expectation: if he expects to see a traditional fairy, the entity will take on the appearance of a fairy – and so on. Given such unlimited powers of transformation, this theory could account for any and every encounter with other-worldly beings – not only the huge variety of folklore entities, but also visionary beings such as the St Michael who appeared to Jeanne d'Arc in 1425 or the sinister aliens who allegedly abducted Whitley Strieber in 1986.

An interesting variant is that of the Spanish writer Salvador Freixedo, a former Jesuit. He has proposed the existence of a race of beings, intermediate between humanity and the divine, who are responsible not only for visions and encounters but also for virtually every other kind of anomalous phenomenon that has defied investigation, which they encourage because this generates psychic energy, on which they thrive. Unfortunately this hypothesis is no more solidly based than that of the Theosophists; both remain speculative.

Arguing against the physical reality of the encounter stories, behavioural scientists and other sceptics have regarded all such experiences as hallucinations – fantasies projected from within the witness's own mind. They point to the fact that hallucinations occur as a symptom in pathological states such as fevers; in mental states such as hysteria; in consequence of diet deficiency or intoxication; under conditions of stress, anxiety or sensory deprivation; and so on. When doctors observed such states, it was liable to be in patients who were physically or mentally ill. As a result the medical profession tended to regard *all* claims of encounters

with other-worldly entities as morbid symptoms of pathological states. The adequacy of this approach is, however, open to question. There is abundant evidence that many encounter experiences occur to people who are not in a pathological condition, and that the consequences are often highly beneficial. So, while accepting that hallucination is the mechanism of the process, the process itself may be very much more complex – and, moreover, frequently profound and purposeful.

One suggestion is that what is taking place is a kind of 'psychodrama' created by the subconscious mind of the witness, and presented to his unwitting conscious mind as a kind of 'substitute reality'. (That the subconscious mind does present such material to the conscious mind is known from dreaming and other psychological processes.)

The psychodrama takes the form of involving the witness in a fantasy experience (although to the witness it appears real), which presents him or her with the resolution of some personal crisis or meets

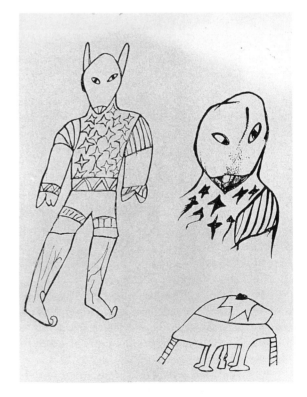

Drawings by schoolboys in Penang, Malaysia, of the ufonauts they saw in August 1970.

some personal need. Thus a teenage girl with a deprived family background may fantasise an encounter with an authority figure such as the Virgin Mary or a Spacewoman, who gives her guidance and reassurance. Similar circumstances forced Petty 'Price' Roach, a divorcée, to move house with her seven children in 1973: finding herself involved in an encounter with extraterrestrial beings provided her with a way of shedding responsibility for her predicament.

According to this approach, the entities need have no objective reality whatever. However, there are some instances in which the evidence is strong for some kind of ephemeral physical substance to the visionary being – notably when the entity is seen by more than one person. While this may perhaps be attributed to a shared hallucination of some kind – another psychological process that has long been debated but not finally resolved – there are some grounds for believing that short-lived projections, having some kind of objective reality, may occur.

The best evidence comes from quite a different kind of experience, in which a person in an alternate state – sleep or hypnosis, for instance – will project himself to some distant place, previously unvisited by him, where he is able to observe the scene and his presence may be detected by others, sometimes to the extent of a visible apparition of himself.

The testimony that this has occurred on several occasions is very strong. Although there is no support for it in anything known to science, it could well be akin to the processes involved in so-called poltergeist phenomena, and such other examples of recurrent spontaneous psychokinesis (RSPK) as the ability to switch off street lamps, to cause UFOs to manifest, or to influence their movements.

If it is a fact that short-lived materialisations can be fabricated in some manner, it is arguable that this could be extended to other kinds of entity experience, and that many of the entities reported do in fact possess some degree of physical reality, being fabricated by the individual or even by the collective mind. However, this is no more than speculation. Until such time as more evidence is available on the physical nature of the entities, the view that they are simply hallucinations must remain the explanation that involves the least speculation and is most consistent with observed experience.

Whichever model we choose, however, one thing is clear: the experience of encountering an other-worldly entity is generally – perhaps always – a meaningful and often valuable event, and no dismissive explanation that ignores this dimension can be regarded as adequate. Entities may not be what they seem, but in some sense or other they exist; and on some level, if not that of everyday reality, they are important to us.

SEE ALSO *Angels; Apports; Balls of light; Case of Ruth; Church of Jesus Christ of Latter Day Saints (Mormons); Consensus reality; Cosmic Joker; Cottingley fairies; Creative visualisation; The Devil; Doppelgängers; Dragons; Ectoplasm; ESP; Explanations; Fairies; Fantasy-prone personalities; Foaflore; Formative causation; Eileen Garrett; Ghosts; Hallucinations; Hypnosis; Hysteria; Jung and the paranormal; Limits of science; Mass hysteria; Men in Black; Modern ufology; Multiple personality; Other dimensions; Phantom hitch-hiker; Philip experiment; Possession; Remote viewing; Ritual magic; Seance-room phenomena; Shamanism; SORRAT; Telepathy and the ganzfeld; Traumas and psi; Tulpas; UFOs; Visions of the Virgin Mary; Werewolves; Witchcraft.*

MEN IN BLACK

The appearance of Men in Black (MIB) in the specific context of extraterrestrial visitation is a vivid demonstration that there is more to folklore than peasant tradition and old wives' tales. At the same time, this new addition to the lore demonstrates the perpetuation of old themes in new guises; for the Man in Black is a traditional stereotype of evil power, just as its counterpart, the Lady in White, is a stereotype of wronged innocence. If the 'white lady' has yet to make any significant appearance in this context, this may be because most encounters with extraterrestrials are told by people who feel themselves to be the wronged victims.

Black is inevitably associated with the sinister,

the diabolic, the evil. There is no question that the great majority of UFO-related MIB are all those things, and moreover foreign, if not downright inhuman, into the bargain. There is, however, some ambiguity as to who exactly the MIB are: in some versions of the myth they purport to be government officials, in others they seem to be extraterrestrial beings. However, this ambiguity may be more apparent than real, for some extraterrestrials may be masquerading as officials.

Finally, the MIB story demonstrates yet another aspect of folklore: an ambivalence about what core of fact, if any, there may be at the heart of the stories. Are they misinterpretations of actual events? Are they pure imagination? Or did they actually happen as described?

No two MIB stories are the same, but the following scenario embodies most of the aspects that characterise the genre:

1. The witness is generally a person who has seen and reported sighting a UFO. The encounter with the MIB takes place soon after – often too soon afterwards for it to be credible that the visitors could know of it by normal channels.

2. Almost invariably, the witness is alone when the encounter occurs. Often the visit is timed very precisely to this end: in the classic 1976 Dr Hopkins case, the MIB arrived when the rest of the family had gone to the movies.

3. The visitors are most commonly three in number. Often they are all men; if there is a female among them, there is never more than one, and she plays a subordinate role. They usually arrive in a large black car, which is a prestigious model such as a Cadillac in the USA, or a Rolls Royce or a Jaguar in Britain. Often it is not the latest model, but it is invariably in perfect condition and may even look and smell new. If the witness is sufficiently in command of himself to note its registration number and later to check it, he is likely to be told that no such number exists.

4. In appearance the MIB conform to the popular image of a CIA or MI5 agent – slightly too well dressed, in what amounts to a uniform of dark suit, dark shoes and socks, and immaculate white shirt. Another bizarre touch is that they wear hats, like stereotypical movie gangsters and secret agents. Albert Bender describes his three 1953 visitors in

The legendary 'Men in Black' who appear to hound those too interested in the UFO phenomenon.

these words: 'All of them were dressed in black clothes; they looked like clergymen, but wore hats similar to Homburg style.'

5. In their physical appearance the MIB are often described as 'foreign' – characterised by dark skin and slightly slanted eyes – and sometimes they speak with accents to match. However, their speech is apt to be over-precise, again like a stereotypical Hollywood villain, and the language they use is in keeping. Actual examples include, 'Again, Mr Stiff, I fear you are not being honest', and 'Mr Veich, it would be unwise of you to mail that report.'

6. Apart from specific details, the MIB often behave in a way that suggests they are not human. Their physical movements may be stiff and clumsy; in one classic scenario the MIB comprise a male and a female, who sit awkwardly together during

the interview with a couple, while the male paws the female, asking the husband if this is all right and if he is doing it correctly. When the husband goes out of the room, the male MIB asks the wife if she has any nude photographs of herself. When they leave, the male seems unable to move, and the female has to ask the witnesses to help her get him to his feet.

7. Certain MIB go to some lengths to establish their identity as official investigators, producing identification cards and even giving their names. Needless to say, later enquiry reveals that no such persons exist.

8. The reason for the visit is curiously unspecific. Often it purports to be a warning not to reveal information or a threat about the consequences of such revelation. If it is a UFO investigator who is being visited, he is likely to be told to abandon his interest. But there seems to be no force behind the threats, and on those occasions where they have been ignored, though violence may be threatened ('If you want your wife to stay as pretty as she is, then you'd better get the metal back!' was the warning given to UFO witness Robert Richardson in 1967), follow-up reprisals have rarely, if ever, been reported.

No single MIB case involves all these eight aspects. But the differences are clearly variations on a theme, however wide the divergence in detail.

It can be seen how each component of the stereotype carries certain sinister implications. Thus the promptness of the encounter suggests that the MIB obtain their information by paranormal means. Their choice of vehicle implies that they have newly fabricated a replica of a car that they believe to be appropriate – unaware that it is an out-of-date model – perhaps because they have seen it in a monitored television transmission. Other details also suggest that the MIBs have modelled themselves on what they have learned from our media, copying Hollywood gangsters, lovemaking and clothing under the illusion that these are representative of everyday behaviour.

At the same time, a witness will generally stress that the bizarreness of the incident struck him only later, and that at the time it all seemed natural. This might encourage us to think that most MIB cases are misinterpretations of real events, perhaps visits by UFO investigators masquerading as government officials, were it not that other details – notably the paranormal aspects of the phenomenon – point in a contrary direction. For instance, if it is true, as claimed, that in the Richardson case only he and his wife, and two senior officials of the investigative organisation APRO, knew that the witness had picked up a metal fragment at the UFO site, this is a strong suggestion that the information was obtained by what we would consider paranormal means.

At the same time, there are aspects of the myth that point to a psychological cause. The fact that a witness tends not to think the visits strange except in retrospect suggests that he may be in an alternate state of consciousness, experiencing some kind of waking dream; this is reinforced by the fact that the visit is rarely, if ever, interrupted, suggesting that it takes place outside real time.

Another circumstance suggests a motivation from within the witness himself. Albert Bender was playing a conspicuous part on the outer margin of UFO research when he received his visit from the Three Men, and immediately abandoned UFOs totally and permanently. This would be understandable if the visit were real; but an alternative explanation is that Bender fantasised the episode – perhaps subconsciously – in order to provide himself with a reason for getting out of his involvement in ufology. If so, the MIB were convenient bogeymen, just as Satan has often been invoked by evildoers who wished to avoid responsibility for their acts. 'The Devil made me do it!' was a plea for centuries before it was used by the Yorkshire Ripper.

In their ambiguity as in their richness of detail, in their continuance of a timeless tradition with specific elements appropriate to our Space Age culture, the MIB are a splendid addition to our stock of folklore entities. But of course the question remains: is that all there is to them? Stories about being harassed by MIB often have an impressively convincing ring – could there truly be a sinister reality underlying the theatrical surface?

SEE ALSO *The Devil; Entity enigma; Fantasy-prone personalities; Foaflore; Hallucinations; Modern ufology; Multiple personality; Other dimensions; Possession; Time; Timeslips; UFOs; Werewolves.*

MODERN UFOLOGY

While for the average man or woman the term Unidentified Flying Object (UFO) is more or less synonymous with 'extraterrestrial spacecraft', this connection is by no means universal among those who have studied them most closely. Serious ufologists, aware of the total lack of decisive evidence for the extraterrestrial hypothesis (ETH), have from the start kept their minds open. As this failure of the phenomenon to produce physical evidence continued, and as tightening standards of investigation revealed the suspect nature of much of the testimony, the trend towards psychosocial explanation – that individual psychology, acted on by social forces, is responsible for many reports – has gained momentum, particularly in western Europe. As a result, today there is little support for the ETH among serious researchers in Europe.

In the USA, on the other hand, the situation is quite otherwise. At the 1988 MUFON (Mutual UFO Network) Conference, the most prestigious annual meeting of American ufologists, veteran researcher Jerome Clark spoke on 'the fall and rise of the extraterrestrial hypothesis', acknowledging the growing gulf between what may be called the 'American' and the 'European' schools (though there are notable dissidents, and many important researchers in Australia and elsewhere, on both sides).

The return to the ETH by American ufologists is based on three events or categories of event, the first of which may be a kind of extraterrestrial Watergate. In December 1984 a researcher named Jaime Shandera, previously little known in the field of UFO investigation, received through the mail an anonymous package containing a roll of undeveloped film. This in turn contained what purported to be a photostat copy of a highly confidential US government document, a briefing paper prepared – in one copy only – for incoming President Eisenhower and dated 18 November 1952. It reveals the existence at that time of a committee of very eminent persons, who were aware of the fact that alien spacecraft had crashed on American soil and that their remains, and those of their occupants, were in custody of the US government.

Though the authenticity of the documents has been questioned in detail by Philip Klass and others, they were, if fakes, created with great skill, arguing a high level of disinformation. Setting aside the essential improbability of the alleged facts, the documents are plausible overall; the one outstanding discrepancy is the appearance, among the list of twelve committee members, of the astronomer Donald Menzel, who was subsequently to write three long and detailed books debunking the UFO phenomenon. Although efforts have been made to account for this on the grounds of Menzel's allegedly devious nature and government affiliations, it is not easy to believe that a busy and highly respected astronomer would, over a twenty-four-year period, waste his time producing three books presenting heavily researched evidence against something that he knew to be true.

Taken together, the objections to the authenticity of the MJ-12 documents are sufficiently strong that there are few outside the USA who accept them, and many even within the country who reject them. None the less, a substantial proportion of the US ufological community continues to give them credence. If genuine, of course, they establish the physical reality of extraterrestrial visitation beyond all possible doubt.

'Gulf Breeze is a solid case,' insist the supporters of this second pro-ETH phenomenon, but the sceptics believe it is a monumental hoax. This case, under massive investigation at the time this book went to press, presents, if genuine, the best photographic evidence yet of alien spacecraft in our airspace.

Towards the end of 1987 a citizen of Gulf Breeze, Florida, calling himself 'Mr Ed', published in a local paper some photographs of UFOs he had seen. Subsequently he made more pictures available to MUFON, the most authoritative investigative organisation in the USA. Tests carried out by experts have failed to detect any sign of fakery in the photographs, which show a luminous structured object low over the landscape at night, often in association with identifiable landmarks.

As UFO photographs go, Mr Ed's are impressive, but a great many aspects of the case are unsatisfactory. Mr Ed has not been consistent in the story

Sceptic Philip Klass beside a display of the alleged pictures of UFOs over Gulf Breeze, Florida, in 1988. These photographs have divided the ufological world.

he has presented, and he has a reputation as a practical joker, often using fake photographs in his tricks. He is also on record as boasting in private, before the first photographs were published, that he was working on the greatest trick of his career.

Such doubts have divided American ufologists sharply, leading to mutual vituperation between supporters and sceptics. If the believers turn out to be right, Gulf Breeze is our best evidence yet for the extraterrestrial origin of UFOs. If the sceptics are right, it is testimony once again to the power of the wish to believe to induce otherwise intelligent people to abandon the reality-testing procedures they would use in normal circumstances.

Neither MJ-12 nor Gulf Breeze has so captured the imagination of the American UFO world, however, as the reports that many hundreds of men and women have been temporarily abducted on board alien spacecraft. Most often the purpose seems to be one of physical/medical examination,

and in some cases genetic engineering, with impregnation of female abductees and forced copulation or sperm sampling of male abductees.

Perhaps because of its sensational nature, no issue has aroused such passionate controversy among serious researchers and general public alike. The great majority of American investigators appear to believe in the physical reality of the abductions, as witness the presentation of the 1988 MUFON annual award for services to ufology for a second time – the only occasion this has occurred – to Budd Hopkins, a prominent New York artist who has made himself the leading investigator of abduction cases and who is totally committed to their reality.

The phenomenon has been given a great popular boost by the publication by fantasy author Whitley Strieber of his account of his own abduction experience. The fact that a person in the public eye should risk his personal and professional reputation by revealing his private experiences has encouraged many to believe that it must be the 'true story' that it claims to be.

The total absence of any convincing physical evidence or supportive testimony that Strieber's or any other abductions have actually taken place; the curious discrepancy between the stories told by subjects who consult Budd Hopkins in New York, speaking of violent personal assaults, compared with those told to Dr Leo Sprinkler in Laramie, Wyoming, whose informants seem generally to have had comforting and reassuring experiences; the inconsistencies, contradictions and implausibilities that confuse every single case record; the fact that there are many parallels in psychological literature, in folklore and in pre-UFO science fiction (as French researcher Bertrand Méheust has brilliantly demonstrated) – these and other factors should provide grounds for approaching the abduction accounts with caution, at the very least. Instead, a great many – perhaps the majority – of American ufologists have committed themselves to belief in the face-value reality of UFO abduction.

Outside the USA, none of these three happenings commands anything like the same degree of belief. It would be true to say that only a small minority of serious researchers outside the United States give credence to the MJ-12 documents, the Gulf Breeze case or the physical reality of abductions. Rightly or wrongly, they continue to believe that the solution to a large part of the UFO phenomenon will be found in its psychosocial dimensions, an approach brilliantly summarised by Australian researcher Mark Moravec in his contribution to the compilation *UFOs 1947–1987* issued by the British UFO Research Association (BUFORA) in 1987.

However, few suppose that UFOs are 'all in the mind'. The on-going investigations at Hessdalen, in Norway, prove beyond reasonable doubt that a physical phenomenon is involved. As a result, considerable study is currently being directed towards the possibility that natural phenomena of a kind as yet unknown to science may be involved.

For Jerome Clark, these approaches have been overtaken by the dramatic events taking place in

the USA. However, ufologists outside the USA note with some misgivings the fact that, like so many sensational UFO events of the past – the contactees of the 1960s, the 'little green men' episode at Kelly-Hopkinsville, the 'crashed saucer' rumours and much more – these current events are all located chiefly in the USA. This coincidence supports the psychosocial position, since it seems to indicate a greater acceptance in the American public – including the informed UFO public – than is to be found elsewhere.

Seen in this light, it is perhaps significant that American ufologists have consistently ignored or derided contributions even from their fellow countrymen that go against current trends. The work of Professor Alvin Lawson, embodied in his 'imaginary contactee' experiment and the 'birth trauma hypothesis' that derives from that experiment, is seldom referred to by US researchers except in scorn. Ironically, it is seen as being of primary significance by researchers outside the United States, who recognise it as one of the few positive contributions to knowledge to have been carried out in the name of UFO research. Another prominent thinker who has been downgraded by his compatriots is veteran investigator John A. Keel, whose seminal book *Operation Trojan Horse* (1972) is arguably the most thought-provoking work to have sprung from the UFO literature.

Ironically, a third victim of the swing of thinking is a further landmark book, *The Unidentified* (1975), which explored possible alternatives to the ETH. This boldly speculative work was the joint work of anomaly researcher Loren Coleman and none other than the same Jerome Clark who has now become so conspicuous a supporter of the ETH.

To change one's mind is no crime, of course. But perhaps if a Gulf Breeze case, an abduction wave or an MJ-12 incident were to occur elsewhere than on American soil, ufologists in other countries might be less suspicious of the current trend.

SEE ALSO *Balls of light; Cosmic Joker; Entity enigma; Explanation; Formative causation; Hypnotic regression; Hysteria; Jung and the paranormal; Other dimensions; Search for extraterrestrial life; UFO classification; UFO paradox; UFOs.*

UFO PARADOX

George Adamski's blond contacts were, they claimed, from Venus, Betty and Barney Hill's abductors were from Zeta Reticuli, Jacques Bordas's from Titan – and Uri Geller's psychic powers are said to come from 'Hoova'. If, as many contactees believe, the purpose of the encounters with beings from UFOs is to promote global and intergalactic harmony, then perhaps the ufonauts ought first to decide on a consistent story.

Often the contactees are given absurd instructions, or ludicrous statements are made to them, such as: 'You will not speak wisely about this night', or even 'You should believe in us but not too much.' Despite this element of charade, to the contactees the encounter experience is shattering, sweeping away all previously held beliefs, hopes and fears, and replacing them with a new purpose and a new reality. A small percentage of these people are so turned about by the experience that they become social drop-outs (sometimes giving rise to the final abduction hypothesis), but most feel the need to develop their understanding of human consciousness, or become mystics and leaders of New Age cults.

Wherever the ufonauts come from, it is clear that they are reaching straight into the minds of the contactees and manipulating their reality. Researchers have suggested that the ludicrous or elusive elements in the encounter drama provide the mental and emotional 'loosening up' needed before the contactees can be programmed into the new reality. The absurd destroys the temporary functioning of the left hemisphere of the brain, tripping the right half into unaccustomed action and opening up the psyche to the profound and archetypal images that the ufonauts seek to implant.

Ufonauts may manipulate human minds, but their craft sometimes leave physical traces. Writer-researcher Jacques Vallée tells the story of a young man who dreamt that a UFO landed in his back garden; small humanoids disembarked and dismantled a mosquito screen that was fixed to his window. They then took him off in their spaceship on a flight into deep space before returning him home. The boy's mother woke him, saying he had obviously had a bad dream, and jokingly asked if he had smuggled a girl into his room during the night because his window was open and the mosquito screen taken down. In the garden were three deep impressions – where the boy had 'dreamt' the craft landed.

Some UFOs, on the other hand, behave like purely psychic phenomena. One woman can summon them at will and make them 'dance' for her appreciative family, including her normally sceptical husband.

If their object in impinging on human consciousness is to distort or improve our reality, then shape-changing from intelligent lights to nuts-and-bolts craft and back again is as good a way as any of going about it. Clearly, they – whoever or whatever they are – need to interact with human beings, and, judging by the reverence with which we treat encounters with them, we need them. Only time will tell whether the relationship remains a balanced, psychically symbiotic one, or whether one reality will gain full control over the other.

One story that may illustrate the fact that the ufonauts are not automatically in control was confided to Jacques Vallée by a young boy who regularly rode in UFOs. On one of the journeys through the skies something flashed past the UFO's windows, causing great alarm among its occupants, who hastily began to press buttons on the console and generally seemed flustered. They asked the boy if he knew what it was that had passed them; the UFO had just seen a UFO.

SEE ALSO *Angels; Balls of light; Case of Ruth; Consensus reality; Cosmic Joker; The Devil; Entity enigma; Fairies; Fantasy-prone personalities; Charles Fort; Uri Geller; Hallucinations; Left and right brain; Men in Black; Modern ufology; Multiple personality; Other dimensions; Search for extraterrestrial life; UFOs; Visions of the Virgin Mary.*

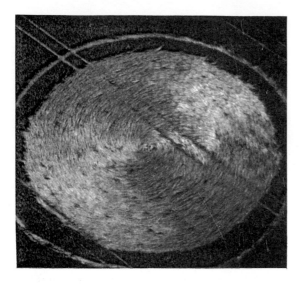 

Circle in the corn at the Devil's Punchbowl, Cheesfoot Head, Hampshire, in August 1986. Two earlier circles can be seen in the background.

CROP FIELD CIRCLES

The phenomenon of crop field circles was first reported in 1946 and became a media event only in the late 1980s. The origin of the completely flat, perfect circles in fields of crops, however, remains a mystery. Misleadingly dubbed 'UFO nests' by the more sensational press, these circles have been reported from Italy, Brazil, France, Canada and the USA, but they seem to have reached epidemic proportions in the south of England in 1988, when over seventy were reported in the first eight months of the year.

Appearing spontaneously, usually overnight, they can be up to 12 metres across; they may be single circles, double or triple, and may be intersected by straight lines. Sometimes the flattened crops show a clockwise swirl, and sometimes anticlockwise or radial bursts. Professor Archie Roy, astronomer and senior member of the Society for Psychical Research (SPR), investigated the circles and stated: 'When you get to the edge [of the circles], you're in flattened crop. An inch further on,

they're untouched. None of these explanations seems to fit.'

However, Dr Terence Meaden, an academic meteorologist who runs the Tornado and Storm Research Organisation in Bradford-on-Avon, believes that the circles are caused by the wind. 'Vortices of air could either suck up or press down,' he says. Statistician and ufologist Paul Fuller also inclines to the air vortices theory. He points out that the flattened crops are layered, showing that whatever caused the effect was moving around. The fact that half the circles are clockwise and half anticlockwise seems to support this part of the theory, but does not in itself provide a watertight explanation for the crop field circles.

Even more fascinating, however, is the reported intelligence of the circles, or their creators. Like the intelligence responsible for poltergeist phenomena, the circles' producers seem to respond to human comment on the phenomenon. One researcher, for example, discussed over the telephone with his brother in Lincolnshire the fact that no circles had been reported there. Just two days later a large circle was discovered in the next village.

SEE ALSO *Explanations; Charles Fort; Cosmic Joker; Other dimensions; UFOs.*

VI Psi Research

Robert Thouless • Propensity for psi • Allergies and psi • Electric people • Traumas and psi • Sex and psi • Ectoplasm • Gustave Geley • Children and psi • Enfield poltergeist • Black Monk of Pontefract • Rosenheim poltergeist • Metal bending • Psychokinesis • Philip experiment • Kenneth Batcheldor • SORRAT • American Society for Psychical Research • Remote viewing • Telepathy • Telepathy and the ganzfeld • ESP • Society for Psychical Research • Parapsychology • CSICOP • Michel Gauquelin • History of Soviet psi • Soviet psi today • Eastern bloc psi • Psi-mediated instrumental response • Eleventh-hour syndrome • Boggle threshold

A chalk-like substance appears in mid-air and floats slowly downwards; a girl is dragged out of bed and thrown across the room by an invisible force; for minutes on end, something telephones the speaking clock faster than it can be dialled. Such things happen without the permission of the laws of nature, and if they happen they should be scientifically investigated. For this reason psi research is arguably the most important study that man can undertake, yet it ekes out a fragile existence, with the most implacable enemies within its own ranks.

Since the Society for Psychical Research (SPR) was founded by a group of Cambridge scholars in 1882, research has repeatedly progressed by a few steps, and retreated by many more. Even in the SPR's early days, personal prejudices, intellectual élitism and a simple refusal to face facts obscured the most remarkable phenomena. Afraid of accusations of gullibility, investigators refused to work with some of the greatest mediums of the day, and shunned colleagues who attempted to do so.

Being a psychical researcher – or parapsychologist, as today's more scientifically minded investigators are called – is no guarantee of open-mindedness. Indeed, the more dramatic the phenomenon, the more its authenticity will be denied – and the more likely it is that those associated with the phenomenon will be subjected to a witch-hunt of which the old Inquisitors would have been proud.

The irony is that paranormal phenomena thrive on simple faith, light-heartedness and belief. The Philip experiment proved that even a piece of furniture becomes imbued with a temporary kind of life (even a personality) when a group of people believe sufficiently. Metal bends to one's will, as long as one believes it is possible – which is why the example of Uri Geller was so inspiring to millions of television viewers, and why psychokinetic activity leapt into being in thousands of homes.

Many attempts have been made to prove the reality of psi functioning in laboratory conditions, although some would say this is as likely to succeed as asking two complete strangers to fall in love with each other to order. Even so, positive results have been recorded among the dreary wastes of statistics that are 'just above chance' expectancy. The American parapsychologist J. B. Rhine proved, if nothing else, that his card-guessers were best at the beginning of the experiment, and less successful as it wore on. This 'decline effect' may be regarded equally as the Boredom Factor, one of the great cautionary tales of psi research.

Unusual successes attended the Cambridge experiments into telepathy, which used the ganzfeld (information deprivation) technique. Less successful researchers, however, believed that positive results suggested fraud and hinted as much – the resulting scandal was reported in the quality national newspapers, and a career was destroyed. There is still no evidence, however, that cheating of any kind ever took place.

The 'boggle barrier' has been resolutely crashed by the work of the Missouri-based group known as the Society for Research on Rapport and Telekinesis (SORRAT), whose experiments began in 1961 and continue today. Film of extraordinary psychokinetic (PK) phenomena produced by the group was greeted with such hostility by the SPR – whose only questions concerned how it could have been faked – that SORRAT continued its pioneering work without support of the 'experts'. The vilification continued, yet so did the phenomena.

The paranormal flourishes when it is respected, which tends to be in spontaneous, rather than laboratory, conditions. The extraordinary success of the Stanford Research Institute's remote viewing – which is essentially field work – and the telepathy experiments of Sherman and Wilkins, in the early years of the century, attest to the power of the unfettered mind.

The work of the late British researcher Kenneth J. Batcheldor into the induction of PK reminds the observer how patience and belief combine to produce dramatic effects. His groups were encouraged to believe that paranormal things were happening, their attitude being not, 'Was that paranormal?' but 'It is!' Like SORRAT, the Batcheldor groups became experts at inducing extraordinary PK, but the work of neither group is deemed scientifically respectable.

Some members of the SPR are also affiliated to the Committee for the Scientific Investigation of Claims of the Paranormal (CSICOP), a singularly hostile and influential international group of rationalists that includes among its members famous conjurers, scientists, writers and parapsychologists. Yet some researchers have reason to be grateful to CSICOP; its early condemnation of the work of French statistician Michel Gauquelin revealed the group's bias, and drew attention to some remarkable work.

The study of astrology, however scientific, is deemed outside the scope of parapsychology; it is with some sense of daring that Gauquelin is given a place in this section. Yet his work is a shining example to the psi researcher – he set out as an unbeliever, yet when his results showed astrology in a favourable light he was not afraid to say so, even when put on the rack by CSICOP and its friends.

Psi research requires courage, stamina, belief and a sense of child-like wonder. Researchers with such qualifications are hard to find and harder to keep – yet there are, perhaps, just enough of them to encourage a timid optimism about the future of this vexed subject.

ROBERT THOULESS

Dr Robert Thouless, President of the Society for Psychical Research (SPR) between 1942 and 1944, was undoubtedly one of the most objective and pioneering of parapsychologists. He was trained as a psychologist, and his greatest contribution to the field of psychical research was the coining of the term *psi*. This is the twenty-third letter of the Greek alphabet and the first letter of the Greek word *psyche* meaning soul or mind. Thouless felt it to be a more useful term to cover apparently paranormal phenomena than 'ESP' or 'psychokinesis', both of which implied a suggestion about the nature of phenomena.

Together with his colleague B. P. Wiesner, Thouless also developed the idea of *shin* (the twenty-first letter of the Hebrew alphabet), which may be taken as the soul or spirit, but is not confined to a religious or Spiritualist context. *Shin* operates on all levels of cognisance, including the nervous system, which may account for psychokinetic abilities.

Thouless experimented endlessly with card guessing and dice throwing (he was a long-time friend of J. B. Rhine) and discovered for himself the importance of the 'decline effect' – the tendency for subjects in psi experiments to score increasingly badly. He recognised that this was due to boredom, and devised ways of creating more engrossing tests.

In his later years Thouless became progressively more fascinated by the problems of proving survival of bodily death. He developed a 'cipher test' through which he hoped, if he survived, to prove the continued existence of his personality. A mess-

SEE ALSO *American Society for Psychical Research; Cross-correspondences; ESP; Life after death; Near death experience; Palm Sunday case; Parapsychology; Psychokinesis; Society for Psychical Research; Telepathy.*

PROPENSITY FOR PSI

The late Professor Robert Thouless, inventor of ingenious cipher tests to prove the continuing consciousness of the personality after death.

Although the evidence is by no means conclusive, it does seem that certain physical, mental, emotional and cultural conditions tend to give rise to psychic abilities more than others. In laboratory tests young children scored significantly higher than other children, who in turn scored higher than adults. Women are arguably more open to spontaneous phenomena than men, and less technically advanced communities readily accept psi as part of their everyday lives.

Total acceptance of psi in the West is rare, although most people experience at least one example of its direct influence in their lives – precognitive dreams are common, as are instances of crisis telepathy. Hostility to psi is widespread, perhaps even implicit in Western culture; most rationalist or scientific bodies such as CSICOP avowedly aim to crush any interest in the subject. Other groups, including several churches, operate a selective scepticism – accepting paranormal phenomena that seem to arise from their religion ('miracles') and ascribing any others to the influence of the Devil.

In fact, acceptance and expectancy of psi has been proved conclusively to encourage further, 'macro', phenomena. Where psi is totally accepted, as by the Kalahari bushmen, there are no obstacles to its place in their lives, and it flourishes – literally as a useful 'sixth sense'. A National Geographic film of the 1960s recorded an instance of a bushman knowing that his child had been born at a certain moment even though he was 1000 kilometres away.

Primitive societies tend to be 'right-brained' – that is, they draw more frequently on the intuitive, creative, right hemisphere of the brain than on the analytical, 'educated' left half. In the West, women

age was prepared in code, the key to which was not recorded in any form or confided to any living being, and which Thouless was to take to the grave with him.

After his death in 1984 several attempts were made to contact him through reputable mediums, none of whom knew the purpose of the sittings. Although evidence accumulated that Thouless did indeed still exist in some form and was communicating with them, he could not remember the key that would 'unlock' the cipher message. The discarnate Thouless said he knew he had to remember to do something, but could not recall what it was. He added that, for the dead, being alive was like having had a dream.

It may be that the problems of communicating with the living are almost insuperable, as F. W. H. Myers had said, but the Thouless cipher tests continue to be used among researchers. Perhaps one day they will provide near-watertight proof of survival.

Bushmen of the Kalahari, like most 'primitive' peoples, have highly developed telepathic powers.

have been found to be considerably more right-brained than men, especially in a crisis, and to be better able to utilise both halves fluently, perhaps giving rise to the higher incidence of spontaneous psi in women than men.

Belief in psi seems to be inborn, then swiftly educated out of us. The consensus in the West is that psi is stupid, harmful or wicked. There may even be a case for suggesting that belief or non-belief in various cultures arises as a result of formative causation; the invisible morphogenetic fields that shape the evolution of each species and determine its collective unconscious, as argued by Dr Rupert Sheldrake, may also help to create the consensus reality shared by human groups.

Certain altered states of consciousness can raise psychic awareness; hypnosis has been shown to create telepathic situations, while trance and sleep lower resistance to psi. Tests on healer Matthew Manning revealed that, when he was concentrating on healing, the 'Stone Age' part of his brain, which is dormant in most modern peoples, was activated. This suggested that Manning's abilities were once common to man – and that they remain potentially within the grasp of all of us.

Research indicates that physical traumas may trigger latent psi abilities – blows to the head or electric shocks can, it appears, endow 'normal' people with a wide range of psychic talents. For example Uri Geller's PK abilities began after he suffered an electric shock while trying to repair his mother's sewing machine.

In parapsychological research it appears that a combination of expectancy and patience can produce dramatic results, as in the work of SORRAT and Kenneth Batcheldor's group. As Batcheldor said, no doubt must be permitted. If apparently paranormal phenomena occur, the attitude must not be 'Is it . . .?' but rather 'It is!'

Striving too hard for positive results can actually inhibit psi; often the longed-for PK occurs at the precise moment when a coffee break has been suggested. It seems that the sudden release of the accumulated tension induces the phenomenon. Another inhibiting factor in parapsychology is the 'decline effect' the sheer boredom involved in say, Zener card guessing in ESP experiments. When even gifted psychics become bored, positive results tail off dramatically. This factor is particularly significant in the replication of experiments, and is a major stumbling block in setting up academically respectable parapsychological work.

Many examples of spontaneous psi are reported by people on holiday or otherwise relieved of the stresses involved in their everyday work, although very monotonous activity, such as that of the assembly-line worker, often creates the trance-like state that can induce sudden flashes of intuition or precognition. The information deprivation of the 'ganzfeld' technique encourages significantly 'above chance' hits in telepathy tests – but usually only when the experimenters are fully expectant, cheerful 'sheep' (believers). In the ultimate analysis, psi only occurs where it is both wanted and needed.

SEE ALSO *Allergies and psi; Kenneth Batcheldor; Boggle threshold; Children and psi; Consensus reality; CSICOP; The Devil; Electric people; Eleventh-hour syndrome; ESP; Experimenter effect; Formative causation; Uri Geller; Healing; Hypnosis; Inspiration in dreams; Jung and the paranormal; Left and right brain; Limits of science; Matthew Manning; Parapsychology; Philip experiment; Precognition in dreams; Psi-mediated instrumental response; Psychokinesis; Sex and psi; Society for Psychical Research; SORRAT; Telepathy; Telepathy and the ganzfeld.*

ALLERGIES AND PSI

There is increasing evidence to show that psychics or sensitives are more prone than others to suffer from allergies. 'Poltergeist children' in particular tend to show allergic reactions – which is significant in view of Dr Jean Monro's work with allergy sufferers at the Breakspeare Hospital in Hertfordshire.

She has shown that many such reactions are caused by hypersensitivity to electricity; in some cases even sitting within a few metres of a light bulb will produce allergic migraine, lethargy, skin rashes, breathing difficulties or dramatic mood changes. But these patients also show the ability to affect electrical equipment in some cases, causing light bulbs to 'blow' or inducing anomalous sounds on televisions or radios – classic 'poltergeist' activity. The allergic patient seems to have a heightened sensitivity to electricity, and possibly to what is generally thought of as 'paranormal' activity.

Healer Matthew Manning has noted a distinct connection between repressed anger and allergic reactions; anger has often been seen as the mobilising force behind some psi ability. The anger of Anne-Marie almost certainly caused the tumult known as the Rosenheim poltergeist, and sporadic outbreaks of psychokinetic effects such as the teleportation of objects, or the interference of electrical equipment in many otherwise ordinary lives can be directly linked to frustration and anger. It seems that the explosive psi activity is produced to defuse a personal crisis, and often has the secondary 'payoff' of attracting attention to the focus.

Allergies alter the chemistry of the body, no matter how fleeting, perhaps producing a force field that is in some way more attractive to anomalous phenomena. Just as the colorant tartrazine is now known to produce hyperactivity in some children, so many other chemicals (including food and pollutants) may go further and produce *paranormal* hyperactivity. The adherents of holism may yet live to see the day when, in order either to cure an allergy or to banish a poltergeist, the sufferer's medical, emotional, social and environmental conditions must be taken into account.

SEE ALSO *Electric people; Formative causation; Healing; Holism; Matthew Manning; Psi-mediated instrumental response; Psychokinesis; Rosenheim poltergeist; Sentient machinery; Sex and psi.*

ELECTRIC PEOPLE

The first signs of poltergeist activity are often disturbances in the electrics of the house – typically, malfunctioning televisions and telephones and exploding light bulbs. Investigators may find their recording equipment mysteriously damaged. Some people even become 'electric', capable of giving off shocks.

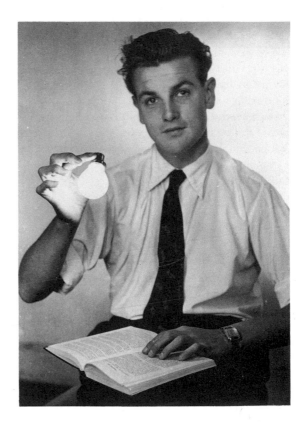

Welshman Brian Williams is so electric that he has only to hold light bulbs for them to light up.

In 1883 Lulu Hurst of Georgia, Alabama became aware of loud rapping sounds near her; crockery smashed itself in her vicinity, and she discovered that she could suddenly control or neutralise force in a way that suggested she had become 'electric'. Unlike many poltergeist children, fifteen-year-old Lulu was astute enough to realise that her strange powers originated in some way from her and not from the spirits of the dead.

Developing her abilities into a stage act, she toured the world as 'The Georgia Wonder'; holding one end of a billiard cue, she would push and pull a group of strong men – no matter how hard they resisted her efforts (although this is an easily learnt feat, relying on balance and leverage for its effect). Objects over which she held her hands would be drawn upwards to them, despite the fact that the items were not made of metal and therefore not susceptible to magnetism – as it is generally understood.

Following the metal bending craze in the 1970s, Dr S. Sasaki of Denki Tshushin University in Japan discovered that some of his metal benders were electric. One twelve-year-old could recharge batteries just by holding them.

Occultists and mystics have long known of the weak force field that surrounds every living creature – its 'aura' – and that under certain circumstances it may be strengthened or weakened. The technique known as Kirlian photography seems to capture the aura on film. British researcher Harry Oldfield also demonstrated how simple it is to give someone greater physical strength, or deplete their energies instantly, by 'windmilling' one's arms behind them in either outward or inward circles. The demonstration provided light relief at one weekend conference, but also pointed to the existence of some invisible force field that surrounds each individual and can be manipulated only too easily by others.

Similarly, healer Matthew Manning encourages those who attend his workshops to trust the 'intuition' of what they feel through the palms of their hands. Some of his exercises are designed to reveal the reality of the force field and its use in locating physical and emotional problems.

Embryologist Professor Harold Burr described his discovery of electrodynamic force fields surrounding living creatures in Blueprint for Immortality (1972). He believed that they provide 'moulds' or patterns for the organism to grow into. This idea was taken much further by Dr Rupert Sheldrake in his theory of formative causation, and in the idea that the 'laws of nature' are really only just habits.

It may well be that all life is essentially electromagnetic and that all activity, including allegedly paranormal phenomena, is the result of fluctuations in such fields. Poltergeists seem to fit into this category, but it has been suggested by many researchers that some UFO sightings or encounters with beings from another dimension are in some way related to electromagnetic disturbances in the atmosphere. T. C. Lethbridge, the master dowser and theorist, suggested that many encounters with fairies or other-worldly beings take place near water or in damp, oppressive atmospheric conditions that may be connected with electrical discharges in the area.

Strangely, for a civilisation that relies so much on electricity, we know very little about the force – certainly not enough. Disturbing details are only just emerging about the devastating effects of being exposed to low-level non-ionising radiation; even living close to high-voltage cables can make whole communities sick. In 1986 a court in Texas ordered a telephone company that had erected power lines over a school to pay $25 million in damages. In the USSR and the USA laws exist to prohibit non-military buildings from being sited near power cables. No such law exists in Britain.

At the Sunbury Hill Clinic and the Breakspeare Hospital in Abbots Langley, Hertfordshire, Dr Jean Monro treats allergy patients with precisely controlled electrical frequencies (a similar effect is believed to be obtained by the use of acupuncture). She has discovered that many ailments appear to be caused by the patient's susceptibility to electrical equipment. In some sufferers even the proximity of a light bulb causes signs of illness. Significantly, many of these hypersensitive people also affect electrical equipment. Phenomena recorded by Dr Monro include the 'blowing' of light bulbs and the producing of background noises on tape recorders and televisions when the subjects were within 10 metres of them.

With such clear examples of the interaction of human beings with natural energy – even with man-made machinery – the sceptics' case against the existence of poltergeists, psychokinesis and the like is rapidly losing ground.

SEE ALSO *Allergies and psi; Electronic voice phenomenon; Entity enigma; Explanations; Fairies; Fireproof people; Formative causation; Fox sisters; Ghosts; Healing; Limits of science; Matthew Manning; Metal bending; Propensity for psi; Psi-mediated instrumental response; Psychokinesis; Rosenheim poltergeist; Sentient machinery; Traumas and psi.*

TRAUMAS AND PSI

Physical and emotional traumas often precede the onset of psychic abilities or spirituality. Saul of Tarsus was struck blind on the road to Damascus; it was after he recovered that his life changed direction dramatically. Similarly, Sai Baba's mission began after he had been stung by a scorpion, and had lain seriously ill for several days. People have reported becoming psychic after blows to the head, electric shocks or suddenly hearing bad news.

In other cases it seems that a flare-up of paranormal phenomena serves to defuse a personal crisis, especially if they take the form of a miracle. Religious images have been seen to bleed and weep in response to their owner's psychosomatic problems, resulting in a cure and an inspiration for others. Less obviously beneficial is the poltergeist infestation, which may nevertheless serve a similar function as an externalisation of inner conflict (usually connected to hormonal disturbances, particularly those during puberty).

Extraordinary, life-saving phenomena may be called into being by urgent need, as parapsychologist Rex Stanford acknowledges in his model of psi functioning known as psi-mediated instrumental response (PMIR), which others know simply as the answer to a prayer.

SEE ALSO *Allergies and psi; Case of Ruth; Consensus reality; Electric people; Eleventh-hour syndrome; Enfield poltergeist; Fate; Uri Geller; Healing; Images that bleed and weep; Left and right brain; Miracles of St Médard; Moving statues; Multiple personality; Propensity for psi; Psi-mediated instrumental response; Psychokinesis; Rosenheim poltergeist; Sai Baba; Sex and psi; Shamanism; Stigmatics; Visions of the Virgin Mary.*

SEX AND PSI

Sexual energy appears to be a prime mover in many kinds of paranormal activity. Most poltergeist foci are pubescent girls – when puberty is reached, the PK activity tends to cease. Some cases centre on pregnant or menopausal women, indicating a hormonal link.

Most mediums are women, and arguably the greatest sensitive of all, Daniel Dunglas Home, was widely believed to be an effeminate homosexual. Why women should be so favoured is not entirely understood, but recent research shows that, in an emergency, women tend to use the right hemisphere to the brain – the intuitive, creative half – much more than men. The right hemisphere may well hold the blueprint for much paranormal behaviour.

Seance-room phenomena were once tainted with accusations of dubious sexuality. Ectoplasm customarily exuded from all the medium's bodily orifices, and the trance was often accompanied by orgasmic pantings.

Sexual frustration can apparently engender encouraging conditions for a wide range of paranormal phenomena including PK, ESP and changes in consciousness that may be perceived as visions of outside entities, such as the Virgin Mary. Perhaps it was for this reason that the Church's founding fathers decreed that their priests must be celibate; the mysteries must remain in powerful hands.

SEE ALSO *Black Monk of Pontefract; Case of Ruth; Cottingley fairies; Helen Duncan; Ectoplasm; Enfield poltergeist; Fantasy-prone personalities; Hallucinations; D. D. Home; Images that bleed and weep; Katie King; Left and right brain; Parapsychology; Rosenheim poltergeist; Society for Psychical Research; Stigmatics; Visions of the Virgin Mary; Witchcraft.*

ECTOPLASM

Few psychical researchers today deem the subject of ectoplasm even worthy of discussion, let alone go so far as to commit themselves to its serious investigation. To many researchers this elusive substance is always an artefact of fraudulent mediums – being, on investigation, regurgitated butter muslin or chewed-up paper. Yet there is still a persuasive body of evidence to indicate that this controversial substance exists – and is crucial to our understanding of psychic phenomena.

The word ectoplasm comes from two Greek roots – *ektos*, outside, and *plasma*, a thing formed – and is generally taken to refer to the greyish, wispy or viscous material that emanates from the body of entranced materialisation mediums and takes the shape of the dead. Sustained research into its nature and functions began in Paris in 1909 with experiments into the mediumship of Eva C. by Dr Shrenck-Notzing and Madame Alexandre-Bisson. They were later to write:

British medium Jack Webber extrudes ectoplasm from his mouth and solar plexus which form rods that levitate trumpets. Webber was never caught cheating, yet even if the production of ectoplasm is a genuinely paranormal talent, it does not by itself constitute proof of an afterlife.

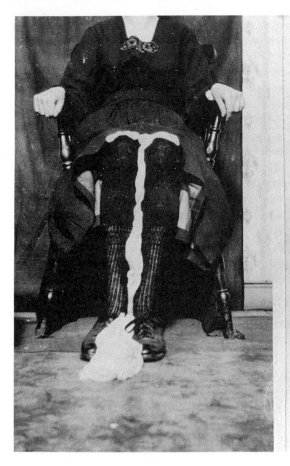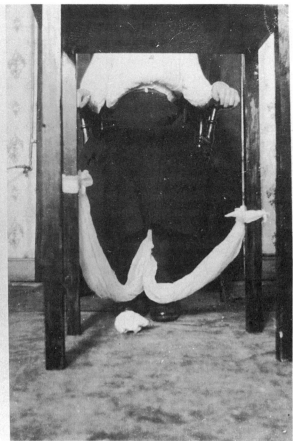

Belfast medium Kate Goligher photographed producing ectoplasm during a series of seances. Thought by believers to be the 'basic building bricks of the universe', ectoplasm has been described variously as greyish-white and viscous, grey and insubstantial, or invisible except to infra-red light. Several mediums were caught extruding buttermuslin from various orifices, but some mediums produced ectoplasm that seemed to be genuine.

We have very often been able to establish that, by an unknown biological process, there comes from the body of the medium a material, at first semi-fluid, which possesses some of the properties of a living substance, notably that of the power of change, of movement and of the assumption of definite forms ... one might doubt the truth of these facts if they had not been verified hundreds of times in the course of laborious tests under varied and very strict conditions.

Subsequent extensive research by Gustave Geley and Charles Richet in Paris, and by W. J. Crawford in Belfast in the 1920s, endorsed the findings of Bisson and Schrenck-Notzing. The full-form materialisations of such mediums as Helen Duncan, Jack Webber and Alec Harris in the 1940s added to the controversy; some of their ectoplasmic revenants walked and talked with the sitters, and were recognised by them.

The researchers made positive contributions to our knowledge of ectoplasm. Crawford considered it to be both visible and invisible; Schrenck-Notzing analysed a portion of it and found common salt and calcium phosphate among its constituents, and Geley described it thus:

The substance separates itself from the medium's body at any point but especially the mouth and natural orifices, as well as the points of the breasts and the fingers. It occurs in various forms: sometimes, most characteristically as a malleable paste, a real protoplasmic mass; sometimes as fine threads; sometimes as straight and rigid strands of various thicknesses, sometimes as a wide flat band; sometimes as a film; sometimes as a kind of thin cloth with vague and irregular edges.

Clearly the substance emanates from the body of the medium, but there was dispute as to whether it is, as Spiritualists believe, manipulated by the subconscious mind of the medium, by the collective or individual minds of the sitters, by discarnate entities or by mischievous entities seeking to deceive.

Some researchers, notably the South African Dr B. J. F. Laubscher, believed that ectoplasm is to be found in everybody, being 'a normal constituent of our bodies'. He particularly endorsed the position of Canadian researcher Dr Glen Hamilton, who died in 1935, and who had made an exhaustive study of seance-room phenomena, which he had photographed. He believed that discarnates used the viscous material to reproduce likenesses of themselves, in order to communicate with the sitters.

The French researchers, however, including Geley, came out against the concept of discarnates manipulating the mysterious fluid. They held that some subconscious force from the medium of sitters acted on it to produce ideoplastic forms capable of movement and communication.

If this is so, it may be a process similar to that unconsciously invoked in the Philip experiment where a table seemed to be temporarily enlivened with a personality. A suggestion of ectoplasm was seen during Kenneth Batcheldor's psychokinesis experiments, forming itself into rods or levers with which to move a heavy table – certainly Eusapia Palladino made furniture move by the production of ectoplasmic rods.

There may be yet further-reaching implications. The hallucinations seen by Ruth were at least once seen by someone else, and the vision of the Virgin Mary over a church in Cairo was visible to thousands of people for many days. Ritual magicians are believed to be able to create thoughtforms or tulpas that assume enough solidity to be perceived as 'real' by others. Are all such projections or externalisations of mental images given form by being clothed in ectoplasm?

SEE ALSO *American Society for Psychical Research; Angels; Kenneth Batcheldor; Black Monk of Pontefract; Boggle threshold; Case of Ruth; Consensus reality; Cosmic Joker; Cottingley fairies; The Devil; Dragons; Helen Duncan; Entity enigma; Fairies; Fox sisters; Gustave Geley; Katie King; Loch Ness monster; Carmine Mirabelli; Eusapia Palladino; Philip experiment; Psychokinesis; Ritual magic; Seance-room phenomena; Society of Psychical Research; SORRAT; Thoughtography; Tulpas; UFO paradox; Vampires; Visions of the Virgin Mary.*

Psychical researchers in Warsaw, 1923. Gustave Geley (centre) remained a believer and was a staunch champion of materialisation mediums.

Polish medium Franek Kluski with a materialisation that resembles a large bird of prey during a seance in 1919.

GUSTAVE GELEY

The eminent French doctor and psychical researcher Gustave Geley was born at Montceau-les-Mines in 1868. He studied in the hospitals of Lyon and at the Faculty of Medicine, where he gained a first prize for his thesis. He subsequently went into medical practice for many years.

Geley had a deep interest in the interaction of soul and matter, and when the Institut Métaphysique International was founded in Paris in 1918 he forsook his practice in Annecy to become its first director. Other important psychical researchers associated with him were Charles Richet, Camille Flammarion and Professor Bonzano.

Sittings with materialisation mediums such as the Poles, Gouzyk and Kluski, produced some of the most remarkable results in the history of psychical research. Sudre described the experimental conditions in these words: '...subject dressed in a special garment, sitters and subject chained together at the wrist, subject held at the wrist and restricted at the legs'. Nevertheless, forms materialised and phenomena were still observed by many French and foreign observers.

J. M. Bird, associate editor of the *Scientific American*, described an afternoon visit to Geley's laboratory in March 1923, the year before the French researcher's untimely death in an air crash (he had been returning from Warsaw, where he had been observing Kluski's materialisations):

Geley conceived the notion of getting a permanent record of the presence of materialised forms. He accordingly had always on hand a supply of melted paraffin ... the extraneous hand (whatever its nature, we may safely call it that) is in point of fact immersed in the vessel of paraffin and at once withdrawn, coated with a thin shell of the liquid which at once congeals. It is from this thin shell, much less a sixteenth of an inch [1.5 millimetres] thick, that the extraneous hand (or foot) is withdrawn, leaving not a mould as one would ordinarily understand this term, but actually a glove of paraffin, of the thickness specified. This is preserved and made more or less permanent by filling it with plaster.

Bird added that Geley did not consider that this proved the agency of discarnate personalities; he preferred to think of a projection of ideas from the medium's mind, in a form that would create these objective images. Geley had collected some twenty moulds, mostly hands, said Bird, and a few feet.

Geley's disposition was somewhat unsociable but his industry was considerable. The daughter of Sir Oliver Lodge, a founder member of the SPR, remembers him as 'difficult to understand but always friendly and kind. He worked much too hard: it seemed as if he was always writing in his study or holding a seance.'

SEE ALSO *Case of Ruth; Helen Duncan; Ectoplasm; Entity enigma; Fantasy-prone personalities; Katie King; Carmine Mirabelli; Eusapia Palladino; Seance-room phenomena; Society for Psychical Research; Thought-ography; Tulpas.*

CHILDREN AND PSI

Writer Lyall Watson tells how a neighbour's young daughter paranormally bent his keys when requested that she do so, 'just like Uri Geller'. Children are in fact considerably more likely than adults to experience paranormal experiences or possess psychic gifts.

Dr Ernesto Spinelli has found that the younger the child the higher (in other words, above chance

Dr Ernesto Spinelli tests young children for psychic ability. He has discovered that the younger the child, the more prevalent such gifts are – perhaps because they have not been conditioned out of them?

expectancy alone) he or she scores in ESP tests. Dr Charles Tart of the University of California, believes that children lose their psi through early conditioning in consensus reality. When small they achieve the impossible simply because they believe it is possible; once doubt or fear is educated or conditioned into them their abilities – with some notable exceptions – cease.

In this context, the common childhood experience of playing with imaginary friends may be of great significance – they may be more 'real' than adults imagine, or remember. The biblical advice that one must become 'as a little child' to enter the kingdom of heaven assumes an extra dimension in the world of parapsychological research.

SEE ALSO *Angels; Boggle threshold; Case of Ruth; Consensus reality; Cottingley fairies; The Devil; Enfield poltergeist; ESP; Fairies; Fantasy-prone personalities; Hallucinations; Lightning calculators; Metal bending; Parapsychology; Philip experiment; Prodigies; Propensity for psi; Sex and psi; SORRAT; Telepathy; Thought-ography; Tulpas; UFO paradox; Visions of the Virgin Mary.*

The children at the centre of the Enfield poltergeist case react nervously to objects flying about. The only known case of its type that was investigated from the start in 1977, it lasted for a year and provided a huge variety of psychic phenomena. The investigators, Guy Lyon Playfair and Maurice Grosse, have been repeatedly accused of gullibility by critics, none of whom investigated the case themselves.

ENFIELD POLTERGEIST

The Enfield poltergeist began on 31 August 1977 and continued for fourteen months – making it one of the longest-lasting outbreaks on record. In the semi-detached council house occupied by Mrs H. (as she is known) and her four children in north London, they and numerous outside witnesses reported practically every type of paranormal phenomenon – from knocking on walls and floors, movement of objects large and small, spontaneous combustion and the passage of matter through matter, to mysterious voices and even human levitation. It is the only case of its kind known to have been fully documented from start to finish: its two principal investigators were Maurice Grosse and Guy Lyon Playfair, both members of the Society for Psychical Research (SPR).

Their findings aroused bitter controversy, some critics insisting that all the phenomena were tricks on the part of the children, especially the two girls, Janet (aged eleven in 1977) and Margaret (then thirteen). Neither girl ever 'confessed', however, despite at least two attempts by newspaper reporters to obtain confessions via a neighbour for substantial financial reward.

Both investigators personally witnessed numerous incidents, including the overturning of large pieces of furniture. They obtained extensive written and tape-recorded testimony from some thirty witnesses including neighbours, social workers, reporters, photographers and the police. They also collected an assortment of objects seen to move without human contact, including a heavy gas fire that somehow was pulled out of a wall. Several incidents were tape recorded.

The most controversial feature was the deep male-sounding voice heard coming from Janet and occasionally from her sister. The voice, over which Janet said she had no conscious control, brought to mind several reports from past centuries of similar voices heard from young girls thought to be 'possessed'. The 'voice' claimed several identities, and among the many hours of obscenity and nonsense it produced there were a few unmistakable instances of paranormally acquired knowledge. A laryngograph test revealed that the voice came from Janet's false vocal folds, normally a potentially painful process. Grosse offered a £1000 donation to charity if any critic could find a girl of eleven who could demonstrate a similar sound for up to three hours of normal conversation. There were no takers.

The investigators made repeated attempts to obtain professional help for the girls, whose lives, especially their school work, were severely disrupted for several months. Local psychiatrists refused even to take their case seriously, but eventually Janet was thoroughly examined during a six-week stay at the Maudsley Hospital in south London, where she was found to be sane and healthy.

She also took part in a number of experiments supervised by Professor J. B. Hasted, then head of the Physics Department at Birkbeck College, London University, and his assistant David Robertson. They obtained chart-recorded evidence for her ability to cause a metal strip to break, and also apparently to gain weight while being monitored on a specially constructed balance.

Graham Morris, a professional news photographer, used a remotely controlled motor-driven camera to obtain several fascinating sequences. In one of them a curtain can be seen twisting into a tight spiral while bedclothes are moved without apparent human agency. Morris himself was struck on the face by a toy brick while taking a picture – providing evidence that the brick was not thrown by anybody visible.

The Enfield case, now widely regarded as the classic poltergeist case of modern times, was the subject of a BBC radio documentary made by Rosalind Morris, and of the book *This House is Haunted* by Guy Lyon Playfair (1977).

SEE ALSO *Black Monk of Pontefract; Children and psi; Cosmic Joker; Explanations; Fox sisters; Uri Geller; Ghosts; Nina Kulagina; Levitation; Matthew Manning; Metal bending; Possession; Propensity for psi; Psychokinesis; Rosenheim poltergeist; Seance-room phenomena; Sex and psi; Society for Psychical Research; SORRAT; Spontaneous human combustion.*

BLACK MONK OF PONTEFRACT

The first signs that something disturbing was happening to number 30 East Drive, Pontefract in Yorkshire came on a September night in 1966. Most of the Pritchard family had gone on holiday to the West Country, leaving fifteen-year-old Phillip and his grandmother, Mrs Sarah Scholes, in the house. The house suddenly became icy cold, and from a point about halfway between ceiling and floor a fine white dust began to fall, which covered

Writer-researcher Colin Wilson, who uncovered the astonishing story of 'The Black Monk of Pontefract', one of the most dramatic poltergeist cases on record.

everything. Mysterious pools of water formed – as fast as they were mopped up others appeared – and a wardrobe 'walked' from its corner.

A phenomenon that seemed to become a regular feature of the haunting first took place that day. A neighbour who knew about poltergeists mentioned that they are fond of tearing up photographs. The family heard a crash; upstairs a wedding photograph had been ripped as if with a sharp knife, its glass shattered. This poltergeist was to prove highly suggestible.

By the time the rest of the family – Joe and Jean Pritchard and twelve-year-old Diane – returned the house was quiet. This peace lasted for two years before the disturbances began again, with pots, and pans, bedding and decorating materials flying through the air and utensils behaving as if alive: a carpet sweeper swung like a club and a roll of wallpaper reared up, swaying like a cobra.

A priest was called in to exorcise the house. At first he was sceptical, but when a candlestick floated before his eyes he announced that there was 'something evil' present, and advised the family to move, something they had no intention of doing. Poltergeists rarely, if ever, succumb to exorcism.

Aunt Maude – Joe's sister – a down-to-earth member of the Salvation Army, believed that the children were playing tricks. As if for her benefit, the poltergeist flung the contents of the refrigerator on the floor, and a reading lamp floated through the air and left the room by the door. The family were terrified by the sudden appearance of disembodied hands, which turned out to be Aunt Maude's fur gloves animated by the poltergeist. One of the hands beckoned to her, but she retorted vigorously: 'Get away, you're evil!' Then one hand formed itself into a fist and shook itself at her, but she responded by singing 'Onward Christian Soldiers' – which the poltergeist mocked by conducting with its 'hands'.

Soon afterwards the family became aware of a shadowy figure in the house and a neighbour first saw what looked like a tall man in a long black robe with a cowl. Before the Black Monk's most dramatic and final visitation, Diane suffered a terrifying experience: she was dragged, screaming, upstairs by an invisible force (her cardigan could be seen being pulled out in front of her). She was abruptly released, but there were red fingermarks on her neck. However, she was otherwise physically unharmed.

A short time after this, Phillip saw the Black Monk – an enormous figure – standing behind some frosted glass. When the boy went to look, the Monk slowly disappeared through the floor. That was the end of the haunting, but not of the story, which came to writer Colin Wilson's ears some years later and which he investigated as thoroughly as he could, given the time lapse.

As he wrote in the weekly series *The Unexplained*:

At the time, I was convinced that a poltergeist is some kind of manifestation of the unconscious mind. . . . After interviewing the Pritchards and talking to neighbours, I reluctantly concluded that the 'unconscious mind' theory is simply untenable. I came round to the view that had been put to me by psychical researcher and writer Guy Lyon Playfair – that a poltergeist is some kind of disembodied spirit with a taste for mischief. . . .

Wilson concluded that the shape chosen by the poltergeist – the Black Monk – was a result of overhearing the family discussing an old story about the ghost of a monk (which had no foundation in fact), in the same way that the phenomenon reacted to ideas about how a poltergeist should behave – slashing photographs, for example.

The investigator added: 'The reasonable explanation is, it seems to me, that some kind of "spirit" lies latent in the house in East Drive, waiting for someone to provide the energy it needs to manifest itself.' This energy was available twice within a couple of years, when first Phillip, then Diane, began to go through puberty, a notoriously energetic time for poltergeist manifestations.

SEE ALSO *Apports; Enfield poltergeist; Fox sisters; Ghosts; Propensity for psi; Psychokinesis; Rosenheim poltergeist; Seance-room phenomena; Sex and psi; Spiritualism; Tulpas.*

ROSENHEIM POLTERGEIST

In 1967 a Bavarian lawyer, Herr Sigmund Adam, was mystified by telephone malfunctions in his offices at Königstrasse 13, Rosenheim. Even though the lines were dead, all the receivers would ring simultaneously, or calls would be cut off for no apparent cause.

When technicians from Siemens, the company that had installed the equipment, began to investigate, yet more mysteries were uncovered. Dozens of undialled calls registered on their meters, including many calls to the speaking clock. In just fifteen minutes on one afternoon for example, forty-six calls to the speaking clock were registered, although it would normally take seventeen seconds to make one such call. This went on for months; in one day the speaking clock was called eighty times.

In October 1967 the electricity board was called in to investigate the strange behaviour of the light fittings – among other anomalies, fluorescent tubes had unscrewed themselves and bulbs were found disconnected. It was at this point that 'witchcraft' was first mentioned in connection with the events.

When Paul Brunner, auxiliary works manager for the electricity board, arrived to investigate Herr Adam's story it became clear that something paranormal was happening. During one morning in November a full fifty amps suddenly surged through the office electrics – but not a single fuse blew, while fluorescent tubing shattered in Herr Adam's office. Computer print-outs of the electrical supply showed loops instead of straight lines.

While the entire electricity supply of Rosenheim was being checked, bulbs exploded one after the other at the office; then the overhead lamps began to swing. By December they were swinging so violently that they smashed into the plaster of the ceiling.

Dr Karger of the Max Planck Institute of Plasma Physics and Dr Zicha, an eminent physicist from Munich University, were called in. After thorough investigation they concluded that fraud was impossible, but they speculated that some form of intelligence was manipulating both power supply and telephone equipment. Meanwhile paintings on the walls were seen to turn up to 360°, twisting the string around the hooks as they did so. The physicists, having made their report, left. Significantly, they had both noted that all the phenomena happened during office hours.

Professor Hans Bender of the Freiburg Institute, a renowned investigator of paranormal phenomena, was called in. He and his team noticed that their Unireg pen trace showed the most violent deflections at 7.30 a.m. – when eighteen-year-old Anne-Marie Schneider arrived at work. She was also seen to become tense when the poltergeist attacks began – Bender had no doubt of the nature of the phenomena – and grew increasingly distressed as they grew in ferocity around her.

After the Christmas holidays the attacks diversified, but always centred on Anne-Marie. Desk drawers were pulled out by invisible forces, pictures and calendars sent spinning on the wall, and a 180-kilogram cabinet moved 30 centimetres from the wall. All the female office staff, especially Anne-Marie, complained of receiving electric shocks during the poltergeist attacks. After adjustable typing chairs had been seen to sink and rise unaccountably when Anne-Marie was sitting on them, she was told to leave. The accumulated damage to the office over the previous few months had cost 15,000 Deutchmarks.

Bender investigated Anne-Marie's psychokinetic talents in his laboratory at Freiburg, but the results were disappointing. It seemed that she had to be under immediate stress in order to create disturbances at a distance. A doctor's report mentioned her unusual nervous condition, in which she would cry out with painful leg cramps and her eyes would glaze over. A psychologist confirmed Bender's own suspicions that she loathed working for Herr Adam and that the outbreaks of paranormal activity reflected this. Bender linked the calls to the speaking clock with her subconscious, fervent clock-watching.

Events in her personal life came to a head when she and her fiancé (who was an electrical engineer) attempted to go bowling and the electronic scoreboard went berserk. He blamed her and told her that 'under the circumstances, marriage would be quite impossible'.

Bitter and resentful, Anne-Marie found a job in another lawyer's office, but her reputation had preceded her and she was asked to leave. Shortly after she began working at a paper mill there was a fatal accident. The word 'witch' was constantly muttered in her hearing; she took the hint and left.

In the mid-1970s she moved to Munich and married. For a while it seemed as if all was quiet, but domestic upheavals caused ripples of arguably paranormal phenomena – none, however, as dramatic as those inflicted on Herr Adam in his Rosenheim offices.

SEE ALSO *Allergies and psi; Black Monk of Pontefract; Electric people; Enfield poltergeist; Uri Geller; Hysteria; Nina Kulagina; Matthew Manning; Metal bending; Carmine Mirabelli; Eusapia Palladino; Parapsychology; Propensity for psi; Psychokinesis; Seance-room phenomena; Sex and psi; Witchcraft.*

METAL BENDING

Psychokinetic metal bending (PKMB) was first demonstrated to a mass audience on 23 November 1973 when Uri Geller appeared on the BBC television programme David Dimbleby's *Talk-In*. A piece of cutlery held by Dimbleby and lightly stroked by Geller appeared to become plastic and bent almost double. Geller became a household name overnight, and controversy began to rage. Was this genuine mind over metal, or merely clever conjuring? Even professional stage magicians were divided on the question.

In a typical performance – subsequently repeated before millions, live or on television – Geller holds a spoon, fork or key in his left hand and strokes the stem with the fingers of his right. The object is then seen to bend upwards. Numerous witnesses have described metal objects continuing to bend after Geller has let go of them.

Geller regularly encourages viewers, listeners or newspaper readers to repeat his feats in their homes. After a 1973 experiment in which he was to beam his powers across Britain at an appointed

Alison Lloyd, aged 11, showing off the metal objects she bent after watching Uri Geller on television.

time, 293 readers claimed that their cutlery had duly bent or broken. Several similar mass experiments were held in other countries, and some were carefully followed up. In South Africa, parapsychologist E. Alan Price discovered that the 'Geller Effect' could continue to operate up to twenty-four hours after a radio or television performance.

The effects were occasionally unwelcome. A West German man complained to police after fifty-one pieces of his cutlery and his birdcage had become distorted after Geller appeared on a television show. He demanded compensation. A Swedish woman threatened legal action after her intra-uterine device had bent, thereby causing an unwanted pregnancy. In general, however, people seemed to enjoy the brief intrusion of psychokinesis (PK) into their lives.

Of more interest to parapsychology than the

Professor John Hasted, formerly of Birkbeck College, London, with the 'paperclip scrunch' that resulted from a metalbending experiment. Dozens of whole paperclips were dropped into the glass ball through a hole in the top, then it was held by metalbender Stephen North. The paperclips became this 'scrunch sculpture' (above).

unpredictable side-effects of Gellermania was the prospect of inducing PK abilities in ordinary people. This was pursued in 1981 by aerospace engineer Jack Houck, who predicted that if a 'peak emotional event' could be created in a relaxed and informal atmosphere, and a specific task suggested, results could be immediate, provided all resistance to the idea of success were eliminated. Houck accordingly hosted a 'PK party' at which guests were encouraged to visualise a force flowing through their arms and into their spoons and to be confident that these could – and would – bend. Five years later, he had entertained a total of more than five thousand guests, many of whom reported an improvement in their physical and mental well-being as a result of their newly discovered PK abilities. The potential for putting such abilities to constructive use, as in healing, seems considerable: one of Europe's most successful healers, Matthew Manning, was a proficient metal bender in his youth.

Although physicists and metallurgists have studied PK-distorted metal under electron microscopes and detected unusual signs of hardening, softening and cleavage, there is as yet no sign of an explanation of how minds and spoons interact. Professor J. B. Hasted, former head of the Physics Department of Birkbeck College, London University, studied PKMB more thoroughly than most other researchers. Although he was convinced that the answer lay 'embedded in quantum theory', he urged that 'the spearhead of research must not be in theoretical formulations but in physical observations'. Metal-bending party-givers and their guests thus have a chance to contribute to science while at the same time having a lot of fun.

SEE ALSO *Uri Geller; Nina Kulagina; Matthew Manning; Parapsychology; Psychokinesis; Quantum mechanics and the paranormal; SORRAT.*

PSYCHOKINESIS

Psychokinesis (PK) means motion caused by the mind. It has generally replaced the older word telekinesis – action at a distance – and is used in parapsychology to describe any phenomenon with a physical effect. The word is also used in psychiatry to mean 'uninhibited maniacal motor response', which is a fair description of poltergeist activity.

Although PK has been widely reported down the centuries from many cultures, its inherent improbability and its violation of such physical laws as we think we understand has led to its general rejection by science. The often excessively maniacal nature of PK has made it impossible to investigate satisfactorily. Yet a large mass of evidence exists to support J. B. Rhine's claim that, 'Mind is what the man in the street thought it was all along – something of a force in itself.'

PK has been studied since the 1850s in three

The Polish medium Stanislawa Tonczyk levitating a pair of scissors. Although she later renounced her Spiritualism to placate her Catholic husband, she never could explain how she did her levitations.

generally overlapping areas: spontaneous outbreaks, performances by gifted individuals, and controlled laboratory experiments. Before that time, reports of spontaneous PK were restricted to individual cases of the poltergeist type or of supposed spirit possession that included inexplicable movements of objects.

Following the birth of Spiritualism in 1848, however, spontaneous PK was to some extent tamed and domesticated in the form of the table-tipping seance. When the table tilted, banged a leg on the floor or rose into the air it was assumed that the spirits were trying to get through, although as early as 1854 attempts were being made to study home-entertainment PK from a psychological rather than a spiritual point of view. The first to publish their findings were Count Agénor de Gasparin and Professor Marc Thury in Switzerland, both of whom drew attention to the close connection between the movements of their tables and the states of the sitters' minds. Undeterred by the physicist Michael Faraday's pronouncement in 1853 that table tipping was fully explained by unconscious muscular activity on the part of sitters, scientists who examined the phenomena more thoroughly than he came to other conclusions. In 1855 a retired chemistry professor in the USA, Robert Hare, claimed to have observed what he believed to be psychic force in action on some ingenious weighing and measuring devices of his own design. A few years later, the eminent naturalist Alfred Russel Wallace made similar claims after experiments in his own home.

The most remarkable investigation of its kind was – and still is – that of the medium D. D. Home by one of the outstanding scientists of his time, William Crookes. The PK phenomena observed and described by Crookes after twenty-nine sessions held between 1870 and 1873 included rappings, levitation of objects and alteration of the weight of inert bodies, besides a wide range of other feats. Despite Crookes's reputation – he was already a Fellow of the Royal Society and later became its president as well as being knighted – he met with scepticism and hostility from his colleagues.

His claims were vindicated, however, by later researchers. The most durable and consistent of all PK mediums, Eusapia Palladino and Rudi Schneider, were extensively investigated over long periods by many different scientists who achieved consistently positive results. Other individuals whose PK abilities were well witnessed and described in print include Franek Kluski and Stanislawa Tomczyk in Poland, Marthe Béraud in France, members of the Goligher family in Belfast and Stella Cranshaw in England. Performances by these and other gifted individuals have provided strong evidence for PK, despite inevitable allegations from the sidelines of cheating or malobservation. Yet the extreme strangeness of PK and the total lack of an explanation for it has led some to reject the evidence of their own eyes. 'I saw, but did I see aright?' Charles Richet remarked after a lively meeting with Palladino. And if researchers – even Nobel Prize winners like Richet – are not sure what they saw, how can they convince anybody else?

In 1934, in an effort to find a way out of this impasse, J. B. Rhine began a long period of experimental PK trials in his new laboratory at Duke University in Durham, North Carolina. His aim was to record statistical evidence rather than still more anecdotal accounts. He succeeded, although not quite as planned. When his initial findings were published in 1943 the overall statistical significance was not high, but an intriguing detail emerged: results tended to be best at the start of a session. This 'decline effect' has been called parapsychology's only truly repeatable experiment, though it must be examined in tandem with the 'experimenter effect' – whereby researchers influence the outcome of their experiments by their attitudes and expectations, thus making independent replication of any PK experiment almost impossible.

A major advance in laboratory PK research was pioneered by Helmut Schmidt, who used 'random event generators' to test subjects' ability to alter a wholly unpredictable process (radioactive decay) by PK. His initially very successful results seemed to build a bridge between PK and quantum physics, thus making the former almost respectable. Positive replications of his work at Princeton University and in several other laboratories added to his reputation, although Schmidt himself lamented in 1988 that 'quantum theory can be wrong when applied to systems that include a human subject'.

The appearance on the scene of Nina Kulagina and Uri Geller led to a sudden revival of interest in star-performer PK. Another unexpected revival was that of the traditional Victorian table-tipping session by psychologist Kenneth Batcheldor, who concentrated on the conditions under which spontaneous PK can be predicted to occur and formulated hypotheses about its elusiveness.

Is PK an entirely new force in nature, or an interaction of existing ones? Or is it perhaps the only force? Batcheldor liked to speculate that it was the fundamental stuff of the universe, echoing the scientist Sir James Jeans's famous remark about the universe being a 'great thought'; while a century earlier Alfred Russel Wallace had noted that, since no primary cause of force was known to exist other than the human mind, it was possible that 'all force may be mind-force.'

SEE ALSO *American Society for Psychical Research; Kenneth Batcheldor; Black Monk of Pontefract; Boggle threshold; Case of Ruth; Consensus reality; Cosmic Joker; CSICOP; Divination; Helen Duncan; Ectoplasm; Electric people; Enfield poltergeist; ESP; Experimenter effect; Explanations; Fireproof people; Fox sisters; Gustave Geley; Uri Geller; Healing; D. D. Home; Images that bleed and weep; Incorruptibility; Katie King; Nina Kulagina; Levitation; Limits of science; Metal bending; Carmine Mirabelli; Moving statues; Eusapia Palladino; Parapsychology; Philip experiment; Psi-mediated instrumental response; Psychic music, art and literature; Quantum mechanics and the paranormal; The Resurrection; Ritual magic; Rosenheim poltergeist; Sai Baba; Society for Psychical Research; SORRAT; Stigmatics; Telephone calls from the dead; Thoughtography; Robert Thouless; Tulpas; Turin Shroud.*

The 'Philip group' of the Toronto Society for Psychical Research, led by Dr A. R. G. Owen and his wife Iris, created a 'ghost' (right) through activating the group's imagination, raising many questions about the nature of reality.

PHILIP EXPERIMENT

The Philip experiment, conducted by the Toronto Society for Psychical Research in the 1970s, is arguably the single most significant piece of modern parapsychological research. Based on the view of English researcher Kenneth J. Batcheldor that successful psychokinesis depends on the experimenters' sense of belief and expectancy, a group of researchers led by Dr A. R. G. Owen and his wife Iris tried to create, and communicate with a non-existent 'ghost'.

First, they met regularly to agree on the details of his life; 'Philip' had been an English aristocrat of the seventeenth century, whose mistress had been burnt as a witch, and who had committed suicide after her death. One member of the group drew his portrait and another wrote his biography, which they all memorised. Then they tried to contact him in classic seance-room fashion. At first they had no success, but discovered that a light-hearted atmosphere and heightened sense of expectancy worked best – eventually paranormal raps greeted them and, using the time-honoured system of 'one rap for yes and two for no', the group held question-and-answer sessions with Philip.

Soon, however, it became apparent that the table around which they sat had become the focus for the paranormal activity; in effect the piece of furniture had become Philip. It even jumped up and down in time to their sing-songs, and once chased Dr Owen across the room. The quality and quantity of PK effects seemed directly linked to the belief of the group. On one occasion when a member remarked: 'We only made you up, you know', the PK ceased abruptly.

In 1974 the group were invited to take part in a half-hour programme for Toronto City Television; 'Philip' (the table) astonished the studio audience by 'walking' up the three steps to the platform and by rapping out answers to questions put to him. Shortly afterwards the experiment, deemed a success, was terminated.

The Philip experiment's greatest gift to parapsychology lies in the number of questions it raises, particularly those about the nature of reality and the far-reaching implications of the experimenter effect.

SEE ALSO *Kenneth Batcheldor; Boggle threshold; Case of Ruth; Children and psi; Consensus reality ; Creative visualisation; Experimenter effect; Fantasy-prone personalities; D. D. Home; Limits of science; Matthew Manning; Carmine Mirabelli: Eusapia Palladino; Psychokinesis; Seance-room phenomena; Society for Psychical Research; SORRAT; Thoughtography; Tulpas.*

KENNETH BATCHELDOR

Kenneth J. Batcheldor, born in 1921, became a psychical researcher almost by accident. At a social gathering in 1964 he and three friends decided, as he recalled later, 'to have a go at table-tipping, just for fun', after one of the group had told some Irish ghost stories. The first sitting was uneventful, but the group met again around the table and were rewarded with a loud bang that they could not ascribe to any normal source. Thus encouraged, they kept going, and at subsequent sittings the table began to slide around, tilt and finally leave the ground. Each sitter testified in writing that the levitation was not due to his or her physical force.

Batcheldor was delighted to have repeated some of the phenomena of the Victorian seance without an *a priori* belief in spirit agencies. In September 1966 his first published work appeared in the *Journal of the Society for Psychical Research*; it was on the subject that was to preoccupy him for the rest of his life: large-scale psychokinesis or 'macro-PK'. He not only claimed to have experienced just about every kind of seance phenomenon reported by the Victorian Spiritualists, but encouraged readers to 'suspend disbelief long enough to attempt experimentation for themselves'. Those who did so successfully included the late Colin Brookes-Smith and the Revd Alan Barham in England, and the 'Philip' group in Toronto headed by the experienced researchers Dr George Owen and his wife Iris.

In 1976 Batcheldor took early retirement from his post of senior clinical psychologist for a group of Devon hospitals, and devoted himself to macro-PK research. His laboratory was his own sitting room, and his subjects were friends and neighbours, none of whom claimed any mediumistic gifts. His main aim was to identify the conditions under which PK took place, and he soon found that the state of the participants' minds had a direct effect on the outcome of any experiment. To generate PK, he found, it was essential for those involved to have total faith in its imminent occurrence – and to harbour no resistance to such a prospect. This attitude, he knew, went against the traditional

The late British researcher Kenneth Batcheldor discovered that an atmosphere of light-heartedness and expectancy creates the most dramatic psychokinesis (PK).

objectivity of conventional science.

One of his theoretical insights, repeatedly confirmed in practice, was that macro-PK can follow what he termed 'induction by artifact'. In other words, if a group of people fully believe that PK is already taking place – even when it is not – it will, in fact, occur as a consequence of this belief. It makes no difference if this group faith is induced by a normal incident, or even by deliberate trickery.

Most of Batcheldor's sittings were held in total darkness, which he found essential if sitters were to achieve doubt-suspension. This made verification difficult, but not impossible – he introduced a number of techniques, such as luminous markers on the table and a pocket torch that he would flash without warning. Several of his later sittings were filmed with infra-red-sensitive video equipment; although he failed to obtain a clear shot of a table in mid-air, several sequences show movements that do not seem normally produced, while some show what looks remarkably like ectoplasm.

Although the problem of full verification eluded him, Batcheldor came close to achieving parapsychology's main goal; the repeatable experiment. Before his death in 1988 he also left precise and well-argued instructions for those wishing to replicate his findings.

A good introduction to his work is included in

J. H. Brennan's *Mindreach* (1985), and a more detailed first-hand account is to be found in Guy Lyon Playfair's *If This Be Magic* (1985). Batcheldor himself revised and approved the relevant passages of both these books.

SEE ALSO *American Society for Psychical Research; Apports; Boggle threshold; Ectoplasm; Experimenter effect; D. D. Home; Levitation; Limits of science; Parapsychology; Philip experiment; Psychokinesis; Seance-room phenomena; Society for Psychical Research; SORRAT.*

SORRAT

Since 1961 the Missouri-based group known as the Society for Research on Rapport and Telekinesis (SORRAT) has produced such an enormous range of large-scale psychokinesis (PK) that its work has either been totally ignored, or dismissed as fraud. Yet if only a fraction of SORRAT's phenomena are taken seriously, it must be admitted that the work of the group is at least on a par with the best PK experiments ever recorded – and therefore it presents a significant challenge to present scientific paradigms.

The group was formed in 1961 by Professor John G. Neihardt, an award-winning literary figure whose lifelong interest in mysticism and psychical research was less well known. Profoundly influenced by the Sioux shaman Black Elk, Neihardt set out to discover how belief, and the power of the group mind, can produce apparently paranormal phenomena.

Until his death in 1973 Neihardt led regular meetings of the group, which was about fifteen-strong, at his home, Skyrim Farm near Columbia, Missouri. Among the members were Dr John Thomas Richards and his wife Elaine, at whose home in nearby Rollo the group were to meet after Neihardt's death and where the most impressive phenomena eventually took place. Dr Richards is also SORRAT's archivist and biographer.

From his research into the history of seance-room phenomena, Neihardt concluded that (in Richards's words): 'a light approach to paranormal phenomena was more likely to put us into the best psychological frame of reference for positive results . . .'. Accordingly, the group met in normal daylight or full electric light, sang, joked and chatted inconsequentially – but with full expectancy that something unusual would happen. Neihardt believed that the single most important factor in achieving positive results was the 'rapportment' among the members of the group, a belief that was to be supported by Dr A. R. G. Owen's Philip experiment some years later in Toronto.

After a lengthy fallow phase, SORRAT began to achieve paranormal raps – usually the first seance-room phenomenon to manifest. They developed from random, anomalous noises to on-demand phenomena that rapped out coded replies to the group's questions.

But of SORRAT's astonishing history, the most impressive phenomena occurred when the group called in W. E. Cox. He was not only a seasoned psychical researcher who had worked with J. B. Rhine but also a skilled amateur conjurer (and therefore, it was believed, likely to be able to detect fraud). Although Cox and individual members of the group did not always harmonise, his contribution to its work was incalculable. By the time he had joined them, extraordinary phenomena were taking place spontaneously, both during SORRAT's meetings and between them, at the Richards's home.

In order to 'trap' the phenomena Cox built a 'minilab' – an upturned aquarium, sealed around the bottom, and containing various objects for the paranormal forces to operate upon. Each of these objects was wired to a clock and a movie camera outside the minilab. If something moved, then the camera would be switched on and any subsequent PK in the minilab would be recorded on film. The results may be deemed to have 'crashed the boggle threshold' and led, inevitably, to accusations of fraud.

Film from the SORRAT archives shows a variety of phenomena. Inside the sealed minilab a pack of cards sorted itself into suits; a piece of card spontaneously combusted; a balloon (its neck tied, and facing upwards) inflated and deflated; a pen wrote

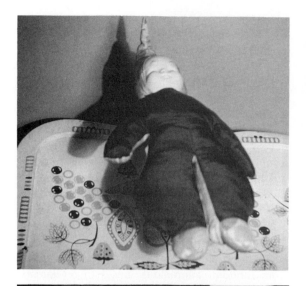

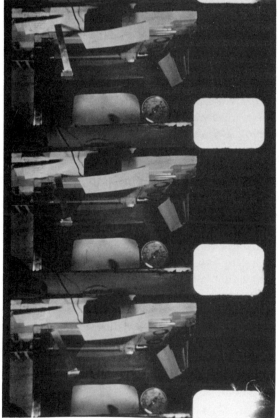

Some of the most spectacular psychic phenomena ever deliberately induced were produced by the Society for Research on Rapport and Telekinesis (SORRAT). Based in Rolla, Missouri, they have met regularly for nearly thirty years. One of their first psi successes was the levitation of objects (above), but it was the phenomena that centred in and around their 'minilab' – a glass box wired to a movie camera – that attracted the most virulent controversy. An aluminium bar can be seen (left) to emerge through the solid glass between frames of the film.

In the early 1980s, film of events inside the SORRAT minilab was shown in Britain to members of the Society for Psychical Research (SPR) by then Aston University parapsychologist Julian Isaacs. It was greeted by a stunned silence. The only questions raised on that occasion concerned the protocol of the experiments and the opportunities for fraud. At the 1982 SPR centenary conference at Cambridge a film was shown that satirised SORRAT's achievements.

Undaunted, Julian Isaacs set up his own network of minilabs in Britain largely in the homes of the Spiritualists and metal benders on whom he based much of his parapsychological research. Although some phenomena were recorded, his work was unfinished when he left to live in the USA.

But SORRAT's phenomena continued and diversified. Their meetings were frequently assailed by

messages purporting to be from several different entities; and two solid leather rings linked and unlinked – before one of them teleported through the glass of a minilab, between frames of the film.

pungent, unexplained odours, ranging from the stench of rotting meat to the fragrance of powerful incense. Apports (objects that appear suddenly, apparently from nowhere, during a seance) such as rings, pens and even, on one occasion, a lady's frilly garter, regularly manifested both during meetings and inside the minilab (by now a permanent feature in the Richards's basement). Sometimes objects from inside the minilab appeared elsewhere.

Through the rap code, and later through spontaneously written notes, various entities gave the group information, which ranged from the frivolous – asked 'What is an apport?' the entity replied: 'An apport is the place where the applanes land' – to the profound. One message, laboriously rapped out, concerned the natural laws governing the manifestation of paranormal phenomena:

The rotation of the Earth sets up force fields, some helping and some inhibiting levitation. We can come through easier when the fields are tilted, for the northern hemisphere, in Fall, Winter and Spring, and your psi output is hurt by hot, moist weather's effect on your bodies.

The group received messages from entities purporting to be 'John King' (father of Katie King, the spirit manifestation researched by William Crookes in the 1870s) and '3 times 3', accepted as a creation of Cox's subconscious mind. They also received detailed information from and about a discarnate being called Myra Cavanaugh, who claimed to have been a student at the University of Missouri-Columbia in the late 1860s and to have died shortly after her graduation. SORRAT tried to trace her but failed – the university records had perished in a fire. But while they were researching 'Myra' she gave them instructions on how to capture her on film. The experimenter who took the photograph saw nothing except grass and sky, but the resulting print clearly showed a girl sitting on the grass, her parasol beside her, smiling at the camera. Although trees in the corner of the picture cast shadows normally, the girl did not.

In 1981 Cox played a trick on SORRAT during a related experiment at the McDonnell Laboratory for Psychical Research in St Louis, Missouri. An alleged psychic was brought in to influence con-sciously, but without touch, a sealed bottle containing a pencil stub, a piece of paper, a safety pin and two pipe cleaners. The safety pin closed, the pipe cleaners made themselves into a stick man and the pencil wrote 'Freedom, love, faith' on the paper. The psychic was then revealed to be a fraud – nevertheless the phenomena had occurred. Perhaps SORRAT's collective strength overcame such minor problems.

The group has never disbanded and continues to produce spectacular PK. Once savagely attacked by other psychical researchers, SORRAT is now largely ignored. Perhaps it is worth remembering that, until Cox joined them, the group did not seek publicity and therefore had considerably less of a motive for fraud.

It may be that the SORRAT experience holds the key to many mysteries.

SEE ALSO *Apports; Kenneth Batcheldor; Boggle threshold; Children and psi; Consensus reality; CSICOP; Entity enigma; Experimenter effect; Uri Geller; Images that bleed and weep; Katie King; Levitation; Limits of science; Metal bending; Paranormal portraits; Parapsychology; Philip experiment; Psychokinesis; Quantum mechanics and the paranormal; Ritual magic; Seance-room phenomena; Shamanism; Society for Psychical Research; Thoughtography; Tulpas.*

AMERICAN SOCIETY FOR PSYCHICAL RESEARCH

The American Society for Psychical Research (ASPR) began its chequered history just over a hundred years ago. It was set up largely due to the enthusiasm of Sir William Barrett, the Dublin physicist so instrumental in starting the London-based Society of Psychical Research (SPR) in 1882.

ASPR's first President was Simon Newcomb, an astronomer, which William James thought an excellent choice. After the discovery of a brilliant medium in Leonore Piper, Dr Richard Hodgson came over from England to investigate her. The new society set out with high hopes of success.

However, that all was not well became clear as early as Professor Newcomb's inaugural address, when he revealed overt disbelief in telepathy (one of the great enthusiasms of the SPR's founders). It seemed that under his direction the society would be incapable of sustained, positive effort, while its financial standing left much to be desired.

On the other hand, Dr Hodgson became Secretary and threw himself into his work with Mrs Piper, convincing himself and others of the reality of the paranormal in general and of survival after death in particular. But such euphoria did not last, and by 1889 the ASPR was in such a bad way that it had to swallow its pride and become merely a branch of the SPR. Then in 1905 tragedy struck with the sudden death of Richard Hodgson.

Relations between the council of the SPR and the sorry remnant across the Atlantic were strained by squabbling over the rights to the Piper records, and the sensitive question of whether or not the ASPR should be liquidated. The California-based Hereward Carrington made a bold move, however, and invited the Neapolitan medium Eusapia Palladino to the USA to be investigated. She was undoubtedly the queen of physical mediumship, just as Mrs Piper ruled mental mediums, but Eusapia entranced could be wily, and had to be watched carefully. When Carrington took her on an American tour it proved disastrous; she was 'exposed' (not for the first time, and by some doubtful investigators, but the damage was done). Carrington himself became *persona non grata* with the fastidious psychical research establishment because of his commercial involvement with Palladino at a time when investigators were expected to work for next to nothing.

Another medium, Mina Crandon – known as 'Margery' – was the unwitting cause of the society's Watergate. Her all-embracing and unique mediumship 'crashed the boggle barrier' so effectively that it led to much internal dissension. Dr Eric Dingwell, the British researcher who often tended towards scepticism, wrote that her work was 'the most remarkable hitherto recorded', and penned a glowing account of a sitting he had attended. Yet J. B. Rhine, writing on the basis of a single sitting – and flying in the face of not only Dingwell

but also Hereward Carrington – condemned her utterly as a fraud.

In 1941, however, there took place what Karlis Osis has dubbed 'the Palace revolution', led by the editor of the *Journal*, Jocelyn Kennedy. A Boston Society had sprung into existence, supported by men more interested in the experimental approach than in the phenomena of the seance room; this move was clearly influenced by the fact that J. B. Rhine had now become synonymous with parapsychology. The Margery investigation was finally abandoned (to the relief of the medium as much as anyone else concerned), and the ASPR acquired a new, less populist image with George Hyslop and Gardner Murphy endeavouring to integrate its work with 'straight' science.

Other luminaries of this time were Margaret Mead, C. G. Jung (who inexplicably had his membership suspended in 1943), William James and William McDougall. Hyslop, as President, became obsessed with financial detail, quibbling even over the purchase of a clock for the society. Laura Dale, by contrast, was a driving force. They were lucky in attracting the membership of Gertrude Schmeidler, best known for her 'Sheep and goats' experiments, which were designed to assess subjects by their overt attitude to the paranormal, and for her critical assessment of cases of ostensible haunting. She was later to become the ASPR's President.

In 1948 the Society was enriched by the addition of a 'medical section' whose influence proved seminal. It included such famous names as Jan Ehrenwald, Jule Eisenbud and Montague Ullman. One of the most exciting post-war developments was the creation of the Maimonides Dream Laboratory to test clairvoyance during sleep – but, like most brilliantly conceived innovations in psychical research, it failed to live up to its promise.

The study of spontaneous cases was resumed after a conference on the subject at Cambridge in 1955, which had the whole-hearted support of Gardner Murphy and others of the ASPR establishment. J. G. Pratt conducted valuable case studies of poltergeist infestation, and others concentrated on field-work in their efforts to find genuine psi phenomena.

As a direct result of Murphy's presidency enough funds were forthcoming to see Karlis Osis

American medium Mrs Leonore Piper, who provided some of the most persuasive evidence for communication between the living and the dead.

appointed as Director of Research. One of his first major investigations was conducted, with Dr Erlandur Haraldsson, into death-bed observations. It provided much of the impetus for the significant research now being carried out on both sides of the Atlantic into the near death experience (NDE), and may turn out to be parapsychology's greatest contribution to the man in the street.

Gardner Murphy resigned in 1971, giving rise to an air of retrenchment and stagnation. However, research into out-of-the-body experiences (taken up more enthusiastically by the media than by the parapsychologists), Professor Ian Stevenson's monumental work on reincarnation, and lately Jahn's work with random number generators hold out some promise of greater things to come.

SEE ALSO *Black Monk of Pontefract; Boggle threshold; Cross-correspondences; Ectoplasm; Enfield poltergeist; ESP; Experimenter effect; Ghosts; Inspiration in dreams; Jung and the paranormal; Life after death; Multiple personality; Near death experience; Out-of-the-body experiences; Eusapia Palladino; Parapsychology; Precognition in dreams; Psychokinesis; Reincarnation; Remote viewing; Rosenheim poltergeist; Society for Psychical Research; Telepathy; Telepathy and the ganzfeld; Thoughtography.*

REMOTE VIEWING

The term 'remote viewing' was coined in 1972 by researchers Harold Puthoff and Russell Targ of Stanford Research Institute (later renamed SRI International) at Menlo Park, California, to describe their experiments in travelling clairvoyance, or the obtaining of information at a distance without the use of normal sensory channels. Their procedure was simplicity itself. One of them would go to a location selected by a random process while the other remained in the laboratory together with the viewer, who would simply describe such impressions of the location as came to mind.

Two viewers who showed unusual ability were New York artist Ingo Swann and Pat Price, a retired Californian police commissioner. Each repeatedly produced accurate descriptions or drawings of distant target locations. In a 1973 experiment, Puthoff went to the Hoover Tower on the Stanford University campus while Targ tape-recorded Price's impressions; they included the words: 'Seems like it would be Hoover Tower.' On another occasion, Price provided specific and accurate information about the target location twenty minutes before the travelling experimenter arrived at it. In this way 'Precognitive remote viewing' was discovered.

Price's work was included in the scientific paper published by Targ and Puthoff in *Nature* (18 October 1974). Following his death in 1975 an unexpected tribute to his talents came from CIA director Admiral Stansfield Turner, who confirmed that agency scientists and officials had taken part in some of the Stanford tests.

They must have been particularly intrigued by the work of Ingo Swann, who virtually took charge of experiments in which he was involved. He introduced a new technique of remote viewing and described distant locations after being given no more than their geographical co-ordinates. Swann also collaborated with the veteran psychic Harold Sherman in an ambitious attempt to describe planets before spacecraft had visited them.

Another successful remote viewer is Keith 'Blue' Harary, a trained psychologist with many years' experience in several laboratories as both subject and experimenter. He helped develop the technique of 'associative remote viewing', whereby a token object or scene is randomly associated with one of a number of possible future events. This method was put to the test in a series of attempts to predict movements in the price of silver. After nine consecutive correct predictions, Harary had made a profit of $120,000. Unfortunately, the next two predictions were wrong and the project was abandoned, although an independent Stanford Research Institute team reported a gain of $25,000 after thirty silver dealings that had been based on the reports of seven viewers using the associative method.

Several other groups have replicated the Stanford work, the first to publish positive results being Chicago psychologists John Bisaha and Brenda Dunne. Following visits by Stanford researchers to the Soviet Union, remote-viewing groups were set up in Moscow and at the University of Yerevan in Soviet Armenia. An international experiment has also been held, with the Georgian healer Dzhuna Davitashvili in Moscow successfully describing the location in California visited by Harary.

Remote viewing is not a skill restricted to star performers. As Puthoff and Targ discovered, anybody can do it – even sceptics. No previous experience, training or beliefs are needed, although participants benefit from regular practice. At least one team, the Mobius Society of Los Angeles, headed by Stephan Schwartz, has gone into business on a professional basis and reported successful application of remote viewing in many fields, including archaeology and crime detection.

No remote viewer is, as yet, infallible and much remains to be learned about the conditions required for success and the separation of 'noise' from signal. Thanks to its simplicity and its wide-ranging potential, remote viewing is one of the most pro-

mising areas of current parapsychology research.
SEE ALSO *American Society for Psychical Research; Doppelgängers; ESP; Healing; Mesmerism; Near death experience; Out-of-the-body experiences; Parapsychology; Shamanism; Society for Psychical Research; Soviet psi today; Telepathy; Telepathy and the ganzfeld.*

TELEPATHY

The word 'telepathy' was coined by Frederic Myers, founder member of the Society for Psychical Research (SPR), in the early 1880s. He defined it as the communication of ideas from one mind to another without the use of any of the recognised channels of sense. It was hoped that research into this phenomenon might lead to the demonstration of levels of human consciousness other than the physical. Myers wrote in the SPR *Proceedings*: 'The Society for Psychical Research was founded with the establishment of thought transference – already rising within measurable distance of proof.' In the years following Myers's death in 1902, such optimism proved premature.

While raising many interesting questions of experimental protocol, J. B. Rhine's card-guessing tests have done little to establish telepathic communication as a fact. Their results are widely ascribed to chance, subconscious clues between experimenter and subject, and so on.

More promising are the experiments into telepathy using the information deprivation of the ganzfeld. But even here experimenters have fallen foul of internal politics, jealousies and the experimenter effect.

Raw data about spontaneous cases, however, has mounted. Telepathic impressions arising from crises – point-of-death, accident, emotional upheaval – have been copiously noted, and the experiences of primitive tribesmen are justifiably legend.

Current debate centres not on anecdotal, but scientific, evidence, which is proving elusive. However, there are already well-authenticated experiments on record that may serve as models

Telepathy as a parlour game. Often a light-hearted approach facilitates greater success.

for other enthusiasts. In the late 1930s the researcher Harold Sherman and the polar explorer Sir Hubert Wilkins co-operated with the psychologist and member of the American Society for Psychical Research, Gardner Murphy. At fixed times in the evening, Sherman in New York would attempt to 'tune in' to Wilkins's distant environment and record his impressions of it. He would date and time his written statements and post them to Murphy, who then had them registered with an attorney. Murphy later compared Sherman's words with those from the log, or Wilkins's verbatim recollections. Many impressive 'hits', entirely beyond chance, were registered over the sixty-eight evening sessions. On 30 November 1937, between 11.30 and 12 p.m., Sherman wrote down: 'Strong impression pingpong balls – is there a table in town where people can play? Can't account for this unusual impression.' Wilkins later wrote:

'Two of the men, Cheeseman and Dyne, were playing pingpong in the school gymnasium, but I was not there.'

On 21 December, between 10.30 and 12 p.m., Sherman wrote: 'You have had some rare wine offered to the crew and you tonight ... I seem to see you all partake.' To which Wilkins responded: 'Blueberry wine – not bad!'

Sherman noted between 11.30 and 12 on 14 February 1938: 'Word "Mackenzie" flashes to mind in connection with flying – is there a company of some sort that supplies you with plane?' Wilkins answered: 'Mackenzie Airways plane brought me out and was preparing to bring me back.'

Such accumulated data is considerable, but – as with many other fields of psychical research – the theory and possible explanations inconsidered and weak. Models of the telepathic process have tended to follow the prevailing paradigms of the time –

thus the 1920s' model notion of brainwaves (akin to radio signals) beamed forth from sender to receiver dies hard. Ideas of some sort of subconscious transmission have been popular, but the workings of the mind remain elusive.

Analytical attention, however, has shifted down the years from agent (sender) to percipient (receiver). Pioneering psychical researcher Mrs Sidgwick was one of the first to draw attention to this area, writing in the SPR *Proceedings* of 1915: 'It may be that the role of the so-called agent is purely passive and that it is the percipient who plays the active role in extracting a combination of ideas from the mind of the agent.'

The observation was endorsed by the French researcher René Warcollier, who has shown that when the percipient does not attempt to receive, transmission does not generally take place. 'He has to place himself in the correct condition – half asleep, mental vacuum, silence – akin to the first stage of hypnosis. In deep hypnosis – perfect transmission has been observed.'

This perspective is reflected in Sherman's description of the passive state he entered during his linking with Wilkins (*Thoughts Through Space*, 1971):

> Make your mind as clear and passive as a pool of water so that it will reflect the vaguest shadow or so it will react to the tiniest pebble which may cause a ripple on it – I was able to bring to each sitting a natural enthusiasm and eagerness to receive messages from him. This attitude seemed to create in me an energy I needed to get results.

SEE ALSO *American Society for Psychical Research; Creative visualisation; Cross-correspondences; ESP; Experimenter effect; Formative causation; Ghosts; Hypnosis; Inspiration in dreams; Left and right brain; Parapsychology; Remote viewing; Society for Psychical Research; Telepathy and the ganzfeld.*

TELEPATHY AND THE GANZFELD

Ganzfeld is a German word meaning a whole or uniform field. In parapsychology it describes an experimental method of inducing receptivity to psi by creating an artificial visual and auditory environment. This is usually done by placing halved ping-pong balls over the subject's eyes and feeding white noise to the ears through headphones. Thus deprived of normal sensory input, the subject is forced into an 'internal attention state' while remaining fully conscious.

The ganzfeld state is not, as often claimed, one of sensory deprivation, but one of information deprivation. The senses remain fully operative, but since they have no incoming information other than uniform light and sound, their attention is turned to ideas and images either produced spontaneously by the subconscious or – it is claimed – transmitted from a distance by telepathy.

It was found in the early 1960s that this state encouraged the manifestation of hypnagogic imagery (images perceived when falling asleep), and in 1974 the American parapsychologist Charles Honorton reported the first attempts to use it for controlled laboratory experiments in telepathic communication. Given the previous lack of any repeatable experiment in psychical research, the ganzfeld studies were an important breakthrough.

Evidence that genuine information was being exchanged was compelling. In an early experiment, one of Honorton's subjects described 'a large hawk's head in front of me . . . the sense of sleek feathers'. Meanwhile, the experimenter was concentrating on a sequence of slides of birds. Another subject spoke of 'all these different circles', while the target image was of rare coins.

Honorton's results were successfully replicated by others including William Braud in the USA and Carl Sargent at Cambridge University's Psychological Laboratory. Others, including Adrian Parker and Susan Blackmore, failed to achieve positive results. This led to one of the bitterest controversies the parapsychology community has yet known. The two conflicting hypotheses are that Sargent (and presumably also Honorton and Braud) were

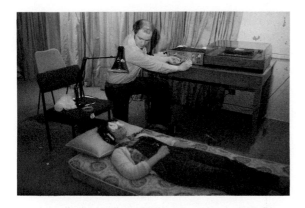

Dr Carl Sargent of Cambridge University sets up a ganzfeld experiment with assistant Heidi Bartlett. The subject records her stream of consciousness while in a state of information deprivation, and elsewhere in the building target images are being transmitted to her telepathically.

Heidi evaluates the success of the experiment. Dr Sargent maintained a significant level of 'psi hitting' among his subjects – a clear case of positive 'experimenter effect'?

either cheating or merely incompetent in their procedure; and that positive results in ganzfeld studies, as in many other fields of psi research, are a direct consequence of the 'experimenter effect'. The latter is the more plausible, since there is abundant evidence for the existence of such effects.

Fortunately, the controversy is easily settled – at least on an individual basis. While a fully controlled laboratory ganzfeld experiment is complex, involving random selection methods and pre-

cautions against sensory leakage, informal experiments can be done at home. The subject is prepared as described above, while the 'sender' goes into another room and concentrates on a picture. The subject describes such impressions that come to mind to a tape recorder – one side of a thirty-minute cassette should be long enough. After the session the subject is shown the target picture together with three 'control' pictures, preferably selected and produced by a third party. The tape is then played back and each impression is scored for its applicability to each of the four pictures, the one with the highest score being judged the winner. This has been found to be a more reliable method than merely taking a look at the four and deciding which is the target.

Useful background reading are Upton Sinclair's classic *Mental Radio* (2nd edn. 1962) and René Warcollier's *Mind to Mind* (1948). Though written before the ganzfeld procedure was used, both books explain in non-technical language the conditions that lead to positive results.

SEE ALSO *American Society for Psychical Research; CSICOP; ESP; Experimenter effect; Formative causation; Inspiration in dreams; Left and right brain; Limits of science; Out-of-the-body experiences; Parapsychology; Propensity for psi; Remote viewing; Society for Psychical Research; Telepathy.*

ESP

Extrasensory perception (ESP) is defined as knowledge of or response to an external event or influence not conveyed through known sensory channels – nor indeed through any others. The American parapsychologist J. B. Rhine introduced the term 'general extrasensory perception' (GESP) as an inclusive description to indicate that ESP can be either telepathy or clairvoyance. There is also precognition, which is knowledge of a *future* event which could not have been predicted or inferred by normal means, and retrocognition, which is knowledge of a *past* event which could not have been apprehended or inferred.

The distinction between telepathy and clairvoyance (now also referred to as distant or remote viewing, if induced) is a fine one. Telepathy is extrasensory awareness of another person's mental content or state. Clairvoyance is similar 'awareness' of objects or objective events.

A further distinction is drawn between laboratory experiments of a 'forced' kind (for instance in card guessing), and the frequent spontaneous and intuitive flashes of paranormal insight that are second nature to some people but incomprehensible to others. They often occur in dreams, on the point of falling asleep (hypnagogic visions) or of waking up (hypnopompic impressions), or in trance-like states of altered consciousness. The hothouse atmosphere of the laboratory may reduce and eliminate this faculty altogether.

Despite the popular belief that the critical study of this subject is of recent origin, it has been extensively explored for centuries. In the eighth century BC the prophet Isaiah pre-recorded a prediction upon 'a great tablet' in the presence of multiple witnesses, including 'Uriah, the priest, and Zechariah, the son of Jeberechiah'. Thus he did what SPR members are urged to do in similar situations; record their predictions beforehand, and tell others about them at the same time. (Unfortunately the biblical one is too vague to be impressive.)

From the period when witches were persecuted with fervour in Britain and Europe in the sixteenth and seventeenth centuries there is a wealth of recorded material that suggests psychic activities. While some of it plumbs the depths of superstition and ignorance, it also includes detailed accounts such as the Throgmorton children's awareness of the precise whereabouts of the alleged witch, Mother Samuel: 'Insomuch that she could do nothing almost at home ... but the spirit would disclose it.' Wherever the poor woman might be at the time, and whatever she was engaged on, the girls knew about it. Careful checks were made by immediate inspection following each statement. It would appear, moreover, that the children were equally adept at finding out each other's movements, business and predicament when they were separated by considerable distances – which, as

Luminaries of the Society for Psychical Research in the 1920s. Mrs Sidgwick has been accused of being biased against several leading mediums of the day.

quoted by B. Rosen in his classic *Witchcraft* (1969), was 'proved to be mostly true by the just computation of times, with many such like things'.

Closer to our own time, and meticulously investigated by Richard Hodgson, are the psychic revelations of Mrs Piper of Boston, whose veridical statements persuaded him and others of the truth of survival after death and of communication with the discarnate. Dr Hodgson's findings pose a serious dilemma that remains unresolved. The sceptic's alternatives boil down either to the acceptance of Spiritualism, or the unproved hypothesis of 'super-ESP', according to which mediums subconsciously gather and integrate data so as to suggest the continued presence in spirit of the dead of a boundless and all-embracing 'radar'. This is a tall order, even though the prominent psychical researcher Dame Edith Lyttelton was on the right track when she declared that 'Telepathy does not merely bridge space, it annihilates it – space becomes an irrelevance.' Whatever may be the truth of the matter, doubters cannot have it both ways: either ESP is a fact of nature, or Spiritualism is the answer.

ESP also emerges in automatic writing when the

'Father of parapsychology' J. B. Rhine tests for ESP in card guessing.

sitter is apparently 'taken over' by an external intelligence and is unaware of his or her writing, or at least of its contents. On 11 December 1901 an exceptional exponent of this art, the Cambridge classical scholar Mrs Verrall, received by these means the following cryptic message: 'Nothing too mean the trivial helps, give confidence. Hence this. Frost and a candle in the dim light. Marmontel he was reading on a sofa or in a bed – there was only a candle's light. She will surely remember this. The book was lent not his own – he talked about it.'

On 1 March 1902 she had dinner with a Mr Marsh who had indeed been reading Marmontel's *Memoirs* in Paris by candlelight on a cold night. The book was borrowed from the London Library, and he had talked about it to friends. In a previous message Mrs Verrall had got the names 'Passy' and 'Fleury', which are relevant to the *Memoirs*, but none of this was known to her at the time. She comments: 'It will thus be noted that the script in December, 1901, describes (as past) an incident which actually occurred two and a half months

later, in February, 1902, – a incident which at the time of writing was not likely to have been foreseen by anyone.'

By contrast the history of laboratory ESP is disappointing, as it has failed to live up to its early promise. The idea of putting the paranormal on a proper scientific footing by submitting it to statistical analysis was not altogether novel when J. B. Rhine embarked on his mammoth task in the 1930s. For a time he was remarkably successful: his subjects scored against chance expectation at an astronomical rate, using specially designed 'Zener' cards with five symbols. A leading statistician was satisfied with this aspect of his work, but results in Britain, using the same method, failed to rise above a meagre level of insignificance. The impression gained ground that, as conditions were tightened to exclude sensory leakage, so the scores declined. A curious side-effect noted by Rhine was the 'decline effect' (or 'boredom factor'), but this, he thought, supported his positive findings since it followed predictable and lawful patterns.

The good news to some was that Rhine's most vociferous British critic, the London mathematician Dr S. Soal, was in the 1960s able to duplicate his results with his own star subject, Basil Shackleton. He was equally lucky with a medium, Mrs Blanche Cooper. She did not enjoy a high reputation, but was now able to foretell events which amazed Soal. For a long time the latter, who became President of the SPR, stood head and shoulders above his peers as having put precognition on the map with his remarkable and unique double in the laboratory and the seance room. The parapsychologist Professor Broad could not hide his amazement at his conversion, and wittily enquired whether Soal was 'also among the prophets'. Meanwhile Rhine's good subjects at Duke University tended to fade out. Worse was to come: suspicions gathered about Soal's integrity when it was found that he had misled his colleagues about a table of random numbers. When his records were re-examined by a computer expert, more serious irregularities in his experimental protocol came to light, and even his sittings with the medium were questioned. None the less, even sceptics who were quick to debunk psi on the basis of laboratory experiments, were unable seriously to challenge the positive data from work with such exhaustively tested psychics as Mrs Piper in the USA, or Mrs Osborne Leonard in Britain.

ESP may well have been an everyday part of primeval lives; today it surfaces occasionally to prompt or warn us, although its timing is not always faultless. In some cases it is even doubtful whether one is dealing with genuine foreknowledge, because psychokinesis (PK) presents a viable counter-hypothesis. This dilemma arises even over apparent ESP in the Bible, since the prophets were credited not only with foreseeing, but also with influencing, the future. Dr Jule Eisenbud, among others, argues that PK may be invoked to explain cases of ostensible foreknowledge; in other words it is not what we can know about future events, but rather that we contrive to bring them about. On a minor scale one can often see a type of self-fulfilling prophecy acting to bring about the predictions of fortune tellers – even if the future they paint is grim.

Retrocognition is a relatively rare phenomenon, and usually takes the form of a timeslip, in which scenes from the past are perceived by the subject, who sometimes becomes part of the historical action. Two Englishwomen on holiday in Dieppe in the 1950s heard the sounds of the Normandy landings of 1944; perhaps they unconsciously trespassed upon the dramatic events that, as it were lay in wait in that area for the right sensitives to trigger off a 'replay'.

In laboratory tests for ESP, as in other aspects of parapsychological research, the elusive prize is the repeatable experiment. Much human error and bias has been eliminated from the protocol of long-run guessing tests through the invention by Helmut Schmidt of a random-number generator, while techniques such as hypnosis and the ganzfeld invoke the altered state of consciousness that seems to encourage ESP.

Yet another, controversial, area may prove fruitful in ESP research. In the recent discipline of ufology there are frequent disquieting claims of communication by ESP between the ufonauts (be they extraterrestrials or aliens of another sort) and their contactees. Frequently experients of close encounters and abductions feel that they are being addressed telepathically. Yet in the laboratory no message of more than a single word has ever been transmitted from mind to mind. Here, as elsewhere in parapsychology, it may be that real life outstrips laboratory findings in both content and style, for we are told that in 1987 a UFO landed at an American Air Force base in Norfolk to disgorge small humanoid creatures – who conversed with the commander by ESP. This incident is unlikely to be followed up by even the most positive and open-minded parapsychologists, however – for, with very few exceptions, they do not acknowledge ufology.

SEE ALSO *American Society for Psychical Research, Astrology; Divination; Entity enigma; Experimenter effect; Inspiration in dreams; Old Testament miracles; Other dimensions; Parapsychology; Precognition in dreams; Prophecy and prediction; Psychic music, art and literature; Psychokinesis; Society for Psychical Research; Telepathy; Telepathy and the ganzfeld; Time; Timeslips; UFO classification; UFO paradox.*

SOCIETY FOR PSYCHICAL RESEARCH

The Society for Psychical Research (SPR) was founded in 1882; its leading progenitors were the Cambridge philosopher Henry Sidgwick, the physicist William Barrett, the journalist E. Dawson Rogers and the classical scholar, poet and psychologist Frederic W. H. Myers, who was to dominate its first twenty years of activity. In its first year it had exactly one hundred members and associates including three Fellows of the Royal Society, three Members of Parliament (one, A. J. Balfour, a future Prime Minister) and a sizeable bloc of Spiritualists who formed the majority of the first Council.

By 1882 there had been more than thirty years of phenomena associated with Spiritualism, physical and mental, genuine and false. Yet apart from the pioneering work of William Crookes with the medium D. D. Home and the enquiries of the short-lived London Dialectical Society, no systematic attempt had been made to investigate these phenomena scientifically. Indeed, at his first presidential address Sidgwick declared that the fact that the debate about their reality was still going on was 'a scandal', one that he urged members to remove 'in one way or another'. Debatable subjects targeted for special investigation were hypnotism, clairvoyance, thought-reading (for which Myers coined the word 'telepathy') and apparitions in haunted houses, in addition to 'the various physical phenomena commonly called Spiritualistic'.

Early progress was rapid in both practical and theoretical areas. This was mainly due to the energy of Myers and his colleagues Edmund Gurney and Frank Podmore, with whom he compiled the largest collection of spontaneous cases ever assembled (*Phantasms of the Living*, 1886). His main work, *Human Personality and Its Survival of Bodily Death*, published posthumously in 1903, remains the cornerstone of the psychical researcher's library.

The outstanding medium studied during the early years of the SPR was Leonore Piper, whose trance writing produced some of the best evidence ever recorded for survival. She even managed to persuade the highly sceptical Richard Hodgson of the possibility of communication with disembodied consciousness. Hodgson, best remembered for his still controversial debunking of the founder of the Theosophical movement, Madame Blavatsky, went on to become an apparent communicator himself following his death in 1905.

Despite the SPR's declared objectivity and insistence on the absence of any corporate views, some unfortunate prejudices soon became apparent. The most serious of these concerned physical mediumship of any kind, and was explicitly stated by Frank Podmore in his otherwise invaluable historical survey *Mediums of the Nineteenth Century* (reissued in 1963). It marred the visit to Cambridge in 1895 of Eusapia Palladino, following which the SPR announced its intention to ignore mediums accused of fraud. The Society also showed the illiterate Neapolitan woman an attitude of academic élitism, something that has unfortunately survived to this day.

However, SPR members could, and still can, do what they like, and in 1908 made amends for the society's shameful treatment of Palladino when a team headed by the Hon. Everard Feilding visited her on her home ground – and produced the most detailed and positive report of its kind ever published. Even Podmore found his scepticism somewhat dented as a result.

There were to be more scandals. The SPR's denunciation of the Crewe 'spirit photographer' William Hope was based on allegations and prejudices alone, rather than on fact, and it led to mass resignations, including that of Sir Arthur Conan Doyle. The poet W. B. Yeats spoke for many when he complained that 'if your psychical researchers had been about when God Almighty was creating the world, He couldn't have finished the job'. In fairness it must be said that when SPR members caught one of their own members, S. G. Soal, falsifying his data, the whole affair was published in great detail by the Society itself – showing that it was able to keep its house in order without the help of the professional debunkers.

When members gathered in Cambridge in 1982 to celebrate their centenary, some asked what, if anything, had been achieved. The scandal lamented by Sidgwick had not been removed.

Instead, the SPR had provided new scandals of its own devising. Psi phenomena were still not accepted by the scientific establishment, nor even by some diehard sceptics among the SPR membership. Had it all been a waste of time and effort?

The answer must be a firm no. True, the SPR had not solved all the remaining mysteries of life, death and the universe, as had seemed its original intention. Yet it had achieved a great deal, most notably in its publications, with more than a hundred book-length volumes of its *Journal* and *Proceedings*, offering a wide range of material for study. This includes exhaustive documentation on everything from haunted houses and lengthy card-guessing experiments to outstanding individuals such as Gladys Osborne Leonard, Winifred Coombe-Tennant and the Schneider brothers, Rudi and Willi. It has also provided a multi-disciplinary forum for many distinguished scientists and philosophers from Sir William Crookes, Sir Oliver Lodge, and Henri Bergson to C. D. Broad, H. H. Price and Sir Alister Hardy.

If the SPR had not existed, it is unlikely that parapsychology would ever have been accepted as an academic field in its own right. The very fact of its survival testifies to the validity of its chosen area of enquiry. Yet a former SPR President, John Beloff, wrote that, for all its past successes, psychical research was 'caught in a bind' and he explained why: 'Without official recognition it lacks the means for the kind of large-scale concerted attack on the problem that appears necessary in order to gain such recognition.' Whether it breaks free from this bind depends on its present and future membership.

SEE ALSO *American Society for Psychical Research; Kenneth Batcheldor; Boggle threshold; Consensus reality; Cosmic Joker; Cross-correspondences; CSICOP; Doppelgängers; Eastern bloc psi; Ectoplasm; Enfield poltergeist; ESP; Experimenter effect; Eileen Garrett; Gustave Geley; Ghosts; History of Soviet psi; D. D. Home; Katie King; Nina Kulagina; Left and right brain; Limits of science; Matthew Manning; Metal bending; Carmine Mirabelli; Out-of-the-body experiences; Eusapia Palladino; Palm Sunday case; Parapsychology; Philip experiment; Psi-mediated instrumental response; Psychic music, art and literature; Psychokinesis; Remote viewing; SORRAT; Soviet psi today; Telepathy; Telepathy and the ganzfeld; Robert Thouless.*

PARAPSYCHOLOGY

Parapsychology is defined as the study of phenomena that cannot be explained in terms of known natural laws. It can be popularly described as psychical research carried out by professional scientists according to the accepted standards of science. Although the word was coined in 1889 (by Max Dessoir), it first became widespread in the English language with the founding of the Parapsychology Laboratory at Duke University in Durham, North Carolina, following the appointment there in 1927 of the Scottish psychologist William McDougall as professor. In the same year he was joined by two young plant physiologists, J. B. Rhine and his wife Louisa, and experimental work in parapsychology began in 1930.

Rhine's intention was to show that psi faculties – clairvoyance, telepathy, precognition and psychokinesis (PK) – could be demonstrated under controlled laboratory conditions and not merely by star performers. He set out to make psychical research respectable; his book *Extra-Sensory Perception* (1934) reached a wide public and popularised the term 'ESP'.

Rhine produced results that could not be challenged on statistical grounds. Using specially designed packs of 'Zener' cards (five each of a star, square, cross, circle and wavy lines), he showed repeatedly that some subjects were able to guess more than the average of five hits per run than could be expected by chance.

One of his assistants, Betty Humphrey, later found that results tended to be at their best at the start of a test and would then decline, picking up eventually if the test went on long enough. This became known as the U-curve or decline effect (or, as some would have it, the boredom factor), and it has been claimed as parapsychology's first repeatable finding.

New York parapsychologist Gertrude Schmeidler discovered what she called the sheep–goat effect: people who believed in ESP (the sheep) tended to score better in controlled tests than those who did not (goats). This would explain Rhine's early successes at Duke which others failed to repeat later elsewhere. His subjects were all sheep, at least at the start. It is likely that Rhine himself may have been exercising a strong experimenter effect on them as well, since he was well aware of the human side of his work, such as the atmosphere in the laboratory and the way subjects were treated. He was also a religious man, committed to the recognition of the human mind as a creative force in itself.

On Rhine's retirement in 1965 Duke University cut off formal connections with his laboratory, although it continued off-campus. It is now known as the Institute for Parapsychology. In 1969 the subject to which Rhine had devoted his career received a major boost when the Parapsychological Association, the professional body founded on his initiative in 1957, was accepted as an affiliate of the American Association for the Advancement of Science.

Research in the post-Rhine period explored new areas. The random event generator replaced the Zener card pack as the laboratory researcher's standard piece of equipment, and physicist Helmut Schmidt showed the possibility of detecting PK effects on such unpredictable physical processes as radioactive decay. His work was successfully replicated by a team headed by Princeton University engineer Robert Jahn, one of the most highly respected workers in the field.

Real-life psi was not overlooked (as indeed it had not been by Louisa Rhine, who published several books of original spontaneous cases). At Maimonides Hospital in New York, experiments in 'dream telepathy' by Montague Ullman, Stanley Krippner and Charles Honorton showed that it was possible to convey information to the mind of a sleeping person. Part of this work is generally believed to have been funded by the CIA, although the researchers were not aware of this at the time. Honorton later developed the 'ganzfeld' technique as an aid to eliciting telepathy under controlled conditions; his work was repeated at Cambridge University by Carl Sargent. Another promising real-life development was the remote viewing work at SRI International in California, where Harold Puthoff, Russell Targ and Keith Harary demonstrated that almost anybody can be successful in psi experiments, given the right conditions.

Despite formal recognition of parapsychology in the USA only one American university, John F. Kennedy at Orinda, California, has a department devoted to it (although postgraduate study is available at a handful of psychology departments at other universities). In Britain prior to 1983 postgraduate study in parapsychology was offered on an individual basis at three universities (Edinburgh, Surrey and Aston), and half a dozen psychology graduates had managed to earn Ph.D. degrees with theses on psi-related subjects. The death of the writer Arthur Koestler in that year led to Britain's first chair of parapsychology, funded by his bequest of an estimated £700,000. This was eventually accepted by Edinburgh after only one other university (Cardiff) had agreed to the stipulated terms, and in 1985 Robert L. Morris was appointed the first Koestler Professor. With the closure of the laboratory at the University of Utrecht, the first of its kind in the world, the Edinburgh department is now the only one in Europe.

Parapsychology remains the most under-funded and under-staffed of any field of study. All its full-time workers can fit comfortably into one room, as they do at the annual meetings of the Parapsychological Association (membership about 275, including a number of non-professional associates). The total annual budget for all open research has been estimated at £500,000 or less. Career prospects for young researchers are poor, and chances of publication in such journals as *Science* or *Nature* are minimal (unless negative results are reported). To add to their problems, parapsychologists have to put up with considerable hostility from their academic colleagues, not to mention the professional witch-hunters.

To some, parapsychology represents a threat. If psi faculties were fully understood, demonstrable to order and generally accepted, they would create havoc in the world of mechanistic and behaviourist science. The spectre of Dark Age superstition would doubtless return, aided by lunatic fringe practitioners, ever willing to exploit public gullibility, and by the media, who have rarely attempted to explain what parapsychologists actually do.

What they are doing is studying the whole nature of man, and they are not going to give up. Many are personally convinced of the reality of psi faculties, while others are intellectually satisfied by the vast body of positive evidence from a century of research that now includes more than fifty years of academic study. The toughest problem parapsychologists face today is not how to elicit psi phenomena or to explain them, but how to persuade others to accept the existing evidence and face its implications.

SEE ALSO *American Society for Psychical Research; Kenneth Batcheldor; Boggle threshold; Cosmic Joker; CSICOP; Eastern bloc psi; ESP; Experimenter effect; Explanations; Formative causation; Eileen Garrett; Michel Gauquelin; Gustave Geley; Uri Geller; Healing; History of Soviet psi; Nina Kulagina; Left and right brain; Limits of science; Metal bending; Philip experiment; Propensity for psi; Psi-mediated instrumental response; Psychokinesis; Remote viewing; Society for Psychical Research; SORRAT; Soviet psi today; Telepathy; Telepathy and the ganzfeld; Robert Thouless.*

CSICOP

In 1975 the American magazine the *Humanist* published a manifesto entitled 'Objections to Astrology' signed by 186 scientists, including several Nobel Prize winners. This was followed in 1976 by the founding of the Committee for the Scientific Investigation of Claims of the Paranormal (CSICOP) under the co-chairmanship of Paul Kurtz, philosophy professor at the State University of New York and editor of the *Humanist*, and sociologist Marcello Truzzi of Eastern Michigan University. CSICOP's stated intention was to 'investigate *carefully* the extraordinary claims of true believers and charlatans of the paranormal world'.

The first major claim to be investigated was that of French psychologist and statistician Michel Gauquelin, concerning a supposed correlation between planetary configurations at birth and subsequent success in certain professions. Two astronomers, George Abell and Dennis Rawlins (both founder

members of CSICOP) and statistician Marvin Zelen duly carried out a large-scale replication of one of Gauquelin's surveys, coming up with similarly positive results. Thus Kurtz, promoter of the anti-astrology manifesto, now had to face evidence *for* astrology at the outset of his crusade against the allegedly irrational.

There followed acrimonious in-fighting, well-documented accusations of cover-ups, and a spate of resignations by such prominent members as Richard Kammann of New Zealand, veteran British sceptic Eric Dingwall and Rawlins himself, who revealed the full story of the Gauquelin affair in the October 1981 issue of *Fate* magazine, in which he expressed doubts about 'the integrity of some of those who make a career of opposing occultism'. The editor of the magazine was less restrained, describing CSICOP as 'a group of would-be debunkers who bungled their major investigation, covered up their errors, and gave the boot to a colleague who threatened to tell the truth'.

Co-founder Truzzi also departed early on after becoming disillusioned by CSICOP's apparent policy of 'tarring everybody with the same brush'. He later founded his own research group, the Center for Scientific Anomaly Research (CSAR), winning the respect of parapsychologists and honest sceptics alike for his open-minded and scholarly approach.

For a group boasting the words 'scientific investigation' in its name, CSICOP's pronouncements are sometimes unusual. A 1985 fund-raising letter read in part 'Belief in the paranormal is still growing, and the dangers to our society are real. . . . Your contribution, in any amount, will help us grow and be better able to combat the flood of belief in the paranormal.'

This statement implies not only that CSICOP's first decade of activity was not very successful, but also that belief in anything not explained by conventional science represents a threat to society. In his book *Science in a Free Society*, Paul Feyerabend likens the manifesto that preceded CSICOP's foundation to the Papal Bull of Innocent VIII in 1484, which ushered in the age of witch-hunting. Even a sceptical *Guardian* reporter covering a CSICOP meeting in London noted 'a most unattractive intolerance to ways of thinking other than their own' among members attending, who had 'shown some swift footwork in changing the ground rules of an investigation when it suits them', while a writer in the *Sunday Times* suggested that 'the time has come for some scientific investigation into the claims of this bizarre committee'.

SEE ALSO *American Society for Psychical Research; Astrology; Boggle threshold; Consensus reality; Explanations; Charles Fort; Michel Gauquelin and the Mars effect; Uri Geller; Limits of science; Metal bending; Parapsychology; Propensity for psi; Psychokinesis; Society for Psychical Research.*

MICHEL GAUQUELIN (AND THE MARS EFFECT)

Born in 1928, Gauquelin graduated as a psychologist from the Sorbonne in Paris. During the early 1950s he and his wife, Françoise, began an extraordinary and unprecedented research programme into the complex workings of astrology that is still continuing today, but at the start they simply wanted to find out whether astrology had any scientific basis.

Gauquelin had studied astrology since he was a boy, and was able to cast a horoscope when he was just ten years old. His statistical examinations of the sun signs of more than twenty-five thousand celebrities failed to find any definite evidence linking birth date and profession. Indeed, at one time he said that 'Astrology is doomed, since its attempts to understand people and their fate are based on nothing but superstition; its roots lie in magic and the model of the world out of which it grew is long out of date' (*The Spheres of Destiny*, 1980). However, his examination of planetary positions for the time of birth (something every astrologer considers essential for an accurate horoscope) reveals a very different picture.

He divided the diurnal motion – that is, the astronomical rise, upper culmination, set and lower culmination points – for each planet into thirty-six sectors, beginning with the rising point. He also used larger divisions of eighteen and twelve. There are traditionally twelve houses in the horoscope, and Gauquelin has stated that his own system is astronomically very similar to the Placidus system of house divisions used by most astrologers. By noting the number of times a planet appears in any one sector for a particular group of births, he was able to see whether there were any correspondences between planetary position and subsequent profession.

The first evidence appeared in 1951, when he was examining the birth data for 576 members of the French Academy of Medicine. Mars or Saturn were rising, or culminating at the hour of birth, in a high percentage of cases. He repeated the experiment with 508 different, but equally eminent, French doctors and achieved the same result. Taking success in their chosen field as his criterion, he went on to examine the birth times of scientists, sportsmen, writers and actors. The evidence grew; writing in *Planetary Heredity* (1988) he says: 'To my surprise, the more calculations I performed, the more the initial trend was confirmed. On top of that, a more-and-more precise statistical relationship appeared to emerge between the time of birth of great men and their professional success.'

The ensuing controversy threw both astrologers and sceptics into confusion. Dennis Rawlins, an astronomer and former member of CSICOP, was perhaps the most vociferous of the sceptics. He argued that Gauquelin's methods and procedure were faulty and that his statistics only demonstrated effects that might be expected by bias – amongst other complaints. However, the Belgian Comité Para used Gauquelin's data and were able to replicate his famous 'Mars Effect' results. (That is, top sportsmen show a marked tendency to be born when Mars is either rising, or at the zenith of the horoscope.) Gauquelin's work has also been endorsed by eminent psychologist Professor Hans J. Eysenck of the University of London. Professor Eysenck has also conducted independent astrological research, notably with astrologer Jeff Mayo and sociologist Joe Cooper.

Since the mid-1960s Gauquelin has devoted

much of his time to the question of planetary heredity; are we born under the same kind of planetary configurations that prevailed at the time of our parents' birth? Some of his findings suggest that this may be the case.

SEE ALSO *Astrology; CSICOP; Divination; Limits of science.*

HISTORY OF SOVIET PSI

In 1875, the eminent Russian chemist D. I. Mendeleyev set up a commission of enquiry at the University of St Petersburg following a visit by the medium D. D. Home. This was seven years before the founding of the Society for Psychical Research (SPR) in Britain, and it was followed by the launching of the journal *Rebus*, which was devoted to the paranormal.

Continuity after the 1917 Russian Revolution was provided by the distinguished academician Vladimir Bekhterev (1857–1927), founder and first head of the Brain Research Institute at the renamed University of Leningrad. There in 1922 he founded a Commission for the Study of Mental Suggestion, making the Soviet Union the first country in the world to boast a state-backed psi research programme.

In 1914 Bekhterev had begun a long series of practical experiments in telepathy and clairvoyance. These were originally suggested by the popular circus artiste Vladimir Durov, who, while training his performing animals by conventional means – making skilful use of ultrasonic whistles – became convinced that he was also able to communicate with them telepathically. By 1920 Bekhterev had the confidence to state in print that 'the behaviour of animals, especially that of dogs trained to obey, may be directly influenced by thought suggestion'.

The similar suggestibility of people was clearly demonstrated at the 1924 meeting of the All-Russian Congress of Psychoneurology. After reading a paper entitled 'The Force of Visual Fixation', Konstantin Platonov (later to become a distinguished

Vladimir Bekhterev, founder of the Commission for the Study of Mental Suggestion at the University of Leningrad in 1922 – the first state-backed psi research programme in the world.

Soviet scientist) gave a practical example, sending a young woman to sleep on the platform and waking her up again without saying a word. 'When I employed the method of forming a representation of the desired end, this proved to be perfectly effective,' he wrote later.

Bekhterev and his colleagues expanded their field of interest to include precognition, psychokinesis, hypnotism and spontaneous phenomena reported by members of the public. The death of Bekhterev in 1927 caused little interruption in Soviet psi research. By then his colleague Leonid Vasiliev (1891–1966) had emerged as an imaginative and successful experimenter with a special interest in 'mental suggestion' and a distance, using human subjects. Having had personal experience of telepathic communication with his mother when he was twelve, Vasiliev began his career (in physiology) convinced of its reality. He demonstrated it himself in a long series of experiments in which he showed that both conscious and unconscious movements of the human body could be caused by unspoken suggestion, both at close range and at distances of thousands of kilometres.

In 1932, with Stalin firmly in control, the Brain Research Institute 'received an assignment to initiate an experimental study of telepathy', as Vasiliev later recalled. From whom this directive came, he never revealed. The research continued until 1938 and concentrated on the search for a physical explanation for telepathy, which was not found. Indeed, experiments using a Faraday cage to screen electromagnetic radiation from both sender and receiver served, in Vasiliev's words, 'to cast doubt upon the electromagnetic theory of telepathic phenomena'.

Vasiliev, like Bekhterev, was a survivor. He continued working until the end of his life, and lived to enjoy the 'thaw' that followed the death of Stalin. Vasiliev's popular book *Mysterious Phenomena of the Human Psyche* (1959) broke a twenty-year silence on telepathy in the Soviet media, and, together with his more technical *Experiments in Mental Suggestion* (1962) (reissued in English in 1976), inspired a whole new generation eager to carry on his work.

Vasiliev's experimental investigation of telepathy was described by SPR member Anita Gregory (on whose initiative the first English translation of one of his books was made), as 'pioneering work of the utmost importance'. Like the majority of those who came both before and after him, he was far more successful as a practical experimenter than as a theoretician. Indeed, the strong emphasis on practical aspects of psi has led to much speculation concerning secret research that may have potential applications in military and intelligence fields. Fragmentary accounts from a handful of emigrants lend some support to this possibility.

SEE ALSO *Eastern bloc psi; ESP; D. D. Home; Hypnosis; Psychokinesis; Remote viewing; Society for Psychical Research; Soviet psi today; Telepathy; Telepathy and the ganzfeld.*

SOVIET PSI TODAY

Parapsychology has never been recognised as a discipline in its own right in the Soviet Union. The official position was made clear in a statement by four leading psychologists, including A. R. Luria, which was published in the journal *Questions of Philosophy* in 1973. 'Obviously', they said, 'some so-called parapsychological phenomena do happen.' However, 'there are no legitimate bases for the existence of parapsychology as a special science' and it is 'necessary to suppress the activity of unqualified and militant parapsychologists' – a clear reference to the most enthusiastic publicist of the subject in the USSR, Eduard Naumov. Coincidentally, Naumov was arrested a few months after the statement was published and sent to a labour camp, although after a vigorous international protest he was released early.

The psychologists went on to criticise the scientific establishment for not paying more attention to psi phenomena, thereby 'demystifying' them. They even recommended the setting up of special laboratories for 'the study of people actually possessing unusual abilities'.

Soviet healer Dzhuna Davitashvili in action.

The most widely studied Soviet citizen with such abilities is undoubtedly Nina Kulagina, discovered by Vasiliev in the early 1960s and investigated in depth by a neurophysiologist, Gennady Sergeyev, in addition to several other Soviet and Western scientists including J. Gaither Pratt from the USA and the Czech Zdenek Rejdak. Kulagina, who specialised in making small objects move without contact, often surprised investigators by performing such feats as stopping the heart of a frog and causing a strong burning sensation on human skin. Sergeyev even had to have eye surgery after getting in the way of what he called her 'powerful superconductive channel of interaction with an object'.

Curiously, in 1973 a 'special laboratory' was set up, devoted to psi-related areas on a more or less full-time basis – the Moscow-based Bioinformation Laboratory of a scientific and technological society named after A. S. Popov. The 'Popov group', as it was known, was headed by one of the leading theoreticians in Soviet psi research, Ippolit Kogan, but it also carried out practical research, notably in the field of healing or 'bioenergy transfer'. Two of its best-known researchers were Larissa Vilenskaya (now a resident of the USA) and Barbara Ivanova, an influential healer and teacher, many of whose articles and papers have been published in the West.

The Popov laboratory was closed down in 1975, for reasons never made clear. In 1978 a similar-sounding laboratory was opened under a stricter regime. Vilenskaya left the country in 1979, while Ivanova remained unemployed, carrying out her teaching at what became known as the 'Park University' – the open air.

According to a survey carried out by the new Popov group, research in psi-related areas was taking place in ten or more Soviet laboratories; Vilenskaya has estimated at least twice that number. Since some of the largest, such as those at Novosibirsk and Alma-Ata, are off-limits even to Soviet visitors, the extent of the work undertaken there can only be guessed on a basis of their infrequent (and usually incomplete) publications. Of special

Davitashvili addresses a seminar of Soviet doctors. Known as 'the woman who healed Brezhnev', she is given a hearing even by sceptics.

interest, however, are reports of telepathic communication between mice at the former, from toxicologist Sergei Speransky, and similar work involving animals, plants and humans by biophysicist Viktor Inyushin and his colleague Alexander Romen at Alma-Ata.

No mention of psi finds its way into any Soviet scientific journal, and it has been left to the popular press to report any developments. This it does more frequently and thoroughly than the Western press. Even *Pravda* has printed readers' letters about 'unusual' experiences, and an interesting consequence of Gorbachev's reforms was the appearance of accounts of spontaneous phenomena, including poltergeists, in the media. Even such journals as *Stroitelnaya Gazeta (Building Gazette)* have published articles on the popular healer Vladimir Safonov, one entitled 'Never Wish Evil on Anybody'. The activities of the Georgian healer and medium Dzhuna Davitashvili have been extensively published both at home and overseas.

There is a strong emphasis in all known Soviet psi research on the practical applications of 'bio-energy transfer' (healing), 'biocommunication' (telepathy) and the 'biophysical effect' (psychokinesis). Many Westerners have repeatedly been urged by their Soviet colleagues to ensure that psi is used only for the common good, although it is a widespread assumption that some have other ideas. Even in the open literature, one cannot help noting the frequency of such terms as 'distant influence' and 'transfer of motor impulses'. Perhaps Lenin himself foresaw his country's psi research programme in his dictum: 'Human intelligence has discovered much in nature that was hidden, and will discover much more, thus strengthening its domination over her'?

SEE ALSO *Curses; Formative causation; Healing; History of Soviet psi; Nina Kulagina; Parapsychology; Psychokinesis; Remote viewing; Telepathy.*

EASTERN BLOC PSI

Attitudes to the study of psi in the eastern European countries vary widely. In those with predominantly Slavic populations and traditions (Poland, Czechoslovakia and Bulgaria), popular interest in psychic matters is very strong. Poland's Psychotronic Society is by far the largest of its kind in the world, with around eight thousand members in affiliated groups all over the country. Its annual conferences in Warsaw attract audiences of more than a thousand. Scientists, priests and the medical profession engage in lively debates and present papers on both theoretical and practical topics, with a strong emphasis on healing. Reports of spontaneous phenomena began to appear in the press in the mid-1980s, further stimulating interest in the paranormal. Some of these have been well investigated by scientists and reported at international meetings.

Bulgaria can claim two world 'firsts'; it is the only country in the world with an officially sponsored parapsychology institute, and the only one with a state-sponsored psychic medium. The former, operating under the Ministry of Education with its own building in central Sofia, is better known for the work of its affiliate body, the Institute for Suggestology. Dr Georgi Lozanov, a medical doctor and research director of both institutes, was also instrumental in promoting the career of Vanga Dimitrova, a remarkable blind clairvoyant from the small town of Petric. Despite such state involvement, Bulgaria tells the world next to nothing about its research findings, apart from those in the field of suggestology and rapid learning, neither of which can be considered paranormal.

Czechoslovakia is considerably more open, at least in this respect. Thanks to its leading champion of 'psychotronics' (the officially accepted Eastern bloc term for parapsychology), psychologist Zdenek Rejdak, psi research has acquired a degree of respectability and status. International conferences with many Western delegates were held in Prague (1973) and Bratislava (1983), at which Czech researchers reported on a wide range of topics from dowsing and healing to clairvoyance, with special

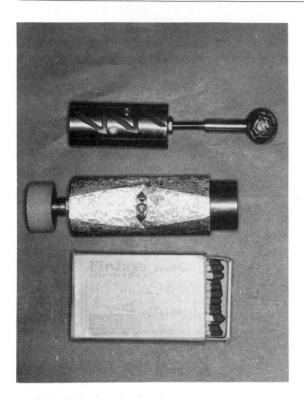

Devices developed by Czech engineer Robert Pavlita for the measurement of psi power. Two small discs (left) change their magnetic properties during the course of the 'activation', and (right) the conical rotor starts to rotate under the influence of strong mental concentration.

emphasis on 'earth energies'.

Hungary presents a paradoxical state of affairs: until the remarkable upheavals of late 1989, the most liberal political regime in the Eastern bloc, it has the most rigidly conservative scientific establishment. Thus, while Hungarians are able to visit the West and keep abreast of research, they receive no kind of official encouragement, much less any support. Even so, a promising start was made in the early 1980s by a small group of physicists and psychologists whose research is of a very high quality by Eastern bloc standards.

Romania is another paradox. The erstwhile most repressive political system in the bloc contrasts with a lively interest among scientists in subjects considered 'fringe' (or beyond) in the West. The Romanian contribution to the subject of high-frequency photography and its use in medical diagnosis has been considerable. An international conference on acupuncture was held in Bucharest in 1977 with many contributions from Romanian researchers, some of whom showed interest in parapsychology. They have, however, little hope of developing it on an official basis until the post-liberation economy settles down.

East Germany treats the whole subject of parapsychology with a hostility matched only by the members of the Committee for the Scientific Investigation of Claims of the Paranormal (CSICOP). Its only contribution to the subject is the regular diatribes against it in the party media. As for Albania, where religion is totally banned, it is unlikely that anything resembling psi research exists there.

If a generalisation is possible, it can be said that, at least in the Slavic republics, psi research is tolerated, provided it is kept free from any religious, occult or 'idealist' tendencies. Its researchers tend to be more enthusiastic and positive than their

Western counterparts, but also, with the notable exception of the Hungarians, less meticulous about their scientific procedures.

SEE ALSO *CSICOP; Healing; History of Soviet psi; Parapsychology; Soviet psi today*.

PSI-MEDIATED INSTRUMENTAL RESPONSE

In 1974 American parapsychologist Rex Stanford created a new model of ESP functioning, which he termed psi-mediated instrumental response (PMIR). His researches had unearthed a strong theme of psychic interference in everyday life, of which even those who most benefited from it were often unaware. The two main strands in this model are that the subject does something to benefit himself, and that there is a purely psychic component in bringing about the desired aim.

One American laboratory experiment showed how even superficial rewards can be detected psychically, and influence the result of the experiment. A group of male students were asked to guess which Zener cards were in opaque, sealed envelopes. Unknown to any of the students, some of the envelopes also contained erotic photographs of women. The students scored significantly higher at guessing the right envelopes when they also held the photographs.

However, PMIR seems to work best in natural, everyday situations; it arises spontaneously in answer to a need, and often makes use of an individual's interests and habits. A woman who prided herself on dressing elegantly and appropriately for every occasion found herself suddenly moved to try on her most festive hats; the next day she heard of her daughter's impending wedding. Similarly, an urge to try on a black skirt preceded the news of her mother's death. In this case the psi-functioning found the most acceptable outlet for the fashion-conscious woman.

Many of the cases of PMIR collected by British parapsychologist Dr Julian Isaacs were concerned with the telephone. There were many cases of friends who tried to telephone each other at the same time (although they had not been in touch for years), or of a friend who could actually hear the other party calling his name before telephoning – there was never any need to ask who was at the other end of the line.

One of the more remarkable telephone stories of recent years concerned a woman who, in deep distress about her financial situation, finally plucked up courage to telephone a friend and ask for a loan. Strangely, the dial on her apparatus seemed to be stuck and it was impossible to use. Gradually, as the day wore on, her distress diminished and she worked out a financial scheme that would avoid her having to ask the friend. Instead, she decided to telephone her just for a chat. This time the dial moved smoothly. Her friend said: 'I hope you haven't been trying to call me. My phone was broken – the dial was sticking, but it seems to have righted itself now.'

Many instances of PMIR involve machinery, such as the invalid car that stalled, embarrassing its owner, at a busy crossing. A moment later a runaway lorry passed the spot where the invalid car would have been. Immediately afterwards the car functioned perfectly once again.

Throughout history there have been many recorded examples of clocks stopping at the moment their owners died, or of alarm clocks ringing at an unaccustomed hour when some tragedy had befallen the family. Inanimate objects apparently become animated, often violently, during poltergeist attacks or change their molecular structure in the hands of a psychic – Uri Geller's bent metal has been shown to have changed its molecular arrangement, and objects held by Carmine Mirabelli were reported to become fluid.

Mind over matter is a huge and controversial subject of which PMIR may be a small, but significant, part. Or it may be that, as with much of parapsychology – or science in general – one aspect of a much larger phenomenon is merely given a label which is also taken as an explanation.

Certainly the SORRAT and Philip experiments have shown how belief in phenomena produces them to order – given time and patience. Clearly both of these psychical research groups regarded their work as experimental, which perhaps slowed down the manifestation of the phenomena (SOR-RAT's major successes came only some fifteen years after its inception).

But the devout do not experiment with their faith; they believe, and miracles just happen. When images of Christ or the Virgin Mary, or the photograph of a dead grandmother, begin to bleed or weep the observers feel comforted. Their faith is reinforced, and therefore the likelihood of further miracles is strengthened. Significantly, many of these phenomena occur in the home of a devout person who is undergoing a personal crisis, often culminating in mysterious illnesses. The statues that bleed and the photographs that weep are signs of psychological release. In some way not understood, the subject's tormented mind has interacted with inanimate objects to bring about a miracle.

Rex Stanford believes that PMIR may be responsible for the answers to prayers; psi functioning depends very largely on the belief of the subject, so religious people with simple faith that their prayers will be answered tend to receive the desired 'pay-off'. Perhaps, Stanford suggests, their need, together with their faith, has mobilised the PMIR.

SEE ALSO *Boggle threshold; Eleventh-hour syndrome; ESP; Experimenter effect; Fate; Foaflore; Uri Geller; Ghosts; Images that bleed and weep; Metal bending; Carmine Mirabelli; Parapsychology; Philip experiment; Psychokinesis; Sentient machinery; SORRAT; Telephone calls from the dead; Visions of the Virgin Mary.*

ELEVENTH-HOUR SYNDROME

Folklore – and history – is rife with stories of people who have been saved from disaster at the last minute by apparently paranormal means. This is known as the 'eleventh-hour syndrome'.

Often apparitions of the dead manifest at critical moments and give the necessary advice or information to get out of a tight spot. There are several stories of airmen who seem to be heading for certain death by flying into mountains, for example, who are saved by the sudden appearance of their dead brothers or fathers in the cockpit. The ghostly companions give advice and comfort, and bring with them a feeling of confidence and superhuman strength or knowledge – they may even appear to manipulate the controls themselves. When the outcome is so satisfactory, it hardly matters whether the apparition was created by the subject's mind, or whether it was an authentic manifestation of the dead.

Writer-researcher Hilary Evans suggests that the mind has a 'producer', an aspect of the subconscious whose function it is to create, just for the sake of it. Its hand is seen in hallucinations, hypnosis, creative visualisations and, arguably, many sorts of projections such as visions, apparitions or encounters with beings from other dimensions. Its usual outlet is in dreams, where even familiar people and places are subtly, almost perversely, changed.

If this device creates the helpful crisis apparitions of the eleventh-hour syndrome, then it has far-

Florence Nightingale was just one of many whose lives were completely altered after being called by a mysterious voice.

reaching implications. Everyone dreams, therefore everyone has a 'producer' – the necessary knowledge and power to save himself from disaster. The problem is knowing how to mobilise this potential.

Sometimes purely physical resources are produced to save the day. The foaflore story of the puny mother who lifts a car off her child is well worn, yet is probably based on fact. If paranormal forces can be called into being in a crisis, then surely the same can apply to physical means?

Emotional crises also appear to bring about their own manifestations of the eleventh-hour syndrome; unbearable inner conflict seems to trigger the bizarre phenomenon of multiple personality, where the appearance of separate parts serves to diffuse the crisis. In the case of Ruth, emotional trauma created apparently 'real' hallucinations that she learnt to control.

Similarly, severe inner struggle usually precedes religious conversion, as with Saul of Tarsus on the road to Damascus, religious visions, or the hearing of God's voice or those of the saints. A complex example of this phenomenon was the case of Florence Nightingale's 'voice'. She was reading a newspaper account of the appalling conditions in the Crimean War and said aloud: 'Someone must do something about it.' She distinctly heard a voice say: 'You will.' With her cultural background she believed she had been called by God, and the rest is history. Yet 'the call' came primarily in answer to her own frustration. It also came in answer to the prayers of the sufferers in the Crimea.

Psi-functioning may come to our aid more commonly than is supposed; Rex Stanford's model of psi-mediated instrumental response (PMIR) suggests that self-interest often mobilises latent ESP and psychokinetic forces and may provide the mechanism for the answers to prayers. Faith, open-mindedness – and need – seem to be the factors that trigger the eleventh-hour syndrome, the most useful weapon in mankind's hidden armoury.

SEE ALSO *Autosuggestion; Case of Ruth; ESP; Fate; Foaflore; Ghosts; Healing; Multiple personality; Propensity for psi; Psi-mediated instrumental response; Psychokinesis; Traumas and psi; Visions of the Virgin Mary.*

BOGGLE THRESHOLD

It is perfectly acceptable in parapsychological circles to talk of 'crossing the boggle threshold' or even 'crashing the boggle barrier' when referring to the witnessing of ostensibly paranormal events that seem frankly incredible. The term 'boggle threshold' was coined by a senior member of the Society for Psychical Research (SPR), Renée Haynes, in the 1970s and has become part of parapsychological jargon.

It has been noted that many members of the SPR and of the Parapsychology Association are inherently sceptical about paranormal experience. Indeed, some are also members of the Committee for the Scientific Investigation of Claims of the Paranormal (CSICOP) – a situation that has given rise to accusations that the SPR is being infiltrated by sceptics in order to undermine the positive research being carried out by its members. The fact remains that, like most people, many parapsychologists are happier with experimental results that are only just a little above chance expectancy. Dr Charles Tart, among others, has suggested that very positive results – that is, way above chance – frighten parapsychologists into denying psi functioning. They then tend to blame the results on poor experimental protocol, or fraud. Results that crash the boggle barrier provoke the deepest suspicion, a fact that led some of the world's most famous psychics, such as Matthew Manning, to give up working with scientists altogether.

When dramatic evidence of psi is likely to lead to suspicion of the scientists involved, even – or especially – from their own colleagues, it is hard to see how parapsychology will ever come of age as a discipline in its own right. Meanwhile paranormal events continue to occur spontaneously, outside laboratory conditions.

SEE ALSO *Kenneth Batcheldor; CSICOP; Experimenter effect; Matthew Manning; Metal bending; Parapsychology; Society for Psychical Research; SORRAT; Telepathy and the ganzfeld.*

VII Frontiers of Science

Beginning and end of the universe • Sunspots • Search for extraterrestrial life • Time • Biorhythms • Timeslips • Other dimensions • Quantum mechanics and the paranormal • Formative causation • Case for God • Consensus reality • Left and right brain • Experimenter effect • Limits of science

Imagine being an inhabitant of Flatland, a two-dimensional world in which a circle would represent a barrier, preventing us from seeing inside it. To such creatures an inhabitant of a three-dimensional world, such as ourselves, would seem supernatural. Tricks could easily be played upon the Flatlanders, such as removing an object from inside the circle and placing it outside – to them it would seem as if the object had dematerialised and rematerialised.

The problems that inhabitants of this hypothetical world would have in perceiving ordinary objects and events may well be similar to those we have when confronted by the paranormal. When objects appear mysteriously during poltergeist attacks, or during psi-induction experiments, they may, in fact, be put in one place and then another by invisible forces – just as the psychics have always claimed. D. D. Home and Carmine Mirabelli were always convinced that their levitations were due to the action of the spirits lifting them up; perhaps this unsophisticated view has some substance. It would be arrogant to dismiss the notion of other dimensions, and the concept of influence of beings from those other planes, especially since modern theoretical physics allows for a huge variety of other dimensions.

A Flatlander who proposed that there were other beings beyond the familiar two-dimensional environment might become the object of popular derision, or worse. Nothing succeeds like success, and the greatest success one can have is the unquestioning maintenance of a consensus reality, a framework within which a predictable (if limited)

life can be led, and which poses no threat to anyone.

In our world we are taught that enquiring minds make good scientists; unfortunately this is only true up to a point. If one enquires too closely into subjects that lie outside the consensus, then beware the wrath of scientism (the religion of the rationalists). Galileo not only claimed that he could see extraordinary worlds through his telescope, but he offered to let any other interested party have a look. No one took up his offer, and his work was condemned from a safe distance.

Today we see parapsychological work rejected by influential committees of dedicated rationalists, who refuse to look for themselves. And when a brave fellow scientist challenges a sacred tenet, such as Darwinism, his book is recommended for burning. This happened to Dr Rupert Sheldrake, whose *New Science of Life* (1980) proposed the idea of formative causation, with its central notion of a morphogenetic (that is, invisible) field that acts as a group mind within a species, shaping its evolution and learning abilities. The Editor of *Nature* had no hesitation in denouncing the book as heretical and condemning it to the flames.

Dr Sheldrake had committed several heinous crimes, but perhaps the greatest was to propose that the mind is different from the brain, and to point to an organising intelligence behind the patterns of life. He cut materialist reductionists to the quick, and they tried to destroy him. They failed.

It is hopelessly outdated to be materialist reductionist in a climate where common sense is assaulted by the conclusions of the quantum physicists, whose sub-atomic worlds are beautiful with uncertainty – a constant display of transformation. As the physicist Sir William Bragg quipped: 'Electrons seem to be waves on Mondays, Wednesdays and Fridays, and particles on Tuesdays, Thursdays and Saturdays.' Quantum mechanics is fashionable, yet the strange world it describes is far more bizarre than most paranormal happenings. Perhaps the secret of its acceptability lies in the fact that quantum physicists stand a chance of winning a Nobel Prize; parapsychologists do not.

Part of our grave limitation as human beings is inflicted upon us by time. Lip service is paid to the notion that time is merely a man-made concept, yet experience shows us that people grow old and die, that tomorrow will come, with or without us there to see it. But there are anomalies; many people have experienced a timeslip, where time is dislocated and they find themselves in the past – or perhaps in the future – interacting quite naturally with the people who live in that time. Are we ghosts from the future? How many timeslips do we experience without knowing it? Perhaps the tyranny of time is something else that is held in place only by the force of consensus reality.

Time becomes truly problematic when one considers the beginning – and end – of the universe. Where were the laws of nature, and where was time before the universe was created? And was it created, rather than randomly thrown together by forces that came from nowhere? There are many fairy tales of the universe told quite solemnly by cosmologists, whose general tolerance for the bizarre is at the same level as a Flatlander's.

The search goes on for extraterrestrial life; many scientists feel that, because we have not been contacted by aliens, we must be the only sentient life in the universe. Yet many mystics and psychics will attest that beings from other dimensions regularly visit us, so that one is led to wonder: would the average scientist recognise extraterrestrial intelligence if he found it?

It all comes down to problems of perception, and of the impossibility of objective research. The experimenter effect demonstrates that scientists with positive attitudes tend to get positive results, while those with negative attitudes get nothing. Nowhere is this more true than in parapsychology, where experiments into psi-functioning tend to be disrupted by psi-functioning, and where, as a result, accusations of fraud proliferate among the researchers.

Many people think psi a subject unfit for the laboratory; their ranks include a number of True Believers. The problem is that the perception of psi operates through the right hemisphere of the brain, whereas the scientific protocol needed to organise respectable experiments is produced by the left hemisphere – the analytical, reasoning and sceptical part. However, there is every reason to believe that, unconfined by anyone's brain, spontaneous psi continues to happen.

BEGINNING AND END OF THE UNIVERSE

Either the universe had a beginning or it has always existed. And either it will have an end or it will continue to exist. As man's knowledge of the universe has increased, especially with the aid of twentieth-century technology, such considerations have occupied the lives of more and more cosmologists struggling to derive satisfactory theoretical models that answer these questions and agree with astronomers' and nuclear physicists' observations of the ultra-large and ultra-small.

It is a brave goal for the human race, which has arrived so recently on the stage of the universe. If the life of the universe so far were expressed as one year, so that it came into existence on 1 January, then on the same scale human beings in recognisable form would have been around only since 11 p.m. on 31 December. Our last brilliant century of science and technology would have occupied the final one-tenth of a second on 31 December.

During the twentieth century, two main theories of the nature of the universe have competed for acceptance. They are the steady-state and the big-bang theories. The steady-state theory, formulated by Hoyle, Bondi and Gold in the 1950s, neatly side-

The Great Spiral Galaxy, Messier 31, in Andromeda. Taken with the 24–36-inch Jewett Schmidt Telescope of the Agassiz Station of Harvard College Observatory, Massachusetts, on the night of 6/7 September 1945. If man is the only intelligent race to evolve in the universe, then not only are we condemned to loneliness but we may conclude that we are merely a temporary and highly improbable accident.

stepped paradoxical considerations such as: 'If the universe had a beginning, what was before the beginning?' and 'If there is an end to the universe, what comes after it?' Questions like these are linked to other awkward questions such as 'Does time exist before the universe begins and after it ends?'

The steady-state theory postulated that there is neither beginning nor end to the universe. It does not evolve; so an observer, stationed anywhere in it at any time, would see the same behaviour of stars and galaxies no matter how distant they were. He would also see the same types of objects. It was, however, an observed fact that the galaxies seemed to be rushing away from each other – the

so-called 'red shift' – so that the average density of material in the universe was decreasing. But that would seem to imply a changing universe – in other words, one that evolved.

To avoid this implication, Hoyle, Bondi and Gold suggested that matter was continually being created, with hydrogen atoms popping into existence in just such numbers as to keep the density of the universe constant. The new material then collected into galaxies to fill the gaps left by the receding galaxies.

According to the big-bang theory, on the other hand, the universe originated about twenty thousand million years ago in a colossal explosion. The resulting fireball, of enormous temperature and density, expanded at speeds that approached the velocity of light. Various kinds of sub-atomic particles came into being, creating matter as we know it. Great clouds of gas and dust were formed, and became galaxies and stars. The expansion is still proceeding and has led to the universe we know today, which is composed of giant and dwarf stars, regular and irregular galaxies, quasars, pulsars, black holes, and at least one planetary system with a life-bearing planet, the Earth.

In recent years the discovery of further features of the universe has led astronomers to discard the steady-state theory, in spite of its aesthetic appeal, in favour of the big-bang theory. It had been predicted in 1948 by Gamow, Alpher and Bethe that if the universe began with a primordial fireball – the big bang – then even now some of the radiation it generated would still be observable. This 'three degree Kelvin radiation' was discovered in 1965 by Penzias and Wilson.

In addition, evidence that the universe is evolving can be deduced from a study of the numbers of different kinds of object such as quasars and galaxies found at different distances from our own galaxy. Light travels with a finite speed, and so observations of increasing distances are really observations going further and further back into time, since the light from more distant objects must have begun its journey that much earlier.

While astronomers accept that the universe must have had a beginning, they are not at all sure if it will have an end – or, if it does, what kind of end it will be. In some scenarios the universe will continue to expand for ever, with ageing galaxies pursuing lonelier and lonelier existences, their sources of dust and gas exhausted, and no new stars being born. Other theories suppose that if the mass of the universe is big enough, the expansion will progressively slow down until it stops. Then contraction will begin, accelerating up to the moment of the final cataclysmic implosion – the big crunch! – which will destroy everything.

Astronomers' knowledge of the actual mass is surprisingly imprecise. Some methods of measurement give one figure, while other lines of argument suggest ten times that figure – more than enough to produce the collapse of the universe. The true value is at present one of the great research problems.

But if the big crunch does come – what then? Some astronomers believe that, although it would certainly be the end of our universe, there may arise phoenix-like from the annihilation a new universe which will go through a similar cycle of existence. This implies that our universe may not have been the first one, an idea astonishingly like age-old Eastern teachings. In the *Bhagavad-Gita* Krishna says: 'For all the worlds pass away ... they pass away and return.' And 'At the end of the night of time all things return to my nature; and when the new day of time begins I bring them again into light.'

Even if they do not know the exact mass of the universe and its fate, cosmologists have been able to trace its history to within a fraction of a second after the big bang. Radiation would have begun to be converted into matter; and evolution of the universe to the state in which we find it would be well on its way, with protons, neutrons, electrons, positrons and all the other sub-atomic particles engaging in their strange transactions under the laws of quantum mechanics.

It is conceivable that there have been many universes in which the starting conditions, and perhaps the laws of physics, were such that life as we know it could not have existed. Scientists have pointed out that even very small changes in these fundamentals would produce a universe totally hostile to life.

Certainly the universe we inhabit today is at once fearsome and wondrous in its explosive origin and possible catastrophic end; its suitability for life is apparently the result of the flukiest chance. And yet the extraordinary thing is that it is more hospitable to age-old spiritual ideas and the findings of parapsychology than was the nineteenth century's model of the universe. That universe was a hard material world of solids, liquids and gases with no place for the paranormal. At least the universe of the late twentieth century is composed of entities that we call sub-atomic particles, in their properties little more substantial than ghosts, with no precise positions in space, obeying bizarre quantum mechanical rules that make the findings of parapsychology seem positively prosaic.

SEE ALSO *Case for God; Formative causation; Ghosts; Limits of science; Parapsychology; Quantum mechanics and the paranormal.*

SUNSPOTS

Sunspots have intrigued scientists ever since they were first observed, by the Chinese, some two thousand years ago. They are seen from Earth as dark blobs on the surface of the sun, arranged in more or less symmetrical bands on either side of the solar equator. They vary greatly in both size and number: the largest are many times the diameter of our planet, and they come and go in cycles. Their cause is not precisely understood, but they are thought to be eruptions of radiation resulting from internal stresses.

Their effects are much easier to identify. Each

Sunspots – literally heavenly activity – may influence human lives, individually and collectively.

sunspot group acts like a huge magnet, and serves as the point of origin of solar flares – especially intense eruptions of radiation that have immediately visible effects on Earth as the auroras in the northern (borealis) and southern (australis) skies. These spectacular displays of light are the only directly visible effects of solar spots and flares. There are a number of other effects, however.

A dramatic example of the potential force associated with a sunspot was the interruption of the Skylab mission in 1979. The space satellite, weighing 80 tonnes, was slowed down by drag resulting from an unexpected increase in solar activity in the middle of that year, and eventually fell to Earth. Exceptionally powerful solar flares have even been known to cause changes in the Earth's rotation, though fortunately these are too small to be generally noticed.

The most important effect of the solar flares is their alteration of the Earth's magnetic field. This in turn has a number of effects on living beings, from insects to humans. These can be observed both on a day-to-day basis and in terms of cycles matching that of the sunspots, which has averaged about 11.1 years since accurate records were first kept in the seventeenth century. The cycles have been found to correspond with a number of observable biological effects, from the thickness of tree rings to the incidence of epidemics.

The pioneering research of Japanese scientist Maki Takata and the Italian Giorgio Piccardi has shown that, in the former's words, 'Man is a living sundial.' After more than two decades of study, Takata found that there was a direct correlation between solar activity and the rate of blood clotting. His work was repeated by Piccardi, who found a similar correlation in precipitation rates of a chemical compound in water.

In the Soviet Union, 'heliobiology' is now accepted as a branch of biophysics, and the first laboratory in the world to specialise in it was founded in Irkutsk in 1968. The pioneer in the field was the versatile scientist Alexander Chizhevsky (1897–1964), who claimed that the solar cycle even influenced historical events such as wars and revolutions. 'We must assume that there exists a powerful factor outside our globe which governs the development of events in human societies,' he wrote in 1926. He noted that the Bolshevik Revolution of 1917 and the unsuccessful 1905 uprising both took place at times of maximum solar activity (as later did the invasions of Hungary in 1956, Czechoslovakia in 1968 and Afghanistan in 1979).

Another distinguished Soviet scientist, A. P. Dubrov, believes that 'magnetic storms' (sudden changes in the Earth's magnetic field caused by solar flares) are a direct cause of heart attacks. His claim was supported by the results of a six-year survey carried out in India, in which it was found that hospital admissions of heart cases closely matched magnetic field readings (*Nature*, 22 February 1979).

Canadian scientist Michael Persinger believes that geomagnetism may even affect psi phenomena such as clairvoyance and telepathy. While this awaits confirmation, it would not be surprising if there were mental as well as physical effects attributable to solar eruptions.

SEE ALSO *Astrology*; *Balls of light*; *ESP*; *Spontaneous human combustion*; *Telepathy*.

SEARCH FOR EXTRATERRESTRIAL LIFE

Since the Second World War, the runaway progress of astronomy and the thousands of reports of Unidentified Flying Objects – UFOs – have forced mankind to consider seriously the possibility that other intelligent species may be found elsewhere than on Earth, and may be taking an interest in us. The popularity of science fiction stories and films have encouraged that idea. Surely among the billions of stars scattered throughout the universe there must be some planets with life – in some cases intelligent life? And if so, surely some of these species would be interested in exploring the universe, or at least in getting in touch with other intelligent species?

It has, however, been suggested that UFOs and their attendant phenomena – witnesses seeing landed spacecraft, with aliens working on them as

if repairing them; and occasional reports from people who say they have been kidnapped and examined by aliens in a spacecraft before being released, sometimes after many hours – are actually more paranormal in origin than extraterrestrial. The psychologist C. G. Jung suggested that in our modern, post-religious age people would still like to believe that benevolent, advanced and powerful beings exist 'up there', who, if we show signs of acting with terminal stupidity, will step in to save us from our folly.

As a result, human beings create hallucinatory UFO fantasies to substantiate this extraterrestrial myth. Even the presence of physical signs such as the landing marks of UFO spaceships in grass or blips on radar screens are attributed in some versions of the paranormal theory to the use of psychokinesis to provide 'detail to lend verisimilitude to an otherwise bald and unconvincing narrative'. Other theories speculate that, whatever the nature of the aliens, it is so different from ours that their well-meaning attempts to contact us simply produce hallucinatory experiences embodying our current science fiction ideas and fears of alien monsters. Because of these theories, many psychical researchers believe that UFOs come within the province of parapsychology rather than astronomy.

Nevertheless, astronomers have embarked on a programme to try to detect the presence of extraterrestrial life. At the 1979 General Assembly of the International Astronomical Union, some of the world's experts in SETI (Search for Extra-Terrestrial Intelligence) debated the subject; and a Commission was set up which now has some hundreds of members.

It was pointed out that the only civilisation of which we know – namely our own – has already reached the stage where it has sent two Pioneer and two Voyager spacecraft to venture out of the solar system. At this rate of progress, it was argued, the entire colonisation of the galaxy would be achieved in something like ten million years. Now the galaxy is at least ten thousand million years old, so colonisation time is only one thousandth of that figure (as eight hours compared to one year). And yet billions of years ago, millions of planets in the galaxy should have evolved to the stage

Artist's impression of our galaxy, the Milky Way. Can we ever be dogmatic about the number of evolved *planets?*

reached by our planet just before life appeared on it. If life did appear on just some of the others, the argument goes, the whole galaxy should have been colonised long ago – extraterrestrials should be walking the streets of our cities! And yet there is no hard evidence that they exist.

It is, of course, possible that we are the first intelligent race to evolve in the universe. If so, not only are we condemned to loneliness, but on such evidence as we have about the enormous size of the universe, its innumerable stars and planets, and our very recent appearance, we would probably have to conclude that we are a purely temporary and highly improbable accident.

If, however, life has appeared on a large number of planets in the galaxy over the past few thousand million years, surely some of them, once they had arrived at a high scientific and technological level, would have decided to explore and colonise the galaxy? Or do they all evolve to some spiritual level

at which colonisation of other planets is irrelevant? Or do they all destroy themselves, as we seem to be in danger of doing?

Two different kinds of search for extraterrestrial life are now going on. Within the solar system, the planet Mars is the one least hostile to life as we know it on Earth. The temperature on its surface is never too low, and there is plenty of water – although most of it is locked within the crust as permafrost or in the form of ice and snow at the planet's north and south poles. It also has an atmosphere about 1 per cent of the density of the Earth's atmosphere. If life originated in the planet's youth, it could well have adapted over long ages to the harsh but not impossible conditions present now.

Life is astonishingly adaptable. On our own planet some blue-green algae are found in water at a temperature of 85°C (185°F), while some plant seeds can be taken to temperatures as low as

−190°C (−310°F) without dying. Living creatures have been found at the bottom of the deepest oceans on Earth, where no sunlight penetrates and the pressure is many tonnes to the square centimetre.

Thus when the two Viking spacecraft were sent to Mars in the 1970s, they were equipped with sophisticated equipment to test for the presence of life in the soil around their landing places. The results were ambiguous. On future missions the plan is to land mobile laboratories that will decide once and for all whether any form of life still exists on Mars. The discovery of even the most primitive form would be of staggering importance. The existence of life on two planets – Earth and Mars – would imply that, given the right conditions, life arises. Since it is probable that such planets exist in their millions, life would be common throughout the universe.

The other way of searching is to look for civilisations on the planets of other stars. If they are only a little ahead of us in science and technology, they may be transmitting radio signals to space. We have begun to do that ourselves, using our powerful radio telescopes as transmitters. For years now we have also been using some of these telescopes to search the heavens, not only for deliberate signals, but also for the electronic garbage that such civilisations will be emitting. Our presence on Earth could be detected at distances as far away as the stars because of our ultra-powerful military radar systems and our television broadcasting stations. For years our planet has emitted stronger radio waves than the sun. If an alien civilisation had receivers big enough to pick up such signals, it could calculate how far the Earth is from the sun and measure the lengths of our day and year.

There is no doubt that in the near future we too will have the technology to enable us to eavesdrop on any civilisations comparable to our own, on planets orbiting stars out to a distance of some 250 light years. Within that sphere there are some million stars. If we find nothing, it could be that we are the only technical civilisation in this part of the galaxy; or it could be that others exist but are so advanced that they use physical laws and processes we are still too primitive to have discovered. Perhaps, also, they do exist but are concealing them-

selves, waiting to see if this civilisation will destroy itself or finally come to its senses.

If we ever contact other intelligent species, will we find that they also report paranormal phenomena? Indeed, could it be that only by paranormal means will they be contacted in a way that overcomes the vast gulfs of space and the finite velocity of light? Only the future will tell.

SEE ALSO *Entity enigma; ESP; Other dimensions; Parapsychology; Psychokinesis; Telepathy; Time; UFO paradox; UFOs.*

TIME

In the Concise Oxford Dictionary, twelve words are allocated to the definition of 'time': 'Duration, continued existence; progress of this viewed as affecting persons or things'. But time is, of course, a far more complex subject than that brief definition might suggest.

Scientists and philosophers have wrestled with the problem of time in a variety of ways. For some it is an illusion; for others it is a linear process measured by clocks, a convenient mathematical or dynamical device used in science; yet others consider time to be multi-dimensional. Physicists such as Minkowski and Dirac explored the concept of the 'block universe', in which 'time' is but one dimension of a four-dimensional static, unchanging iceberg universe through which our individual consciousnesses move. The findings of quantum mechanics, nuclear physics and relativity have led other scientists to conceive of even stranger universes in which time, if it passes, can flow at different rates in different places and may even, for some atomic particles, reverse its direction of flow.

The everyday picture of time, in which past and future do not exist and only the present moment is real, is ludicrously inadequate. How 'thick' is the present moment – a second, a millisecond, a nanosecond? We have instruments that can actually measure the passage of time to a picosecond – which, compared to a second, is as a second compared to thirty thousand years!

If we continue to put time through such a theoretical bacon-slicer we are surely in danger of reducing reality to nothing. In fact there are good grounds for believing that in some strange way both the past and the future have some kind of reality; the essential difference between them and the present is that it is the present that is perceived by the individual, while both past and future are usually unperceived. But there are many well-authenticated cases of people who have had precognitions (glimpses of the future), or retrocognitions (glimpses of the past).

Such cases are scattered through the *Proceedings* and *Journals* of the Society for Psychical Research (SPR) and other societies devoted to the paranormal. Professor Ian Stevenson collected a large number of premonitions of the sinking of the *Titanic*. Dame Edith Lyttelton also obtained many premonitions of the crash of the airship R101. Later, Dr Ralph Barker, the first medical man to arrive on the scene of the Aberfan disaster, when a coal tip buried a Welsh school and suffocated over one hundred children, found scores of well-authenticated precognitions of the disaster.

Psychometrists like Peter Hurkos or Gérard Croiset were able on occasion to view the past as if it were still there. Other people may experience only one, never-to-be-forgotten episode in which they see past events. Mrs Buterbaugh, secretary to Dean Sam Dahl at the Nebraska Wesleyan College, was sent on an errand to a neighbouring building. She entered a suite of rooms where she saw the motionless figure of a woman in old-fashioned clothes. When Mrs Buterbaugh looked out of the window, the buildings that should have been there had disappeared, and all she could see were fields. The mystery woman was subsequently identified from old photographs as a former lecturer, who had died in that building many years before. Dr James McHarg investigated the case of a woman who, returning home in Letham village late one night, had to walk some miles along country roads after her car broke down. In the fields she saw flickering torches held by men in strange clothes as they examined a multitude of dead bodies. Various other details made it likely that the woman was witnessing a re-enactment of the battle of Nechtansmere, fought in 685 AD in that area.

Another, similar, case was witnessed by many people hundreds of years earlier. Some weeks after the battle of Edgehill in 1642, villagers, and officers sent by King Charles I to investigate, saw the battle being refought.

Is the past still there, recapturable under the correct conditions? Much more disturbing than that: is the future already there and occasionally glimpsed? And if so, is it unalterable, so that free will is at best a comforting illusion? Or is it a plastic, malleable future of which we have precognitions – so that, by taking the proper steps, we can avoid a disaster or prevent it happening?

One theory of time that goes some way towards accommodating free will and precognitions supposes that all events are contained in a static block universe. The consciousness, like a little spotlight, travels along a path chosen by free will through this block universe, illuminating small segments of it in succession. The person experiences the illusion that things happen. The theory also postulates that the 'spotlight' of the person's unconscious mind is bigger, and always encloses the consciousness' spotlight. Thus, whatever is in the immediate 'future' of the person's experience is already being 'seen' or 'illuminated' by the person's subconscious. If there is a potential disaster (for instance, a plane crash) within the subconsciousness' wider spotlight, that spotlight can – probably in a dream – warn the person, who can either act upon it or dismiss it as a dream. He may cancel his flight, or travel in the plane. The two future events of either reading that the plane has indeed crashed, or of being in the crash, are both equally real in the block universe of all possible events. But whichever one the person actually experiences will depend upon his decision.

J. W. Dunne and H. F. Saltmarsh, among others, have published theories of this type that try to make sense of the clues given us by cases of precognitions and retrocognitions regarding the nature of time. A different kind of theory from the block universe kind tries to avoid the idea of backward causation implied by a future event not yet real producing a premonition. It suggests that a kind of super-psychokinetic process is at work, in that the person dreams of a disaster and then tampers with events to produce it by psychokinesis. The proponents of this type of theory argue that in our dark and total ignorance about the limits of psychokinesis – mind over matter – we cannot dismiss such a possibility.

Indeed, in our similar dark ignorance regarding the true nature of time we can only hope that continued study of the paranormal will lighten that darkness.

SEE ALSO *Astrology; Divination; Fate; Ghosts; Hypnotic regression; Lexilinking; Life imitates art; Precognition in dreams; Prophecy and prediction; Psychokinesis; Society for Psychical Research; Timeslips.*

BIORHYTHMS

Our lives, like those of all living creatures, are affected by numerous cyclic events. The most familiar of these is the twenty-four hour day/night cycle, caused by the rotation of the Earth. It times the most important functions of our bodies, and the distressing effects of a sudden alteration in this predominant cycle are all too well known to travellers as jet-lag. The fact that people can quickly adapt to a new day/night phase indicates to what extent living beings are influenced by external factors.

Experiments in artificial environments, such as underground bunkers, have shown that many of our familiar biorhythms are less securely locked into the twenty-four-hour cycle than they may seem. Left to their own devices without familiar external stimuli, our circadian biorhythms (rhythms with a period of approximately a day, but not always exactly) show a tendency to lengthen. There is evidence to suggest that this lengthening is due to the influence of the lunar day – the time of one lunar orbit of the Earth – which is 24.84 hours. In 1977, Californian medical researcher Dr Laughton Miles reported an unusual case in which the circadian biorhythms of a blind patient seemed to be phase-locked with the moon.

Wilhelm Fliess, German doctor who advocated further study of biorhythms.

The moon also provides us with the month period. There are in fact five different months, varying in length from 27.21 to 29.53 days; the most visibly influential of these is the anomalistic one of 27.55 days that causes tides as the moon moves closer to or further from the Earth. Lunar periods are known to have a direct effect on the mating or spawning of a variety of fish, crabs and animals; and the moon, at least in popular imagination, is responsible for the female menstrual cycle of about twenty-eight days.

Early in this century, Viennese psychologist Hermann Swoboda and Dr Wilhelm Fliess in Berlin independently put forward a theory that human lives were regulated by two cycles, a physical one of twenty-three days and an emotional one of twenty-eight days. Later, an Austrian engineer named Alfred Teltscher came up with another universal cycle of thirty-three days, which was supposed to drive intellectual performance. A number of large-scale surveys have been carried out that seem to indicate the reality of these three biorhythms, whereas other surveys have failed to reveal anything of the kind.

It is possible that both the promoters of pop-biorhythm and its critics are wrong; that we do have physical, emotional and intellectual cycles, but that they are not of exactly twenty-three, twenty-eight and thirty-three days. Moreover, they are not the same for everybody. In one of the most careful studies of its kind, conducted by Dr Rexford Hersey at the University of Pennsylvania in the 1930s, the emotional moods of twenty-five factory workers selected for their stable personalities were studied for a whole year. Hersey found that emotional cycles did emerge, averaging about thirty-five days – quite close to Teltscher's thirty-three day cycle. However, among individuals the cycles could be as short as sixteen or as long as sixty-three days. A 1977 survey undertaken at the Biocron Systems Co. of California revealed an even wider spread in a group of two hundred subjects – from fifty-four days down to only two.

If our lives were governed by the twenty-three/twenty-eight/thirty-three-day cyclic triune, something would have to cause each of the cycles. A twenty-seven- to twenty-nine-day cycle driven by one or other of the moon's movements has some plausibility, yet no possible cause for the other two has yet been identified. The best way to settle the argument is for individuals to test themselves for overall physical, emotional and intellectual rating and work out their personal biorhythm charts.
SEE ALSO *Astrology*; *Experimenter effect*.

TIMESLIPS

Timeslips happen quite suddenly; the only warning may be a prickling of the skin and a sense of physical and mental oppression. These sensations heralded the most famous of all apparent timeslips – what was to become known as the Trianon 'Adventure' of two scholarly English ladies, the Misses Moberley and Jourdain, in the early years of the twentieth century. They were walking in the grounds of the palace at Versailles, near Le Petit Trianon, when a feeling of profound oppression assailed them, accompanied by a dead stillness in the air. A man ran past dressed in eighteenth-century clothes and spoke to them in archaic French; they saw a fair woman in the costume of the same era, and had an overwhelming feeling of the dislocation of time and personal dissociation. Then it was over, and they were back in the twentieth-century world.

They wrote down separate accounts of their 'Adventure', but were unprepared for the hostility that was to greet their publication. Even today the case remains controversial; elaborate counter-explanations are put forward, including the idea that a contemporary pageant, unknown to the visitors, was being enacted in the grounds. But many other apparently sincere and perplexed people have had similar experiences, adding weight to the belief that the Misses Moberley and Jourdain could indeed have had a paranormal experience at Versailles.

In the early 1960s a social club visited Rievaulx Temples – eighteenth-century follies overlooking Rievaulx Abbey in Yorkshire. One of the party, a teenager named Lisa, was enjoying the summer evening and chatting with an older woman in the group as they sauntered around the follies. 'Suddenly it seemed as if I was encased in cotton wool,' she recalls.

> I could no longer hear what my companion was saying, although I could make out her lips moving as if through a mist. We both seemed to be walking in slow motion and I was dimly aware that there was no one else around, although a few seconds before half a dozen of the others had been with us. There was no sound whatsoever except for a slight buzzing noise, and what seemed to be a horse and carriage coming up the road behind. Then a man and a woman in eighteenth-century dress walked silently by, hand in hand, ignoring us. Almost immediately it was as if the spell broke and my companion was suggesting tea in the most down-to-earth fashion. She had not seen or felt anything unusual, but I certainly needed that tea!

Both sets of women may have projected on to their surroundings an exteriorisation of extra-sensory impressions. In both the Trianon and Rievaulx

Le Petit Trianon – scene of one of the most dramatic apparent timeslips ever recorded.

In the early years of the twentieth century the Misses Jourdain (left) and Moberley (right) experienced a remarkable – and controversial – timeslip while visiting Le Petit Trianon.

cases others in the area had stayed firmly in the present, sensing nothing unusual. But there was a difference between them; one of the historical figures spoke to the Misses Moberley and Jourdain as if he perceived them to be as real as those who inhabited his own space-time. It may be that the only major distinction between a true timeslip and seeing a ghost is the interaction of the percipient and the perceived, although, as always in investigations of the paranormal, there are striking exceptions to the rule.

In the 1960s an apprentice heating engineer, Harry Martindale, was working alone in the cellars of York's medieval Treasurer's House when he was startled to hear the sound of a trumpet close to him. Then the figure of a man carrying a round shield emerged through one wall and walked slowly through the cellars, preceding a line of about fifteen bedraggled-looking men. Martindale could see them in detail, but just from the knees up – the only time he saw their feet was when they walked through a hole in the ground. It seemed that they were Roman soldiers retracing their steps over a road that was now below the cellar floor. When Martindale told his story historians were puzzled by the detail of the round shield, but it was later discovered that the Sixth Legion, based at Eboracum (Roman York) had used auxiliary troops – who carried round shields.

There was no tradition of a ghost story involving Roman soldiers marching through time in the Treasurer's House, and there have been no further 'replays'. Yet if their appearance were somehow staged for Martindale's benefit they showed no sign that they perceived him; if it were a one-way timeslip, then the Treasurer's House and the young man would not have existed for them.

Yet there have been two-way timeslips that crash 'the boggle barrier' by their sheer matter-of-factness. One of the many dramatic timeslips in Joan Forman's book *The Mask of Time* (1978) concerned a party of eight skiers from the British and American Embassies in Oslo in 1950. Brigadier K. Treseder and an American friend were walking towards their cars after skiing near Oslo Fjord. Suddenly an old lady spoke sharply to them, in English with a strong Scottish accent, saying that it was private land and they had no right to be there. She was dressed in a quaint Edwardian-style cycling habit. The Brigadier's wife joined them as the old lady brushed aside their apologies and continued to harangue them until they sheepishly turned to go. The rest of the party, it was revealed, had seen no old lady and suggested that the others had been talking to a ghost.

Subsequent enquiries revealed that the local farmer's great-grandfather had married 'the Girl from Scotland', who may have been the lady in the cycling suit who told the skiing party off so briskly. Yet there was nothing ghostly about her, there was no local ghost story concerning her, and she had engaged in conversation with three living people. Did she, back in her own time, wonder about their strange clothes and the odd machines they were about to climb into?

Are we ghosts from the future to past generations, while they are simply oddly dressed strangers to us? It may be that space-time is considerably more flexible than we imagine, and that individuals come and go as a matter of course.

SEE ALSO *ESP*; *Ghosts*; *Matthew Manning*; *Other dimensions*; *Time*.

OTHER DIMENSIONS

Our experience of the world conditions us into believing that objects – houses, trees, cars and so on – are three-dimensional: they have length, breadth and height. We therefore feel that we live in a three-dimensional universe. Many of us also believe that time may be considered some kind of fourth dimension – duration – but that it is essentially different from the other three. For one thing, although we can travel within the three space-like dimensions, we are unable to slow or accelerate our progression along the time-like dimension, or to travel into the past or jump into the future.

Cosmologists – who consider problems concerning the true nature of space and time, the origin of the universe and its evolution – find themselves compelled to consider the possibility that the universe may have more than four dimensions; some of them may be space-like and some of them time-like. Limited by their five senses, human beings may not be able, except under very special circumstances, to perceive the consequences of most of these other dimensions. It is possible, in fact, that these circumstances involve the paranormal.

The Victorian writer Edwin A. Abbott considered the behaviour and experiences of creatures confined to a two-dimensional world with no knowledge of a third dimension. Abbott's book *Flatland* is still entertaining and thoughtful reading even now, more than a century after it first appeared. To the Flatlanders, a circle would be a barrier preventing them from seeing what was inside it. If they were inside it, they could not see out or get out unless part of the circle was made of transparent material and another part could be opened as a door. Flatlanders' anatomy would be different from ours: two-dimensional creatures could not have a digestive system with two end openings, or they would fall apart!

They could not create the complicated machinery or electric circuits we use, because they lacked the freedom given by the third dimension. If a three-dimensional cylinder intersected their plane they would see a circle or an ellipse appear, depending on the angle the cylinder made with the Flatland plane; this circle or ellipse would persist while the cylinder was passing through their 'world'. Likewise, if a sphere passed through Flatland the Flatlanders would first see a point expanding into a circle that would grow for a time before shrinking to a point and vanishing.

A three-dimensional creature like a human being, looking into their world, could play all kinds of 'supernatural' tricks on them. To lift an object from within a circle in Flatland and return it outside the circle would bewilder them. They might even deny that it could have happened. It would be the equivalent to us of an object disappearing from within a closed room and reappearing outside it – teleportation, or dematerialisation and rematerialisation. In his book *Psychokinesis* the parapsychologist John L. Randall points out that the variety of actions that a being with access to a third dimension could perform in Flatland would produce phenomena such as extrasensory perception, psychokinesis, apports, levitation and so on. By analogy, he continues, they could be produced in our three-dimensional world by a being who had access to a fourth dimension.

One of the first people to explore such possibilities was Johann C. F. Zöllner. A brilliant experimental and theoretical physicist, Zöllner devised four experiments, any one of which, if successful, would provide proof of the reality of the fourth dimension. They involved wooden rings, seashells, a continuous loop of dried gut, a hollow glass ball and a candle. For example if the two rings, each turned in one piece from a different wood, became interlinked with no sign of breakage, this could be explained by supposing that the 'spirits' had lifted them into the fourth dimension. As has often been the experience of psychical researchers, the results he witnessed were unexpected, remarkable – and ambiguous. Later attempts to discredit Zöllner and his work were unjust, and characteristic of those who refuse to consider the weight of evidence for the paranormal.

The latest theories in physics are known as string theories. They try to achieve a grand universal theory embracing all known phenomena in the universe (particles and forces), and seem to be consistent only if space-time has ten or twenty-six dimensions. According to the theorists, the reason we experience only three space-like dimensions and a single time-like one is that all the other dimensions are curled up into regions so tiny that we just do not notice them.

Psychical research theorists who postulate two time-like dimensions – in order to avoid paradoxes in accepting the existence of precognitions – seem positively modest compared with the theoretical physicists. Whatever the true number of dimensions, however, there is no doubt that many of the paranormal phenomena reported from antiquity seem less unbelievable given the freedom of operating in even one more dimension than the familiar three.

SEE ALSO *Apports; Consensus reality; CSICOP; ESP; Explanations; Limits of Science; Mysterious appearances; Parapsychology; Psychokinesis; Seance-room phenomena; SORRAT; Time; Timeslips.*

The quantum theory suggests that the 'solid' world as we know it is a mass of changing dimensions. Danish physicist Niels Bohr (left) and Lord Rutherford – the first man to split the atom – (right) believed that reality was an ever-changing structure.

QUANTUM MECHANICS AND THE PARANORMAL

The late nineteenth-century scientific model was outstandingly successful in explaining a host of natural phenomena and integrating them into a seemingly universal theory of the physical world. It also looked as if the functions of plants and animals could ultimately be resolved into electro-physico-chemical processes. Mind was merely the brain in action.

The model therefore had no place within it for the paranormal. Unexpectedly, however, the paranormal did not go away. What happened was the demolition of that model and its replacement by a new model based on quantum mechanics and relativity.

The first suspicions that nature was not as it had seemed came when the Michelson-Morley experiment failed in its attempt to detect the Earth's movement through the ether. Lorentz and Fitzgerald suggested that the explanation lay in assuming that physical objects actually had sizes that depended on their speeds in comparison to the velocity of light. Likewise the measurement of the passage of time by a clock depended on the clock's velocity. Later on, Einstein showed that this curious velocity effect also altered the mass of an object. As its velocity approached the velocity of light its mass began increasing, and it would reach the mass of the whole universe when its speed reached that of light – which it never would, for the velocity of light could never be attained by a physical object.

Treating space and time as separate and independent quantities was also shown to be false. In 1908

Herman Minkowski suggested that the concept of space-time could remove the barriers to our acceptance of such strange effects as time and size alterations. Worse assaults on common sense were to follow.

J. J. Thomson showed that the electron was an entity over a thousand times smaller in mass than the hydrogen atom. Other experimenters discovered the proton and the neutron. Bohr and Rutherford postulated that any atom consisted of a nucleus of protons and neutrons surrounded by electrons circling the nucleus like miniature planets moving round a miniature sun. Like our solar system, the atom now became largely composed of nothing. If it had been a sphere the size of the Earth, then the nucleus would be the size of a cathedral at its centre, with the electrons the size of bungalows pursuing their lonely orbits about that centre.

But Bohr and Rutherford went further. Using Max Planck's idea, formulated in 1905, that in atomic processes energy comes in multiples of a basic energy unit, the quantum, they showed that for the electrons in atoms only certain orbits were possible. The physicists were able to explain the pattern of lines or narrow gaps in the spectra of visible light that had passed through gases as being due to the electrons absorbing just enough energy to jump from a lower orbit to a higher one. The gaps occurred precisely where the researchers predicted they would be. And so, even though some of the theory's assumptions seemed against all common sense, it became accepted because it worked.

Other researchers were now demonstrating additional strangenesses about sub-atomic particles. The electron was a wave as well as a particle. This possibility, suggested by de Broglie in 1924, was fully confirmed by experiment and was developed a short time later by Erwin Schrödinger and Paul Dirac in the theory of wave mechanics.

This dual quality of particles is recognised in Werner Heisenberg's Principle of Complementarity: 'The concept of complementarity is meant to describe a situation in which we can look at one and the same event through two different frames of reference. These two frames mutually exclude each other, and only the juxtaposition of these con-

tradictory frames provides an exhaustive view of the appearance of the phenomena.'

Heisenberg's Principle of Indeterminacy states that for sub-atomic entities it is impossible to know exactly their position and velocity. And if sub-atomic particles are wave-like, it is not possible to talk about position in any precise fashion. In fact the equations of theoretical physics refer merely to possibilities or probabilities, not to facts. As Professor Henry Margenau said: 'The equations say nothing about masses moving; they regulate the behaviour of very abstract fields, certainly in many cases non-material fields, often as tenuous as the square root of a probability.'

This field theory implies that matter is composed of wave-like processes – that the seemingly hard material universe perceived by our physical senses is an illusion. In addition, the seeming separateness of objects within that universe is also an illusion. On the sub-atomic scale, there are no 'objects' of invariant 'mass' and given 'volume' separated by 'distances' and acting on each other with 'forces' of the simple push-pull type of mechanics. The entity we conveniently call an electron has no definite position at a given time, no definite velocity and no isolation from the rest of the universe. Quantum theory states that there is a small but finite probability of the electron being anywhere. It is in some way related to every part of the universe. This inter-relatedness property is also applied to other sub-atomic particles.

Instinctively we react against these totally unfamiliar and strange ideas, assuming that the uncertainty in our knowledge of position, velocity and so on is simply due to the imprecision of our measurements. But this is not so. The uncertainty is built into the microworld because of the nature of sub-atomic particles, of which over one hundred types are now known.

This strange and beautiful sub-atomic universe is forever hidden to our senses, geared as they are to the macroworld of seeming reality. The entities of this universe elude everyday concepts: they are related to each other in a web of mathematical probabilities in a shadow game whose rules are the laws of relativity and quantum physics. The statements of physicists about the nature of reality and about the immediate sensory world have come to resemble more and more the statements of mystics, from both East and West, and those of mediums regarding the operations of their psychic faculties. As a result the medium, the mystic, and the physicist find themselves in unexpected accordance. The odd man out is the person who still believes that the nineteenth-century hard material world comprises the whole of reality – not realising that that house was demolished almost a century ago.

The principle of complementarity, forced on theoretical physicists because of the dual nature of sub-atomic particles – sometimes particles, sometimes waves – can be usefully employed in the paranormal. The sensory viewpoint of everyday life is evidently only one aspect of reality, a bread-and-butter viewpoint geared towards a human being's immediate physical survival. The modern physicist's viewpoint, seen to be totally different from the sensory one, scans nature in a different way, revealing aspects of reality quite different from those possessed by the sensory world. Instead of importance being conferred on objects, masses, positions, distances, a linear time of past, present and future and so on, the emphasis is on patterns, fields and an intimate relationship of space with time that ordinary language totally fails to describe. From this second point of view, the physicist is able to construct experiments that reveal new aspects of nature and confirm his theories or force him to modify them. The viewpoints are complementary. Each works in its own fields.

Can one then hope that psychic phenomena such as telepathy, clairvoyance, psychometry, precognition and retrocognition will fit a body of theory analogous to the theories of quantum mechanics and relativity? Like these theories, it may have to begin by agreeing that, in the world of the paranormal, ordinary concepts of space and time are inadmissible.

What might correspond in 'psychic mechanics' to the non-material fields of quantum mechanics? Strangely enough, the first steps along the road to such a concept were taken by certain researchers in that same period when the demolition and reconstruction men were moving into the late nineteenth century's world model edifice.

Men such as William James, Sigmund Freud and C. G. Jung were exploring another world invisible to sense-geared man – the world of the unconscious mind, whose strange, often paradoxical operations impinge sneakily yet influentially on man's thoughts and actions. All three were interested in the paranormal – James and Jung intensely so – for the light it might shed on the dark, invisible continent of the psyche. Jung introduced the concept of the collective unconscious. A major feature of the Jungian collective unconscious was that it was not merely a passive record, but a reactive, dynamic one.

The existence of the collective unconscious and its structures – archetypes (the instincts of the unconscious), forms, and the collective racial memory of mankind – is supported by dream comparison and analysis, by the universality of myths and by paranormal phenomena. It looks too as if this great, submerged continent of the psyche exists outside space and time. Like islands isolated by the ocean, human beings' consciousnesses lie separate, above the threshold of the unconscious. But just as all islands joint below the ocean surface, so Jungian teaching suggests that, although each human may have a personal subconscious, at greater and greater depths of his psyche there is a merging.

The pioneers of quantum mechanics replaced gross matter with non-material fields, accepting that their nature was indefinable and that only their operational laws could be sought. So the depth psychologists for the most part ignore questions regarding the nature or 'whereabouts' of the collective unconscious, seeking merely to discover and understand its laws by studying its transactions with human beings. Just as the theoretical physicists have recognised various kinds of sub-atomic particles within the fields they study and have deduced their laws of interaction, it may be expected that the explorers of the psyche – psychologists, psychoanalysts, psychical researchers – will discover more about the structures of the collective unconscious.

Various researchers have even attempted to generalise the field theories and particle theories of quantum mechanics to include paranormal phenomena. Martin Ruderfer suggested that the 'neutrino sea' might be a possible form of energy

Professor John Taylor, mathematics expert of London University. In 1974 he made public his whole-hearted support of Uri Geller's apparently paranormal feats. Within months he had retracted his beliefs – some say because his colleagues threatened to 'excommunicate' him due to his provocative views. Perhaps in such cases science is seen to be uneasy in the presence of such 'damned data'.

that could initiate psychic phenomena. Mathematical physicist Adrian Dobbs put forward a two-dimensional model of time and postulated the existence of 'psitrons', particles of imaginary mass that can travel faster than light, in accordance with orthodox relativity theory. In his closely argued theory (no more bizarre in its properties than much of quantum mechanics) he tried to account for telepathy and precognition.

Physicist and parapsychologist Helmut Schmidt persuaded volunteers to try to predict events triggered by radioactive decay, use being made of single quantum processes (electrons from a strontium-90 source were individually registered). The time of occurrence of such an event is completely unpredictable, and yet Schmidt's volunteers obtained scores that would only have been expected to happen by chance once out of every thousand million experiments. It is extremely difficult to explain Schmidt's experiments without invoking precognition and/or psychokinesis. If they involve the former, the mind is acquiring future information; if the latter, then the mind is

operating on the sub-atomic level in a manner recalling the astronomer Sir Arthur Eddington's saying: 'The stuff of the world is mind stuff.'

We are still at the beginning of our understanding of such matters. It may be that quantum mechanics will only be of value to the study of the paranormal because of its shining example of success achieved by the courage of its creators in postulating totally new and seemingly irrational concepts. On the other hand, some new Einstein or Newton may already be waiting in the wings before appearing on the world's insubstantial stage to show how a more generalised quantum mechanical model will embrace the paranormal.

SEE ALSO *Kenneth Batcheldor; Cross-correspondences; CSICOP; Doppelgängers; Helen Duncan; Ectoplasm; ESP; Explanations; Formative causation; Ghosts; Inspiration in dreams; Jung and the paranormal; Katie King; Nina Kulagina; Metal bending; Near death experience; Eusapia Palladino; Palm Sunday case; Parapsychology; Philip experiment; Precognition in dreams; Prophecy and prediction; Psychokinesis; Remote viewing; Society for Psychical Research; SORRAT; Telepathy; Telepathy and the ganzfeld; Time; Timeslips; Tulpas.*

FORMATIVE CAUSATION

Conventional science has so far concentrated on explanations in which forces and movements serve as the causes of change; in other words it has mainly confined itself to the study of energetic causation. But this mechanistic approach is of limited value in understanding formative processes, in which structures and patterns of organisation come into being. Consider, for example, the building of a house. The materials of which it is made – bricks, cement, timber, and so on – can be chemically analysed, and the amount of energy used in constructing it can be measured but the *form* of the house is not determined just by the building materials and the energy used in building it; it depends on an architect's plan. With the same building materials and the same amount of energy,

Manchester Grammar School pupil Antony Rix (aged 14) demonstrates his computing skills to visiting technologists. According to Dr Sheldrake, new skills become easier for an individual the more they are practised by others elsewhere.

a house of different structure could have been built instead, according to a different plan. The plan acts as a kind of cause of the form of the house.

In the case of man-made objects, the form is in general determined by human ideas, plans or designs. But in the case of self-organising structures, such as crystals and living organisms, there is no externally imposed human plan or design. So what acts as their formative cause? This question has been debated by philosophers ever since the time of ancient Greece. The Pythagoreans believed that forms were determined by eternal mathematical principles. Plato thought they were copies or reflections of transcendent archetypes, which in Christian neo-Platonism were taken to be ideas in the mind of God. Aristotle thought they were shaped by the non-material souls inherent in all living beings, rather than by archetypes beyond time and space. Mechanistic science lies in the Pythagorean-Platonic tradition, in so far as it ascribes all form and order in the world to the operation of external, non-material laws of nature transcending time and space, existing even 'before' the origin of the universe in the Big Bang.

The hypothesis of formative causation, first proposed in 1981 in Rupert Sheldrake's *A New Science of Life* and further developed in *The Presence of the Past* (1988), proposes that the formative causes of

chemical, biological, social and mental organisation are fields inherent in all such systems. These fields, like magnetic fields, exist within and around the material systems that they shape and organise. Such fields are called morphic fields, from Greek *morphe*, meaning form. Like electromagnetic, gravitational and quantum matter fields, morphic fields are regions of physical influence, but they are not the same as any of these already recognised fields of physics. Nor are they fixed in nature, like Aristotelian souls, or Platonic archetypes, or the eternal mathematical laws of mechanistic science. Rather, they evolve in the course of time.

The structure of morphic fields depends on the actual form and organisation of previous similar systems; such fields contain an inherent memory. Any given morphic system, say a hedgehog embryo, 'tunes in' to all previous similar systems, in this case previous developing hedgehogs. Through this process, called morphic resonance,

Dr Rupert Sheldrake, whose theories of formative causation provoked extreme hostility in scientific literature to the extent that his A New Science of Life *(1980) was labelled 'a book for burning'.*

A Great Tit pecks through a foil milk-bottle top to get to the cream. It was noticed that Great Tits all over Europe began to do the same within weeks of the first recorded attack on milk bottles. But Tits do not communicate or travel widely – so how was the knowledge made known to all individuals within the same species?

morphic fields come to contain a kind of pooled, or collective, memory. Because of morphic resonance, the nature of self-organising systems becomes, through repetition, increasingly habitual. In its most general terms, the hypothesis of formative causation enables the regularities of nature to be seen as habits, rather than as fixed by eternal laws of nature.

This hypothesis gives rise to a wide range of experimentally testable predictions. For example, when a new chemical compound is synthesised for the first time, it may be difficult to crystallise because there is no already existing morphic field for the lattice structure of its crystals. However, after it has crystallised for the first time, it should be easier to crystallise again, because of morphic

resonance from the first crystals. Through repetition, it should on average become easier to crystallise all over the world.

In fact, newly synthesised chemicals are in general slow to crystallise at first, and as time goes on do tend to form more easily all around the world. The usual explanation that chemists give for this phenomenon is that fragments of previous crystals get carried around the world on the beards of migrant chemists, and thus serve as seeds or nuclei for crystallisations in other laboratories. Alternatively such seeds are supposed to be wafted around the world as microscopic, invisible dust particles. The hypothesis of formative causation predicts that it should be possible to observe these accelerations in the rate of crystallisation even when bearded chemists, or migrant scientists in general, are excluded from the laboratory, and when dust particles are filtered from the atmosphere.

The hypothesis makes many other predictions in the chemical and biological realms. For example, when animals such as rats learn a new trick in one place, animals of the same kind – other things being equal – should be able to learn the same trick more readily in other parts of the world. The more rats that learn it, the easier it should become for others. There is already evidence from laboratory experiments in different parts of the world that this effect actually occurs.

Similar effects would be expected in the realm of human learning: it should, on average, be easier to learn what many other people have already learned. Thus, for example, wind-surfing and computer programming should be easier to learn now than they were twenty years ago, other things being equal. Of course, in the human realm other things are rarely equal, and so it is difficult to know to what extent improvements are due to morphic resonance as opposed to other factors, such as changes in motivation and better teaching methods. Nevertheless, special experiments can be devised to test for morphic resonance effects in human learning, and several have already been carried out. In an international competition for the best test of this hypothesis sponsored by the Tarrytown Group of New York in 1986, all three winning entries involved experiments using languages unfamiliar to the subjects; and all showed effects consistent with the hypothesis; details are given in *The Presence of the Past*.

This hypothesis has striking implications for the understanding of memory. Morphic resonance takes place on the basis of similarity, and the most specific and effective resonance acting on any particular organism will in general be from its *own* past, since in general organisms are more like themselves in the past than like any other organisms. In the realm of form, this self-resonance helps to maintain an organism's structure in spite of the fact that its material constituents are continually changing. In the realm of behaviour, self-resonance enables an animal to tune into its own past patterns of activity and can thus provide the basis of memory.

Hence our own memories, including those underlying our habits and the memories of particular events, may depend on our tuning in to ourselves in the past. These memories need not be stored as material traces within the brain. Indeed, despite decades of effort to locate memory traces, they have continued to elude detection; contemporary neuroscientists usually assume that memories must be distributed over relatively large regions of the brain in order to account for the fact that they seem to be both 'everywhere and nowhere in particular', as one researcher put it. One well-known theory postulates that memory traces are stored holographically. However, the recurrent failures to find memory traces in brains may have a much simpler explanation: such traces may not exist, any more than your television set contains traces of the programmes you watched last week.

Why, then, can brain damage lead to a loss of memory? Think again of your television set. If some of its components were cut out, various defects would ensue; there could be a loss or distortion of sound or pictures, while damage to the tuning circuit could lead to the loss of the ability to receive entire channels. But this would not prove that the programmes you see on your television are stored within the circuitry. Likewise, the fact that some memories can be lost as a result of brain damage does not prove that these memories are stored inside the brain; it could be that the damage interferes with the 'tuning' or 'reception' of memories

transmitted by morphic resonance from the same person in the past. Nor does the fact that in certain circumstances memories can be evoked by the electrical stimulation of the temporal lobes of the brain prove that they are stored there. The evocation of programmes on other television channels as a result of the electrical or mechanical stimulation of the tuning circuit of a television set does not prove that they are stored inside these material components.

If we tune into our own memories by morphic resonance, why do we not also tune into other people's? According to the hypothesis of formative causation, we do; we all draw upon and in turn contribute towards a collective human memory. This idea closely resembles C. G. Jung's concept of the collective unconscious.

What would happen if for some reason someone turned in by morphic resonance to a particular person who is now dead? They would gain access to memories of a past life. Such past-life memories, for which there is in fact empirical evidence – especially in the case of spontaneous memories by young children – are usually interpreted as evidence for reincarnation. But accessing someone else's memories by morphic resonance need not necessarily imply reincarnation.

The idea that memories are not stored as material traces inside brains also changes the context of the age-old debate about the possibility of survival of bodily death. Almost all traditional conceptions of survival, be they in terms of reincarnation, ancestor spirits in the underworld or Purgatory, Heaven and Hell, imply the survival of personal memory, even if only of habitual tendencies and moral dispositions. Yet if memories are stored materially inside brains, no personal survival would be possible because the decay of the brain after death would entail the wiping out of all memory. But if memories are not stored in the brain, they would not necessarily be lost at death. If the brain is only the tuning system, then personal survival would not be possible – not because the memories themselves decay, but because the tuning system is lost. But if there is a non-material aspect of the self that survives the death of the brain, then it could still perhaps gain access to the memories by some kind of resonance. Thus the hypothesis of formative causation leaves the question of survival open, whereas the conventional theory leaves it closed.

Apart from the memory of past lives, the parapsychological phenomenon to which formative causation seems most relevant is telepathy. In a world in which morphic resonance is taking place, telepathy would seem normal rather than paranormal; after all, the ability of rats to learn more readily what other rats elsewhere had already learned could be thought of as a kind of mass telepathy. Morphic resonance might also help to account for the extraordinary similarities shown in the lives of identical twins separated soon after birth. At present these similarities are conventionally interpreted in terms of detailed 'genetic programming'; but a morphically resonant connection between these very similar individuals would seem to provide a simpler explanation.

The hypothesis of formative causation is only a hypothesis, so far supported by little direct experimental evidence. But meanwhile, at least it serves to show how much of the conventional scientific world view depends on questionable assumptions, such as the reality of eternal, non-material laws of nature and the existence of memory traces. And it reminds us that what seems paranormal in one theoretical context may seem normal in another.

SEE ALSO *Afterlife*; *Case for God*; *ESP*; *Explanations*; *Eileen Garrett*; *Jinxes*; *Jung and the paranormal*; *Left and right brain*; *Limits of science*; *Near death experience*; *Out-of-the-body experiences*; *Quantum mechanics and the paranormal*; *Reincarnation*; *Telepathy*; *Telepathy and the ganzfeld*; *Twins*.

CASE FOR GOD

One model of a human being, much favoured by the so-called rational realist, is of an electro-chemico-physical mechanism with five senses that enable it to obtain information from, and transmit it to, the environment and its fellow mechanisms. And that is all. The instruments of science are merely extensions of these five senses.

Such a realist usually explains the age-old beliefs in demons, angels and gods as primitive attempts to provide explanations for natural, terrible and unexpected events – fire, earthquake, flood, disease. These beliefs were also comforting. Man could petition and placate such supernatural beings so that they became allies against nature. Within such a belief system a specialist class could flourish enabling those people – shaman, witch-doctor, medicine-man, priest – who professed to have control of the hot-line to Heaven to act (for a fee) as spiritual middlemen. It was natural that, apart from the squalid lower classes of supernatural beings, gods and goddesses should be imagined to resemble different types of human being. They could be proud, powerful, capricious, vicious, covetous, revengeful and so on. Far from the Christian belief being true that God made man in his own image, the reverse was nearer the mark.

Those with religious beliefs spurn such a bleak picture, yet it is undeniably the case that many who still profess a belief in a particular religious system in reality merely pay lip service to it; in their heart of hearts they think otherwise. This is particularly so in the West, and is exemplified by the businessman who, faced by the psychical researcher Frederic Myers's question, 'What do you think will happen to you when you die?' answered: 'Oh, I suppose we will enter into the joy of our Lord, but why talk about such an unpleasant subject?'

And yet, throughout recorded history, human beings have testified that in the right circumstances they have made contact with a source outside themselves which has given help, comfort, inspiration and advice, and has so influenced their lives that from that moment on their actions have demonstrated to their fellow human beings that something momentous has happened to them. Many of these human beings have been very ordinary people, and their experiences have influenced only themselves and their immediate circle. Others have gone on to lead lives of great prominence: they have founded great religions and left bodies of teachings in their efforts to describe to the world what their experiences have taught them and demanded of them.

Among those who have greatly influenced the

world are Lao-tzu, the Buddha, Confucius, Jesus Christ and Mohammed.

The teachings of Jesus in the New Testament talk persuasively of a loving God, able and willing to be contacted, and from whom help can be obtained. From the East have come the *Upanishads* and the *Bhagavad-Gita*. The former are to the Hindu what the New Testament is to the Christian – a spiritual treatise of great wisdom; while the *Bhagavad-Gita*, a marvellously guiding poem of love, light and life, is the glory of Sanskrit literature.

Mystics also have spoken of their experience of a realm of spirit, of a meeting with the Ground of All Being, of a deeper understanding of the nature of time and human existence. Again these peak experiences have proved impossible to translate into the expressions of everyday speech: it is more a case of what it is not, than of what it is. The halting descriptions of the experiences are often couched in the cultural symbols of the subject's upbringing, but whether the mystic is from East or West, the underlying experience seems universal. It should also be noted that the commonly held image of mystics is that of unworldly, vague, woolly-minded if not weak-minded people, yet throughout history they have shown an above-average capacity for practical problem-solving and resilience in the face of difficulties that would have broken most people.

Recent research into the near death experience (NDE) also supports the idea of a spiritual level of existence. Thousands of cases are now known of people who have been so near to death that they would have died in former times when the level of medical skill was poorer. In a large proportion of such cases – irrespective of intelligence, education, religious upbringing or cultural environment – the subjects found themselves having the same core experience. They were released from the suffering body, viewed the terrestrial proceedings around the body, travelled through a tunnel and exited into a landscape of ineffable beauty; and they were conscious of the presence of a Being of Light, who gently and lovingly took them through a review of their life so far. Attempts by some researchers to 'explain' the experience as a protective form of self-delusion caused by one of a variety of factors are not convincing.

Also relevant is the testimony throughout history, from philosophers, poets, novelists, scientists and composers, that their greatest achievements have in fact been given to them. Although they may have to strive beforehand and struggle afterwards, in order to capture the work and present it to the world, they invariably believe that what may have created comes to them from a source beyond themselves. Wordsworth, Socrates, Dickens, Chopin, Goethe and Kekulé are a few of those who have experienced this intrusion from somewhere else – an intrusion so powerful, so imperative, so awesome that it often terrifies the recipient. As Frederic Myers put it: 'The influence rises from no discoverable source; for a moment it may startle or bewilder the conscious mind; then it is recognised as a source of knowledge, arriving through inner vision; while the action of the senses is suspended in a kind of momentary trance.'

One result of a century and more of psychological research, hypnotic studies and psychoanalysis was to establish the existence of a subconscious mind. At times it produces dreams; it delivers information to us; it is the repository of our memories; and it is, like a servant, responsible for much of the smooth running of our bodies while we, undisturbed by such domestic chores, are left free to make major decisions.

Four pioneers in particular – Frederic Myers, Professor William James, Sigmund Freud and C. G. Jung – established beyond doubt that a human being's mind is made up of conscious and unconscious. In the light of the existence of paranormal phenomena, Myers, James and Jung believed that the concept of mind had to be extended further. Myers talked about the subliminal (below the threshold) mind as by far the more important part of personality. James accepted the existence somewhere of a store of all human experience that on occasion could be tapped. Jung suggested the idea of the collective unconscious, a level of mind in contact with every living person but that did not belong to any individual, that had its own drives and purposes.

It is impossible to deny that some source exists, which under the right circumstances can be massively influential in people's lives. To the genius it is inspiration; to others it is religious in effect. In

1969 Professor Sir Alister Hardy founded the Religious Experience Research Unit in Oxford to find out why people have spiritual, transcendental or religious experiences. When do they have them? What do they mean? How do they affect people's lives?

Now called the Alister Hardy Research Centre, it holds over five thousand accounts of first-hand experiences of people who report being aware of the presence of God; or of a presence that is not necessarily named as God; or of having a feeling of guidance and answer to prayer; or of sensing a presence that generates awe and wonder; or of experiencing light, joy, a sense of oneness and abiding love. Professor Hardy's hypothesis was that 'there is some profound reality behind religion', and believed that this hypothesis should be 'made the subject of prolonged and thorough research'. That research is now being carried out.

Whether we call that profound reality the collective unconsciousness, or the Ground of All Being, or the World Mind, or God, it is there. The great religious teachers, the mystics, the psychics, ordinary men and women, inspired geniuses – all have much to tell us concerning its nature and its purpose regarding mankind. A human being can certainly act like an electro-chemico-physical mechanism with but five senses to receive information, but sooner or later the spiritual knock at the door must be answered.

SEE ALSO *Afterlife; Buddhism; Consensus reality; Cross-correspondences; Formative causation; Hypnosis; Inspiration in dreams; Jung and the paranormal; Karma; Left and right brain; Near death experience; Quantum mechanics and the paranormal; Reincarnation; Shamanism; Society for Psychical Research.*

CONSENSUS REALITY

David Bohm, Professor of Theoretical Physics at the University of London, believes that all apparent matter is illusory, the result of an implicate order which he calls 'the holomovement'. Writing of Bohm's theories, Professor Arthur Ellison says: 'Our ordinary science gives theories which are only approximations for local conditions. We look at nature through lenses and try to objectify and so alter what we hope to see.' Thus what is observed depends on the observer's place in space and time – and in the everyday world, on his fears, prejudices and conditioning. When the first European ships reached what was to become New Zealand the Maoris literally did not see them. They did not exist in the physical world for them – because they did not exist in the Maoris' consensus reality.

In order to illustrate that people see only what they are 'programmed' to see, Professor Ellison carried out a simple experiment. Using straightforward electromagnetic principles, he arranged for a bowl of flowers on the table in front of him to rise into the air while he lectured, then slowly return to the table top. He would not draw attention to this happening. The flowers rose according to plan, but it was only in question time that comments were forthcoming. A few people bravely stated that they had seen the bowl rise and fall. A few added that they had seen 'spirit hands' lifting it. But a significant number – the rationalists – poured scorn on the whole event, saying that they had seen nothing.

It has been suggested that perception and consciousness may change over the centuries, that Homer's 'wine-dark sea' may, in fact, have been a literal, rather than a poetic, description of what his generation perceived. But whether or not the ancients were colour-blind, their expectations – and therefore their experiences – were limited. A disembodied voice could never have been, for them, that of a radio announcer, although it may have been an oracle.

The human brain is a highly selective receptor; it only allows us to see, and remember, what can be assimilated by our cultural and personal inheritance. As illustrated by Professor Ellison's experiment, many people literally do not see events or objects that contravene their world-view. Others embellish them to taste. And out of those who perceived a bizarre, 'impossible' happening, many will suffer from what Brian Inglis calls 'retrocognitive dissonance'. This is a common fate of those who witness paranormal events; the more time that passes after the event is observed, the less likely the observer is to believe it. Time is the great enemy of positive results in parapsychology.

When confronted with the paranormal, rationalists frequently behave with a hostility that borders on the hysterical. Scientists in particular urge its destruction, for they fear it ushers in a new Dark Age of superstition. In fact what they fear is the expansion of reality and therefore the necessity for a new scientific paradigm with which to deal with it. Non-scientific rationalists have a more basic fear: that consensus reality will break down and that madness will become sanity – and vice versa.

However, not everyone has a paranormal experience, even though they may seek them. Gifted 'sensitives' such as D. D. Home are rare, and, despite the extraordinary results of the Philip experiment, most tables stay on the floor. Even among would-be believers consensus reality is so strong that many paranormal events may well simply go unnoticed. Given the phenomenal capacity of the human brain for ignoring the unacceptable, perhaps many bizarre events take place all the time and are instantly ignored.

In the world of the occult, reality is manipulated by the adept, using trance, hypnosis and projected thoughtforms. Allegedly age-old rituals provide the template for a new reality; 'the right words' uttered at the right phase of the moon and on a certain day at a certain time will bring about the desired result. Sympathetic magic seeks to bring together the world 'out there' with the world of the imagination, and make them one. A doll may be named and dressed as a certain person and life breathed into it by the ritual magician before it is set in a tableau that mimics the desired result. Named dolls placed back to back, for example, might symbolise a quarrel that the magician wishes two people to have.

Many occultists and mystics believe that anything one imagines is imprinted on an ideoplastic plane. Fervent and deliberate visualisation will bring it into this plane, so that it may be perceived with the physical senses – any strong belief or desire makes a thoughtform that, theoretically, can impinge on consensus reality, although it rarely does. Thus, for example, visions of the Virgin may be the projected thoughtforms of believers – most

of whom have been young girls, the prime receptors for paranormal experience. As far as it is known, the Virgin has never addressed herself to anyone other than a believer.

Occultists claim that thoughtforms may, if imbued with enough energy from their visualiser, take on a life of their own. This could be the reason that the Virgin of Medjugore has become uncharacteristically ecumenical: she has praised a local woman for her especial holiness – yet this woman is a Muslim. This is not a traditional feature of visions of the Virgin.

The visions also raise another question about their manifestations. Since Bernadette Soubirous saw her 'lady' in the 1850s, successive visionaries have developed tumours and died young. One of the visionaries of Medjugore became sick shortly after the first visions and remains very ill. If energy were being drawn from the visionaries in order to create the thoughtform, one would expect at least one of them to experience debility and lowered immunity to illness.

Those who admit to unusual perceptions have often ended their days at the stake or in psychiatric institutions. Even today, it is a rare doctor who encourages the apparent aberration, but Morton Schatzman's work with 'Ruth' in the 1970s was a watershed in our understanding of what we call 'reality'.

SEE ALSO *Boggle threshold; Case of Ruth; Children and psi; Cosmic Joker; Creative visualisation; Cryptozoology; Entity enigma; Fantasy-prone personalities; Ghosts; Hallucinations; Left and right brain; Miracles of St Médard; Other dimensions; Parapsychology; Philip experiment; Quantum mechanics and the paranormal; Ritual magic; SORRAT; Thoughtography; Tulpas; UFO paradox; Vampires; Visions of the Virgin Mary.*

LEFT AND RIGHT BRAIN

The brain is composed of two halves connected by a bridge of two hundred million nerve fibres known as the corpus callosum. The right hemi-

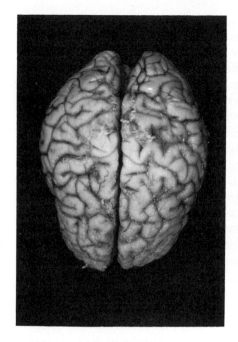

The brain: to materialists it is the sum of the personality. When it dies, so does the individual. But supposing it is only the receiver for signals culled from far wider sources? And even within a reductionist framework, the left and right hemispheres are understood to cope with very different aspects of consciousness. The left half deals with the rational, analytical type of thinking, whereas the right side of the brain governs intuitive, psychic and creative thinking. Sometimes total appreciation of an artistic event, such as listening to a concert (right) involves both halves of the brain – the left half begins by registering the notation and individual performance of the instruments, and the right half – the holistic hemisphere – appreciates the entire thing.

sphere controls most of the functions of the left-hand side of the body, and vice versa. The two halves deal with different functions; the right with the intuitive, artistic and non-verbal ones, the left with the analytical, logical and 'educational' ones. In some activities the cognitive processes will shift from one half to the other; when listening to music, for instance, we begin by appreciating it as a whole experience (right brain), then begin to pick out the different instruments (left brain).

On the whole, modern Westerners are predominantly left-brained, emphasising all activities that require logic and reason – a situation that is constantly reinforced by an educational system that relies on facts and analysis. Yet this education is actually at odds with certain talents – the meticulous analysis required to pass examinations in music and literature manifestly does little to encourage musical or literary talent. More controversially, the type of medical training offered in the West effectively destroys the average doctor's intuitive healing potential. British healer Matthew Manning does not diagnose as a matter of principle, because he believes that he, like any other intelligent person in this society, has read enough about illness for his left brain to interfere with his right; reason may taint or confuse a purely intuitive response.

The hostility and suspicion generally accorded to mystics and psychics in the West is largely due to the ingrained idea that anything right-brained is 'sinister' (the Latin for 'left'), as in the right brain's influence on the left side of the body. Hence witchcraft, healing, mediumistic talents, mystical union with God and even genius are regarded as a threat to the equilibrium of society. Part of this antagonism is reinforced by the puritan work ethic that rejects 'unearned' success – such as that which is the result of inspiration in dreams or trance. Yet ironically, it is by 'letting go' of the rigidly confining left brain that we can get in touch with our greatest potential, and arguably with other beings, even the gods themselves.

The right brain is holistic, grasping the broad idea, seeing the whole rather than working laboriously through a problem from beginning to end. The answer to a persistent question may come to us when we are in a state of reverie, or even asleep (when the left brain is largely off duty) – yet in Western society children are rigorously discouraged from day-dreaming.

Right-brain functioning is very vulnerable to left-brain interference. Thus if we have an overwhelming paranormal experience our belief in it tends to diminish with time – a common phenomenon called 'retrocognitive dissonance' by writer Brian Inglis, and one that militates against the long-term impact of parapsychological experiments. The mentally unbalanced, however, may be so right-brain dominant that they simply cannot function in the physical world without constant assistance. The pictures in their head may be beautiful, but they find it impossible to dress themselves or go through the logical steps involved in making a simple meal.

The phenomenal capacity of idiots savants, the 'foolish wise ones', to be artists or lightning calculators despite being seriously subnormal in other ways, can be seen as right-brained dominance at its most idiosyncratic. There may, however, be many other factors present in such cases, such as residual memories from previous incarnations. Most of these mono-talented people rely entirely on relaying the whole picture or piece of music or set of numbers, for that is how they receive them. The process is instant and cannot be explained.

It may be that telepathy happens when a strong right brain speaks to another strong, or unusually receptive, right brain. One method of inducing dramatic telepathic results in the laboratory is the ganzfeld, where the recipient relaxes in a state of information deprivation, all outside 'noise' stilled. This seems to alert the right brain and switches the left brain off. But in general parapsychological experiments suffer from the problems implicit in replication; logic and reason must be involved, and right-brain receptiveness will diminish.

The experimenter effect, in which the expectations of the researcher are reflected in the results of the experiment, is also vulnerable to the influence of the left brain. The left brain does not even conceive of a boggle barrier, let alone permit any experience to crash it. Many of the researchers who bring parapsychology into disrepute are unrepentantly left-brained; they have no intention of using methods such as biofeedback or meditation in order to contact their right brains. Such people are wasting everyone's time, whereas the work of such researchers as the late Kenneth Batcheldor was highly successful because he encouraged the child-like expectancy produced by the right brain.

Even in the case of spontaneous psi-functioning there are problems in permitting the right brain to be heard. Automatic writing, for example, requires total dissociation on the part of the medium if his or her own habitual modes of thought are not to contaminate the results, a state of mind that is exceptionally difficult to achieve. Some psychic artists and writers, however, such as Mrs Pearl Curran and Luiz Gasparetto, have managed to do so. The discarnates involved in the Cross-correspondences deliberately engaged a system that could not be tainted by the conscious minds – or the left brains – of the mediums involved.

But if genius, inspiration and psychic functioning are located in something as mortal as the brain, does this mean that there can be no survival of death? When the brain dies, is that truly the end? It seems not; the right brain appears to be a highly tuned receiver, a channel for information from elsewhere – be it the collective unconscious or the individual 'mind' that is made so much freer by the death of the physical body.

SEE ALSO *Afterlife; Kenneth Batcheldor; Boggle threshold; Cross-correspondences; CSICOP; Experimenter effect; Formative causation; Healing; Holism; Inspiration in dreams; Karma; Matthew Manning; Near death experience; Parapsychology; Prodigies; Psychic music, art and literature; Sex and psi; Society for Psychical Research; SORRAT; Telepathy; Telepathy and the ganzfeld; Chico Xavier.*

EXPERIMENTER EFFECT

Anybody who learns Latin at school will soon have to recognise the distinction between *num*?, which implies that a negative answer is expected, and *nonne*?, where the expected answer is 'yes'. People are more likely to make the expected than the unexpected reply. Accordingly, the results of scientific experiments may be affected if questions are put in such a way that expectations, one way or the other, are aroused in subjects who are required to answer them. And such expectations may be conveyed not just by *num*? or *nonne*? or their latter-day equivalents, but also by inflections in the questioner's voice or the expression on his face.

This is only one of the many forms in which the experimenter effect can operate to distort research results. Obviously they can also be influenced by what the subjects have been conditioned to accept as a *possible* outcome of an experiment. The stock assumption in scientific circles has long been that, although there may be errors of this kind – as in the notorious example of the astronomers who refused to look through Galileo's telescope for fear that what they saw would upset their preconceptions – in the long run, the truth will out. It is only recently that the fear has surfaced that the truth is not being allowed out because of the way in which experimenters, consciously or unconsciously, are ensuring that findings provide whatever they hope will be provided.

The first attempt at a comprehensive study of the effects that experimenters can have on the course of their experiments, and consequently on the results, was made as recently as 1966 by Robert Rosenthal in his *Experimenter Effects in Behavioral Research*. Rosenthal had made his name a few years earlier with experiments in which he had given one group of students 'genius' rats, bred for their ability to run fast through mazes, and another group of 'stupid' rats. The students' findings revealed that the geniuses did indeed do distinctly better in maze tests. Only then did Rosenthal reveal that both sets of rats had come from the same stock.

The obvious explanation was unpalatable to scientists: that the rats were picking up the bias that had been implanted in the researchers' minds. Ironically, it was also unpalatable to psychical researchers. They had been trying to prove the reality of extra-sensory perception (ESP) in elaborately controlled trials – far more carefully controlled to prevent experimenter bias, Rosenthal had to admit, than the bulk of conventional psychology trials – and had come up against what appeared to be psychic intervention. Believers in ESP, 'sheep', on balance tended to do better in trials for ESP than disbelievers, 'goats', as if belief and disbelief were influencing the results.

This suggested that scientific controls to prevent straightforward experimenter effect might be rendered inadequate by psi experimenter effect, which could bypass them by transmitting information from mind to mind. Problems had arisen in psychical research earlier, when some researchers appeared to obtain positive results quite readily, while others' results were consistently negative. Could it be that there were 'sheep' and 'goat' investigators, as well as subjects?

The idea was put to the test by two members of the Society for Psychical Research (SPR) in the 1950s. When Dr D. J. West, the Society's Research Officer, was involved in experiments, the results were disappointingly negative; whereas those conducted by G. W. Fisk, a member of the Council of the SPR, produced some positive results. In one series, Fisk sent out to volunteers, in sealed opaque envelopes, cards printed with clock faces. In their replies they told him what they thought was the hour recorded on each card; a few of them appeared to be able to 'tell the time' more consistently than could be explained by chance guessing.

Fisk sent these subjects another batch of cards, without mentioning that in half of them the hour on the clock face had been set by West – in a random order, as were those set by Fisk. When the cards were returned, they were divided according to experimenter. West's proved to be generally negative; Fisk's, as usual, positive. A further test in 1958 provided a similar result.

It was left to Julie Eisenbud, one of the most respected of American psychical researchers, to point out ruefully that this was precisely what they should have expected. They had been striving to make their investigations acceptable to orthodox scientists by eliminating experimenter effect; but if psi existed, it had to be assumed that it would be capable of evading physical controls of the kind designed to ensure that subjects did not pick up clues through the five senses. Everybody had been behaving as if there could be a kind of gentleman's agreement not to employ ESP on trials of ESP, which was absurd.

Absurd it might be, but what were psychical researchers to do? They had committed themselves to seeking proof for the reality of ESP and PK by experimental procedures acceptable to orthodox science; and since orthodox scientists declined to accept ESP, they would not be impressed by findings apparently revealing the existence of psi experimenter effect. Since Rhea White related the evidence for psi experimenter effect in two long papers in the *Journal* of the American SPR in 1976, it has been rather grudgingly adopted as a complication by most researchers; but there are still a few who have declined to come to terms with its implications.

One of those implications, however, has recently begun to give rise to alarm in orthodox scientific circles. There have been a number of cases recently when apparently well-established ideas have been upset because researchers, after first providing robust results, have later begun to obtain disconcerting findings.

In the 1960s, for example, Texas researchers claimed that when planarium worms were cut in half, both halves retained certain 'memories' of lessons they had learned. For a time, other researchers obtained the same results, which were published in *Science, Nature* and elsewhere. But just as they seemed to be growing well established, other researchers began reporting negative results; eventually the impression grew that there was no substance to those initially obtained.

Much the same happened to the work of Neal Miller, Professor of Psychology at the Rockefeller

University of New York. In the 1960s, with the help of standard behaviourist methods, Miller taught laboratory rats to control their blood pressure and temperature; these results were repeated in other laboratories. But just as the case seemed proved, laboratories elsewhere began to report negative results.

These were extreme examples; but it is far from unusual for attempts to repeat the results of experiments to provide anomalous results which have to be explained away. And in some cases – as in Miller's – it is very difficult to account for what has happened by any known, accepted form of experimenter effect. Could psi be responsible, acting through the desire to obtain results impressing itself on the rats and worms? If psi turns out to be responsible, it will explain much that has been disconcerting in laboratories all over the world.

SEE ALSO *American Society for Psychical Research; Consensus reality; Cosmic Joker; CSICOP; ESP; Formative causation; Levitation; Limits of science; Parapsychology; Psychokinesis; Society for Psychical Research; Telepathy and the ganzfeld.*

LIMITS OF SCIENCE

In his essay on the limits of science Sir Peter Medawar argued that nothing could impede or halt the advancement of scientific learning except a failure of nerve: 'There is no limit upon the ability of science to answer the kind of questions that science *can* answer.' Nevertheless there was a limit of a different kind, he admitted: 'It is logically outside the competence of science to answer questions to do with first and last things.' Science is not going to answer the question 'why?' about, say, the way the world began, however much information it may provide about 'how' it began.

In connection with psychical research, the problem has been limits – or, rather, limitations – of another kind. At any given time, scientists accept a collection of what used to be considered laws of nature, but which are now more cautiously described as models. A century ago, when research into extrasensory perception (ESP) and psychokinesis (PK) was being conducted by some world-renowned scientists, they had to contend with the orthodox dogma that communication and action at a distance without the application of some known physical force was impossible. Telepathy did not happen, because it could not happen.

Dogmas of this kind breed what has come to be known as 'scientism': in effect a faith, held as firmly, and often as blindly, as any religious belief. What psychical researchers still have to contend with is not so much science, as scientism; and its limitations take two main forms.

'The most heinous crime a scientist can commit', Medawar claimed in his essay entitled 'Scians', 'is to declare to be true that which is not so.' But there is another crime that is hardly less venial: to denounce as fraudulent phenomena that the scientist has not himself investigated. This has been the stock-in-trade of the Committee for the Scientific Investigation of Claims of the Paranormal (CSICOP), set up with the barely disguised intention of demolishing those claims.

Its members made one full-scale investigation, of the Gauquelins' astrological findings. CSICOP's results confirmed those of the Gauquelins; whereupon CSICOP asserted that the Gauquelins' findings had been overturned. When this in turn was exposed, the decision was taken to hold no more such investigations; since then most of the contributions to its journal, the *Skeptical Inquirer*, have been of the marginally less heinous type – denunciations of psychical research by individuals who have not cared to undertake it themselves.

One other limit of science has to be taken into consideration: the possibility, and indeed the likelihood, that forces are at work that can be recognised, and perhaps up to a point allowed for, but that cannot be fitted into the framework of science as we know it. An obvious example is the poltergeist. Not merely does it perform in ways which upset the current model of gravity (itself an unexplained type of action at a distance, which nobody has been able to account for); but the way in which objects move as if carried or thrown by an invisible hand also suggests that a disembodied intelligence is at work.

Medawar noted another of the limitations of science: a failure of nerve. In the course of research a scientist may hit upon some anomaly that seems unaccountable in the light of his faith. The temptation then may be to ignore it, or to explain it away as best he can. If, like Galileo, he goes ahead and confirms that it is not an anomaly, the faithful may prefer to do as they did when he invited them to look through his telescope for themselves and make excuses for declining the invitation.

This happened to William James when his investigation of the Boston medium Mrs Leonore Piper convinced him that she had genuine supernormal powers. She knew things in her trances, he had found, 'which she cannot possibly have heard in her waking state'; but he could not persuade colleagues to come and test her for themselves. If she had failed to impress them, they would have been wasting their time. If she *had* impressed them, they would have had to face the unwelcome fact that the foundations of their faith were shaky.

Occasionally a scientist would agree to investigate, admit to being convinced, but then retract – as Sir David Brewster did, following sessions with the medium D. D. Home. T. H. Huxley took a different course; after a demonstration by another medium, Charles Williams, he offered an explanation of the way Williams *might* have been able to cheat, which enabled him later to claim that he had witnessed 'as gross an imposture as ever came under my notice'. More recent is the interesting spectacle of the two books by Professor John Taylor: *Superminds*, accepting the genuineness of the psychokinetic phenomena associated with Uri Geller, published in 1975; and *Science and the Supernatural*, five years later, drawing diametrically opposite conclusions from basically the same set of investigations.

Gravity at least behaves reasonably consistently; as does magnetism, another unaccounted-for type of action at a distance. Poltergeists appear to be influenced by a 'mind' that is unpredictable, but, on the evidence, capable of mocking gravity, and of performing many other feats which conventional science cannot begin to cope with.

The bulk of psychical research over the past half-century has been devoted to attempts to prove the reality of ESP and PK through trials of the type which, if they produce positive results, will compel the respect of orthodox scientists. But they have remained unconvinced, as Richard Broughton conceded in his presidential address to the Parapsychological Association in 1987. The question had to be faced, he said, whether the experimental method was adequate, as over the decades it had proved to be 'rather less productive than we would have liked or perhaps expected it to be'.

The expectation was understandable, as the evidence which has accumulated would ordinarily suffice to secure the recognition of psi. But it has been rejected, in the last resort, because the researchers cannot produce consistently repeatable results: 'mind' gets in the way. Although attempts will doubtless continue to be made to demonstrate psi to the satisfaction of scientists, it is becoming increasingly likely that it will be demonstrated only to their *dis*satisfaction – by the discovery of ways in which psi can intrude in conventional scientific experiments. As a result the accumulating anomalies will no longer be able to be brushed aside, and science will have to set new limits, looser than scientists care even to contemplate.

SEE ALSO *Apports; Boggle threshold; Consensus reality; Cosmic Joker; CSICOP; Curses; Enfield poltergeist; ESP; Experimenter effect; Explanations; Fate; Formative causation; Michel Gauquelin; Uri Geller; Ghosts; Healing; D. D. Home; Hypnosis; Images that bleed and weep; Incorruptibility; Jinxes; Nina Kulagina; Levitation; Lexilinking; Loch Ness monster; Matthew Manning; Mesmerism; Metal bending; Carmine Mirabelli; Near death experience; Other dimensions; Philip experiment; Psi-mediated instrumental response; Psychokinesis; Quantum mechanics and the paranormal; Remote viewing; The Resurrection; Sai Baba; Society for Psychical Research; SORRAT; Stigmatics; Suspended animation; Telepathy; Telepathy and the ganzfeld; Thoughtography; Tulpas; Turin Shroud; UFO paradox; Vampires; Werewolves.*

VIII Life After Death

Cross-correspondences • Palm Sunday case • Direct voice • Electronic voice phenomenon • Ghosts • Telephone calls from the dead • Out-of-the-body experiences • Near death experience • Life after death • Vampires • Reincarnation • Karma

American writer Nathaniel Hawthorne wrote: 'We sometimes congratulate ourselves at the moment of waking from a troubled dream; it may be so the moment after death.' It may also be that we do not wake from the process of dying, that the atheists and rationalists were right and that the death of the brain means the death of the personality. And after that, nothing. However, modern man has access to privileged knowledge about life after death.

By far the most persuasive body of evidence for an afterlife comes not from the mystics or mediums, but from the medical profession. In these days of advanced resuscitation techniques, many more people are being brought back to life from the state of clinical death where once they would have remained – and what tales these travellers have to tell! After the process of dying, with its attendant distress, agony and discomfort, the near death experience (NDE) reveals a world of light, love and bliss. These people are shown a little bit of Heaven, given advice and warnings about their own lives and that of the globe – and then sent back, despite their pleas to stay, because it is not yet their time to die. Sceptics try to explain the experience by ascribing it to drugs (but not every NDEr has been given them), or to wishful thinking (although many of them have hoped for oblivion) or cultural expectation (but many were atheists). It seems that at last we have some hard information about what it is like to die, and some reason to believe in the age-old promises of heavenly joy.

Sir Arthur Conan Doyle remarked that a man does not automatically fall 'into the honeypot' when he dies, and, if we consider the second most persuasive body of evidence for an afterlife, we must acknowledge that being dead can seem like hard work. The automatic scripts, purporting to come from discarnate founders of the Society for Psychical Research (SPR) through the mediumship of various ladies, were spread over thirty years and three continents. Any fraud or collusion may effectively be ruled out. Yet these fragmentary scripts – known as the Cross-correspondences – show that the SPR founders were still active intelligences, that they were still 'alive' in a real sense after their bodily deaths. They had, apparently, invented the scheme when they met in the afterlife, and had deliberately designed it to rule out, as far as possible, interference from the mediums' own minds. The Cross-correspondences remain a monumental body of evidence for an afterlife, and go some way towards explaining why communication between that plane of existence and ours is frequently so distorted. The discarnate Frederic Myers, founder of the SPR, likened his feeling when trying to send a message to that of 'standing behind a sheet of frosted glass'.

The mediums involved in the Cross-correspondences were women of high integrity; one suspects they were chosen as such by the discarnate gentlemen for this purpose. Not all pronouncements of mediums are quite so unequivocal, however.

The phenomenon of direct-voice communication, practised by Leslie Flint and a few other mediums, is fraught with problems. Mr Flint was exhaustively tested and, it seems, could not have cheated, yet the voices of Oscar Wilde, Amy Johnson and others 'came through' and were recorded in his seances. On the whole, the voices are convincing, but the words less so. It is as if a competent impersonator is thrust on stage without a script and has to get by on the voice alone. Such hollow performances are typical of the seance room, and leave one wondering about the true nature of the spirit impersonators.

Certainly anyone who has tried to capture the voices of the dead using the electronic voice phenomenon technique (basically letting a tape recorder run to record anything or nothing), may be alarmed by what might be picked up. Most of the time the anomalous sounds turn out to be explicable in rational terms, but occasionally the sound of approaching footsteps or even a full-blown Nuremberg rally cannot be explained.

Ever since there have been machines, especially those concerned with communication, there have been suspicions of ghosts lurking in them. One phenomenon that is guaranteed to awaken the sceptic in the most ardent True Believer is that of telephone calls from the dead. Yet, if the dead continue to exist, and communication, although difficult, is not impossible, why should we not receive calls from the departed? There is evidence that it happens, and that such incidents are not merely auditory hallucinations created by grief or wishful thinking – and if it happens, then it should be taken seriously. The ultimate frustration, however, remains the fact that we have no number on which to call them back.

To an increasing number of people, life on Earth means a series of incarnations, each dependent for its conditions upon the last. The doctrines of reincarnation and karma (the law of cause and effect) are gaining ground in the West. The evidence for reincarnation is strong, and a belief in it can be used in a variety of practical ways, such as psychotherapy – if phobias and fears from past lives are interfering with the present life, they can be erased by hypnotic regression. Sceptics say that it is all psycho-drama – false creation to please the therapist. Nevertheless it works.

There is a school of thought that says that, in the matter of an afterlife, one gets what one believes. Thus a Catholic will find a Purgatory, a Red Indian a Happy Hunting Ground, and so on. Although this theory does not bode well for either those with a lively fear of vampires, or those who believe in oblivion, the near death experience does not bear this out. We do not get what we believe, we get what actually exists.

CROSS-CORRESPONDENCES

By 1906 a number of prominent members of the Society for Psychical Research (SPR), among them Frederic Myers, Edmund Gurney and Professor Henry Sidgwick, were no longer alive. In 1910 Professor Henry Butcher, Professor of Greek at Edinburgh University, died, while the death of Dr A. W. Verrall, a noted classical scholar at Cambridge, occurred two years later. They are all relevant to the unfolding puzzle of the Cross-correspondences, which are considered by many psychical researchers to be the best evidence yet that human beings survive death.

In 1906 the Society's research officer, Miss Alice Johnson, was investigating the output of a number of women who were able to produce automatic writing. Among them were Mrs Holland, who was in fact Mrs Fleming, the sister of Rudyard Kipling, and lived in India; Mrs Willett (in reality Mrs W. Coombe-Tennant); Dame Edith Lyttelton; and Mrs Verrall, lecturer in classics at Newnham College, Cambridge, and wife of Dr A. W. Verrall. The famous medium Mrs Piper in the USA was also a member of the group, and a number of other people were involved, such as the Verralls' daughter Helen.

It was discovered that the automatic scripts from different automatists bore certain significant resemblances to one another and to the material produced by Mrs Piper. From then on, efforts were made by the Society to keep the automatists in ignorance of one another's output. Geography helped, for the mediums were in three widely distant countries. Alice Johnson and Mr J. G. Piddington collated and studied the scripts, helped

Discarnate founders of the Society for Psychical Research (SPR), such as F. W. H. Myers (left) and Edmund Gurney (right), are believed to have met in the afterlife and invented the ingenious Cross-correspondences, fragments of automatic script channelled through different mediums on different continents, that only make sense when put together. The experiment lasted over thirty years and many believe it provides the second-best evidence for an afterlife after the near death experience.

by people such as Sir Oliver Lodge and Gerald William Balfour. The investigation went on for many years, requiring great patience and a wide classical knowledge.

The scripts were signed and purported to come from the deceased founders and members of the SPR. The communicators said that they were producing the scripts because a single theme distributed between various automatists, none of whom knew what the others were writing, would prove that one mind, or group of minds, was at the back of the whole phenomenon. In other words, it could not easily be explained by cross-telepathy among the automatists. Also, recondite points in classical literature were introduced to prove the identity of the authors, for Myers, Verrall and Butcher had

all been front-rank classical scholars.

The scripts often contained fragments from several themes, distributed among the automatists, often in a variety of ways. On 16 April 1907, Mrs Holland in India wrote: 'Maurice, Morris, Mors. And with that the shadow of death fell upon him and his soul departed out of his limbs.' The following day Mrs Piper spoke the words 'sanatos' and 'Tanatos'; then on 23 April the word 'Thanatos' and on the 30th this word three times. On 29 April Mrs Verrall wrote: 'Warmed both hands before the fire of life. It fails and I am ready to depart.' She also wrote: 'Come away, Come away' and the Latin sentence: 'Pallida mors aequo pede pauperum tabernas regumque turres (put in) pulsat' [Pale death with equal foot the huts of the poor and the towers of the rich (put in) strikes]. Thus the theme of death was given by all three in different languages.

When the Cross-correspondences really got going, they became increasingly intricate. Sometimes the investigators became baffled and had to ask for 'clues' to the solutions of the current literary and classical puzzles being teasingly farmed out in the scripts. Hints were given by what became known as the Script Intelligence.

An analogy, poor as it is, may give some idea of the bizarre situation. Suppose that three famous painters disappear from their homes and studios. As the years pass, no one knows whether they are dead or alive. And then, without warning, through the letter-boxes of a number of people living in different countries come envelopes. Each envelope contains a piece of a jigsaw puzzle. As the days and weeks pass, the envelopes, each containing its piece of jigsaw, continue to arrive at irregular intervals. But the pieces arriving at any particular address make no sense and do not fit when an attempt is made to put them together. Ultimately, however, it turns out that when all the pieces delivered to all the people are brought together, they are parts of three different jigsaws. Moreover, each jigsaw carries an original oil painting totally characteristic of one of the missing artists, as if this is the way the three artists, wherever they are, have decided to let the world know they are still alive.

Unfortunately the Cross-correspondences were much more complicated than that, so that it is difficult to single out for display any of the themes. Some of the themes or puzzles were delivered over several years.

The objection that Mrs Verrall, herself a classical scholar and anxious to prove the survival of her husband, could have concocted the puzzle subconsciously and secreted bits and pieces of it in the automatists' subconsciousnesses, has to overcome the fact that after her death in 1916 the Cross-correspondences continued just as vigorously and ingeniously as before.

In addition, a number of the Cross-correspondence cases involve a two-way process, the investigators' efforts at decipherment producing a reaction on the part of the Script Intelligence when it saw it had to make things easier for the investi-

gators to produce a solution. In fact, the necessity to invoke the operation of telepathy, clairvoyance and precognition on a massive scale in order to avoid the simple hypothesis that the communicators were who they said they were, shows the power of the Cross-correspondences in displaying the paranormal in action.

The mediumship of one of the automatists, Mrs Willett, was studied closely over the years by Sir Oliver Lodge, Gerald William Balfour and Mrs Sidgwick. Because of Mrs Willett's particular gift of 'seeing' and 'hearing' the communicators, it was possible for the investigators to have long direct conversations with them. The opportunity to test and assess the communicators' statements and responses to questions, together with their personality traits as revealed in these conversations, enabled the investigators to form firm opinions as to the nature of these unseen entities, which claimed to be the spirits of Frederic Myers, Henry Sidgwick, Edmund Gurney and various others. They spoke of their plan to prove their survival after death, and described the experiments they were carrying out to try to improve the means of communication. They maintained that the Willett method was better than the trance-medium method, but it was still immensely difficult to get the medium's mind to deliver the right words or expressions.

Whatever the communicators were – whether they were who they say they were, or something else – they certainly acted as if they were intelligent and knowledgeable. They had convincing and consistent personalities, very strongly reminiscent of the people they claimed to be.

They also claimed that their new state was in many ways bewildering. The Gurney entity, communicating through Mrs Willett, said on one occasion: 'You never seem to realise how little we know ... sometimes I know and can't get it through, but very often I don't *know*', while on another occasion the Frederic Myers entity, communicating through Mrs Holland, wrote, in something like despair:

The nearest simile I can find to express the difficulties of sending a message – is that I appear to be standing behind a sheet of frosted glass

– which blurs sight and deadens sounds – dictating feebly to a reluctant and somewhat obtuse secretary. A feeling of terrible impotence burdens me – I am so powerless to tell what means so much – I cannot get into communication with those who would understand and believe me.

St Paul wrote: 'For now we see through a glass darkly, but then face to face.' If some of the communicators of the Cross-correspondences are to be believed, the view from the other side is not much clearer.

SEE ALSO *ESP: Life after death; Palm Sunday case; Psychic music, art and literature; Society for Psychical Research; Telepathy.*

PALM SUNDAY CASE

One of the most famous Cross-correspondences cases, the Palm Sunday case, takes its name from the death from typhus on Palm Sunday in 1875 of a young woman, Mary Catherine Lyttleton, shortly before her twenty-fifth birthday. Her death was a tragic loss to Arthur Balfour, who was in love with her. He never married, and for the rest of his life until his death in 1930 he spent every Palm Sunday in seclusion with Mary's sister in remembrance of her.

When Mary died he had given his mother's emerald ring to her sister to be buried on her finger. He had also had a silver box made for a lock of Mary's hair, cut off during her illness; this box was lined with purple and engraved with periwinkles and other spring flowers. In addition, a photograph existed of Mary standing at the foot of a staircase and holding a candlestick with a candle in it. Throughout Arthur Balfour's long career, during which he became British Prime Minister, he kept these matters to himself.

The Palm Sunday scripts were produced by Mrs Verrall, her daughter Helen, Mrs Holland and Mrs Willett. They seemed to contain evidence that Mary Lyttleton and Francis Maitland Balfour (Arthur's

Mary Lyttleton, who died at the age of twenty-five and was adored by Arthur Balfour (later British Prime Minister). He never married, and became convinced of her continuing personality through the persuasive evidence of the Cross-correspondences.

younger brother, killed in a mountaineering accident in 1882) were trying to convince the living that they had survived their bodily deaths and that Mary's love for Arthur was as strong as ever. The investigators who studied the scripts were Arthur Balfour's elder brother Gerald, Mrs Henry Sidgwick and Mr J. G. Piddington.

Between 1901 and 1912 scripts were obtained by Mrs Holland and the Verrall women that contained numerous cryptic fragments – words, phrases, symbols and drawings, many of them classical and easily recognised – but without any understanding of why they should have been inserted in their automatic writings. There were references to the Palm Maiden, May Blossom, the Blessed Damozel and Berenice. Candles and candlesticks appeared; mention was made of a lock of hair, something purple, a metal box, a periwinkle. It was as if these years formed a long period of preparation during which the essential clues were scattered profusely among other material. The denouement came in 1916, when every fragment fell into place.

By that year Mrs Willett too had begun producing scripts, and had developed her distinctive style of mediumship in which she could 'see' and 'hear' the communicators while still being able to talk to the investigators. The intelligence behind the script now implored Arthur Balfour (who was only marginally interested in psychical research) to sit with Mrs Willett. The resulting script referred explicitly to Mary and to the hitherto unintelligible fragments or clues. For the first time Arthur now told his brother about the casket he had had made for Mary's lock of hair. From then on, in the years that remained to him, his hope that the girl he had loved so shortly in her life and so long in his memory was still waiting for him strengthened to a firm conviction.

The case was studied for many years by people of high intelligence who saw in it, at the very least, paranormal activity on a massive scale. For some it also showed survival after bodily death.

SEE ALSO *Cross-correspondences; ESP; Ghosts; Life after death; Near death experience; Psychic music, art and literature; Society for Psychical Research; Telepathy.*

DIRECT VOICE

One of the most controversial forms of spirit communication is that known as direct voice, when the discarnate communicators use the vocal equipment of the medium in order to speak to the sitters. All too often the gruff or squeaky voices uttered by the entranced medium seem like amateur imper-sonations, to be believed only by the most credulous or grief-stricken.

One of the most famous of the few British mediums to practise direct voice was Leslie Flint, who retired in 1976 and whose forty-two-year career was rigorously, and regularly, investigated. Brought up as a member of the Salvation Army, Flint nevertheless showed marked psychic talents which he developed with a local Spiritualist group. At first the spirits, using his energy, amplified their voices through a trumpet, but as his powers grew, the voices simply happened in the air about him. One of the first of many dead celebrities to use his gifts was 'R. V.', who appeared to Flint in Arab dress. A German woman, unknown to the medium, wrote to him about a message passed to

The discarnate Oscar Wilde is one of the many famous spirits who are said to have communicated through 'direct voice' medium Leslie Flint. Being dead seemed to have robbed the writer of his sharp wit – and his slight Irish accent.

her Spiritualist group by the spirit of Rudolf Valentino, who had given them Flint's name and address. This corroboration of the contact was greatly appreciated by the fledgling medium.

Over the years a galaxy of film stars and literary lions spoke through Flint and were duly recorded, while investigators from the media and the Society for Psychical Research took every opportunity to try to catch him out in perpetrating a fraud. Although he was searched, bound and gagged with sticky tape, and once had his mouth filled with coloured water in an attempt to prevent ventriloquism, the voices still came through. Infra-red camera techniques picked up the outline of an 'ectoplasmic voice box' hovering 60 centimetres in the air above the medium, through which the communicators spoke, but which dissolved when Flint came out of his trance.

Two sitters in particular built up a comprehensive library of recordings from the seances. George Woods and Betty Greene taped their sittings with Flint for over fifteen years, accumulating some five hundred tape recordings. These were believed to include messages from Oscar Wilde, Amy Johnson, George Bernard Shaw, pioneering female doctor Elizabeth Garratt Anderson and a host of lesser known people such as 'Mickey', Flint's young Irish spirit guide.

As the years passed, new celebrities 'came through'; they included Marilyn Monroe, who revealed that she had not committed suicide but had taken an accidental overdose of barbiturates. However, it is here that suspicions about the true nature of the communicating entities are compounded. In the last few years extremely persuasive evidence has come to light about the conspiracy surrounding Marilyn's death. Whatever happened that night in August 1962 it was considerably more complicated than a simple overdose – yet the spirit purporting to be the sex goddess did not even refer to those events, as might be reasonably expected.

Neither are the tapes particularly impressive; 'Oscar Wilde' seems to have lost the keen edge of his wit, although mercifully his bitterness about his disgrace has also disappeared. Dr Garratt Anderson's medical advice to a sitter consisted of urging him to 'take things easy', and spirit guide 'Mickey' sounds like an actress playing a child for the radio. Yet 'Amy Johnson', although she appears to have no technical knowledge of flying, sounds remarkably like the living woman as recorded in the 1930s.

If we reject the fraud hypothesis, are we to assume that these vocal impersonations are somehow the result of Flint's exteriorisation? Are they split-off parts of his unconscious making mischievous drama? Or does death rob us of so much of our knowledge and mannerisms that we seem like poor radio actors trying to convince?

The answer may lie in another direction, although it poses many more questions. It may be that objective outside entities, not necessarily what they claim to be, use the channels provided by entranced mediums – the better to deceive.

SEE ALSO *Cosmic Joker; The Devil; Helen Duncan; Ectoplasm; Electronic voice phenomenon; Entity enigma; Fairies; Eileen Garrett; Ghosts; Katie King; Life after death; Carmine Mirabelli; Ouija board and planchette; Eusapia Palladino; Philip experiment; Psychic music, art and literature; Psychokinesis; Seance-room phenomena; Society for Psychical Research; SORRAT; Doris Stokes; Visions of the Virgin Mary.*

ELECTRONIC VOICE PHENOMENON

In 1959 Swedish film-maker Friedrich Jurgenson discovered anomalous voices on his tape recording of birdsong, which he interpreted as messages from dead relatives. In the succeeding thirty years Jurgenson and his Latvian-born colleague Dr Konstantin Raudive have accumulated vast stores of such tapes, and have persuaded many others of the authenticity of the 'electronic voice phenomenon', (EVP), although most parapsychologists remain sceptical about their claims.

One of the problems involved is that the messages 'come through' in fragments and may be jumbled with static and other noise. Critics have pointed out that not enough control was exercised on the experiments; transmissions from radio and the police have often been interpreted by the faithful as messages from the Other Side. Indeed, the subjectivity of interpretation remains the greatest problem with the phenomenon – sounds made by the accidental brushing of the tape recorder with fingers have been 'recognised' as the voices of the dead. With the very weak and fragmentary nature of the voices, a short tape recording of about fifteen minutes requires many hours of painstaking analysis, which is not always very fruitful, and the concentration involved may lead itself to auditory hallucination.

In 1972 Richard Sheargold wrote in *Psychic News*: 'There is no longer room for doubt that the science of psychics has at last achieved its first real breakthrough.' But after some further years of research, Sheargold, while admitting that the voice phenomenon is 'beyond any doubt objective', said that he was 'ever more sceptical of its weak and ambiguous results', and thought extended periods of time spent listening to the tapes 'very unwise'.

Yet unambiguous, unexplained sounds on tape are not unknown, although many of them – perhaps perversely – arise spontaneously rather than during EVP recording sessions. Many people have captured curious, metallic, sing-song voices on tape. These may be the result of the unimaginable difficulties involved in discarnate communication, or they may be the voices of alien intelligences or elementals engaging in a charade.

Some sounds are only too unmistakable, however. One psychic found himself listening to a Nuremburg rally, complete with ranting dictator and goose-stepping feet. A journalist who left a tape recorder running in Borley church later heard chanting and footsteps approaching; there had been no one there but himself.

There have been cases of radios picking up old wireless messages – some listeners, to their horror, heard the SOS from the *Titanic*, over forty years after it sank. It seems that radio waves simply go on for ever, being invisibly present continually; a suitably tuned receiver may pick them up years after their broadcast. In a similar, but less understood, fashion, events that encompassed great emotion (such as the Nuremberg rallies) may be imprinted on the ether and replayed in the future.

Or it may be that an individual has unacknowledged psychic gifts that react with a discarnate entity who chooses to communicate via that person's radio or tape recorder, using a form of psychokinesis.

Many of the voices, with their almost nonsensical, fragmentary messages, are reminiscent of the output of a ouija board or planchette, both notorious contraptions for attracting the denizens of lower astral worlds – elementals. There is a real danger of becoming mentally contaminated by these negative forces, which may fasten on to the EVP to masquerade as discarnate loved ones.

SEE ALSO *Allergies and psi; Boggle threshold; Cosmic Joker; Cross-correspondences; Electric people; Entity enigma; Ghosts; Life after death; Men in Black; Ouija board and planchette; Psychokinesis; Rosenheim poltergeist; Telephone calls from the dead; Timeslips; UFO paradox.*

GHOSTS

Professor H. H. Price, a former President of the Society for Psychical Research (SPR), wrote:

The tea-party question, 'Do you believe in ghosts?' is one of the most ambiguous that can be asked. But if we take it to mean 'Do you believe that people sometimes experience apparitions?', the answer is that they certainly do. No one who examines the evidence can come to any other conclusion. Instead of disputing the facts, we must try to explain them.

In its early years the SPR (founded in 1882) devoted considerable energy to the Ghost Question. In 1889 the society undertook a mammoth *Census of Hallucinations*, with the full approval of the International Congress on Experimental Psychology. The question was put: 'Have you ever, when believing yourself to be completely awake, had a vivid impression of seeing or being touched by a living being or inanimate object, or of hearing a voice; which impression, so far as you could discover, was not due to any external cause?'

Of the seventeen thousand replies, nearly 10 per cent reported such an experience; one in twenty of these had seen a convincing apparition, while one in thirty recognised it. There were a few provocative cases of partial hallucination – where the witness saw only a hand or legs. There were twenty-five reports of animal hallucinations, one a horse with a coach. Roughly twice as many apparitions of the living were reported compared with true 'ghosts' (apparitions of the dead), and over a hundred cases were collective.

Apparitions of the living may be labelled as reciprocal out-of-the-body experiences, doppelgängers (or doubles), or simply (as in the case of Ruth), hallucinations. They may be deliberate projections by a dreamer, occultist or curious researcher, or they may apparently wander off on their own without the knowledge of their 'original'. They may be taken as real by percipients, or believed to be ghosts due to the incongruity of the time, place and circumstances of their appearance.

Apparitions of the dead may be 'crisis apparitions' – in which the percipient has a hallucination of a relative or friend at the moment of their death or a great trauma. Many of these cases show a marked sense of reality; during the First World War a young woman was working in her kitchen when she heard the door open. Turning, she saw her brother come in. He was, as far as she knew, battling in the trenches of Flanders, but soldiers did come home quite suddenly on leave. He was deathly white and his uniform was covered in mud. He said: 'Put the kettle on, Maud. I'm dead tired.' She complied with his request, came back to the seat he had taken – and there was no one there. She later discovered her brother had died at the very moment she saw him.

There are hundreds of such cases on record, and thousands more are part of family legends the world over. Sometimes these apparitions speak, as did this soldier; sometimes they are wearing unfamiliar clothes or bear some mark or wound that they were in the process of sustaining when their vision was seen. Occasionally they are seen in the position in which they were later discovered to have died; one man was seen apparently kneeling – in fact he had been killed propped up in this

The woman who casts no shadow was photographed by members of the SORRAT group. Believed to be the ghostly apparition of 'Myra', who had been communicating with them, she took them to that location and suggested they take a photograph – although they saw no one there at the time.

position by the weight of other bodies.

One of the most remarkable cases on record of a crisis apparition is that of Lieutenant McConnel, who was killed when his plane nose-dived in thick fog on 7 December 1918. At 11.30 that morning McConnel set off on a duty flight for Tadcaster, about 100 kilometres from his Royal Flying Corps base at Scampton, Lincolnshire. He told his roommate, Lieutenant Larkin, that he expected to be back for tea. At about 3.15 Larkin heard McConnel clatter into the living quarters and utter his typical greeting of 'Hello, boy!' Larkin looked up and saw McConnel in the doorway, in normal flying clothes but, oddly, wearing his naval cap. They exchanged a few pleasantries, then McConnel said: 'Well, cheerio!', closed the door and left the room. A Lieutenant Garner-Smith came in and enquired whether or not McConnel was back; Larkin said he was. A little later he discovered that McConnel had died at the very moment he had apparently come back and talked to him.

Various theories are put forward to account for

the phenomenon of crisis apparitions. In the McConnel–Larkin case it has been suggested that Larkin subconsciously worried about his friend flying in such thick fog, and externalised an image of him as a kind of wish-fulfilment that he was safe. Or perhaps the dying man, in whatever split second he had before death overtook him, projected himself safe and happy to his destination. Yet, in the other case mentioned above, the soldier was not perceived as well and happy by his sister, but rather deeply fatigued in the most realistic way.

Many 'ghosts' are, of course, well and truly dead when they are perceived, although some may appear solid and lifelike and others insubstantial. The remarkable haunting of the Despard home in Cheltenham in the 1880s by a woman in black began with the sound of her footsteps; then her apparently solid form was seen repeatedly by the household for several years – but during that time she began to lose substance. The last time she was seen she was distinctly transparent. Yet at the height of her powers of manifestation she even seemed real to a dog, who wagged his tail and fawned at her – until her true nature dawned on him, when he ran away trembling.

Sometimes the percipient seems imbued with paranormal powers. There are cases where people have seen details of dress that, at the distance they were standing from the ghost, they could not normally have noticed. One little girl who saw the apparition of her grandfather in a mirror 'noticed' his footwear, although his feet were out of sight, and described his manner of walking, despite the fact that he took just one step as she watched. These cases are reminiscent of some encounters with UFOs, where the percipient believes he has dreamt the experience but later discovers physical evidence of its occurrence. The merging of states of consciousness in the witness is taken by some researchers to indicate a manipulation of reality by

Ghost in Raynham Hall, Norfolk.

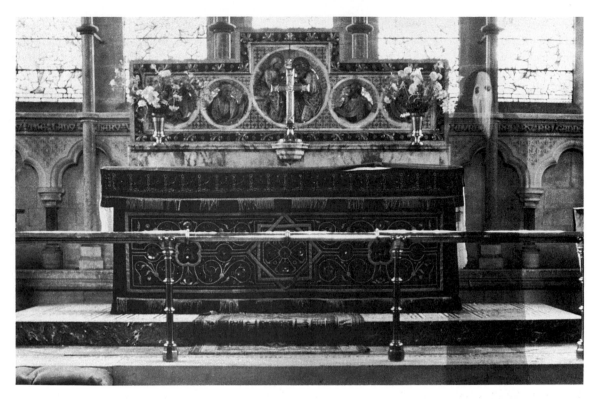

Ghoulish figure that appeared on the developed print of a photograph taken by the Rev. K. F. Lord of the interior of Newby Church, near Ripon, North Yorkshire, in the early 1960s.

the controlling entities – this may be true in some cases of haunting.

Some witnesses to ghostly visitations describe an edgy or oppressed feeling just before the encounter, similar to that experienced by the Misses Moberley and Jourdain during their apparent timeslip at Versailles. Other witnesses feel drained after their experiences, as if some vital force has actually been used by the entity in order to manifest.

In the case of haunted houses or specific places associated with ghosts, it has been suggested that great emotion, such as the despair preceding suicide, may somehow imprint on the surroundings an image of the person or event involved, which is then 'replayed', like a video tape, over and over again. The ghost is not, it is comforting to know, really the soul of the dead person, but rather an empty shell, a kind of hologrammatic representation of their former selves.

Pioneering psychical researcher Frederic Myers wrote that

the behaviour of phantasms of the dead suggests dreams dreamt by the deceased person whose phantasms appear. The actions of these phantasms may therefore be expected to be vague and meaningless, or at any rate to offer little response or adaptation to the actions of the persons who observe them.

Dr Raynor C. Johnson agrees, writing that 'an apparition of a human being is not a centre of consciousness; it is, so to speak, a psychical marionette given temporary life by some quite separate centre of consciousness'. Ghosts can be fascinating and should be a valid subject for study, but one must look elsewhere for evidence of an afterlife.

SEE ALSO *Case of Ruth; Consensus reality; Doppelgängers; Entity enigma; Hallucinations; Life after death;*

Near death experience; Out-of-the-body experiences; Society for Psychical Research; Timeslips; Traumas and psi; Tulpas; UFO paradox; Visions of the Virgin Mary.

TELEPHONE CALLS FROM THE DEAD

A phenomenon guaranteed to crash the boggle barrier is that of receiving a telephone call from someone who is dead. American researcher D. Scott Rogo collected enough data on this subject to write his *Phone Calls from the Dead* (1980). Strangely, the book received little attention from either the popular press or the parapsychological fraternity. It seemed too outrageous to take seriously.

Yet at least one respected parapsychologist became involved in the paranormal because of just such an 'impossible' telephone call. Walter Uphoff's secretary, due to go into hospital for a minor operation, reminded him to call his insurance broker. When Uphoff eventually called him he was told that the secretary had already done so; it was then discovered that she had, in fact, died under the anaesthetic some hours before she made the call. There was no doubt about the time of her death, the time of the call, her identity (as given to the insurance office) and the fact that the details of the insurance transaction were those regarding Uphoff's business and no one else's.

Uphoff, telling the story to the College of Psychic Studies in London in the early 1980s, said that that single incident proved to him that post mortem survival, if only for a short while, was a fact. Since the telephone call, he and his wife Mary Jo have become enthusiastic researchers of the paranormal, specialising in macro-PK such as thoughtography and metal bending. (Their book *Mind Over Matter: Implications of Masuaki Kiyota's PK Feats with Metal and Film* was published in 1980.)

With the inventions in the nineteenth and early twentieth centuries of photography, sound recording, movie film and the telephone, Spiritualists – such as Sir Arthur Conan Doyle – welcomed the new potential in communicating with the dead. Yet the use of such technology in this respect has been highly controversial and very limited, as experiments with the Electronic Voice Phenomenon (or 'Raudive voices') have shown. As for photography, some genuinely paranormal photographs have been taken, although the 'extras' have usually appeared spontaneously rather than to order, and fakes have outnumbered the genuine many times over.

One theory suggests that the telephone is the ultimate symbol of communication, almost its archetype, and therefore the perfect channel for discarnate messages. Using the telephone is – theoretically, at least – less threatening and arguably less difficult than utilising the services of even the best medium. It also has the psychological advantage of seeming more matter-of-fact and having no quasi-religious overtones.

However, discarnate entities talking over the telephone is not a phenomenon that lends itself to laboratory testing; after all, there is no number the researchers could dial to summon up the dead. One has to wait for the message that might never come, or may not come telephonically.

Sceptics point out that auditory hallucinations are very common, especially among the bereaved, and being mistaken about hearing the telephone ring is an everyday occurrence. Put the two together with a desperation to talk to a loved one, and perhaps the result is a belief that the dead really have made a telephone call. There is also, of course, the possibility of cruel hoaxes.

On the other hand, only a few generations of the living have had the experience of using a telephone. Perhaps the discarnate will find the increasingly sophisticated apparatus easier to manipulate, although we may never be able to return the calls.

SEE ALSO *Boggle threshold; Case of Ruth; Direct voice; Electronic voice phenomenon; Eleventh-hour syndrome; Experimenter effect; Explanations; Hallucinations; Life after death; Limits of science; Mediums; Parapsychology; Psi-mediated instrumental response; Sentient machinery; Thoughtography.*

OUT-OF-THE-BODY EXPERIENCES

Between one person in ten and one person in twenty is likely to have had an out-of-the-body experience (OOBE) once in his or her life. The literature of psychical research is full of stories of both spontaneous and induced OOBEs, and rigorous methods have been devised by parapsychologists to test the claims of those who have them.

Typically, spontaneous OOBEs might occur as a result of a physical trauma – a blow to the head, for example. Experients report the sensation of floating above their bodies, which they perceive with disinterest or even amusement. A slight buzzing noise often accompanies the 'going out', and some people experience the sensation of being let out on a piece of elastic – 'the silver cord' – which links their consciousness to the top of the head. Many people report conversations they overheard while out of the body, or distant scenes they could not normally know, and later discover these details to be correct. The most frequent emotions accompanying the experience are euphoria and a sense of well-being, although a small percentage feel that they must get back into their bodies or they will be possessed by other entities.

Occultists have long believed that we experience OOBEs during sleep, and that dreams are the garbled recollections of our adventures when out of the body. Flying dreams in particular are taken as proof that this happens, but modern dream research indicates that the consciousness still resides in the body during sleep. It may be that some element of consciousness, however, can split off and rove about, for this appears to happen during remote viewing, a similar phenomenon to that which used to be known as 'travelling clairvoyance'.

Occasionally the 'astral body' can be seen by others, and is often taken as the real person – these are known as 'reciprocal' cases. One American woman who dreamed she floated nearly 1500 kilo-

metres to see her mother discovered that she had been working in the kitchen at the time of the dream, and had seen her daughter, dressed as she knew she had been and with her hair 'combed nice' in a pony tail. The dogs also saw the girl and became excited.

Psychics and occultists can induce OOBEs, often using a method similar to self-hypnosis, and have scored highly in laboratory tests designed to explore the extent of their travelling clairvoyance. In the USA Ingo Swann and Keith 'Blue' Harary have proved successful at remote viewing and inducing OOBEs, picking up target information while out of the body that they could not have learned in any other way. Dr Charles Tart and, in Britain, Professor Arthur Ellison have devised rigorous tests for the 'travellers', and have concluded that some form of consciousness does leave the body and is capable of reporting new information.

One disturbing aspect of such experimental work is its implication in espionage. Indeed, some wit has coined the term 'ESPionage' for the phenomenon that may allow invisible secret agents to enter foreign establishments for the purpose of spying.

Sceptics about OOBEs point out that the phenomenon can be induced by the taking of certain drugs, such as LSD, and that it merely gives the illusion of travelling, gleaning information paranormally and so on. Yet there is no convincing evidence that drug-induced sensations akin to OOBEs are, in fact, similar to the spontaneous phenomena, and the veridical evidence for reciprocal and 'ESPionage-type' cases is very strong.

Those who have a near death experience (NDE) report, without exception, having had an OOBE as a component of the experience. It is, as it were, mandatory to have one in order to rid oneself of the encumbrance of the body and its pains. Alan Gauld, in his *Mediumship and Survival* (1983), says: 'Undergoing an NDE may change a patient's whole religious and philosophical outlook. He has, it seems to him, learned by experience what it is like to die.'

SEE ALSO *Near death experience; Possession; Parapsychology; Remote viewing; Shamanism; Witchcraft.*

NEAR DEATH EXPERIENCE

Today, when the dying are wired to life-support systems and those at the point of death are shunted out of the way of the living, death is the greatest taboo, and dying the greatest failure. Yet those very resuscitation machines that seem so impersonal have achieved a remarkable side-effect – they have enabled the clinically dead to come back and tell us what it is like to die. Since Dr Elisabeth Kubler-Ross's pioneering work with the dying became widely known in the early 1970s, the near death experience (NDE) has been seen as one of the major breakthroughs in our understanding of the greatest mystery.

One of the most significant aspects of this deeply personal experience is its consistency; those who have reported NDEs come from different cultures and have varying religious expectations about an afterlife – yet the experiences they had are remarkably similar. The 'core experience' appears to have five stages: an altered state of feeling; separation from the physical body; entering the darkness, typically a dark tunnel; seeing the light; and entering a beautiful, inner world, which is frequently described as 'Heaven'.

The first stage may come quite suddenly in the midst of the subject's pain and distress. Pure bliss seems to flood the patient's whole being – as one NDEr said: 'I felt more truly alive than ever before.' A woman who had 'died' recalled: 'I then passed into another dimension. I felt no pain any more and was conscious of the most wonderful golden light. A feeling of absolute peace and bliss flooded over me.'

Over half of those who have reported having had an NDE had an out-of-the-body experience in which they saw themselves apparently lying dead. Accompanying emotions included relief, curiosity and even amusement. One woman who witnessed the medical staff desperately trying to resuscitate her said: 'I was amused at all this fuss going on with my body, as it did not concern me a bit.'

Many of those who have this experience remember having listened to the conversations of those around them, or having floated off to other rooms

Durdana Khan with paintings of heaven – painted from memory. As a young child she died for a few minutes and later described going to heaven and meeting God. Many people who have been resuscitated have described a similar near death experience.

in the building. Later investigation often reveals that the conversations they had overheard had actually taken place, and that the knowledge about the layout of the hospital was paranormally acquired.

The next stage involves travelling, often at incredible speed, down a long black tunnel. The experience is one of peace or growing euphoria. Light appears at the end of the tunnel, towards which the individual consciousness is being propelled. The light is unimaginably intense, but not painful or threatening. Several NDErs report the presence of a being of light who can be sensed rather than seen at this stage. Total happiness accompanies this perception.

The last stage involves entering the world of light, which is so transcendentally beautiful that it is literally beyond words. Many people report sensing 'the music of the spheres' and the colour blue. Little Durdana Khan 'died' for fifteen minutes while her father, a doctor, worked desperately to save her. When he succeeded, she reported that 'God is blue'.

Many of the NDErs come back with precognitive knowledge. One woman described meeting on 'the other side' her mother, who was preparing to receive her Aunt Ethel. When the woman returned to normal consciousness she discovered that her aunt had, indeed, died suddenly.

A controversial aspect of the NDE is that of negative, or terrifying, experiences while being 'dead'. Some researchers deny that any such states have been reported, while some cardiologists, such as Michael Rawlings, maintain that a small percentage of those who 'die' are glad to return. Common feelings associated with negative NDEs are panic, terror and complete desolation and loneliness. Archetypal hellish horrors assail them, or in some cases, the experiences relate more to the notion of purgatory. Many of those who report negative NDEs are attempted suicides.

Most people who return from death, however, do so with the utmost reluctance, yet with a strong sense of purpose. Commonly they had been told while undergoing the experience that their work on Earth was not yet completed and they were urged back. Sometimes they made the decision to return, but in most cases they had no choice. Most NDErs are completely changed by their experience, becoming less materialistic and more God-centred, loving and compassionate. None of those who reported a positive NDE continued to fear death.

Sceptics have described all the 'symptoms' of the NDE as 'the brain's last fling' before complete extinction – as a way of hypnotising the subject into quiescence before the great trauma of death. Many of them believe that the inner visions are drug-related – yet a high proportion of the reported NDEs do not involve medication in any form. Straining to fit the facts into the ultimate rationalist reductionism, some sceptics assert that the NDEs represent wishful thinking, overlooking the fact that many NDErs wished for oblivion and did not have any expectations about an afterlife – yet they still experienced such a state. As the founder of the International Association for Near Death Studies (IANDS), Professor Kenneth Ringer, says: 'The wishful thinking explanation is . . . just wishful thinking!'

The NDE is one of the most exciting revelations in the history of mankind. It has provided comfort for thousands, besides adding to our knowledge about the fallacy we call death.

SEE ALSO *Cross-correspondences; Explanations; Formative causation; Healing; Left and right brain; Life after death; Out-of-the-body experiences; Palm Sunday case.*

LIFE AFTER DEATH

Shakespeare called it 'the undiscover'd country from which no traveller returns'; certainly any statement about the nature of the afterlife must remain a matter either of faith or of some scepticism. Yet there is a solid body of evidence – although not proof – of a post mortem survival in the trance utterances and automatic (or 'directed') writings of mediums. Willingly suspending disbelief, one may extrapolate from the most cogent of these communications a consistent pattern for the nature of the afterlife.

In his important book *Living On* (subtitled: *A study of altering consciousness after death*), Paul Beard takes the posthumous communications of such notables as T. E. Lawrence, Sir Oliver Lodge and Frederic Myers to the élite band of mediums – such as Geraldine Cummins and Rosamond Lehmann – to illustrate what we may expect after death.

Often the nature of our death determines our immediate experience of the afterlife. Violent or sudden death may lead the individual to suffer a kind of post mortem shock, or even to deny his death altogether. An illusory hospital ward may be created to lull the newcomer into quiescence, or the newly departed soul may discover – the hard way – that he is really dead. The discarnate Edgar Wallace became angry at what he considered to be a joke in very bad taste – a papier mâché effigy of himself in a coffin – before realising its true nature, and relinquishing his hold on Earth life.

But the overwhelming majority of those who die awake to a bright, blissful world (described most convincingly by those who have had a near death experience), where they are greeted by dead relatives and friends. There is often a great need for sleep, and consciousness comes and goes as the spirit acclimatises to the new world.

Several communicators, notably Frederic Myers, refer to the first stage of posthumous life as 'Summerland'. This sphere is essentially mindstuff, an ideoplastic plane where even a casual thought may become 'real'. To many unambitious souls this will no doubt seem like Heaven, for the mindstuff happily creates villas by the seaside and illusory dinners, complete with fat cigars afterwards.

T. E. Lawrence, 'Lawrence of Arabia', spoke after death, it is claimed, on the nature of the afterlife.

Nobler-minded souls have little involvement with Summerland.

At this level there are also Hells, or 'Winterland', where those in the grip of strong negative emotions or addictions exist in utter desolation. But, as the discarnate former nun Frances Banks said, 'No one is ever left comfortless unless he wishes it.' The only power that keeps the individual in Hell is that of his own helplessness. Regular visits from higher beings may or may not help him to realise he can move upwards if he wishes.

Then comes the Judgement, which bears little resemblance to the medieval concept of Judgement Day, but appears to be yet more devastating. The person's life unrolls before him like a video recording, but he appears to play all the other parts in his life, feeling all the slights and injustices heaped upon them by himself throughout his incarnation.

One can discover three or more levels of spiritual

awakening that are known as 'Heavens'. To a lower soul, however, they would be beyond appreciation, and are not even sought by them. In these rarefied spheres the spirit learns from his group soul, whom he has known in many lifetimes, and discovers more about the fine attunement of spirituality. It is here that it is decided – with his full co-operation – whether or not he will be reincarnated, and if so, under what circumstances.

Not everyone finds the higher planes comfortable. T. E. Lawrence ('Lawrence of Arabia') discovered relationships with women to be just as fraught with misunderstandings as in life. (Although there can be no sex or lust, there is a union of soul-bodies that is greatly prized among discarnate lovers.)

In the light of the afterlife experience, perhaps not surprisingly, many people change their minds about certain cherished views. Significantly, Conan Doyle's notions of Spiritualist communications underwent a radical re-evaluation. As Paul Beard says: 'After his death he says he found many communications to be less valid and accurate than he had supposed, and this disquieted him.'

SEE ALSO *Cross-correspondences; Eileen Garrett; Ghosts; Karma; Near death experience; Other dimensions; Out-of-the-body experiences; Palm Sunday case; Psychic music, art and literature; Reincarnation; Society of Psychical Research.*

VAMPIRES

The dead who rise from their graves to suck the blood of the living – vampires, the undead – fall into the grisly twilight world between the occult and the paranormal. Some, such as occultist Dion Fortune, believed that vampires are Earthbound spirits who feed on the living in order to maintain some kind of consciousness, or are the deliberately animated thoughtforms of the magical adept. But most researchers tend to see the myriad vampire legends as hysterical misreporting of natural events, such as the results of premature burial.

Yet such was the ubiquity of vampire reports

from the Balkans during the sixteenth, seventeenth and eighteenth centuries that contemporary commentators wrote of a 'vampire epidemic'. Stories abounded, especially in Romania, of whole villages being terrorised by the undead, who rose out of their graves to suck the lifeblood of the villagers. Inevitably, posses of clergy, medics, lawyers and locals would trace the individual vampire to his or her grave and find the monster lying as if asleep in the coffin. The procedure was then to drive a metal stake through its heart and hack off its head.

Many vampires were said to utter terrifying shrieks as the stake was hammered home, and they would gush blood, or other body fluid, from the wound. This would not be surprising if the 'vampire' were not, in fact, dead at all. Premature burial was, until very recently, horrifyingly common – one eighteenth-century graveyard that was dug up to make way for a car park in Paris in the early 1980s was discovered to have a third of its graves occupied by the corpses of those who had tried to break out of their coffins.

Occult novelist Dennis Wheatley believed that many rumours of vampirism arose because vagabonds often broke into graveyards to seek shelter in times of hardship. Terrified locals catching sight of these ragged and skinny intruders might well come to believe that they were vampires. Yet it was not merely superstitious peasants who believed in the reality of the undead: the philosopher Jean-Jacques Rousseau wrote: 'If ever there was in the world a warranted and proven history, it is that of vampires. Nothing is lacking: official reports, testimonials of persons of standing, of surgeons, of clergymen, of judges; the judicial evidence is all-embracing.'

Very strange things do happen to dead bodies. Some saints develop post mortem stigmata, move their hands as in ritual blessing, give off fragrant oils that have curative properties, or are proven to be incorruptible – often despite having been buried in conditions that should, if anything, have hastened decomposition. Because few bodies, except those of putative saints, are ever exhumed, it is impossible to estimate the number of incorruptible corpses. Some of them may have been mistaken for vampires.

Most people today associate vampirism with the fictional character Dracula, inspiration of many films, who was the anti-hero created by Irish novelist and theatre manager Bram Stoker in 1897. Stoker set his tale of Gothic horror in Transylvania, then in the Austro-Hungarian Empire but now part of Romania, and based his aristocratic vampire on legends about Vlad Dracula, a fifteenth-century prince whose bloodthirstiness reached epic proportions. 'Dracula' had two possible meanings: Vlad's father was called Dracul, so his name may merely have meant 'son of . . .' But it could also mean devil. Vlad's nickname was 'the Impaler'; his greatest pleasure was to have a banquet under a forest of spikes on which thousands were impaled – taking days to die. He was a monster certainly, but there is no evidence that he actually drank blood; a descendant of his family, however, did.

The Countess Elisabeth Bathory was a seventeenth-century noblewoman of Slovakia, whose perverted belief that her youth would only remain if she bathed in the blood of virgins led to the torture and death of six hundred local girls. She was walled up alive in 1611; it is said that her ghost still screams.

Christopher Lee portrays the 'blood count', Dracula. Vampirism, however, is not merely a silver-screen creation; it provided one of the most well-attested epidemics of paranormal menace in Eastern Europe in the seventeenth century.

The 'Blood Countess' became the prototype for Sheridan le Fanu's bestseller *Carmilla*, and prepared the Victorians for the horrors of *Dracula*. Stoker had researched the topography of Transylvania at the British Museum, and had spent many hours in discussion with a Hungarian professor, Arminius Vambery. He may also have had occult knowledge on the matter, for records show that Stoker was a member of the Hermetic Order of the Golden Dawn. *Dracula* was an instant and lasting success, the fascination of its subject lying in its heady mixture of the supernatural and of the seduction of the innocent.

While theatre-goers and film fans enjoyed their innocent vampire evenings, the likes of John George Haigh, the 'acid bath murderer', felt drawn to drink the blood of others in order to sustain themselves. On one occasion, Haigh killed a young man called Swann and tapped a vein, drinking about 'a wineglassful' of the victim's blood. Haigh was hanged in 1949.

In 1973 fear of vampires killed a Polish immigrant who lived in Stoke-on-Trent. Demetrious Myicura was found dead amid great squalor; bags of salt had been placed between his legs and behind his head; dishes containing excrement mixed with garlic were found on the window-ledge and under the bed. The man had died, said the coroner, by choking on a pickled onion, but the prevalence of garlic, ritually placed, reminded one of the investigating officers of vampire stories. The 'pickled onion' was found to be a clove of garlic; terrified of a vampire attack, he had tried to sleep with one in his mouth.

The widespread belief in the power of garlic as a prophylactic against vampires may arise from its authentic biochemical properties. When garlic 'sweats' it gives off moisture that repels flies, once believed to carry the plague. But if eaten it has the effect of being a blood purifier.

Dion Fortune believed that many dead Hungarian soldiers became vampires – in the spirit – in the First World War, feeding on the blood of the wounded. It was easier for them than for others to become the undead, for Hungary has a continuing belief in vampirism. Belief always encourages any kind of paranormal phenomenon, no matter how outrageous, as the Philip and SORRAT experiments have shown, and the manipulative reality of belief is seen clearly in the case of Ruth.

More acceptable, however, than the notion of the dead feeding on the living in this literal sense is the idea of psychic vampirism, a common phenomenon where certain people leave one feeling unaccountably drained. A similar principle may apply to Earthbound spirits or elementals, whose only hope of remaining attached to this planet is to draw off the vitality of the living.

Yet there are instances of wounds and blood inexplicably appearing on living people. Stigmatics exhibit what are believed to be signs of the grace of God, and some poltergeist victims, such as the Hungarian Eleanore Zugun, often broke out in spontaneous red weals, as if being scratched or lashed. In 1960 a South African farm worker, Jimmy de Bruin, became the focus for poltergeist activity and was witnessed to scream in agony and terror as bloody wounds spontaneously opened up on his body.

All over the world cattle and other animals are mysteriously torn apart, but these mutilations are generally ascribed to ravening aliens. UFOs are frequently reported in the area before the attacks.

It may be that the vampire phenomenon relies on the fashionable paranormal beliefs of the day. It may be that an outside agency – the Devil, magical adepts or aliens – reanimate the dead. Or it may be that creating vampires is yet another deadly ability hidden in the human psyche.

SEE ALSO *Black Monk of Pontefract; Case of Ruth; Consensus reality; The Devil; Entity enigma; Images that bleed and weep; Incorruptibility; Philip experiment; Ritual magic; Stigmatics; UFO paradox; UFOs; Werewolves; Zombies.*

REINCARNATION

A recent Gallup poll showed that 25 per cent of the British population believe in reincarnation, and similar surveys in the USA and France show an equal commitment to the belief. Yet the doctrine

Belief in reincarnation is rapidly gaining ground in the West as an alternative to the orthodox Christian view of one life followed by heaven or hell. Here Ray Bryant looks for what he believes is his own grave.

of reincarnation – the idea that a human soul may be reborn time and again in different bodies – is not part of mainstream Western culture.

Despite the widespread idea that Christians do not believe in reincarnation, the Church has never officially opposed the belief, and many churchmen today are privately committed to the doctrine – some even publicly sanction it, pointing to certain New Testament texts to support the idea. Although there is not one unequivocal statement about reincarnation in either the Old or New Testaments, there are several that may be interpreted as a reference to it, such as Matthew 17: 9–13: 'His disciples asked him saying, ''Why say the scribes that Elias must come first?'' And Jesus answered ''Elias is come already, and they knew him not.'' And the disciples understood that he spoke to them of John the Baptist.'

One of the main problem areas of the Christian faith concerns the manifest unfairness of life – how

are we to be judged on the merits and sins of one life when one person lives just a few weeks in dire poverty, and another lives to a ripe old age in happiness and splendour? Professor Geddes MacGregor, speaking to the Wrekin Trust's 1988 conference on reincarnation, likened this situation to an examination presided over by an erratic schoolmaster. Although there was no known time limit for the examination, he stopped one student writing after five minutes and others after hours, yet all would be judged equally on the scope of their work. He also quoted St Paul's statement: 'As a man sows, so he shall reap,' pointing out that it means nothing unless it refers to reincarnation and the doctrine of karma, or the law of cause and effect; it is manifest nonsense if taken to refer to one life. Not all who 'live by the sword' die by it, either, in the context of a single earthly existence.

Parapsychology largely ignored claims of spontaneous memories of former lives until Dr Ian

Stevenson of the University of Virginia won the William James essay contest in 1960 with his *Evidence for Survival from Claimed Memories of Former Incarnations*. Since then Dr Stevenson has collected two thousand 'reincarnation type' case histories, of which sixty-five have been published.

Most of these case histories concern young Indian children who begin to call themselves by other names, and claim to come from entirely different families in distant locations, almost as soon as they can talk. Often they describe a violent-death ending to their former incarnation, and some of these children exhibit birthmarks or scars in the same place as the wounds they claim to have sustained previously. One boy, for example, had a very unusual birthmark on his abdomen where he claimed his former self had been shot; it was consistent in formation with a bullet wound. Some of these birthmarks even bear serrated edges, like the knife wounds they are believed to represent.

A typical scenario of Stevenson's case histories follows this pattern: the child assures his current family that he is really someone else – he gives the full name and nickname of this person – living at a certain village unknown, except perhaps by name, to his current family. He is obviously unhappy in his present body and wishes to go 'home'. Eventually his present family take him to the distant village where he runs ahead, knowing his way to the house where he lived before, greeting 'his' widow and offspring with joy, using their pet names and mentioning incidents that only they could have known. The evidence for such cases seems water-tight, but they are not without their critics.

Ian Wilson, author of *The Turin Shroud* and *Time Out of Mind?*, points out that most of the children involved in such cases are from very poor homes and that their 'previous' families were wealthy. Moreover, many of the details of these deaths were made public because they involved some degree of notoriety – a murder in a prominent family would make banner headlines. Wilson suggests that the child's family may have colluded with him in order to gain financially from the 'previous' family. Yet this theory does not take into account three factors. In some Hindu sects, to remember a past life is a bad omen, and rather than fostering it, such children are often punished to the point

British writer Ian Wilson. A Catholic, he finds most of the evidence for reincarnation seriously flawed, and accuses some researchers of bias.

of torture. Secondly, it is more likely that a reincarnated spirit would remember a life that made headlines than one that did not. Finally, not all of Stevenson's two thousand cases could be accused of systematic and calculated fraud. On this scale it would be an industry, and would have been exposed as such long ago.

Memories of past lives may also arise spontaneously in Western adults: the present suddenly 'melts away' and the individual finds himself temporarily in another body at another time and place. This phenomenon may be a timeslip rather than a personal memory, but, judging by the accompanying feelings of recognition, many reported cases seem likely to be 'far memory'.

Hypnotic regression can seem the royal road to past lives, but there are hidden dangers, as subsequent researchers discovered after reading about the work of Arnall Bloxham and Joe Keeton, whose hypnotised subjects recalled dramatic and detailed previous lives. In almost all cases the past lives were found to be culled from buried memory – cryptomnesia – of historical novels read years before. Yet some of their cases remain unexplained, and it seems likely that there are genuinely paranormal elements in most of them. The cryptomnesia theory simply will not fit a high proportion of all hypnotic regression.

Many theorists believe that the energies from the

hopes and fears of past lives are carried on in this incarnation, for better or worse. Several psychiatrists and psychotherapists use far memory therapeutically; Dr Denys Kelsey has used this method for thirty years to achieve 'instant, complete and permanent' cures for many present psychosomatic and emotional problems, such as phobias.

One young woman went to Dr Kelsey deeply distressed by a fear of flying, which was particularly upsetting as she had been newly promoted to a job that required her to travel widely. Under hypnosis she relived the last flight of a young RAF officer, shot in the neck and trapped in a burning plane, terrified of hitting the ground. Once she had recalled that life, her fear left her instantly. The energies of unresolved distress, such as that experienced in the process of dying, may be seen to accompany the spirit into a new body, emerging as unexplained aversions and terrors.

The details of rebirth are by no means universally accepted. Some cultures believe that one is always reborn as the same sex; others think rebirth happens only within the same family; while others think reincarnation is reserved for those who have suffered a violent death, and need another life in order to wreak their vengeance. Some researchers find this variety of belief suspicious, while others find it completely understandable that a discarnate spirit will want to be reborn according to the teachings of his last culture.

There are problems with the doctrine of reincarnation, such as the notion of an infinite regress. Was it God's fault that our first incarnation was less than perfect, requiring a long line of future incarnations to put it right? Then there is the matter of numbers: today's population explosion must accommodate more souls than the total of those who have lived before – where have they all come from? Other planes of existence, or even other planets, are offered as answers to this question, and the creation of new souls cannot be ruled out.

Yet however many theological or theoretical questions remain to intrigue us, the evidence for reincarnation as a fact of life and death is strong. For those who prefer a just world, that is comfort indeed.

SEE ALSO *Fantasy-prone personalities; Hypnotic regression; Karma; Life after death; Near death experience; Timeslips.*

KARMA

The idea of karma is said to have originated in India two or three hundred years before the advent of Buddhism. Karma – from the Sanskrit meaning 'action' – is the accumulation of the causes we make and their effects. Every thought, word and deed creates a latent force or energy that is stored in the depths of our life as a karmic seed. Karma is an inescapable chain of causality that stretches back through past incarnations and forward into the infinite future. According to this ancient principle of retributive justice, actions in the past shape the present and actions in the present determine the future. Good karma is formed by positive mental functions such as altruistic love and compassion; evil karma by hatred, greed and anger. Thoughts translated into action create a much heavier karma. For example, hatred confined to the heart brings lighter retribution than if it is expressed verbally or physically.

Karma is adjustment rather than punishment, and does not preclude free will. All through our lives we find ourselves confronting situations the foundations of which have been laid by our actions in the past. Whether we do so with wisdom and courage, or with folly, cowardice and brutality, depends on us. But every time we respond negatively, we will be obliged to face similar situations many times over until the essential lesson is learnt.

Karma explains all seemingly unjust suffering, all seemingly unmerited rewards. In the words of George Eliot:

Our deeds still travel with us from afar,
And what we have been makes us what we are.

SEE ALSO *Buddhism; Curses; Fate; Jinxes; Life after death; Prodigies; Reincarnation; Spontaneous human combustion.*

Index